SAP MM Invoice Verification
Technical Reference and Learning Guide

P. K. AGRAWAL

Formerly Program Manager
Tata Technologies Limited
Pune

SAP MM INVOICE VERIFICATION: Technical Reference and Learning Guide
P. K. Agrawal

PHI Learning Private Limited

Delhi-110092
2015

₹ 725.00

SAP MM INVOICE VERIFICATION: Technical Reference and Learning Guide
P. K. Agrawal

Warning and Disclaimer
While every precaution has been taken in the preparation of this book, the author and the publisher do not guarantee the accuracy, adequacy, or completeness of any information contained in this book. Neither is any liability assumed by the author and the publisher for any damages or loss to your data or your equipment resulting directly or indirectly from the use of the information or instructions contained herein.

Trademark Acknowledgements
SAP, SAPconnect, SAPNet, SAPoffice, SAPscript, ABAP, Basis, ECC are registered or unregistered trademark of SAP AG.

All product and service names mentioned in this book are registered or unregistered trademarks or service marks of their respective companies. Use of any product or service name in this book should not be regarded as affecting the validity of any trademark or service mark.

ISBN-978-81-203-5040-3

The export rights of this book are vested solely with the publisher.

Published by Asoke K. Ghosh, PHI Learning Private Limited, Rimjhim House, 111, Patparganj Industrial Estate, Delhi-110092 and Printed by Rajkamal Electric Press, Plot No. 2, Phase IV, HSIDC, Kundli-131028, Sonipat, Haryana.

This book is dedicated to
SAP consultants and users
who deserve to understand SAP much better

Table of Contents

Each section is rated for its importance and relevance for functional consultants (FC), users (US), business process owners (PO) and senior managers (SM). In MR, you can keep your own rating and in UL, your understanding level. These ratings are repeated at the beginning of each section, so that at the beginning of each section you know whether to read it, or skip it, without having to go back to the Table of Contents.

SAP Menu

Sequence number	SAP Menu (ECC 6)	Where covered	Why not covered
	▽ 🗇 SAP menu		
1	▷ 🗀 Office		OoS
2	▷ 🗀 Cross-Application Components		OoS
3	▷ 🗀 Collaboration Projects		OoS
4	▽ 🗇 Logistics		
4.1	▽ 🗇 Materials Management		
4.1.1	▷ 🗀 Purchasing		OoS
4.1.2	▷ 🗀 Inventory Management		OoS
4.1.3	▷ 🗀 Excise Duty		OoS
4.1.4	▽ 🗇 Logistics Invoice Verification		
4.1.4.1	▽ 🗇 Document Entry		
4.1.4.1.1	📦 MIRO - Enter Invoice	4.1	
4.1.4.1.2	📦 MIR7 - Park Invoice	11.5	
4.1.4.1.3	📦 MIRA - Enter Invoice for Invoice Verifi	11.7	
4.1.4.2	▽ 🗇 Further Processing		
4.1.4.2.1	📦 MIR4 - Display Invoice Document	11.3	
4.1.4.2.2	📦 MR8M - Cancel Invoice Document	11.8	
4.1.4.2.3	📦 MRBR - Release Blocked Invoices	11.10	
4.1.4.2.4	📦 MIR5 - Display List of Invoice Docum	11.12	
4.1.4.2.5	📦 MIR6 - Invoice Overview	11.7.6	
4.1.4.2.6	📦 MR90 - Output Messages	20.9	
4.1.4.3	▽ 🗇 Automatic Settlement		
4.1.4.3.1	📦 MRRL - Evaluated Receipt Settleme	13.2	
4.1.4.3.2	📦 MRDC - Automatic Delivery Cost Set	13.3	
4.1.4.3.3	📦 MRKO - Consignment and Pipeline	14.1	
4.1.4.3.4	📦 MRIS - Invoicing Plan Settlement	15.1, 15.2	
4.1.4.3.5	📦 MRNB - Revaluation	4.19	
4.1.4.4	▽ 🗇 GR/IR Account Maintenance		
4.1.4.4.1	📦 MR11 - Maintain GR/IR Clearing Acc	18.1	
4.1.4.4.2	📦 MR11SHOW - Display/Cancel Accou	18.1.6, 18.2	
4.1.4.5	▽ 🗇 Archiving		
4.1.4.5.1	📦 MRA1 - Create Archive	21.3	
4.1.4.5.2	📦 MRA2 - Delete Documents	21.4	
4.1.4.5.3	📦 MRA4 - Manage Archive	21.3.8	
4.1.4.5.4	📦 MRA3 - Display Archived Document	21.5	

SAP Customizing Implementation Guide

Sequence number	SAP Customizing Implementation Guide (ECC 6)	Where covered	Why not covered
	▽ 📄 SAP Customizing Implementation Guide		
1	📄 🕒 Activate SAP ECC Extensions		OoS
2	▷ SAP NetWeaver		OoS
3	▷ 📄 Enterprise Structure		OoS
4	▷ 📄 Cross-Application Components		OoS
5	▷ Auto-ID Infrastructure		OoS
6	▷ SAP xApp Resource and Portfolio Managemen		OoS
7	▷ 📄 Financial Accounting		OoS
8	▷ Financial Accounting (New)		OoS
9	▷ Financial Supply Chain Management		OoS
10	▷ Strategic Enterprise Management/Business A		OoS
11	▷ 📄 Controlling		OoS
12	▷ 📄 Investment Management		OoS
13	▷ 📄 Enterprise Controlling		OoS
14	▷ 📄 Real Estate		OoS
15	▷ Flexible Real Estate Management (RE-FX)		OoS
16	▷ 📄 Logistics - General		OoS
17	▷ 📄 Environment, Health & Safei		OoS
18	▷ 📄 Sales and Distribution		OoS
19	▽ 📄 Materials Management		
19.1	▷ 📄 General Settings for Materials Managemen		OoS
19.2	▷ 📄 Consumption-Based Planning		OoS
19.3	▷ 📄 Purchasing		OoS
19.4	▷ 📄 External Services Management		OoS
19.5	▷ 📄 Inventory Management and Physical Inven		OoS
19.6	▷ Excise Duty		OoS
19.7	▷ 📄 Valuation and Account Assignment		OoS
19.8	▽ 📄 Logistics Invoice Verification		
19.8.1	📄 🕒 Define Attributes of System Messages	12.6.3	
19.8.2	📄 🕒 Define Tax Jurisdiction		CS
19.8.3	📄 🕒 Configure Automatic Postings	19	

Reasons for 'why not covered'

Reason	Description
CS	Country specific functionality is out of scope of this book.
OoS	Out of scope.

Preface

If you are a consultant or a user of SAP and feel frustrated because SAP seems impossible to master; this book is for you. It shows that SAP is finite, can be understood well, and that the task is not as daunting as it appears. Moreover, you do not have to worry about forgetting things; you can always find them again, and fairly easily.

This book has evolved from the difficulty that each one of us experiences in 'Managing SAP'. As I constantly struggled, trying to understand the concepts of SAP and explore their linkages with other concepts, I found memory to be a major handicap. So I started taking notes. Before long, I could not find what I had written. Then I started reorganizing my notes. And finally I started feeling more comfortable. I knew where to write when I learnt something new, and I could find things I was looking for.

The notes improved continuously, and then came the desire to share them with others; hence these books. While writing this book, I have tried to be clear, crisp and comprehensive as possible.

This book is also meant for users of SAP, business process owners and senior managers of companies, who have implemented, or are in the process of implementation, or are planning to implement, or are evaluating modules of SAP MM. Their need to understand the subject is not as comprehensive as that of functional consultants. How all these category of readers should use this book is described below.

How to use this book

There are two ways in which you can use this book. You can use it as a learning guide, and you can use it as a technical reference. When you use this book as a learning guide, you have to cover it in several iterations. Each iteration is designed to enhance your knowledge and prepare you for the next iteration.

In terms of job roles one can classify the readers as senior managers, business process owners, users, and functional consultants. Senior managers need to know only the important concepts, and what SAP can do for them. BPOs need to know more of SAP concepts and have a good idea of how to perform different tasks in SAP. Users need to have a thorough understanding of different tasks they have to perform in SAP and the concepts underlying them. Functional consultants need to know everything, or at least everything important.

In the table of contents, each topic is classified in terms of relevance and importance for each category of user. Each topic is given an A, B, C, or X rating for each category of user. During each iteration, you can decide the role and importance level you intend to cover. You can select the role you are going to refer to in an iteration, based on your job role, but that is not essential. For example, if you are going to be a user of SAP, but do not know anything about SAP, you may select senior manager role in your first iteration. Having learnt important concepts, you may select BPO role in the next iteration. Finally you may select user role. Also, once you become a proficient user, you may go through the book from the perspective of a functional consultant. These ratings are repeated at the beginning of each section so that at the beginning of each section itself you know whether to read it, or skip it, without having to go back to the Table of Contents.

In addition to the suggested ratings, I have left two blank columns. Although I have given an importance rating to each topic, you can decide the importance based on your requirements. For example, if 'Consignment and Pipeline Settlement' is not applicable to you, you may mark it as not relevant for you. Similarly, you can decide the importance rating. There is nothing sacrosanct about the rating given by me. You may note this rating in the blank column 'MR—My Rating'. As you read a topic, you will achieve a level of understanding. You can record it in the column 'UL—Understanding Level'. You may use A/B/C/X, or any other rating scale. After you complete an iteration, these columns will help you decide, which topics to revisit.

When you are reading this book, you will need to work on the system. When you are reading only the important concepts as senior manager, it may be possible to read the book without hands-on experience. However, as you go deeper and deeper, working on the system will become more and more necessary.

If you are using this book as a technical reference, apart from the table of contents and index, you can also locate the relevant material by using 'SAP Menu', and 'SAP Customizing Implementation Guide (IMG)'. Expanded tree of both the SAP menu and the IMG (ECC 6.0) is given after the Table of Contents. Once you find the node in these structures, you will be guided to the relevant section. If that node is not covered in the book, that is also mentioned along with the reason for not covering it. In such cases you have to look for information elsewhere; this book will not help you.

You can also use the structure of this book to keep your discoveries in an organized way. You can maintain a Word or an Excel document where you record your discoveries either against page numbers or section numbers.

You can also use the structure of this book for guiding your discussion with the users and recording their input. That document will finally become the configuration manual.

Acknowledgements

I am deeply indebted to Mr. D.V. Prasad, Mr. Hemant Khedkar, and my family, who contributed in different ways to make this book possible. I express my sincere gratitude to my publisher, PHI Learning, for putting their trust in me and for improving the presentation of this book.

Individual social responsibility

There is no doubt that we must excel in our chosen profession. But our responsibility does not end there. Indeed, we have a greater responsibility of making the world a better place to live in—to address the challenges the world faces, to analyze, to find solutions, to share, to network, and to make a difference. You may have wondered about the diagram on the cover page; it is a plan for a City without Traffic Lights. There are five articles at the end of this book. You will perhaps find them interesting to read. In particular, think about Samay Daan to make a difference. It is our Individual Social Responsibility.

P.K. AGRAWAL

Enterprise Structure

1.1 ENTERPRISE STRUCTURE

Functional Consultant	User	Business Process Owner	Senior Management	My Rating	Understanding Level
A	A	A	A		

1.1.1 Organizational Levels

Client

Many customers of SAP are corporate groups having one or more companies. Whereas each company is an independent financial entity, consolidation of financial data is required for the entire enterprise. SAP permits this by keeping data of all the companies in the same set of tables on a single server from which it can be extracted as required.

Apart from the production server, which contains real-life business data, you also need a server for Quality Assurance, Training, etc. While many customers of SAP maintain separate servers for each of these purposes, there are some customers who would like to keep all these data on a single server. To meet this requirement, SAP allows division of a server in multiple clients. The data stored in one client is invisible in other clients. When you log on to SAP, you log on to a client. This determines the data you will see.

1

Company code

Your business may consist of one or more company codes. A company code is a legal entity having its own balance sheet and profit and loss statement.

Plant

In common parlance, a plant is a manufacturing facility. In SAP, it has a wider meaning. Any place of work, be it a manufacturing facility or an office, is called a plant. All goods movements take place in a plant and, therefore, in a company code.

Storage location

A storage location is a physical location where you receive, store and issue materials. You also periodically check the quantity of material stored and compare it with book inventory.

1.1.2   Enterprise Structure

Overview

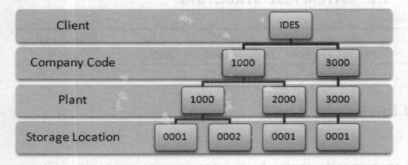

Relationships

The above figure shows the relationships between various organizational levels which may be summarized as under:

➤ A client may have one or more company codes.

➤ A company code may have zero, one, or many plants.

➤ A plant belongs to one and only one company code.

➤ Plant ids are unique in the entire implementation. The same plant id cannot exist in another company code.

➤ A plant may have zero, one, or many storage locations.

➤ A storage location belongs to one and only one plant.

➤ A storage location is identified by the combination of plant id and storage location id. Therefore, the same storage location id can exist in another plant, but it is a different storage location.

1.2   COMPANY CODE

Functional Consultant	*User*	*Business Process Owner*	*Senior Management*	*My Rating*	*Understanding Level*
A	A	A	A		

1.2.1   Purpose

Your business may consist of one or more company codes. A company code is a legal entity having its own balance sheet and profit and loss statement.

1.2.2   IMG Node

SM30 ➤ V_T001

1.2.3   Screen

Company Code	1000
Company Name	IDES AG

Additional data	
City	Frankfurt
Country	DE
Currency	EUR
Language	EN

1.2.4   Primary Key

Company Code

1.3 PLANT

Functional Consultant	User	Business Process Owner	Senior Management	My Rating	Understanding Level
A	A	A	A		

1.3.1 Overview

Plant

In common parlance, a plant is a manufacturing facility. In SAP, it has a wider meaning. Any place of work, be it a manufacturing facility or an office, is called a plant. All Inventory Management transactions take place in a plant and, therefore, in a company code.

Relationship of plant with company code

Each plant belongs to one and only one company code. A company code can have zero, one, or many plants.

Relationship of plant with storage locations

Each storage location belongs to one and only one plant. A plant can have zero, one, or many storage locations.

1.3.2 IMG Node

SM30 ➤ V_T001W

1.3.3 Screen

Plant	1000
Name 1	Werk Hamburg
Name 2	

Detailed information

Language Key	EN	English
House number/street	Alsterdorfer Strasse 13	
PO Box		
Postal Code	22299	
City	Hamburg	
Country Key	DE	Germany
Region	02	Hamburg
County code		
City code		
Tax Jurisdiction		
Factory calendar	01	Factory calendar Germany standard

1.3.4   Primary Key

1.3.5   Important Fields

Factory calendar

Each plant has a factory calendar that determines its working days. You specify the factory calendar of the plant here. Factory calendar can be maintained using transaction SCAL.

Factory Calendar ID	01	Factory calendar Germany standard

Valid	From Year	1990
	To Year	2098

Holiday Calendar ID	08	Public holiday calendar Baden-Württemberg

Special Rules	none exist

Factory Date Start	

Workdays

- ☑ Monday
- ☑ Tuesday
- ☑ Wednesday
- ☑ Thursday
- ☑ Friday
- ☐ Saturday
- ☐ Sunday
- ☐ Public Holiday

1.3.6 Assignment of Plant to Company Code

After you create a plant, you can assign it to a company code in view V_T001K_ASSIGN, or using transaction OX18.

CoCd	Plnt	Name of Plant	Company Name	Status
0001	0001	Werk 0001	SAP A.G.	
0005	0005	Hamburg	IDES AG NEW GL	
0006	0006	New York	IDES US INC New GL	
0007	0007	Werk Hamburg	IDES AG NEW GL 7	
0008	0008	New York	IDES US INC New GL 8	
1000	0099	Werk für Customizing-Kurse SCM	IDES AG	
1000	1000	Werk Hamburg	IDES AG	

1.4 STORAGE LOCATION

Functional Consultant	User	Business Process Owner	Senior Management	My Rating	Understanding Level
A	A	A	A		

1.4.1 Purpose

A storage location is a physical location where you receive, store and issue materials. You also periodically check the quantity of material stored and compare it with book inventory. There may be zero, one or more storage locations within a plant. Storage locations are always created for a plant. Storage location ids are unique within a plant. The same storage location id in another plant is a different storage location.

1.4.2 IMG Node

SM34 ➤ VC_T001L

1.4.3 Storage Locations

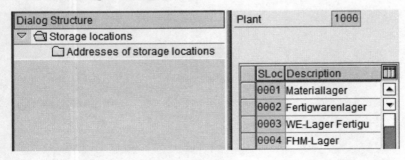

1.4.4 Addresses of Storage Locations

Dialog Structure	Plant	1000
▽ ☐ Storage locations	Stor. Location	0001
☐ Addresses of storage locations		

No.	
	▲
	▼

A storage location can have multiple addresses. You can create an entry and maintain address details. This is useful, if a storage location has multiple entry and exit gates and their postal addresses are not the same.

Edit address: SL1

Name

Title	
Name	

Search Terms

Search term 1/2		

Street Address

Street/House number		
Postal Code/City		
Country		Region

PO Box Address

PO Box	
Postal Code	
Company postal code	

Communication

Language	English		Other communication...
Telephone		Extension	
Mobile Phone			
Fax		Extension	
E-Mail			
Standard Comm.Method			

Comments	

☑ ▽ 🖫 Preview 🔁 🔁 International Versions ✖

Material

2.1 MATERIAL MASTER

Functional Consultant	User	Business Process Owner	Senior Management	My Rating	Understanding Level
A	A	A	B		

2.1.1 Purpose

The material master comprising all the individual material master records stored in the system contains descriptions of all materials that an enterprise procures, produces, and keeps in stock. It is the central repository of information on materials for the enterprise. Materials can be procured and used without a material master record, but they cannot be stocked or produced.

2.1.2 Initial Screen

When you run transaction MM01 to create a material, the system gives the following initial screen.

Create Material (Initial Screen)

| Select view(s) | Organizational levels | Data |

Material	
Industry sector	
Material Type	
Change Number	

Copy from...	
Material	

Material

Material number

Each material is assigned a unique material number, which identifies the material. Although it is called material number, it is actually an 18-digit alphanumeric string.

Old material number

If you want to use your pre-SAP material numbers in SAP, you can do so by using external number range. Alternatively, you can use old material number field for linking pre-SAP material number to the SAP material number.

Internal material number

When you create a material in the system, you identify it through a material number. SAP can automatically assign number from a running serial to the material you create. Further, you can have multiple running serials, called internal number ranges, and different materials may be assigned numbers from different number ranges, depending on their material types.

External material number

➢ Some companies follow a numbering system which can tell you what kind of material it is. For example, you can tell from the material number that it is a raw material, that it is steel, that it is a cold rolled steel, etc. Although this sounds very useful, you may often run out of numbers in your numbering scheme.

➢ Some companies want to retain their pre-SAP material numbers.

In both these, and other scenarios, a company may decide that the user creating the material will specify the material number.

Number ranges

The numbers can be assigned to different materials from different number ranges. For more details, see Section 2.6.

Industry Sector

SAP is used by different industries worldwide as shown in the following screenshot.

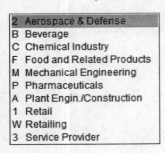

The material data that the mechanical engineering industry needs to maintain would be different from the material data that the pharmaceutical industry needs to maintain. Hence, when you create material data, you specify the industry sector, and the system adjusts the data screens accordingly.

Default Industry Sector

You can set a default value for industry sector by clicking Defaults ➤ Industry sector.... . The system gives the following dialog box.

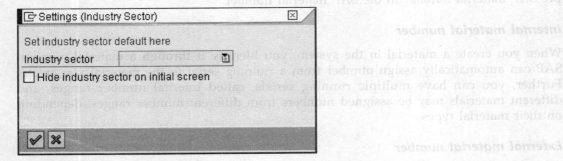

Industry sector

If you set the industry sector here, it is proposed as the default value when you create a material.

Hide industry sector on initial screen

If you set the industry sector and select this checkbox, the system uses this industry sector when you create a material, and does not even show it on the initial screen. This facility is useful for those users who operate in a single industry sector.

Material Type

A material type is a group of materials with similar attributes. The material type allows the management of different materials in a uniform manner. There are different types of materials. A material is assigned a type when you create the material master record. The data you maintain for a material also depends on the type of material. For example, the data needed for manufactured parts would be different from the data needed for perishables.

```
IBAU   Maintenance assembly
HERS   Manufacturer parts
MPO    Material Planning Object
NLAG   Non-stock material
UNBW   Non-valuated material
NOF1   Nonfoods
HIBE   Operating supplies
VERP   Packaging
FRIP   Perishables
PIPE   Pipeline material
```

For details of control functions of material type, see Section 2.7.

Change Number

In your company you can implement engineering change management, and control changes through change master records. If you are using the engineering change management system, you can enter the change number here.

Screen Layout

The screen you get for maintaining a material can be customized to your requirement. You can get different screens based on material type, industry sector, user and transaction.

2.1.3   Views

Selecting the Views

SAP maintains material data in a large number of views. When you change or display a material, you need to select the views you are going to work with. This is because each view has associated organizational levels, and the system prompts you to specify them. By selecting the views, you need to specify only those organizational levels that are needed by the selected views. If you click Select view(s), the system shows you the available views and you can select the views you want to maintain.

View
Basic Data 1
Basic Data 2
Classification
Sales: Sales Org. Data 1
Sales: Sales Org. Data 2
Sales: General/Plant Data
Foreign Trade: Export Data
Sales Text
Purchasing
Foreign Trade: Import Data
Purchase Order Text
MRP 1
MRP 2
MRP 3
MRP 4
Forecasting
Work Scheduling
Production Resources/Tools
General Plant Data / Storage 1
General Plant Data / Storage 2
Warehouse Management 1
Warehouse Management 2
Quality Management
Accounting 1
Accounting 2
Costing 1
Costing 2
Plant Stock
Storage Location Stock

Default Views

You can set default views by clicking Defaults ➤ Views.... The system gives the following dialog box.

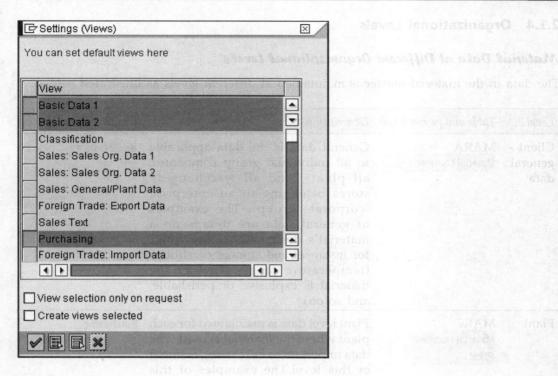

View

Select the views you want to select by default.

View selection only on request

If you select the views and also this checkbox, the system directly displays the material without showing the select view(s) dialog box. Of course, you can always click Select view(s) , and select more or less views to work on.

Create views selected

If this indicator is set, all selected views are created, with the exception of the Sales Text view, the Purchase Order Text view, and the Classification view, when you save the material master record. As a result, you do not have to access and confirm each screen individually. This function is particularly useful when creating a material master record with a reference.

2.1.4   Organizational Levels

Material Data at Different Organizational Levels

The data in the material master is maintained at different levels as illustrated below:

Level	Table and primary key	Description	Example view
Client - general data	MARA Material Number	General data is the data applicable to all individual group companies, all plants, and all warehouses/stores belonging to an enterprise (corporate group). The examples of general data are details on a material's design (CAD drawings, for instance) and storage conditions (temperature range, whether the material is explosive or perishable, and so on).	Basic Data 1
Plant	MARC Material Number Plant	Plant level data is maintained for each plant where the material is used. The data important to Purchasing is stored at this level.The examples of this data are the maximum and minimum order quantities of a material and the reorder point.	Purchasing
Storage location	MARD Material Number Plant Storage Location	Storage location level data is data specific to a storage location. Stock levels are an example of the data maintained for each storage location.	Storage Location Stock

Specifying Organizational Levels

You need to specify organizational levels depending on the views you select. If you select all the views and click   Organizational levels , the system gives the following dialog box.

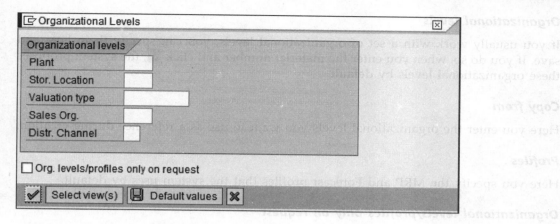

If you do not select all the views, you may not see some of the fields in the above dialog box.

Default Organizational Levels

You can set default values for organizational levels by clicking Defaults ➤ Organizational levels... . The system gives the following dialog box.

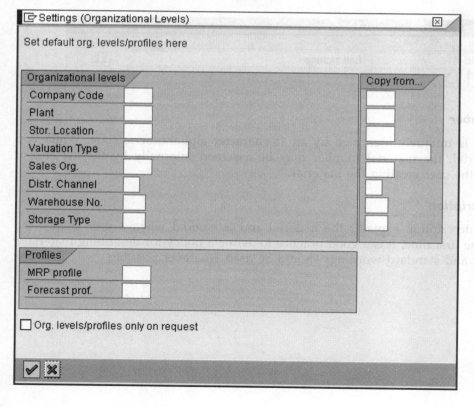

Organizational levels

If you usually work with a set of organizational levels, you can specify them here and save. If you do so, when you enter the material number and click ✅, the system proposes these organizational levels by default.

Copy from

Here you enter the organizational levels you want to use as a reference during creation.

Profiles

Here you specify the MRP and Forecast profiles that the system uses by default.

Organizational levels/profiles only on request

If you select the organizational levels and also this checkbox, the system directly displays the material without showing the organizational level dialog box. Of course, you can always click | Organizational levels |, and change the organizational levels.

2.1.5 Basic Data 1

Material

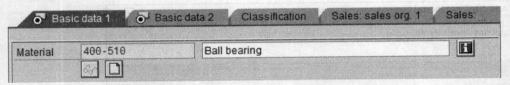

Material number

Each material is uniquely identified by an 18-character alphanumeric code. When you create a material, the material number may be assigned internally by the system, or externally by the user creating the material.

Material description

The material description explains the material and is entered when a user creates the material for the first time. It is a good practice to define a policy for describing materials. Abbreviations and standard wordings should be used wherever possible.

General Data

General data			
Base Unit of Measure	PC piece(s)	Material Group	001
Old material number		Ext. Matl Group	
Division	01	Lab/Office	
Product allocation		Prod.hierarchy	
X-plant matl status		Valid from	
☐ Assign effect. vals		GenItemCatGroup	

Base unit of measure

The base unit of measure is the unit in which stocks of the material are managed. The system converts all the quantities you enter in other units of measure (alternative units of measure) to the base unit of measure. The base unit of measure is the unit satisfying the highest necessary requirement for precision.

Material group

The material group classifies your materials, and thereby helps you locate a particular material. The examples of material groups are steel, non-ferrous metals, fasteners, and lubricants. Material group is an important filtering and aggregating criterion in reporting on materials.

You can also maintain purchasing info record for non-stock material at vendor, material group level. For example, this facility can be used to identify vendors of Stationery items.

You need to differentiate between material type and material group. Material types have a large number of properties associated with them, and you generally use material types predefined by SAP. Material groups do not have associated properties, but you use them for analysis, e.g. total inventory of steels. Material groups also help in searching for a material.

Old material number

When you implement SAP, you may transfer data from existing systems. If you assign the material numbers in SAP independently, you can keep the old material number here. You can use the old material number to systematically search for material master records via matchcodes.

External material group

Sometimes there are material groups defined by external bodies, e.g. CCG material group or the Nielsen material group. Here you can specify an external material group for this material. The master list of external material groups is maintained in view V_TWEW.

Ext. Material Group	Ext. matl grp descr.

Division

Division is a way of grouping materials, products, or services from the point of view of Sales and Distribution. The system uses divisions to determine the sales areas and the business areas for a material, product, or service.

Laboratory/office

Here you can specify the design office, laboratory, or laboratory worker who is responsible for this material. This field is used mostly in chemical industry. The master list of laboratory/engineering office is maintained in view V_024L.

Lab/Office	Text: Lab./engineering office
001	Laboratory 1
002	Laboratory 2
G01	Lab Group 01

Product allocation

The product allocation determination procedure determines how product allocation is carried out.

Product hierarchy

The product hierarchy is used in the Sales and Distribution area for analyses and price determination. It is used to depict the competitive materials of competitor 1 in relation to those of competitor 2. Here, your own company is also regarded as a competitor and its materials as competitive materials. You can use this representation as a basis for market analysis.

Cross-plant material status, valid from

If you do not want the material to be purchased after a certain date, you can set the material status to Blocked for Purchasing with the date from which the blocking is effective. This can be done for all the plants in the Basic data 1 tab or for individual plants in the Purchasing tab.

Assign effectivity parameter values

Here you indicate whether you can assign values to the effectivity parameters or override the date when you explode an assembly or a finished product.

General item category group

Here you can specify the material grouping that helps the system determine item categories during sales document processing. The master list is maintained in view V_TPTM and configured in Sales and Distribution.

Dimensions/EANs

Dimensions/EANs			
Gross Weight		Weight unit	KG
Net Weight			
Volume		Volume unit	
Size/dimensions			
EAN/UPC		EAN Category	

Gross weight, net weight and weight unit

This information can be used to check storage bin capacity in Warehouse Management. It is also used in the Goods Receipt Forecast report generated by transaction ME2V.

Volume and unit

This information can be used to plan storage and transportation. It is also used in the Goods Receipt Forecast report generated by transaction ME2V.

Size/dimensions

Here you can specify the size or dimensions of the material along with the unit of measure. The data you enter is merely for information and is not used by the system.

EAN/UPC, EAN category

The European Article Number (EAN) is assigned by the manufacturer of the particular material. The EAN identifies the manufacturer uniquely. In USA, Universal Product Code (UPC) is equivalent to EAN. With internal number assignment, you enter the EAN category, but not an EAN. With external number assignment, you enter the EAN, but not an EAN category. In this case, the EAN is checked for correctness, and the EAN category is determined by the system automatically.

Packaging Material Data

Packaging material data	
Matl Grp Pack.Matls	
Ref. mat. for pckg	

Material group of packing materials

If this material uses packaging material, here you specify the material group of packaging materials. This information can be used to find all materials that require similar packaging materials. Material groups of packing materials are maintained in view V_TVEGR.

Reference material for packaging

If this material is packed in the same way as another material, for which you have specified detailed packing instructions, you can enter the number of that material here.

Basic Data Texts

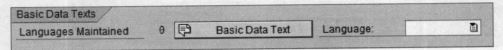

Basic data texts

You maintain detailed description of the material in different languages in the `Basic data text` tab, which you access by clicking `Basic Data Text`. The system shows the number of languages in which the text is maintained.

2.1.6 Basic Data 2

Material

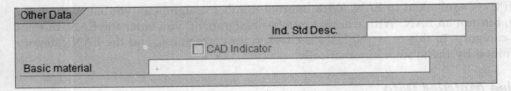

Other Data

Industry standard description

Here you can store description of the material in accordance with the appropriate industry standard (such as ANSI or ISO). This field is purely for information.

CAD indicator

The CAD indicator shows that the material was transferred to SAP from a CAD system. This indicator is only for information but can also be used as a search criterion to find a material.

Basic material

Here you can maintain the basic constituent of the material. The master list of basic material is maintained in view TWSPR.

Basic matl
C 60
CR25
CRNIMO2
Edelstahl / stainless steel
Grauguß 25
Metall / Metal
SPHAEROGUSS
St60
Stahl / Steel
Steel 50 / Stahl 50
Titan / Titanium

Environment

Environment	
DG indicator profile ☐	☐ Environmentally rlvt
☐ Highly viscous	☐ In bulk/liquid

Dangerous goods indicator profile

If a material is dangerous, you can assign it a profile here. The profiles are maintained in view DGV_TDG41. A profile specifies whether the material is dangerous or not and whether it is relevant for dangerous goods checks, dangerous goods documents, template materials and one-time materials.

Environmentally relevant

Here you can specify that this is an environmentally relevant material. This indicator is used in the Sales and Distribution module.

Highly viscous

You can use this indicator to identify highly viscous materials. This indicator can be used to control data output on transport documents.

In bulk/liquid

This indicator shows, if the goods are to be transported in bulk. You can use this indicator to control data output on transport documents.

Design Documents Assigned

Design documents assigned
☑ No link

No link

This checkbox indicates, if design documents are linked to this material.

Design Drawing

Design Drawing			
Document		Document type	Doc.vers.
Page number	Doc.ch.no.	Page format	No. sheets

Document number, document type and document version

A document has a number and a version. When creating a document, you specify a document type, which controls field selection and the available statuses for a document info record.

Page number

Here you specify the page number of the document on which the material can be found.

Document change number

Document change number indicates the change status of the drawing.

Page format

Here you can store the page size of the technical document of this material.

Number of sheets

Here you can store the number of pages that the technical document contains.

Client-specific Configuration

Client-specific configuration	
Cross-plant CM	☐ Material is configurable
☐ Variant	🖉 Configure variant

Cross-plant configurable material

Unlike the plant-specific configurable material, the cross-plant configurable material is valid for all plants.

Material is configurable

Here you can specify that the material is configurable. For example, if you buy envelopes of various sizes, colours, with or without an address window, etc., instead of creating separate material master records for every possible combination (e.g. C5 with window, C6 without window), you can use a configurable material. For a configurable material, you create characteristics, class, material, and configuration profile.

Variant

This specifies that the material is a variant of a configurable material.

Configure variant

Click [🖎 **Configure variant**] to configure variant of this material.

Additionals

[**Additionals**]

You can assign additionals to articles to ensure their effective presentation at sale. Price tickets, security tags, clothes hangers, and shipping materials are all the examples of additionals. Click [**Additionals**] to enter additionals for the material.

Seq	Sa	D	Cl	D	Class	Key	Additionals	Description	Pro	Description	P	Description of pr

Additionals

Material   400-510

Additionals

Additionals

2.1.7 Purchasing

Material, Plant

Sales text	⚙ Purchasing	Foreign trade import	⚙ Purchase order text

Material	400-510	Ball bearing	ℹ
Plant	1000	Werk Hamburg	

Not all data in this view is at plant level. Some data is at material level. These are discussed separately. If a material exists in one plant and you want to create it in another plant, use transaction MM01 (Create), not transaction MM02 (Change).

Material Level General Data

General Data

Base Unit of Measure	PC	piece(s)	Order Unit		Var. OUn
			Material Group	001	
			Qual.f.FreeGoodsDis.		
☐ Batch management					

Base unit of measure

The base unit of measure is not at the plant level. If you change the base unit of measure here, it changes in the `Basic data 1` tab and applies to all plants.

Order unit

Order unit can differ from base unit of measure because the vendors may use a different unit of measure than the unit of measure used by the company internally.

Variable order unit active

Normally you buy material in the order unit defined above. However, for some materials you want the flexibility to buy in different order units from different vendors. You can do so by activating this field. You also need to maintain conversion ratios in the `Units of measure` tab (see section 2.1.8).

Material group

Here you specify the material group. The material group is also displayed in the `Basic data 1` tab.

Qualifies for free goods discount

Here you can specify whether, and for which areas, the material qualifies for a discount in kind. This indicator is presently used only in Purchasing.

Batch management

Here you can specify that the material is managed in batches.

Material Level Purchasing Values

Purchasing values				
Purchasing value key	1		Shipping Instr.	
1st Rem./Exped.	10	days	Underdel. Tolerance	0.0 percent
2nd Reminder/Exped.	20	days	Overdeliv. Tolerance	0.0 percent
3rd Reminder/Exped.	30	days	Min. Del. Qty in %	0.0 percent
StdValueDelivDateVar	0	days	☐ Unltd Overdelivery	☐ Acknowledgment Reqd

Purchasing value key

In the purchasing documents you specify a number of characteristics: reminder days, tolerance limits, shipping instructions, order acknowledgment, etc. These characteristics are combined in a purchasing value key in customizing and assigned to a material here. In the purchasing documents, this data is proposed from the purchasing info record or, in its absence, from the material master record.

Reminder 1, 2, 3

These fields indicate the time interval in days at which reminders are to be issued to the vendor before (if the number is negative) or after the due date. The due date depends on the purchasing document. For example, for RFQ, it is receipt of quotation.

Standard value for delivery time variance

Is one week delay in delivery too much, or too less? The answer depends on the material. In this field, the value in days specifies how many days variance from the planned delivery date is to count as a 100% variance. If the actual delivery is 2 days after the planned delivery date and this field contains 10, then the variance is 20%.

Shipping instructions

This field specifies the packaging and shipping instructions for the item. Shipping instructions are configured in view cluster VC_T027A, which is discussed in Section 2.11.

Under-delivery tolerance

This field specifies the percentage (of the order quantity) up to which an under-delivery of this item will be accepted.

Over-delivery tolerance

This field specifies the percentage (of the order quantity) up to which an over-delivery of this item will be accepted.

Minimum delivery quantity in percentage (%)

This is the minimum percentage of the purchase order quantity that must be delivered for the goods receipt to be included in the vendor evaluation. In this way, you can prevent a vendor from receiving a good score for a punctual delivery, where the quantity delivered was insufficient.

Unlimited over-delivery

This field specifies whether unlimited over-delivery can be accepted for the item.

Acknowledgement required

This field indicates whether the vendor is required to acknowledge the receipt of purchasing document, e.g. purchase order, outline purchase agreement, etc.

Material Level Manufacturer Data

Other data / manufacturer data		
		Mfr Part Profile
Mfr Part Number		Manufact.

Manufacturer part profile

This field contains a profile, if you work with MPN materials. The profile then applies to all MPN materials that are assigned to this firm's own, inventory-managed material.

Manufacturer part number and manufacturer

This field contains the number used by the manufacturer, or by the vendor, to manage a material. If there is just one manufacturer part number for your firm's own inventory-managed material, the manufacturer is specified. In that case, there is no need to create an MPN material. In order to use manufacturer part numbers, it must be enabled in view V_130S.

Plant Level General Data

General Data				
Base Unit of Measure	PC	piece(s)	Order Unit	Var. OUn
Purchasing Group	001		Material Group	001
Plant-sp.matl status			Valid from	
Tax ind. f. material			Qual.f.FreeGoodsDis.	
Material freight grp			☐ Autom. PO	
			OB Management	
☐ Batch management			OB ref. matrial	

Purchasing group

Purchasing group is a buyer or a group of buyers. Here you specify the purchasing group that is responsible for buying this material for this plant.

Plant specific material status, valid from

If you do not want the material to be purchased after a certain date, you can do so by specifying the material status `Blocked for Purchasing` with the date from which the blocking is effective. This can be done for all the plants in the `Basic data 1` tab or for individual plants in the `Purchasing` tab.

Tax indicator for material

The tax indicator is used in the automatic determination of the tax code in Purchasing. The tax code can be determined automatically by price determination using purchasing conditions.

Material freight group

Material freight group determines freight codes and classes in a freight code set. The freight code set is used to determine freight costs. Configuration of the freight groups and codes is in Sales and Distribution.

Automatic PO

Here you can specify that purchase orders can be generated automatically from purchase requisitions using transaction ME59N. To make the generation automatic, a further indicator must be set in the vendor master record of the vendor associated with the purchase order.

Original batch management and original batch reference material

The concept of original batch is used in batch management.

Plant Level Other Data

Other data / manufacturer data			
GR Processing Time	1 days	☐ Post to insp. stock	☐ Critical Part
Quota arr. usage		☐ Source list	JIT Sched. Indicator
			Mfr Part Profile
Mfr Part Number			Manufact.

GR processing time

This field specifies the number of workdays required for inspection of material after its receipt.

Post to inspection stock

By default a material is received in unrestricted use stock. However, if you want the material to be received in quality inspection stock by default, set this indicator. This indicator is copied to purchase order items, and when goods are received, quality inspection stock is proposed by default.

Critical part

This field specifies that this is a critical material, and during stock taking, it should be counted completely.

Quota arrangement usage

Quota arrangement determines which vendor or plant should get the next order. This decision is based on the quantity ordered on the vendor, or the plant, and its share of business. The key question here is what purchasing documents should be included in determining the quantity ordered. Quota arrangement usage determines the purchasing documents that are included in determining how much quantity has been ordered. SAP provides the following preconfigured options.

Q	PO	SLn	PlOr	PReq	MRP	Ord
1	☑	☑	☐	☐	☐	☐
2	☑	☑	☑	☑	☐	☐
3	☑	☑	☑	☑	☑	☐
4	☑	☑	☑	☑	☑	☑

Source list

If this indicator is set for a plant, a source of supply must be entered in the source list before the material can be ordered.

JIT schedule indicator

This indicator determines whether it is possible to generate JIT delivery schedules in addition to forecast schedules for a material specified in a purchase scheduling agreement.

2.1.8 Units of Measure

Sometimes, for a material, you use different units of measures for different purposes. You need to convert quantities from one unit to another. You can maintain this conversion in the material master. If you click **➡ Additional data** in the material master, you get additional tabs in which you can enter data about a material. One of these tabs is the **Units of measure**.

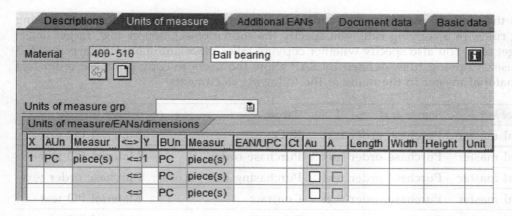

Material

You specify units of measures and their conversion to each other for this material.

Units of measure group

In the tab above, either you can maintain the data yourself, or you can copy sets of predefined conversions, by specifying Units of measure grp. Units of measure groups are defined in view V_006M. If you enter a Units of measure grp in the tab above, all entries for that units of measure group are copied in the tab.

Unit group	Alt. Unit	Measurement unit text	Counter	Denominat.
LAMP	PAC	Pack	50	1
LAMP	PAL	Pallet	1,000	1
LAMP	PC	piece(s)	1	1

Conversion

Here you specify the ratios for converting a quantity of this material from one unit to another.

2.1.9 Material Texts

In the material master you can maintain the texts specified in view V_TTXIDI.

Object	ID	Meaning
MATERIAL	BEST	Purchase order text
MATERIAL	GRUN	Basic data text
MATERIAL	IVER	Internal note
MATERIAL	PRUE	Inspection text

Purchase order text can be entered in the Purchase order text tab. For the other three texts, click ➡ Additional data and go to the appropriate tab. In all these tabs, you can enter the texts in multiple languages.

Texts in the material master can be copied in the items of purchasing documents using copying rules. In a copying rule, you specify the source object, source text, target object and target text. You also specify whether copying takes place automatically or is decided by the user. Copying rules defined by SAP allow the users to copy purchase order text of the material master in the items of the following documents.

Source object	Source text	Target object	Target text
Material master	Purchase order text	RFQ	Material PO text
Material master	Purchase order text	Purchase order	Material PO text
Material master	Purchase order text	Purchasing info record	Purchase order text
Material master	Purchase order text	Contract	Material PO text
Material master	Purchase order text	Scheduling agreement	Material PO text

2.1.10 Plant Data/Storage 1

Material, Plant, Storage Location

Forecasting	Plant data / stor. 1	Plant data / stor. 2	Quality management

Material	400-510	Ball bearing
Plant	1000	Werk Hamburg
Stor. Loc.	0001	Materiallager

Not all data in this view is at storage location level. Some data is at material level, some at plant level, and some at storage location level. These are discussed separately. If you do not specify the plant and the storage location, you will see the material level data in this tab.

Material Level General Data

General data

Base Unit of Measure	PC	piece(s)	
Temp. conditions		Storage conditions	
Container reqmts		Haz. material number	
		Number of GR slips	
Label type		Lab.form	☐ Appr.batch rec. req.
☐ Batch management			

Base unit of measure

The base unit of measure is the unit in which stocks of the material are managed. The system converts all the quantities you enter in other units of measure (alternative units of measure) to the base unit of measure. The base unit of measure is the unit satisfying the highest necessary requirement for precision.

Temperature conditions

Some of your materials may require storage at certain temperatures. In view V_143, you maintain the master list of temperature conditions.

Temp. conditions	Description
20	20° Fahrenheit
30	30° Fahrenheit
40	40° Fahrenheit

Storage conditions

Some of your materials may require special storage conditions. In view V_142, you maintain the master list of storage conditions.

SC	Description
HU	Controlled humidity
RA	Radioactive material
RE	Refrigerator
SU	No sunlight

Container requirements

Some of your materials may require certain containers for storage and transport. In view V_144, you maintain the master list of container requirements.

Container reqmts	Description
B1	Bin 2' x 2' x 1'
B2	Bin 3' x 3' x 2'
P3	Pallet 3' x 3'
P4	Pallet 4' x 4'

Hazardous material number

The hazardous material number indicates that the material is dangerous, making special precautions necessary for its storage and shipment.

Number of goods receipt slips

You may print goods receipt slips that accompany the goods during storage and movement. The goods receipt slip usually has information on the material, vendor, purchase order, goods receipt date, plant, and storage location. The base unit of material is usually a small unit, e.g. pieces. However, the material is usually stored and moved in larger units, e.g. cartons. You need a goods receipt slip per carton, not per piece. In this field, you can maintain the ratio. During goods receipt, you will specify the number of pieces received, and the system will determine the number of goods receipt slips to be printed. If you enter nothing in this field, only one goods receipt slip is printed.

Label type

You may also print goods labels. One label is printed for each unit of goods. Labels may be of different types. Master list of label types is maintained in view V_6WP3.

Label type	Text
ST	Sticker
TG	Tag

Label form

Label form determines the size and layout of the label. Master list of label forms is maintained in view V_6WP4.

Label form	Text
E1	Label quantity in order quantity
E2	Label quantity in stock quantity
E3	Label quantity in order price quantity

Approved batch record required

In process industry, you may approve batches before they can be stored for unrestricted use. For such materials, select this indicator.

Batch management

Here you can specify that the material is managed in batches.

Material Level Shelf Life Data

Shelf life data			
Min. Rem. Shelf Life		Total shelf life	
Period Ind. for SLED	D	Rounding rule SLED	
Storage percentage			

The shelf life data is used for checking shelf life expiration in Inventory Management.

Plant Level General Data

```
General data
  Base Unit of Measure   [PC]    piece(s)        Unit of issue              [    ]
  Temp. conditions       [  ]                    Storage conditions         [  ]
  Container reqmts        [  ]                    Haz. material number       [        ]
  CC phys. inv. ind.      [  ]    ☐ CC fixed     Number of GR slips         [        ]
  Label type              [  ]    Lab.form  [  ]  ☐ Appr.batch rec. req.
                                 OBManagmnt [  ]  OB Ref. Material           [        ]
  ☐ Batch management
```

Unit of issue

Here you enter the unit that the system proposes for goods issues, transfer postings, other goods receipts, and reservations. You should enter a value in this field only, if you want to use a unit of measure differing from the base unit of measure.

Cycle counting physical inventory indicator and cycle counting fixed

These fields are used in cycle counting in physical inventory.

Original batch management and original batch reference material

The concept of original batch is used in batch management.

Storage Location Level Data

```
  Storage Bin        [        ]        Picking area        [    ]
```

Storage bin

Here you specify the storage bin within a storage location where the material is stored. The storage bin is only significant, if you do not use SAP Warehouse Management. It appears on goods receipt/issue slips.

Picking area

The picking area groups together storage bins from the standpoint of picking strategies; that is, the storage bins are arranged in a strategically advantageous manner for the task of picking.

2.1.11 Plant Data/Storage 2

Material, Plant and Storage Location

⚙ Plant data / stor. 1	♂ Plant data / stor. 2	Quality management	Accounting...

Material	400-510	Ball bearing	ℹ
Plant	1000	Werk Hamburg	
Stor. Loc.	0001	Materiallager	⊗ 🗋

Not all data in this view is at storage location level. Some data is at material level, some at plant level, and some at storage location level. These are discussed separately. If you do not specify the plant and the storage location, you will see the material level data in this tab.

Material Level Weight/Volume Data

Weight/volume			
Gross Weight	3	Weight unit	KG
Net Weight	3		
Volume		Volume unit	
Size/dimensions			

Here you maintain the weight, volume, and size of the material. This data can also be maintained in `Basic data 1` tab.

Material Level General Plant Parameters

General plant parameters	
SerLevel	

Serialization level

Serialization level	Short text
	Serialization within the stock material number
1	Keep equipment number and serial number synchronous

You may give a serial number to each item of a material, e.g. a car, or an engine. The serial numbers uniquely identify an item within a material number. These materials are assigned `Serialization level` blank. However, for plant and machinery, you want the serial number to be synchronous with equipment. These materials are assigned `Serialization level` 1.

Plant Level General Plant Parameters

General plant parameters

☐ Neg. stocks in plant   Log. handling group ⬜

Serial no. profile   ⬜   SerLevel ⬜   Distr. profile   ⬜

Profit Center   `1010`   Stock determ. group   ⬜

Negative stocks allowed in plant

Here you specify whether negative stocks are allowed for the material in the plant.

Logistics handling group

The logistics handling group is used in the calculation of working loads such as placement into stock and picking. The master list of logistics handling group is maintained in view V_TLOG.

Serial number profile

A serial number profile must be assigned to each material that is to be serialized. This assignment at plant level is made here.

Distribution profile

Here you can assign a control profile for merchandise distribution. Materials can be distributed among the individual recipients in a plant. The master list of distribution profiles is maintained in view V_TMFPF.

Profit centre

The profit centre you specify here is used in cost accounting.

Stock determination group

Stock determination groups classify materials for stock determination. Here you can specify the stock determination group of a material in a plant.

Storage Location Level Data

There is no storage location level field in this tab.

2.1.12 Plant Stock

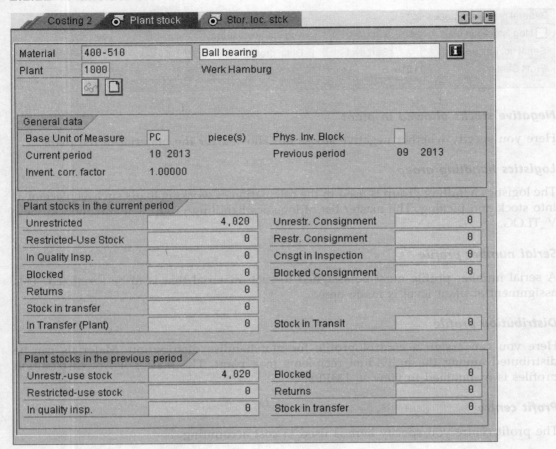

The fields in this tab are the same as the stock fields for a storage location. For stock in transfer and stock in transit, the storage location is not known until they are received in the receiving plant. Hence, they are shown at the receiving plant level.

In transfer (plant)

This field shows the quantity that has already been withdrawn from the issuing plant, but has not yet arrived at the receiving plant. Until the material arrives at the receiving plant, the system manages it as stock in transfer belonging to the receiving plant. This does not include the quantity being transferred on the basis of stock transport orders.

Stock in transit

This field shows the quantity of a material that has already been withdrawn from stock in the issuing plant, but not yet arrived at the receiving plant when stock is transferred using a stock transport order. Stock in transit is managed in the valuated stock of the receiving plant. However, its use is not yet unrestricted.

2.1.13 Storage Location Stock

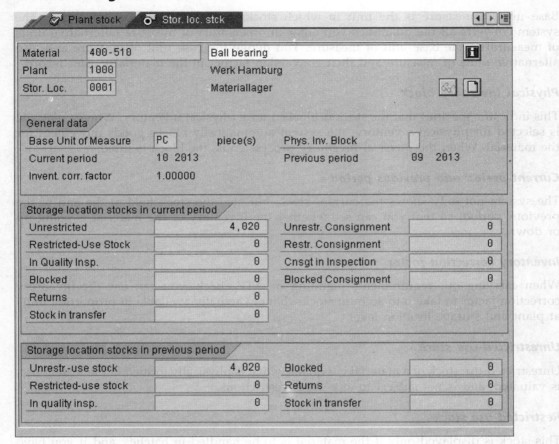

Material

SAP allows you to buy and use a material without a material number, but you cannot stock or produce a material without a material number. You can stock a material only if it has a material number.

Plant, storage location

Normally a material is stocked in a storage location of a plant. Exceptions to this rule are:

➢ Stock held with a vendor, e.g. in the case of subcontracting
➢ Stock held with a customer, e.g. in the case of consignment
➢ Stock in transit
➢ In transfer (plant)

These stocks are held directly at plant level, not at storage location level.

Base unit of measure

Base unit of measure is the unit in which stocks of the material are managed. The system converts all the quantities you enter in other units of measure (alternative units of measure) to the base unit of measure. You define the base unit of measure and also alternative units of measure and their conversion factors in the material master record.

Physical inventory block

This indicator specifies that the stock is blocked for a physical inventory. When a material is selected for physical inventory, the system automatically blocks goods movement for the material. When the physical inventory process ends, the block is lifted.

Current period and previous period

The system not only shows the current stock, but also the stock held at the end of the previous period, so that you can see whether the inventory of the material is going up or down.

Inventory correction factor

When carrying out requirements planning or ATP check, you can use the inventory correction factor to take into account stocks that are actually available in proportion units at plant and storage location level.

Unrestricted-use stock

Unrestricted-use stock of a material is a quantity that is physically located in the warehouse, is valuated, and is not subject to any usage restrictions.

Restricted-use stock

This stock is displayed only if the material is to be handled in batches, and if you have flagged the stock as restricted in the batch master record using the status key. This stock is regarded as available in materials planning.

Stock in quality inspection

This field shows the quantity of material in quality inspection.

Blocked stock

This stock is only shown, if the material is managed in batches. This means that you need to have identified the stock with the appropriate batch status key in the batch's master segment. This stock is considered as unavailable for the purposes of material requirements planning.

Returns (blocked stock)

This field shows customer returns. Because returns from customers normally have to be inspected, they are posted initially to the blocked stock returns where they are not subject to valuation or unrestricted use. If the result of the inspection is that the stock can be released for unrestricted use, you enter this conclusion as a separate step. Valuation then takes place for the goods received.

Stock in transfer (from one storage location to another)

This field shows the quantity that has already been withdrawn from the issuing storage location, but has not yet arrived at the receiving storage location. Until its arrival, the system manages this material as stock in transfer of the receiving storage location. This does not include the quantity being transferred on the basis of stock transport orders.

Consignment fields

Some of your vendors may stock their own material at your premises. You pay for the material only after you use it. This is called consignment. Although the material belongs to the vendor, you are responsible for its safe-keeping and accounting. These fields contain quantity of material with you under consignment. Unrestricted-use, blocked, etc., have the same meaning as your own material.

Previous period fields

These fields display quantities at the end of the previous period. This information is useful in knowing whether the inventory is going up or down.

2.1.14 Accounting 1

Material, Plant, and Valuation Type

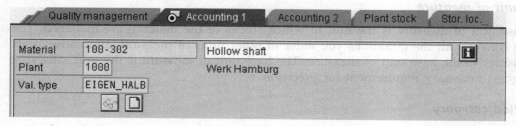

Valuation area

SAP uses the concept of valuation area within which a material has the same price. At the enterprise level, you can decide whether you want valuation area to be at plant level, or at company code level. You make this choice in transaction OX14.

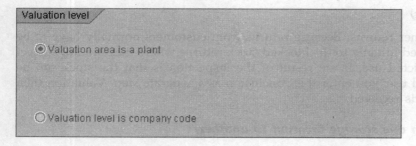

This choice is at client level. Therefore, it affects all company codes.

Level of data in this tab

The data in this tab is at the level of valuation area. In this implementation, valuation area is a plant that is why you see the Plant field here. If the valuation area was company code, you would have seen the Company code field here.

Material with split valuation

If the material has a split valuation, the valuation type field also appears and the data is at material, valuation area, and valuation type level.

General Data

General data				
Base Unit of Measure	PC	piece(s)	Valuation Category	B
Currency	EUR		Current period	12 2013
Division	01		Price determ.	☐ ML act.

Base unit of measure

The base unit of measure is the unit in which stocks of the material are managed. The system converts all the quantities you enter in other units of measure (alternative units of measure) to the base unit of measure. The base unit of measure is the unit satisfying the highest necessary requirement for precision.

Valuation category

You can do split valuation only if the material has a valuation category. If the valuation category for a material is blank, you cannot do split valuation.

ValCat	Description
B	Inhse/ext.proc.
C	Status
H	Origin

In the case of split valuation, the valuation category also determines which valuation types are allowed.

Currency

The system shows the currency for all the values on this tab.

Current period

The system shows the current posting period.

Division

Division is a way of grouping materials, products, or services from the point of view of Sales and Distribution. The system uses divisions to determine the sales areas and the business areas for a material, product, or service.

Price determination

This indicator is only of use, if the material ledger is active.

Material ledger active

This checkbox indicates whether material ledger valuation is active for the material.

Current Valuation

Current valuation			
Valuation Class	7900		
VC: Sales order stk		Proj. stk val. class	
Price control	S	Price Unit	1
Moving price	350.00	Standard price	350.00
Total Stock	495	Total Value	173,250.00
		☐ Valuated Un	
Future price		Valid from	

Valuation class

Valuation classes classify materials so that their inventory is managed in appropriate G/L accounts such as Raw material, Finished goods, WIP, etc. Using this feature, you can post raw materials to one stock account and bought out parts to another. Valuation classes possible for a material are restricted by the account category reference of the material type of the material.

Valuation class: sales order stock

If you want to post sales order stock of a material to an account different from the account to which the standard stock is posted, you can specify a valuation class here. Valuation classes possible for a material are restricted by the account category reference of the material type of the material.

Valuation class: project stock

If you want to post project stock of a material to an account different from the account to which the standard stock is posted, you can specify a valuation class here. Valuation classes possible for a material are restricted by the account category reference of the material type of the material.

Price control

The inventory of a material may be managed at standard price, or at moving average price.

Price control	Short text
S	Standard price
V	Moving average price/periodic unit price

This parameter affects the accounting of goods receipt for storage.

Price unit

Normally the price is for one unit, but sometimes it may be for a number of units.

Moving price

When goods are received, the system calculates the moving average price automatically by dividing the total value of the material in the valuation area by the total stock in the valuation area.

Standard price

You can maintain inventory of a material in a valuation area (plant or company code), at standard price that you specify here. The difference in the value of the material received and that calculated at standard price is charged to the income from price difference account.

Total stock

Here the system shows the stock of the material in the valuation area (plant or company code), or if applicable, for the valuation type.

Total value

Here the system shows the value of the material in the valuation area (plant or company code), or if applicable, for the valuation type.

Valuated unit

Here you can indicate that the valuation is based on batch-specific unit of measure.

Future price, valid from

If you want to change the material's price on a future date, you specify the price and the date.

Previous Valuation and Standard Cost Estimate

Previous period/year	Std cost estimate

Previous period/year

Click [Previous period/year] to display valuation data for previous period and year.

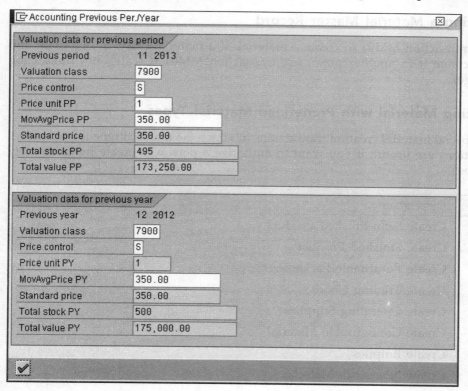

Standard cost estimate

Click [Std cost estimate] to see the standard cost estimate.

2.2 MATERIAL MASTER PROCESSES

Functional Consultant	User	Business Process Owner	Senior Management	My Rating	Understanding Level
A	A	A	B		

2.2.1 Creating a Material Master Record

You can use transaction MM01 to create a material. If a material exists in one plant and you want to create it in another plant, use transaction MM01 (Create), not transaction MM02 (Change).

2.2.2 Creating Material with Predefined Material Types

You can use special material creation transactions in which the material type is predefined. These transactions are useful, if you want to authorize a person to create materials only of specific types.

Transaction	Description
MMB1	Create Semi-finished Product
MMF1	Create Finished Product
MMG1	Create Returnable Packaging
MMH1	Create Trading Goods
MMI1	Create Operating Supplies
MMK1	Create Configurable Material
MML1	Create Empties
MMN1	Create Non-stock Material
MMP1	Create Maintenance Assembly
MMR1	Create Raw Material
MMS1	Create Service
MMU1	Create Non-valuated Material
MMV1	Create Packaging
MMW1	Create Competitor Product

2.2.3 Displaying a Material Master Record

You can use transaction MM03 to display a material.

2.2.4 Changing a Material Master Record

You can use transaction MM02 to change a material. The system logs the changes made. You can see the changes made to a material by selecting Environment ➤ Display changes .

2.2.5 Changing Material Type

If you want to change the material type, use transaction MMAM and specify the new material type because the screen you get depends on the material type.

2.2.6 Mass Maintenance of Material Master

If you want to make similar changes in several materials, use transaction MM17. Here you can select the tables and fields you want to maintain.

Object Type	BUS1001	Materials (industry)
Variant Name		

Tables   Fields

Short Description	Table Name
General Material Data	MARA
Material Descriptions	MAKT
Plant Data for Material	MARC
Material Valuation	MBEW
Storage Location Data for Material	MARD
Units of Measure for Material	MARM
Sales Data for Material	MVKE
Forecast Parameters	MPOP
Planning Data	MPGD_MASS
Tax Classification for Material	MLAN
Material Data for Each Warehouse Number	MLGN
Material Data for Each Storage Type	MLGT

In this transaction, you can make changes for several materials in a single screen.

2.2.7 Displaying Change Documents

You can use transaction MM04 to view the changes that have taken place in a material.

2.2.8   Deleting a Material Master Record

Flagging a material for deletion

You can use transaction MM06 to flag a material for deletion. You may not delete the material data completely. You can delete it for a plant, storage location, etc. If you want to review materials that are without stock, in the initial screen, you can select Extras ➤ Proposal list... to generate the proposed deletion list. You can select a combination of material, plant and storage location from this list, which is then transferred to the initial screen for deletion.

Deleting a material

To actually delete a material, run transaction MM71.

Removing deletion flag

Transaction MM06 can also be used to remove the deletion flag, if transaction MM71 has not been run to actually delete the material. Run transaction MM06, remove the tick, and save.

2.2.9   Scheduling Material Creation, Change, and Deletion

You can schedule creation, change, or deletion of a material. Specify the date when the change would come in effect.

Transaction	Description
MM11	Schedule Creation of Material
MM12	Schedule Changing of Material
MM16	Schedule Material for Deletion

The planned changes do not take effect until you run transaction MM13.

2.2.10   Displaying Scheduled Changes

You can display planned changes and how a material would look on a given date.

Transaction	Description
MM14	Display Planned Changes
MM19	Display Material at Key Date

2.2.11 Activating Planned Changes

If you schedule creation, change, or deletion of a material, you need to activate the changes using transaction MM13. You can use this facility to create a two-step material maintenance process. Several persons may schedule material creation, change, or deletion. A higher level person would periodically review the planned changes and activate them.

2.2.12 Extending a Material to Storage Locations

You can run transaction MMSC to extend a material in a plant to one or more storage locations.

Material	400-510	Ball bearing
Plant	1000	Werk Hamburg
Base Unit	PC	

Storage locations

SLoc	Copy from	Bin	MRP	Reorder Point	Fixed lot size	SPT
0001						

2.2.13 Loading Material Data from a File

You can use program RMDATIND to transfer material master records to SAP for test purposes. Production data is transferred with program RBMVSHOW (transaction BMV0). Program RMMMDE00 can be used to delete all material data in the current client.

2.3   MATERIAL MASTER REPORTS

Functional Consultant	User Process Owner	Business Management	Senior Rating	My Understanding	Level
A	A	A	B		

2.3.1 Materials List

Run transaction MM60 to display the list of materials.

Material	Plant	Material Description	MTyp	Matl Group	Unit	ABC	Pr.	Price	Crcy	PGr
817	1000	Paint	HAWA	004	PC		V	10.00	EUR	
819	1000	Wallpaper	HAWA	00107	PC		S	350.00	EUR	
820	1000	Door	HAWA	00107	PC		S	600.00	EUR	
1157	1000	170DS55001C-184M	HALB	00101	EA		V	4,190.38	EUR	001
100-100	1000	Casing	HALB	001	PC		S	113.76	EUR	100

2.3.2 Stock Overview

You can run transaction MMBE to see stock overview of one or more materials. The stock is displayed at multiple levels, e.g. client, company code, plant, storage location, etc. It is also displayed in various categories, e.g. unrestricted use, quality inspection, blocked, etc.

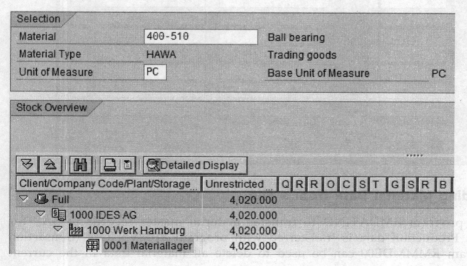

2.4 MATERIAL MASTER SCREEN

Functional Consultant	User	Business Process Owner	Senior Management	My Rating	Understanding Level
A	C	C	C		

2.4.1 Screen Sequence Determination

Purpose

The screen that you get for maintaining the material master is technically called a screen sequence, and can depend on the transaction, the user, the material type and the industry sector. In this view cluster you define how the screen sequence is determined.

IMG Node

SM34 ➤ V_CM2

Screen Sequence Control

The screen sequence used for maintaining material master can depend on the following:

- 📁 Transaction screen reference
- 📁 User screen reference
- 📁 Material type screen reference
- 📁 Industry sector screen reference

For each combination of these four variables, the screen sequence is defined here.

Dialog Structure	SRef. trans.	SRef. user	SRef. matl type	SRef. industry	SSq	Screen seq. description
🗁 Screen sequence control	01	*	*	*	21	Std ind.(short) tab pages
📁 Transaction screen reference	01	*	HERS	*	12	Manufacturer Parts
📁 User screen reference	01	*	PLM	*	PL	Std ind.(short) tab pages
📁 Material type screen reference	01	*	ROH	B	ZB	Excise Duty + VSO
📁 Industry sector screen reference	01	*	ROH	C	EH	Std (short) w/EH&S tabs

Transaction Screen Reference

You can group your transactions in transaction screen references, which are used for determining screen sequence.

Dialog Structure	TCode	Transaction Text	SRef. trans.
📁 Screen sequence control	MAL1	Create material via ALE	01
🗁 Transaction screen reference	MAL2	Change material via ALE	01
📁 User screen reference	MM01	Create Material &	01
📁 Material type screen reference	MM02	Change Material &	01
📁 Industry sector screen reference	MM03	Display Material &	01

User Screen Reference

You can group your users in user screen references, which are used for determining screen sequence.

Dialog Structure		Name	SRef: user
🗁 Screen sequence control		ALBAT	
🗁 Transaction screen reference		ASCHE	EH
🗁 User screen reference		BAESSLER	BA
🗁 Material type screen reference		BATIPPS	EB
🗁 Industry sector screen reference		BLUMOEHR	

Material Type Screen Reference

You can group your material types in material type screen references, which are used for determining screen sequence.

Dialog Structure		MTyp	Material type description	SRef: matl type
🗁 Screen sequence control		ABF	Waste	ROH
🗁 Transaction screen reference		AEM	Samples	ROH
🗁 User screen reference		BLG	BLG Empties External	ROH
🗁 Material type screen reference		BLGA	BLGAEmpties Fixed assets	ROH
🗁 Industry sector screen reference		CH00	CH Contract Handling	ROH

Industry Sector Screen Reference

You can group your industry sectors in industry sector screen references, which are used for determining screen sequence.

Dialog Structure		I	Industry description	SRef: industry
🗁 Screen sequence control		1	Retail	M
🗁 Transaction screen reference		2	Aerospace & Defense	M
🗁 User screen reference		3	Service Provider	M
🗁 Material type screen reference		A	Plant Engin./Construction	M
🗁 Industry sector screen reference		B	Beverage	B

2.4.2 Screen Sequence Definition

Purpose

When you maintain material master, you get a screen. This screen is defined here.

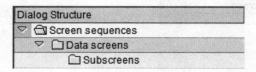

A screen, technically called a `Screen sequence:`, consists of several `Data screens` (tabs in the material master). Each `Data screens` in turn consists of `Subscreens`, whose sequence can be changed. The screen sequence used is determined based on transaction, user, material type and industry sector.

IMG Node

SM34 ➤ V_CM1

Screen Sequences

When you maintain material master, you get a screen. This screen can be customized to your requirement. There are multiple levels in defining this screen. The highest level is the screen sequence. Although SAP provides many preconfigured screen sequences, screen sequence 21 is default. This book also uses screen sequence 21. In this screen sequence, data is grouped in tabs.

Dialog Structure	SSq	Screen seq. description
▽ ◱ Screen sequences	01	Std industry sequence
▽ ▭ Data screens	03	Standard retail sequence
▭ Subscreens	11	Std industry: small scrns
	12	Manufacturer Parts
	21	Std ind.(short) tab pages

Data Screens

The tabs that you see while maintaining material master are defined as data screens here. Screen sequence 21 has the following data screens:

SSq	Scrn	Screen description	T	SC	M	GUI status	TT	R	Alt. screen descrip.
21	07	Basic Data 1	1	4004	K	DATE00	2		Basic data 1
21	08	Basic Data 2	1	4004	K	DATE00	2		Basic data 2
21	09	Sales: Sales Org. Data 1	1	4000	V	DATE00	2		Sales: sales org. 1
21	10	Sales: Sales Org. Data 2	1	4000	V	DATE00	2		Sales: sales org. 2
21	11	Sales: General/Plant Data	1	4000	V	DATE00	2		Sales: General/Plant

Subscreens

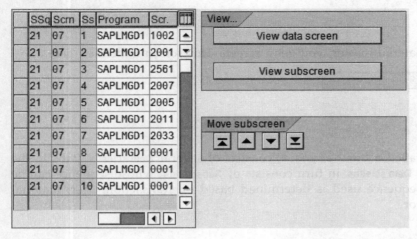

SSq	Scrn	Ss	Program	Scr.	
21	07	1	SAPLMGD1	1002	
21	07	2	SAPLMGD1	2001	
21	07	3	SAPLMGD1	2561	
21	07	4	SAPLMGD1	2007	
21	07	5	SAPLMGD1	2005	
21	07	6	SAPLMGD1	2011	
21	07	7	SAPLMGD1	2033	
21	07	8	SAPLMGD1	0001	
21	07	9	SAPLMGD1	0001	
21	07	10	SAPLMGD1	0001	

A data screen consists of several subscreens. If you click **View data screen**, you see the entire tab, but if you click **View subscreen**, you see only a part of the tab. If you change the sequence of subscreens, the sequence of the fields in the tab changes. You can move a subscreen up or down using the buttons.

Creating Your Own Subscreens

If you want to create your own subscreens, you can create a function group of your own by copying function group MGD1 (for industry) or function group MGD2 (for retail) using transaction OMT3C. The subscreens are not copied, except for two subscreens which are copied for technical reasons. You can use this copy to create subscreens of your own.

2.4.3 Additional Screens

Purpose

In the material master, apart from the main screens, you can go to additional screens by clicking ⇨ Additional data. Here you can specify that a secondary screen appears as an additional screen or is accessed by pushbutton from another main screen or additional screen.

IMG Node

SM30 ➢ V_T133S_ZUORD

Screen

Screen sequence 21   Std ind.(short) tab pages

Scr	Screen description	FCode			Additional			Processing routine
40	Descriptions				1			OKCODE_KURZTEXTE
41	Units of Measure				2			OKCODE_MENGENEINHEITEN
42	Basic Data Text	PB26			5			OKCODE_BDT
48	Consumption	PB09			8			OKCODE_VERBRAUCH

2.4.4 Sequence of Main and Additional Screens

Purpose

If you want to change the sequence of tabs in the material master, you can do that here.

IMG Node

SM30 ➤ V_T133S_REIHF

Screen

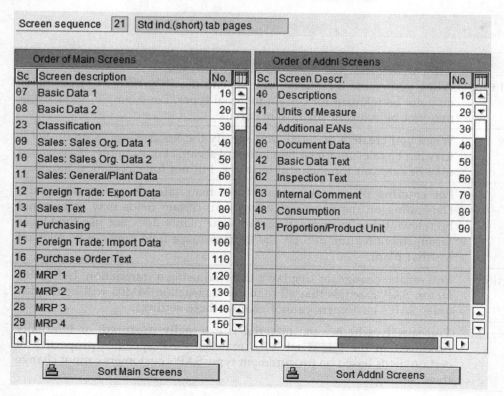

Screen sequence 21 Std ind.(short) tab pages

Order of Main Screens			Order of Addnl Screens		
Sc	Screen description	No.	Sc	Screen Descr.	No.
07	Basic Data 1	10	40	Descriptions	10
08	Basic Data 2	20	41	Units of Measure	20
23	Classification	30	64	Additional EANs	30
09	Sales: Sales Org. Data 1	40	60	Document Data	40
10	Sales: Sales Org. Data 2	50	42	Basic Data Text	50
11	Sales: General/Plant Data	60	62	Inspection Text	60
12	Foreign Trade: Export Data	70	63	Internal Comment	70
13	Sales Text	80	48	Consumption	80
14	Purchasing	90	81	Proportion/Product Unit	90
15	Foreign Trade: Import Data	100			
16	Purchase Order Text	110			
26	MRP 1	120			
27	MRP 2	130			
28	MRP 3	140			
29	MRP 4	150			

Sort Main Screens   Sort Addnl Screens

You get the main screens when you create, change or display material. You go to additional screens by clicking  .

2.4.5 Data Entry Properties of a Field

Overview

Data entry property of a field

In the material master, a field can have one of the following data entry properties:

| Hide | Display | Reqd Entry | Opt. entry |

Factors affecting data entry property of a field

The data entry property of a field is determined by the following factors:

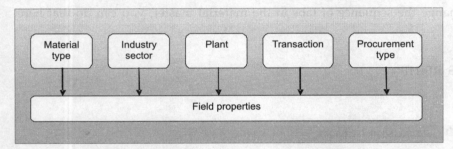

Factor	Determination of the factor and relevance
Material type	When you create a material, you specify the Material Type . Certain fields may not be relevant for certain material types. For example, CAD Indicator may not be relevant for raw materials.
Industry sector	When you create a material, you specify the Industry sector . Certain fields may not be relevant for certain industry sectors. For example, Highly viscous may be relevant for chemical industry, but not for mechanical industry.
Plant	For entering plant specific data for a material, you specify the plant. Depending on the nature of your plant, certain fields may or may not be relevant. For example, if one of your plants does not use the Quota arrangement feature of SAP, the Quota arr. usage field may not be relevant for that plant.
Transaction	You create, change, or display a material using a transaction. Using this factor, SAP specifies that all fields in transaction MM03 will be display only. SAP's customers cannot change these settings.
Procurement type	You specify whether the material is externally procured, or internally produced in the MRP 2 tab of a material. SAP specifies properties of certain fields based on procurement type. SAP's customers cannot change these settings.

Grouping of factors affecting field property (Field reference groups)

If material type influences data entry property of a field, you need to define data entry property of each field for each material type. The same is true for industry sector, plant, transaction, and procurement type. This design would require considerable effort in initial configuration and maintenance of the same. It is also prone to inconsistencies. SAP, therefore, lets you group the factor influences in Field reference groups.

Grouping of fields having identical field properties (Field selection groups)

There are certain fields which have identical data entry properties. You can group them in Field selection group.

Fields (Field selection group 87)	
Field name	Short Description
MARA-BEHVO	Container requirements
MARA-RAUBE	Storage conditions
MARA-STOFF	Hazardous material number
MARA-TEMPB	Temperature conditions indicator

Field properties for a combination of field reference group and field selection group

For each combination of field reference group and field selection group, you specify field property.

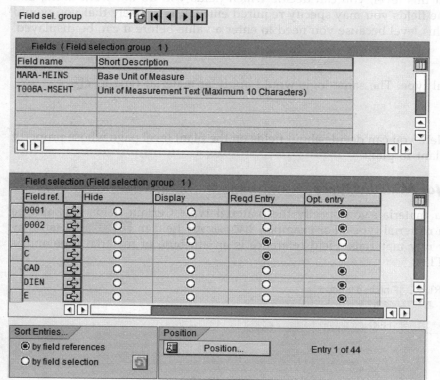

Determination of field property

Field reference groups represent factor influences. Each factor can give you one field reference group. So, you may have five field reference groups, each of which will have a data entry property. The system will use the field property as per the following priority:

Setting	Priority
Hide	1
Display	2
Required entry	3
Optional entry	4

Guidelines for determining properties of a field reference

It might seem daunting to adjust three variables to get the right field property; the other two are predetermined by SAP. But if you can evolve clear policy guidelines, it may be possible to tackle this complex task.

Industry sector

At the highest level is industry sector. A client will usually have one, or at the most a few, industry sectors. At this level, you can decide which fields you do not want at all, and hide them. For some fields you may specify required entry. It is unlikely that you would specify display at this level because you need to enter a value before it can be displayed.

Material type

The next is material type. The same logic would apply at material type level.

Plant

The next is plant. Here you can decide about fields on the plant level page whose property might vary from plant to plant.

Field References for Material Types

When you create a material, you specify the material type. Certain fields may not be relevant for certain material types. For example, CAD Indicator field in Basic data 2 tab may not be relevant for raw materials. Field reference is an attribute of material type and is specified in view T134.

Material Type	FERT	Finished product
General data		
Field reference	FERT	

Field References for Industry Sectors

A group may operate in multiple industry sectors, e.g. Automobiles, Chemical and Steel. There are certain fields that will not be relevant to each of these sectors. For example, the field Highly viscous in Basic data 2 tab may be relevant for Chemical industry, but not for Automobile industry. You may, therefore, decide to hide the field Highly viscous in the material master screen in the Automobile companies. Field references for industry sectors are defined in view V137. Industry sectors are also maintained through this view.

Industry sector	Industry description	Field reference
1	Retail	A
2	Aerospace & Defense	A
3	Service Provider	A
A	Plant Engin./Construction	A
B	Beverage	A
C	Chemical Industry	C
F	Food and Related Products	P
M	Mechanical Engineering	M
P	Pharmaceuticals	P
W	Retailing	A

It is recommended that you do not change the field references for industry sectors defined by SAP. By doing so, you will be able to use the field properties defined by SAP. You may change the field properties if you want to. If you define your own field reference for an industry sector, you must define the properties of all fields. If you change the field reference for an industry sector, you must review the properties of all fields.

Field References for Plants

You can use this feature for implementing plant-specific influence on field properties. For example, if one of your plants does not use the Quota arrangement feature of SAP, the Quota arr. usage field in the Purchasing tab may not be relevant for that plant. Field references for plants are defined in view V_130W. These are applicable only for plant level fields.

Plant	Name 1	Maintenance status	Field reference
1000	Werk Hamburg	KDEVALBPQSZXCFG	0001
1100	Berlin	KDEVALBPQSZXCFG	0001
1200	Dresden	KDEVALBPQSZXCFG	0001
1300	Frankfurt	KDEVALBPQSZXCFG	0001
1400	Stuttgart	KDEVALBPQSZXCFG	0001

Field References for Transactions

Field references for transactions are predefined in table T130M by SAP. There is no maintenance view for maintaining this field.

Transaction Code	Field reference
☐ MM01	MM01
☐ MM02	MM02
☐ MM03	MM03
☐ MM06	
☐ MM11	MM11
☐ MM12	MM12
☐ MM16	
☐ MM18	MM02
☐ MM19	MM03
☐ MM41	MM01
☐ MM42	MM02
☐ MM43	MM03

Field References for Procurement Types

Procurement type for a material

Each material has a procurement type in the MRP 2 view of the material.

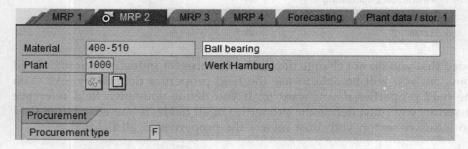

Master list of procurement types

The procurement type field can have the following values:

Procurement type	Short text
E	In-house production
F	External procurement
	No procurement
X	Both procurement types

Field references for procurement types

For each procurement type, the field reference is given below:

Procurement type	Field reference
E	E
F	F
Blank	No field reference
X	No field reference

Field Selection Groups

Fields are grouped in field selection groups. A field selection group is a logical grouping of fields that should have the same data entry property. Fields are assigned to a field group in view V_130F. A field can belong to only one field selection group.

Field name in full	Short Description	Sel. group	
CALP-AUFSG	Actual Markup in Sales Price Calculation	177	⇨
CALP-EKORG	Purchasing Organization	176	⇨
CALP-ENDPR	Final price	180	⇨
CALP-KZPBL	Indicates that prices at plant level are to be deleted	194	⇨
CALP-LIFNR	Vendor Account Number	176	⇨

Field Properties

Field properties are defined for each combination of field selection group and field reference group in view V_T130A_FLREF (transaction OMS9).

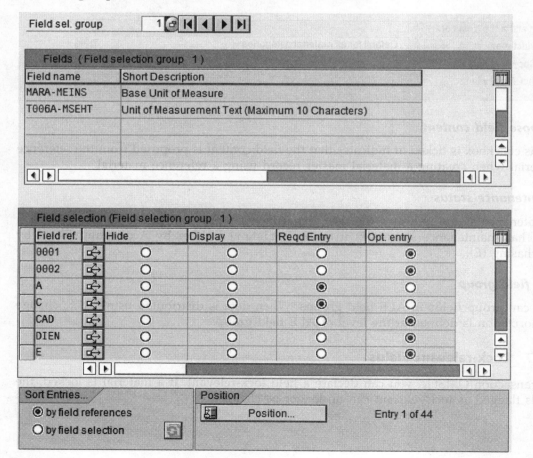

Field references with prefix SAP are valid client-wide and must not be changed. Field reference KB is also valid client-wide, but may be changed.

2.4.6   Field Attributes

Apart from data entry properties of a field, some other field attributes are also defined in view V_130F.

Field name	EINE-EKGRP
	Purchasing Group

Field attributes (industry and retail)

☐ Propose field cont.	
Maint. status	E
ALE field group	GR_E

Field attributes (retail only)

Restrict matl cat.	Default for all material categories
☑ Copy field content	
☐ Incl. initial values	

Propose field content

If this checkbox is ticked, it indicates that the field content is proposed from the reference material when creating a material master record using a reference material.

Maintenance status

Maintenance status indicates the user departments which can maintain this field. If a field has maintenance status BE, it can be maintained either by Accounting (B) or by Purchasing (E).

ALE field group

You can group fields in ALE field groups. When data is distributed using ALE, change authorization is defined at the level of ALE field group.

2.4.7   Lock-relevant Fields

In transaction OMSFIX you can declare a field lock-relevant. If a material is locked, the fields flagged as lock-relevant can no longer be changed.

Field name	Short Description	Lock-rel.
CALP-AUFSG	Actual Markup in Sales Price Calculatio	☐
CALP-EKORG	Purchasing Organization	☐
CALP-ENDPR	Final price	☐
CALP-KZPBL	Indicates that prices at plant level are to	☐

2.5 MATERIAL MASTER COMPLETENESS

Functional Consultant	User	Business Process Owner	Senior Management	My Rating	Understanding Level
A	C	C	X		

2.5.1 Maintenance Status

Since a material master record has so many views, ensuring completeness of material data is a challenging task. SAP provides a method of checking completeness and maintaining the missing data. This method is based on the concept of maintenance status. The data in the material master is divided in 15 functional areas or user departments. Each user department is given a one-character code.

User department	Maintenance status
Basic data	K
Classification	C
Sales	V
Purchasing	E
MRP	D
Forecasting	P
Work scheduling	A
Storage	L
Warehouse management	S
Quality management	Q
Accounting	B
Costing	G
Plant stocks	X
Storage location stocks	Z
Production resources/tools	F

Plant stock and storage location stocks are for display purpose only.

2.5.2 User Departments which have Maintained Data for a Material

When a user department creates its data for a material, the material master record acquires the corresponding maintenance status. The maintenance status is stored in a 15-character field in material master tables, e.g. MARA, MARC, MARD, etc. These fields are not maintained by users; they are updated by the system automatically. Table MARC contains the following data for material 400–510:

Material	Plant	Maint. status
400-510	1000	VEDPLQBG
400-510	3000	EDPLBGVXQ

This shows that sales data, `Maint. status` V , has been maintained for plant 1000, but not for plant 3000.

2.5.3 User Departments which are Required to Maintain Data for Materials of a Material Type

In view T134 (see section 2.7.8), for a material type you specify the user departments which are required to maintain data for a material. This is used for checking completeness of data for a material.

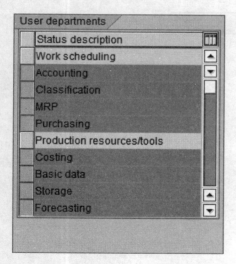

2.5.4 Checking and Completing Material Data

SAP provides transaction MM50 to identify incomplete data. In the initial screen, you limit the range of checking data completeness. For example, you may be interested in completing data for Purchasing department for plant 1000. In that case, you enter E in the Maintenance status field and 1000 in the Plant field in the initial screen. When you execute, you get the following result:

S	Created	Material	MTyp	I	CoCd	Plnt	SLoc	SOrg	DC	WhN	Material Description
E	21.12.2005	RX_5129	HALB	M		1000					Bolt
E	21.12.2005	RX_5170	HALB	M		1000					Drive
E	21.12.2005	RX_5210	HALB	M		1000					Booster Frame
E	21.12.2005	RX_5214	HALB	M		1000					Drive Unit
E	21.12.2005	RX_5221	HALB	M		1000					Rotation Column
E	21.12.2005	RX_5270	HALB	M		1000					Drive
E	18.01.2006	GTS-N2-013	HALB	M		1000					Engine Block
E	16.02.2006	GTS-RES02	HAWA	1		1000					milk powder

You can select one or more lines in this list and click Maintain materials . The system takes you to the material master screen where you can update and save the data. In this way, you can ensure completeness of the material data.

2.5.5 Maintenance Status of a Field

In view V_130F, you can see the maintenance status of a field.

Field name	EINE-EKGRP
	Purchasing Group

Field attributes (industry and retail)

☐ Propose field cont.

Maint. status	E
ALE field group	GR_E

Field attributes (retail only)

Restrict matl cat.	Default for all material categories

☑ Copy field content

☐ Incl. initial values

Maintenance status of a field indicates the user departments that can maintain the field. If a field has maintenance status BE, it can be maintained either by Accounting (B) or by Purchasing (E).

2.5.6 Maintenance Status Determination in Data Transfer

When you transfer material data, how do you determine maintenance status? Do you take into account all fields? You can select from the following options:

1	All fields are considered
2	All are considered except general fields for client/plant
3	Only single status fields are used as far as possible

You specify the value of this key for each screen sequence in view V_T133S.

	SSq	Screen seq. description		Determination type
	01	Std industry sequence	3	Only single status fields are used as far as possible
	11	Std industry: small scrns	3	Only single status fields are used as far as possible
	12	Manufacturer Parts	3	Only single status fields are used as far as possible
	21	Std ind.(short) tab pages	3	Only single status fields are used as far as possible

This setting is required only for data transfer, and only if you have not specified which maintenance statuses are to be created or changed during data transfer.

2.5.7 Maintenance Status for Plants

Maintenance statuses for plants are defined in view V_130W. In this view, you can restrict the maintenance statuses allowed for each plant.

	Plant	Name 1		Maintenance status	Field reference
	1000	Werk Hamburg		KDEVALBPQSZXCFG	0001
	1100	Berlin		KDEVALBPQSZXCFG	0001
	1200	Dresden		KDEVALBPQSZXCFG	0001
	1300	Frankfurt		KDEVALBPQSZXCFG	0001
	1400	Stuttgart		KDEVALBPQSZXCFG	0001

2.6 NUMBER RANGES

Functional Consultant	User	Business Process Owner	Senior Management	My Rating	Understanding Level
A	C	C	C		

2.6.1 Purpose

Here you define number ranges and link them to materials.

2.6.2 IMG Node

Transaction MMNR—Define Material Master Number Ranges

2.6.3 Overview

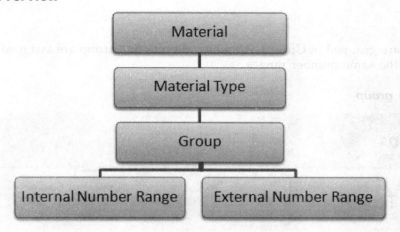

Number ranges in a group

A material can get number from the internal number range, or the external number range, which are accessed via material type and group. A group can be assigned at the most one internal number range, and at the most one external number range.

Internal material number

When you create a material, you have the option of using internal or external number range. If you do not specify a number, the system assigns the next number from internal number range. If an internal number range is not assigned to the group, it gives error.

External material number

If you specify a number or alphanumeric string, the system proceeds as follows:

➤ Checks that the number is not already used.

➤ Checks if ☐ External no. assignment w/o check field is selected for the material type in table T134.

  ➤ If the above field is selected, the system not to check the material number entered on the screen against the number range. In this case, the material number assigned must contain at least one letter, and not consist only of figures.

  ➤ If the above field is not selected, the system checks that the number is within the external number range assigned to the group.

External material number for unassigned material types

If you have not assigned a particular material type to a group, you can create materials of that type only if the ☑ External no. assignment w/o check field is selected for the material type in table T134. For materials of that type, you can use only the external material numbers.

2.6.4 Groups

Groups

Material types are grouped in Groups. All material types in a group are assigned material numbers from the same number ranges.

Materials in a group

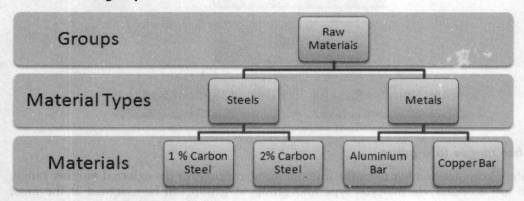

Groups are linked to material types as described below. All material types that are not assigned to a group belong to the group `Not assigned`. When a material is created in the material master, its material type is specified.

Through these linkages, each material belongs to a group.

Number ranges for a group

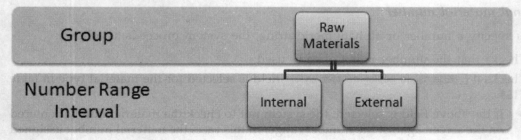

2.6.5 Creation of a Group

Click `✎ Groups` to maintain groups. You can create one or more groups. To create a group and to assign number ranges to it, click `Group ➤ Insert`.

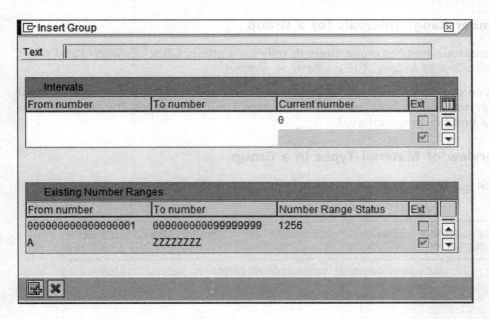

Enter the group name. Enter the range of numbers for internal and external number ranges. Press 'Enter' or click 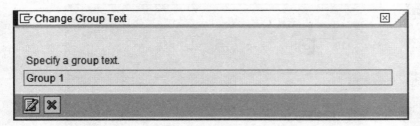 to add the group.

2.6.6 Renaming a Group

You can rename a group by selecting the group and clicking Group ➤ Maintain text .

2.6.7 Material Types in a Group

You can assign a material type to a group. A material type can belong to only one group. When a material type is created, it is automatically put in the group Not assigned. A material type in the Not assigned group, or in any group, can be assigned to another group. Place cursor on a material type and click 🔍 to select it. Then place the cursor on a group and click 🔲 Element/Group to assign the material type to the new group. The old assignment is automatically deleted.

2.6.8 Number Range Intervals for a Group

You should maintain number range intervals only for a group. Click [🖉 Groups] and select a group [☑ Foods and Beverages]. Click [Interval] ➤ [Maintain].

To a group you can assign only one internal number range interval and only one external number range interval. If both internal and external number ranges are assigned, you cannot add a number range interval.

2.6.9 Overview of Material Types in a Group

You can click [⬛] to see material types in a group and the number ranges assigned to the group.

Subobj.val No Year From number				To number	Number Range Status Ext P
Element		No No P			
01	0000000000000000001		0000000000099999999		1256
ABF	01 02				
AEM	01 02				
BLG	01 02				
BLGA	01 02				

2.6.10 Output Format of Material Numbers

You can define the output format of the material numbers in view V_TMCNV. There can be only one format.

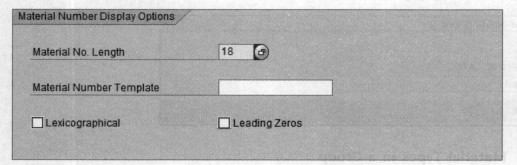

Material number length

Here you can specify the maximum length of the material numbers in your organization. The material number length cannot be more than 18, but you can specify shorter lengths.

Material number template

You can specify a template for the material numbers, consisting of editing characters and selection characters; an underscore (_) denotes a selection character that is replaced by a significant character in the material number. For example, the material number 12345678 (significant characters) with template __-_____-_ is stored as 12-34567-8. The length of the material number includes the editing characters, and is 10 in this case.

Lexicographical

This indicator is relevant only for numeric material numbers. Alphanumeric material numbers are stored as entered and are left justified.

Indicator	Assignment	Storage	Justification	Examples
Not set	Internal as well as external	The material number is padded with leading zeros to the defined length.	Right-justified	123 is stored as 0000000123 (if length is 10 characters).
Set	Internal	The material number is padded with leading zeros to the defined length.	Left-justified	123 is stored as 0000000123 (if length is 10 characters).
Set	External	The material number is not padded with leading zeros. Leading zeros, if entered, are stored too.	Left-justified	The material numbers 123 and 0123 are two different material numbers.

Leading zeros

If you tick this checkbox, a numeric material number is shown with leading zeros to fill up its defined length. If the ☐ Lexicographical indicator is set, then this indicator is ignored by the system.

2.7 MATERIAL TYPE

Functional Consultant	User	Business Process Owner	Senior Management	My Rating	Understanding Level
A	C	C	C		

2.7.1 Purpose

A material type is a group of materials with similar attributes. The material type allows the management of different materials in a uniform manner. The material type defines certain attributes of a material, which have important control functions, including screen layout determination, number range assignment, and material valuation.

2.7.2 IMG Node

SM34 ➤ MTART (view T134)

2.7.3 Material Type

Material Type	FERT	Finished product

Material type and description

SAP provides a number of predefined material types.

MTyp	Material type description
ABF	Waste
AEM	Samples
BLG	BLG Empties External
BLGA	BLGAEmpties Fixed assets
CH00	CH Contract Handling
COMP	Prod. alloc., purchased
CONT	KANBAN Container
COUP	Coupons
DIEN	Service
DOCU	documentary batch
EPA	Equipment Package
ERSA	Spare parts
FERT	Finished product

Select a material type and click 🔦 to see and change its properties. You can also create your own material types.

2.7.4 General Data

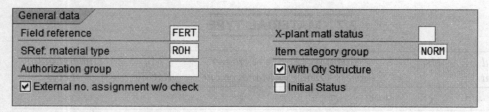

General data			
Field reference	FERT	X-plant matl status	
SRef. material type	ROH	Item category group	NORM
Authorization group		☑ With Qty Structure	
☑ External no. assignment w/o check		☐ Initial Status	

Field reference

On the material master screen you see a number of fields. The properties of these fields can be set as per your requirement based on five parameters as explained in section 2.4.5. Material type is one of the parameters. For a material type, you define the field reference here which is used in setting field properties.

Cross-plant material status

The cross-plant material status restricts the usability of the material for all plants.

01	Blocked for Procmnt/Whse
02	Blocked for task list/BOM
BP	Blocked for Purchasing
KA	Blocked for Costing
OB	Obsolete Materials
PI	Free for Pilot Phase

When you create a material of this type, the value specified in this field is proposed in the `X-plant matl status` field of `Basic data 1` tab by default. You can change the value there.

Screen reference: material type

Screen layout of materials master can differ for different material types. For more information, see section 2.4.1.

Item category group

When you create a material of this type, the value specified in this field is proposed in the `GenItemCatGroup` field of `Basic data 1` tab by default. You can change the value there.

Authorization group

You can give authorization to maintain material master record based on authorization group using authorization object M_MATE_MAT. You can specify authorization group at material type level here. If no authorization group is entered, no specific authorization check is carried out for materials of this material type.

With quantity structure

The value in this field provides the default value in the field `With Qty Structure` in the `Costing 1` tab of the materials master.

External number assignment without check

Internal and external number ranges are assigned to material types via group. If a material type is not assigned to any group, it has no internal or external number range assigned to it. You can tick this field to allow external number assignment without a check against the number range. In this case, the material number assigned must contain at least one letter, and should not consist only of figures.

Initial status

This indicator specifies that the initial status of a batch is "restricted".

2.7.5 Special Material Types

Special material types
☐ Material is configurable
☐ Material f. process
☐ Pipeline mandatory
☐ Manufacturer part

Material is configurable

If you tick this field and create a material of this type, the `Material is configurable` indicator in the material master is automatically set and you cannot change it. If you mark a material configurable, you should not be allowing quantity and value updating.

Material for process

This indicator allows materials of this type to be defined as materials for a process in which there may be co-products.

Pipeline mandatory

This indicator makes pipeline handling mandatory for materials of this type. Neither external nor internal purchase orders are possible for pipeline materials. In addition, neither quantities nor values are updated for these materials.

Manufacturer part

This indicator identifies materials of this type as manufacturer parts. In Purchasing, you can create a material master record for each manufacturer part number and assign it to your company's own material. Only a restricted amount of material master data can be maintained for manufacturer parts. In particular, plant-specific data cannot be maintained.

2.7.6 Internal/External Purchase Orders

Internal/external purchase orders	
Ext. Purchase Orders	1
Int. purchase orders	2

External purchase orders

Here you can specify whether external purchase orders are allowed, not allowed, or allowed with a warning.

Internal purchase orders

Here you can specify whether internal purchase orders, i.e. in-house production of the material, are allowed, not allowed, or allowed with a warning.

Both these indicators together decide which procurement types are available in the MRP 2 view of a material.

2.7.7   Classification

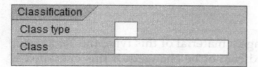

Class type and class

You can use class to extend the industry material master to include a subscreen on which you can maintain the characteristics of the class as additional fields.

2.7.8   User Departments

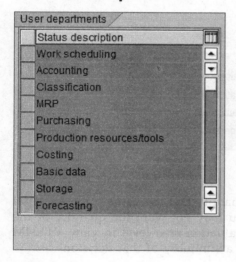

User departments

Here you specify the user departments which are expected to maintain data for material of this type. The system uses this information to identify the user departments which are yet to maintain data for a material. For more information, see section 2.5.3.

2.7.9   Valuation

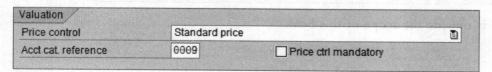

Price control

In the `Price control` field of the `Accounting 1` tab of the material master, you can specify whether the stock is valuated using standard price or moving average price/periodic unit price. The value in this field provides the default value for that field.

Price control mandatory

If you tick this checkbox, when you create or change a material of this type, the `Price control` defined on this screen applies to the material and cannot be changed. If this checkbox is not ticked, the `Price control` defined on this screen is defaulted, but can be changed.

Account category reference

In the `Accounting 1` tab of the material master, you specify a valuation class. Valuation classes are grouped in account category references. Here you specify the account category reference. The system then lets you select from valuation classes of that account category reference only.

2.7.10 Quantity/Value Updating

Quantity/value updating	
Quantity updating	Value updating
○ In all valuation areas	○ In all valuation areas
○ In no valuation area	○ In no valuation area
◉ By valuation area	◉ By valuation area

Quantity/value updating

When a goods movement takes place, usually the quantity and the value of the material is updated. However, for certain material types, you may not want the quantity or the value to be updated. This decision is specified at valuation area level in view VT134M (see section 2.7.12). The fields shown above present a summary of that decision.

2.7.11 Retail-specific Fields

Retail-specific fields		
Material type ID	General material type	🖹
Time till deleted		
☐ Display material	☐ Print price	

SAP Retail is outside the scope of this book.

2.7.12   Quantity/Value Updating for Valuation Areas

In view cluster MTART (view VT134M), you define properties of a material type in a given valuation area.

Val.	Matl	Qty updating	Value Upda	Pipe.mand.	PipeAllowd
1000	ROH	☑	☑	☐	☐
1100	ROH	☑	☑	☐	☐
1200	ROH	☑	☑	☐	☐
1300	ROH	☑	☑	☐	☐

Valuation area and material type

For a given material type, quantity and value updating properties can be different for different valuation areas.

Quantity updating

When goods movement takes place, quantity is updated. However, you can decide that this will not be done for materials of certain type in certain valuation areas.

Value updating

When goods movement takes place, value of the material is updated. However, you can decide that this will not be done for materials of certain type in certain valuation areas.

Pipeline mandatory

Here you specify whether a material assigned this material type is subject to mandatory pipeline handling for this valuation area.

Pipeline allowed

Here you specify whether a material assigned this material type is allowed to have pipeline handling for this valuation area.

2.7.13   Material Creation Transactions for Specific Material Types

For creating material master record, you can use special create transactions which are used to create specific material types. In view V_134K, you assign material types to transaction groups. Transaction groups are linked to transactions in table T130M by SAP. There is no maintenance view for maintaining this field. Both the view V_134K and relevant entries from table T130M are given in the screenshot below.

Grp	MTyp	Material type description
B	HALB	Semi-finished product
F	FERT	Finished product
G	LEIH	Returnable packaging
H	HAWA	Trading goods
I	HIBE	Operating supplies
K	KMAT	Configurable material
L	LEER	Empties
N	NLAG	Non-stock material
P	IBAU	Maintenance assembly
R	ROH	Raw material
S	DIEN	Service
U	UNBW	Non-valuated material
V	VERP	Packaging
W	WETT	Competitive product

Transaction grp	Transaction Code
B	MMB1
F	MMF1
G	MMG1
H	MMH1
I	MMI1
K	MMK1
L	MML1
N	MMN1
P	MMP1
R	MMR1
S	MMS1
U	MMU1
V	MMV1
W	MMW1

2.8 MATERIAL GROUP

Functional Consultant	User	Business Process Owner	Senior Management	My Rating	Understanding Level
A	C	C	X		

2.8.1 Material Group

Material groups are defined in view V023. For a material group you can specify an authorization group, and thereby control authorization to maintain a material using the authorization object M_MATE_MAT. You can also specify a default unit of weight, which is proposed when a material is created. If nothing is specified, the default unit of weight is kg. You can create a hierarchy of material groups by appropriately numbering the material groups, which is evident in the screenshot below:

Matl Group	Material Group Desc.	Grp.	DUW	Description 2 for the material group
001	Metal processing			
00101	Steels			
00102	Steel sheets			
00103	Electronics			
00104	Mechanics			
001041	Fasteners			Mechanical fasteners

You may use the United Nations Standard Products and Services Code (UNSPSC) for configuring your material groups.

2.8.2 Entry Aids for Items without a Material Master

Sometimes you place order for a material group instead of a specific material. In view V023_E, you can assign a purchasing value key and a valuation class to a material group.

Mat. Grp	Mat. Grp Descr.	ValCl	PurValK
001	Metal processing		
00101	Steels		
00102	Steel sheets		
00103	Electronics		
00104	Mechanics		
001041	Fasteners		

2.8.3 Distinction between Material Group and Material Type

You need to differentiate between material type and material group. Material types have a large number of properties associated with them and you generally use material types predefined by SAP. Material groups do not have associated properties, but you use them for analysis, e.g. total inventory of steels. Material groups also help in searching for a material.

2.9   MATERIAL STATUS

Functional Consultant	User	Business Process Owner	Senior Management	My Rating	Understanding Level
A	C	C	X		

2.9.1 Purpose

The material status determines how a material is handled in purchasing, materials planning, etc. For a material in a plant, you can set a material status in the corresponding material master record. In case a material has a material status, the system will issue either a warning or an error message, if the material is used.

2.9.2 IMG Node

Transaction OMS4—Define Material Statuses

2.9.3 Material Status List

Material Status	Description
01	Blocked for Procmnt/Whse
02	Blocked for task list/BOM
BP	Blocked for Purchasing
KA	Blocked for Costing
OB	Obsolete Materials
PI	Free for Pilot Phase

2.9.4 Screen

Material Status	01	Blocked for Procmnt/Whse

Plant-specific settings

Purchasing

Purchasing msg.	B

Production resources/tools

PRT message	

BOMs

BOM header msg.	
BOM item message	

Plant maintenance

Plant maint. message	

Routing/recipe

Routing/master recipe message	

Inventory management

Inventory mgmt msg.	B

Warehouse management

Transfer requirement msg.	

Material requirements

Ind. reqmt msg.	
Forecasting message	B
MRP message	B
LT planning message	

Transfer order message	

Cost estimate with quantity structure

Mat. Cost Estimate Procedure	

Production

POrder header msg.	
PO/network item msg.	

Cross-plant settings

ALE distribution

Distr. lock	
Profile Name	

For each activity, you can assign one of the following:

	No message
A	Warning
B	Error message

In ALE distribution, you can lock distribution of object data for the Integrated Distributed PDM Solution. If you want a material with this status to be distributed, enter a profile that controls change authorizations in ALE systems.

2.9.5 Material Status at Plant Level

The material status can be assigned at plant level in the `Purchasing` tab of the material master.

2.9.6 Material Status for all Plants

You can also set `X-plant matl status` in the `Basic data 1` tab, which applies restrictions to all plants.

2.10 PURCHASING VALUE KEYS

Functional Consultant	User	Business Process Owner	Senior Management	My Rating	Understanding Level
A	C	C	X		

2.10.1 Purpose

In the `Purchasing` view of the material master record, you can store rules governing the following:

➤ The issue of reminders with respect to nearly due and overdue deliveries
➤ The admissibility of over- and under-deliveries
➤ Order acknowledgment requirements for purchase order items
➤ Shipping/packaging instructions

You stipulate these rules in a purchasing value key. In the purchasing documents, the purchasing value key is taken from the purchasing info record. If the purchasing info record is not used, or the purchasing value key is not found there, it is taken from the material master.

2.10.2 IMG Node

SM30 ➤ V_405

2.10.3 Screen

Pur.Val.Key   1

Deadline monitoring
1st Reminder/Exped.   10
2nd Reminder/Exped.   20
3rd Reminder/Exped.   30
☐ Acknowledgment Reqd

GR/IR control
Tol. Underdelivery
Tol. Overdelivery
☐ Unlimited Overdel.
Shipping Instr.

Vendor evaluation
Min.Del.Qty %
StdDelDtVar

2.10.4 Primary Key

Purchasing Value Key

2.10.5 Important Fields

Reminders 1, 2, 3

These reminders specify the number of days representing the time interval at which reminders are to be issued to the vendor before (if the number is negative) or after the due date. The due date depends on the purchasing document. For example, for RFQ, it is the receipt of quotation.

In the case of purchasing documents, the time intervals are defaulted from the purchasing info record or, if the purchasing info record does not exist, from the material master record. In the event of several reminder levels, the days must be set out in ascending order of time, without gaps.

Acknowledgement required

If you want vendors to acknowledge purchase orders, contracts, scheduling agreements, etc., you specify that here.

Under-delivery tolerance

This specifies the percentage (of the order quantity) up to which an under-delivery of this item will be accepted.

Over-delivery tolerance

This specifies the percentage (of the order quantity) up to which an over-delivery of this item will be accepted.

Unlimited over-delivery

This indicator specifies that unlimited over-delivery can be accepted for the item.

Shipping instructions

Here you specify the packaging and shipping instructions for the item.

Minimum delivery quantity in percentage

This is the minimum percentage of the purchase order quantity that must be delivered in order for the goods receipt to be included in the vendor evaluation. In this way, you can prevent a vendor from receiving a good score for a punctual delivery, where the quantity delivered was insufficient.

Standard value for delivery date variance

The number in this field represents the number of days that will be counted as 100% variance. The difference between actual and planned delivery in days is divided by this number to give actual variance. If the actual delivery is 2 days after the planned delivery date and this field contains 10, then the variance is 20%.

2.11 SHIPPING INSTRUCTIONS

Functional Consultant	User	Business Process Owner	Senior Management	My Rating	Understanding Level
A	C	C	X		

2.11.1 Purpose

In the purchasing value key, you specify shipping instructions. When you assign a purchasing value key to a material, the shipping instructions embedded in the purchasing value key are applicable to that material.

In the purchasing documents, the purchasing value key is taken from the purchasing info record. If the purchasing info record is not used, or the purchasing value key is not found there, it is taken from the material master. As a constituent of the purchasing value key, the shipping instructions become a part of the purchasing document.

When the relevant goods receipts are entered, the extent to which the vendor has complied with these instructions can be noted.

2.11.2 IMG Node

SM34 ➤ VC_T027A

2.11.3 Shipping Instructions

Dialog Structure		Shipping Instr.	Dsc. Ship.Instr.	Print Ship.Instr.
▽ 🗁 Shipping instructions		V1	Shipping instruction 1	☑
☐ Compliance with		V2	Shipping instruction 2	☑

Print shipping instructions

If you set this indicator, the shipping instructions will also be printed out on the form when purchasing documents are outputted as messages.

2.11.4 Compliance with Shipping Instructions

Shippg Instr.	V1	Shipping instruction 1

	Comp	Text Compl. w. Shipping Instr.	Pts	Default	Sh. Text GR	Long Txt GR	Text Key
	01	Instruction complied with	100	⦿	☑	☑	
	02	Instruction not complied with		○	☑	☑	

Compliance key

When the goods are received, you may check the vendor's compliance with the shipping and packaging instructions. You may give him a score which is used in vendor evaluation and may want to print the compliance or non-compliance of the shipping and packaging instructions on the goods receipt slip. All these are encapsulated in the compliance key. When you assign compliance key to a goods receipt slip, all the features described here automatically apply.

Text

You assign a compliance key to a goods receipt slip. You select the key, whose text best describes the compliance with the shipping and packaging instructions.

Points for compliance with shipping instructions

When you assign a compliance key to a goods receipt slip, the vendor gets the points specified here for that compliance key.

Default value indicator

You can specify one of the compliance keys as the default key. This key appears in the goods receipt slip by default, and the user can change it.

Short text indicator

If you tick this checkbox, the short description is printed on the goods receipt slip.

Long text indicator

If you tick this checkbox, the long description is printed on the goods receipt slip.

Text key for compliance with shipping instructions

If you specify a standard text here, it is printed on the goods receipt slip.

Procure-to-Pay Cycle

3.1 PROCURE-TO-PAY CYCLE

Functional Consultant	User	Business Process Owner	Senior Management	My Rating	Understanding Level
A	A	A	A		

3.1.1 Procure-to-Pay Cycle

A typical procure-to-pay cycle has the following steps:

Purchase requisition

A user department requests the Purchase department to procure a material. It specifies the quantity and the date by which it is required.

RFQ

The Purchase department requests the vendors to quote for the material.

Quotation

The vendors quote the price for the material. The Purchase department compares the quotations, accepts one quotation, and rejects others.

Purchase order

The Purchase department issues a purchase order to the vendor, whose quotation has been accepted, specifying the material, the quantity, the price, and the delivery date.

Goods receipt

The vendor sends the goods to the plant of the buyer, where it is received and stored. On receipt of goods, two documents are created by the system: a material document and an accounting document. The material document updates the stock in inventory and the accounting document updates the G/L accounts in Financial Accounting (FI). For stock material, the inventory account is debited and the GR/IR account is credited. For direct consumption material, the consumption account is debited and the GR/IR account is credited.

Invoice receipt, verification and posting

The vendor sends the invoice to the Purchase department. The invoice is verified against the purchase order and goods receipt. The system posts a financial transaction, debiting the GR/IR account and crediting the vendor account. Differences, if any, are posted to the inventory account or consumption account as appropriate.

Vendor payment

The vendor is paid, crediting the vendor account and debiting the bank account.

3.1.2 SAP Modules

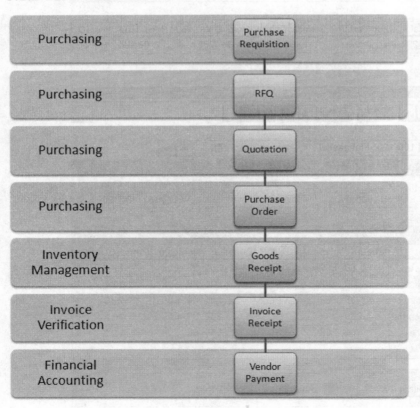

3.2 PURCHASING

Functional Consultant	User	Business Process Owner	Senior Management	My Rating	Understanding Level
A	A	A	A	A	

3.2.1 Purchase Order

Purpose

Purchase order is the most important instrument through which the vendor is instructed to supply material.

Transaction

ME23N—Display Purchase Order

Screen

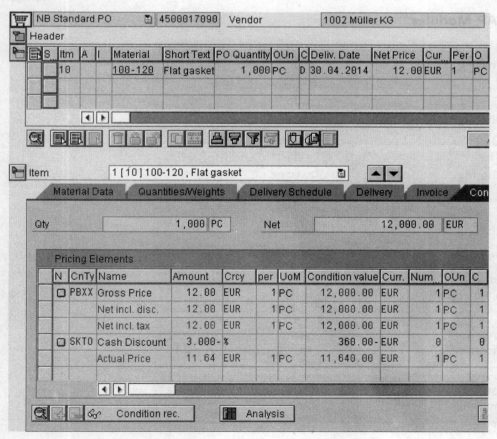

Header

A purchase order has a header and one or more items. The important information in the header includes the vendor. The information in the header applies to the entire purchase order. It is also possible to have conditions at the header level which apply to all the items.

Items

A purchase order has one or more items. The important information in a purchase order item is the material, quantity, delivery schedule, and price. There may be several elements of price; each price element is identified by its condition type.

3.2.2   Scheduling Agreement

Purpose

Scheduling agreement is another instrument through which the vendor is instructed to supply material.

Transaction

ME33L—Display Scheduling Agreement

Initial Screen

In the initial screen, enter the scheduling agreement number.

Header

Click 🖳 to see the header data.

Agreement	5500000130	Company Code	1000	Purchasing Group	000
		Agreement Type	LP	Purch. Organization	1000
Vendor	1002	Müller KG			

Administrative Fields

Agreement Date	06.08.2014	Item Number Interval	10	Subitem Interv.	1
Validity Start	06.08.2014	Validity End	31.12.2014	Language	EN

Terms of Delivery and Payment

Payt Terms	ZB01			Targ. Val.	0.00		EUR
Payment in	14	Days	3.000 %	Exch. Rate	1.00000	☐ Ex.Rate Fx	
Payment in	30	Days	2.000 %	Incoterms	CPT		
Payment in	45	Days Net					

Reference Data

Quotation Date		Quotation	
Your Reference		Salesperson	Mr. Schulze
Our Reference		Telephone	109876543
Suppl. Vendor		Invoicing Party	

Taxes

CtrySlsTxNo.	DE	DE123456789

Item Overview

Click 🔊 to see the item overview.

Agreement	5500000130	Agreement Type	LP	Agmt Date	06.08.2014
Vendor	1002	Müller KG		Currency	EUR

Outline Agreement Items

	Item	I	A	Material	Short Text	Targ. Qty	OUn	Net Price	Per	OPU	Mat. Grp	Plnt	SLoc	D	Texts
	10			100-120	Flat gasket	100	PC	12.00	1	PC	001	1000	0001		

Price

Select an item and click Item ➤ Conditions.

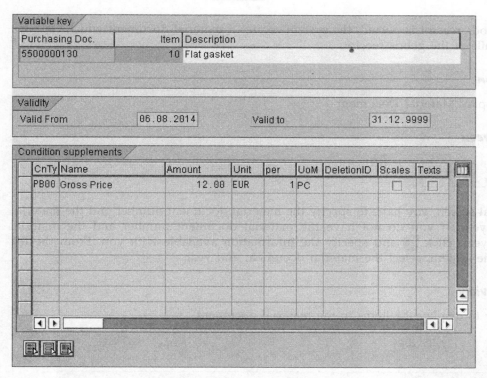

Here you can see the price of the item.

3.3 INVENTORY MANAGEMENT

Functional Consultant	User	Business Process Owner	Senior Management	My Rating	Understanding Level
A	A	A	A		

3.3.1 Goods Receipt

Goods are received in Inventory Management. In Inventory Management, all types of goods movement, including goods receipt are recorded using transaction MIGO. There are different types of goods movement, e.g. goods receipt, goods issue, etc. They are identified by movement type. Most common movement type for goods receipt is 101. When goods movement is posted, a material document and associated accounting documents are created. The material document contains detail of goods movement, e.g. material, quantity, vendor, etc.

3.3.2 Material Document

Purpose

When a goods receipt is posted, the system creates a material document which contains all the details of the goods receipt.

Transaction

MB03—Display Material Document

Initial Screen

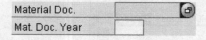

In the initial screen, you have to specify the material document number and the material document year. If you do not have the material document number and the material document year, click 🔗 and specify the information available with you. From the list given by the system, select the material document and year.

Item Overview

Press Enter to display the items in the material document.

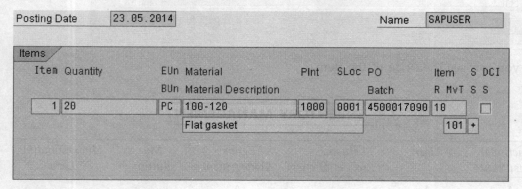

Header

Click 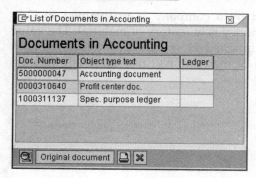 to see the header of the material document.

Document Date	23.05.2014		Posting Date	23.05.2014
Mat. Doc. Year	2014		Time of Entry	16:08:06
Entry Date	23.05.2014			

Transaction/Event				
Trans./Ev. Type	WE	Goods Receipt for Purchase Order		
			Name	SAPUSER

⦿ Individual Slip
◯ Indiv.Slip w.Inspect.Text
◯ Collective Slip

Accounting Documents

Documents in accounting

Click `Accounting Documents...` to see the documents in accounting.

Ʃ List of Documents in Accounting ⊠

Documents in Accounting

Doc. Number	Object type text	Ledger
5000000047	Accounting document	
0000310640	Profit center doc.	
1000311137	Spec. purpose ledger	

Original document

Accounting entries

Select `Accounting document` and click 🔍 to see the accounting entries.

Data Entry View						
Document Number	5000000047	Company Code	1000	Fiscal Year		2014
Document Date	23.05.2014	Posting Date	23.05.2014	Period		5
Reference		Cross-CC no.				
Currency	EUR	Texts exist	☐	Ledger Group		

CoCd	Itm	PK	G/L Acc	Account	Description	Amount	Purch.Doc.	Item	Material	Quantity
1000	1	89	300000	300000	Inventory - Raw Mate	240.00	4500017090	10	100-120	20
	2	96	191100	191100	Goods Rcvd/Invoice R	240.00-	4500017090	10	100-120	20

Accounting entries of goods receipt are particularly important for the person doing invoice verification because the accounting entries of invoice verification complement the accounting entries of goods receipt.

3.4 ACCOUNTING CONCEPTS

Functional Consultant	User	Business Process Owner	Senior Management	My Rating	Understanding Level
A	A	A	A		

3.4.1 Purpose

When goods are received, the value of the material held by the company goes up as also the liability of the company to pay the vendor. This section discusses important concepts in accounting that are needed both for Inventory Management as well as for invoice verification.

3.4.2 General Ledger Accounts

The account of the money raised and deployed by a company is maintained in G/L accounts. One area where the company deploys money is inventory of material. The value of material held by the company is usually maintained in several G/L accounts, each G/L account having the value of a specific type of material, e.g. raw material, finished goods, spare parts, etc.

3.4.3 Debit and Credit

Credit

You get credit for giving.

Goods issue	Material stock credited	Material stock decreases	Stock G/L account credited	Stock G/L account decreases

Debit

You get debit for receiving.

Goods receipt	Material stock debited	Material stock increases	Stock G/L account debited	Stock G/L account increases

3.4.4 Double Entry Book Keeping

In double entry book keeping, debits and credits are always matched. Money always gets transferred, from one account to another; it is never lost or gained. Therefore, in a goods receipt, when the inventory account is debited, the GR/IR clearing account is credited. Later when an invoice is received from the vendor and settled, the GR/IR clearing account is debited and vendor account is credited.

3.4.5 Chart of Accounts

Chart of accounts

A chart of accounts is a list of G/L accounts. For each G/L account, the chart of accounts contains the account number, account name, and control information, e.g. whether the account is a balance sheet account, or a P&L account.

Chart of accounts for a company code

Each company code is assigned one and only one chart of accounts. It may use some or all of the G/L accounts in the chart of accounts. Another company code may use the same chart of accounts, or a different chart of accounts.

Chart of accounts for a group of companies

The use of the same chart of accounts by several group of companies helps in consolidation of the group's financial information.

3.4.6 Company Code

Company code

Inventory management takes place for a plant. The plant belongs to a company code. All financial transactions take place in a company code. Balance sheet and Profit and Loss (P&L) statement is published for each company code. Company code used in this book is 1000.

G/L accounts for a company code

Each company code is assigned one and only one chart of accounts. It may use some or all of the G/L accounts in the chart of accounts. Some properties of a G/L account, e.g. whether the account is a balance sheet account, or a P&L account, is specified at the level of the chart of accounts, and must remain the same for all company codes that use that G/L account. However, there are some properties of a G/L account that can vary from company code to company code.

3.4.7   Important Accounts

Inventory management transactions result in posting to various accounts, e.g.

- ➢ Stock accounts
- ➢ GR/IR clearing account
- ➢ Price difference account

Stock accounts

When goods are received, inventory goes up. Inventory may be classified in several G/L accounts, e.g. raw material, parts for assembly, finished goods, etc. Collectively these G/L accounts are called stock accounts.

GR/IR clearing account

Most companies do not credit the vendor on goods receipt. They credit a GR/IR clearing account. When invoice is received and settled, the GR/IR clearing account is debited and the vendor is credited.

Price difference account

Sometimes a company uses standard price for a material for internal purposes. When such a material is received, there may be difference between the procurement price and the standard price. Such difference is debited or credited to a price difference account.

Other accounts

Depending on the business scenario, several other types of accounts may be posted to, e.g. asset, tax, etc.

3.4.8   Account Determination

SAP does not require you to manually specify G/L accounts every time. It determines them automatically based on the logic specified by you at the time of configuration. However, you can also specify G/L accounts manually in certain situations that are permitted by your company.

3.4.9   Financial Statements

Balance sheet

A balance sheet is a statement of the company's assets and liabilities. Each company is required by law to publish its balance sheet periodically.

P&L statement

A P&L statement is a statement of the company's revenues and expenses for a period. Each company is required by law to publish its P&L statement periodically.

3.4.10   Accounting Period

Accounting divides the financial year into several accounting periods. Accounting periods may be open for posting, or closed for posting. If you try to post a transaction in a period that is closed, you will get an error message.

3.4.11   Price Control

Moving average price

When you receive a material, you pay for it at certain price. You also have the same material, purchased earlier, perhaps at a different price. Usually, companies determine a moving average price by dividing the total value of the material by total quantity. This is the rate charged when goods are issued to a cost object.

Standard price

Some companies do not want the material price to keep changing all the time. They specify the price of a material, which is used for all internal purposes. This is called standard price. SAP supports standard price. You can change the standard price, if required. You can also use standard price for some materials, and moving average price for others.

Price control for a material

You can decide whether a material will be valuated at moving average price or at standard price. This is specified in the material master at plant level in the Price control field.

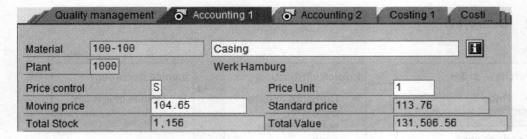

The Price control field has the following options:

Price control	Short text
S	Standard price
V	Moving average price/periodic unit price

Periodic unit price

Periodic unit price is used in Product Cost Controlling. It is out of the scope of this book.

3.4.12 Controlling Area

Controlling area

Several company codes may belong to a controlling area. Company code 1000 used in this book belongs to controlling area 1000.

Controlling area documents

Along with documents for financial accounting, the system also produces controlling documents.

3.5 INVOICE VERIFICATION

Functional Consultant	User	Business Process Owner	Senior Management	My Rating	Understanding Level
A	A	A	A		

3.5.1 Purpose

After supplying material, a vendor presents the invoice to your company. The purpose of invoice verification is to check the incoming invoices in terms of their content, prices, and arithmetic. When the invoice is posted, an invoice document and associated accounting documents are created.

3.5.2 Overview

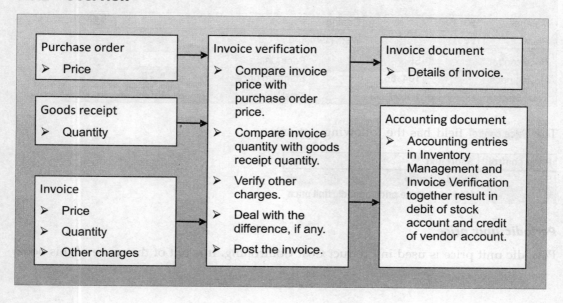

3.5.3 Invoice Verification Process

The invoice verification process is largely system driven. Information in the invoice received from the vendor is entered in the system. The system fetches the related purchase order and goods receipt data. The system also determines the amount payable based on the purchase order and goods receipt data and compares it with the vendor's invoice data. If the two match, the invoice is posted.

3.5.4 Dealing with Difference

The main challenge in invoice verification is to deal with the difference in the vendor's invoice and the system computed amount. Some companies insist on ironing out the difference, either getting a corrected invoice or changing own data, before posting the invoice. But some companies establish policies to deal with the difference and post the invoice nonetheless. SAP supports both practices.

Price difference

If there is a difference in system price and vendor price, usually lower of the two is paid. Accounting entries are passed to that effect and the moving average price of the material may change.

Quantity difference

If there is a difference in system quantity and vendor quantity, usually it is best to resolve the difference. If, however, the invoice is posted without resolving the difference, the system expects further invoice or goods receipt that will clear the difference. Posting an invoice with quantity difference does not change the stock; stock can only change through goods movement.

3.5.5 Accounting Entries

During goods receipt the stock account is debited and the GR/IR clearing account is credited. During invoice posting the GR/IR account is debited and the vendor account is credited. In addition, posting takes place to many other accounts depending on the scenario, e.g. other charges, difference in system computed and vendor amounts, etc.

Invoices having System Amount Matching Vendor Amount

CHAPTER 4

4.1 GOODS RECEIPT BASED INVOICE—MOVING AVERAGE PRICE

Functional Consultant	User	Business Process Owner	Senior Management	My Rating	Understanding Level
A	A	A	A		

4.1.1 Scenario

Invoice verification

After receiving material from a vendor, you receive the invoice. An invoice represents the vendor's claim on the customer for payment of goods supplied. Incoming invoices are verified for quantities, prices, and other charges. When the invoice is posted, the system

➢ Creates an invoice document

➢ Creates an accounting document crediting the amount payable to the vendor

➢ Updates the purchase order history

This chapter discusses scenarios in which there is no variance between the invoice and the amount computed by the system.

Goods receipt based invoice verification

The vendor supplies material against a purchase order item. He may supply the entire quantity in one lot, or in several partial lots. When the vendor sends you an invoice, you may want him to invoice each goods receipt separately (one invoice item per goods receipt), or you may want him to club all goods receipts together. You specify this in the purchase order. For a purchase order item, you can specify ☑ GR-Bsd IV in the Invoice tab.

98

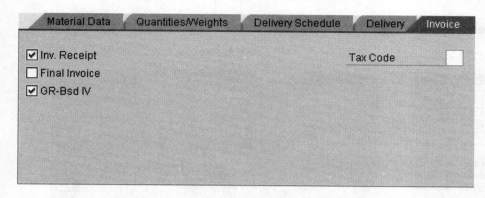

In goods receipt based invoice verification, an invoice contains information at goods receipt level. If an invoice is for multiple goods receipts, each goods receipt is an invoice item.

Moving average price

In Accounting 1 tab of the material master, there is a field Price control V. This field can have the following values:

Price control	Short text
S	Standard price
V	Moving average price/periodic unit price

If the price control of a material is the Moving average price, the total value of goods is debited to the Stock account and credited to the GR/IR account.

If the price control of a material is the Standard price, the value of goods determined at the standard price is debited to the Stock account. The total value is credited to the GR/IR account. The difference is debited or credited to the Price difference account.

4.1.2 Transaction

MIRO—Enter Invoice

4.1.3 Setting the Company Code

In transaction MIRO, you first set the company code.

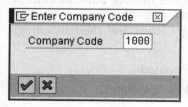

You can change the company code by selecting Edit ➤ Switch Company Code .

4.1.4   Screen

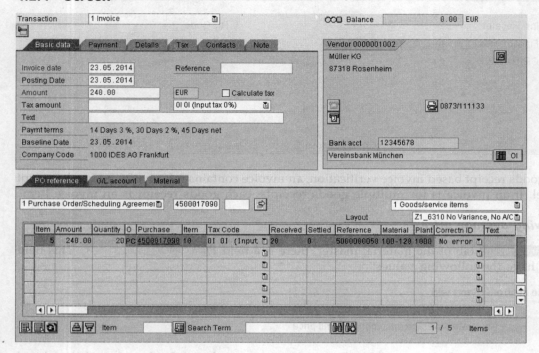

4.1.5   Transaction and Balance

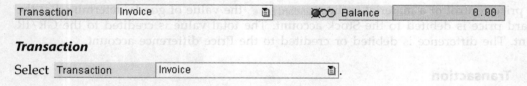

Transaction

Select Transaction [Invoice ▼].

Balance

In this field, the system shows the difference between the invoice amount and the total of amounts calculated for the items + tax amounts + unplanned delivery cost (entered in Details tab). Initially, it shows ⬤○○ Balance [0.00] because the invoice amount is not entered and invoice items are not selected. As you enter the invoice amount and/or invoice items, this field will show the difference between the two. You cannot post an invoice only when the traffic light is red ⬤○○. The traffic light icons and their meanings are given below.

⬤○○   The invoice document contains errors and cannot be posted.

○◐○   The invoice document is correct, but will be blocked for payment.

○○◼   The invoice document is correct and can be posted.

4.1.6   Basic Data

Basic data	Payment	Details	Tax	Contacts	Note

Invoice date	23.05.2014	Reference	
Posting Date	23.05.2014		
Amount	240.00	EUR	☐ Calculate tax
Tax amount		0I 0I (Input tax 0%) 🖹	
Text			
Paymt terms	14 Days 3 %, 30 Days 2 %, 45 Days net		
Baseline Date	23.05.2014		
Company Code	1000 IDES AG Frankfurt		

Invoice date

The invoice sent by the vendor has a date. You enter this invoice date here.

Reference

The vendor may have given the invoice a number or a reference. You can enter that here. The reference document number can be used to search an invoice in transaction MIR5.

Posting date

This is the date on which the invoice is posted. This date determines the period in which the accounting entries will show in your book of accounts.

Amount and currency

Here you enter the invoice amount. This includes taxes and unplanned delivery costs. If planned delivery costs are also a part of the invoice, they are also included.

Tax code

You must select a tax code. For zero tax, select 0I (Input tax 0%) 🖹 .

Tax amount, calculate tax

You may either enter the Tax amount, or select the ☑ Calculate tax checkbox. In the latter case, the system computes the tax amount and populates the Tax amount field. This should be done only after selecting the invoice items.

Text

Here you can enter text that can be printed in the Accounting documents (see Section 4.25).

4.1.7   Vendor

The screen you get initially does not have the vendor. The vendor information appears only after you enter the purchase order, or the `Inv. Party` (alternative payee) in `Details` tab. If the vendor is a one-time vendor, you can enter his details by clicking `OI`.

4.1.8   PO Reference

Reference document category

Select `Purchase Order/Scheduling Agreement` .

Purchase order number, item number

Enter the purchase order number, and if necessary the item number.

Goods/service items

Select `Goods/service items` .

Layout

This field determines the item fields you see. You may select `All information` to see all the fields, or a variant that is appropriate for the scenario. Variants can be defined using transaction OLMRLIST. If you have a number of items, you may like to use an aggregation layout, which combines several lines into one. You can also display items for each aggregation line. How to use aggregation layout is explained in section 12.2.1.

4.1.9 Items

Proposed goods receipts

In goods receipt based invoice verification, the system fetches all goods receipts of the purchase order and inserts them as items in the invoice screen. If a purchase order item is specified, goods receipts of only that item are fetched.

Reference document

Scroll the item fields until you see Reference Doc. This field shows the goods receipt number. In goods receipt based invoice verification, the vendor should specify the goods receipt numbers in the invoice. Ensure that only the goods receipt numbers mentioned by the vendor are selected.

Selecting invoice items

You can select/deselect an item by clicking   .

	Item	Amount	Quantity	O	Purchase	Item	Tax Code		Received	Settled	Reference
	5	240.00	20	PC	4500017090	10	0I 0I (Input	20	0		5000000050

Important item details

Ensure that the Quantity , Amount and the Tax Code fields of the selected items match those in the vendor's invoice. The Correctn ID field should be No error , indicating to the system that the invoice item is error-free.

4.1.10 Simulating Account Movements

When you post an invoice, accounting entries are passed. Before posting the invoice you may want to know which accounting entries will be passed. If the accounting entries are not correct, you may not want to post the invoice. You can see the accounting entries that will be passed by clicking Simulate .

Position	A	G/L	Act/Mat/Ast/Vndr	Amount	Cur	Vendor	Posting Key
1	K	160000	Müller KG / 87318 Rosenheim	240.00-	EUR	1002	31
2	S	191100	Goods Rcvd/Invoice Rcvd (third party)	240.00	EUR		86

4.1.11 Posting the Invoice

If the invoice matches the system data in terms of quantities, prices and other details, the system should show Balance   0.00 . Post the invoice by clicking .

4.1.12 Invoice Document

Display the invoice document using transaction MIR4.

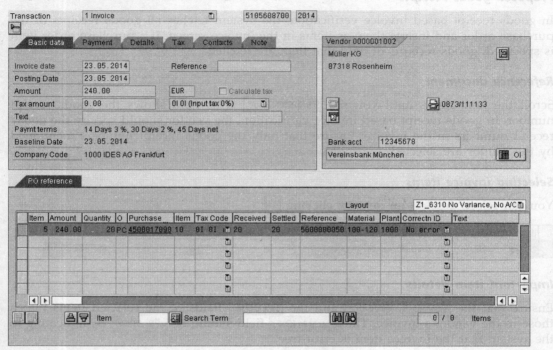

The invoice document has the same format as the invoice entry, except that it cannot be changed, and it has a document number and the financial year of posting.

4.1.13 Accounting Documents

In transaction MIR4, click Follow-On Documents ... . The system displays the list of accounting documents.

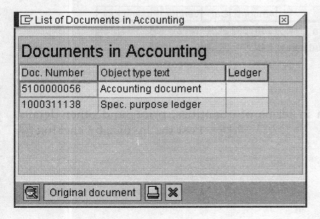

4.1.14 Accounting Entries

Double-click the | Accounting document | to see the accounting entries.

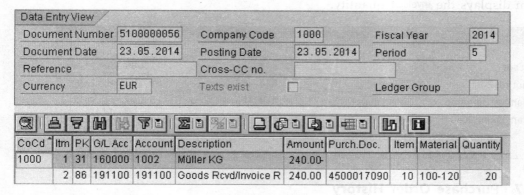

CoCd	Itm	PK	G/L Acc	Account	Description	Amount	Purch.Doc.	Item	Material	Quantity
1000	1	31	160000	1002	Müller KG	240.00-				
	2	86	191100	191100	Goods Rcvd/Invoice R	240.00	4500017090	10	100-120	20

The GR/IR account is debited and the vendor is credited.

4.1.15 Accounting Entries during Goods Receipt

In transaction MB02, display the goods receipt and click | Accounting Documents... |. Double-click the | Accounting document | to see the accounting entries.

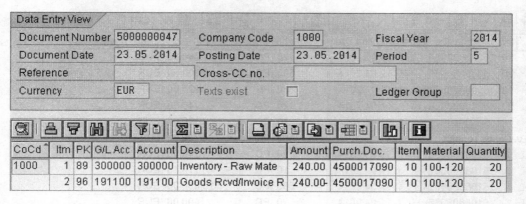

CoCd	Itm	PK	G/L Acc	Account	Description	Amount	Purch.Doc.	Item	Material	Quantity
1000	1	89	300000	300000	Inventory - Raw Mate	240.00	4500017090	10	100-120	20
	2	96	191100	191100	Goods Rcvd/Invoice R	240.00-	4500017090	10	100-120	20

Note that the invoice posting nullifies the entry in | 191100 Goods Rcvd/Invoice R |. After invoice posting, the net effect is debit to the Stock account and credit to the Vendor.

4.1.16   Purchase Order Status

Use transaction ME23N to display a purchase order. In the Status tab of the header, the system displays the Invoiced quantity.

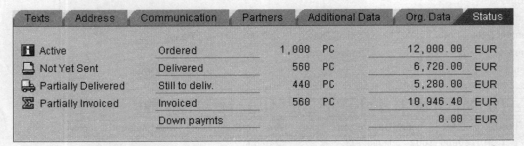

Texts	Address	Communication	Partners	Additional Data	Org. Data	Status

Active	Ordered	1,000	PC	12,000.00	EUR
Not Yet Sent	Delivered	560	PC	6,720.00	EUR
Partially Delivered	Still to deliv.	440	PC	5,280.00	EUR
Partially Invoiced	Invoiced	560	PC	10,946.40	EUR
	Down paymts			0.00	EUR

4.1.17   Purchase Order History

Use transaction ME23N to display a purchase order. In the Purchase Order History tab of item detail, the system displays invoice receipts after goods receipts.

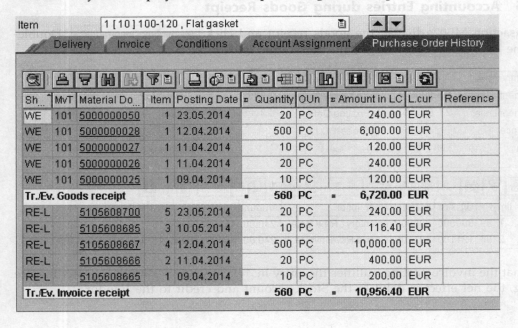

Item   1 [10] 100-120 , Flat gasket

Delivery	Invoice	Conditions	Account Assignment	Purchase Order History

Sh...	MvT	Material Do...	Item	Posting Date	Σ Quantity	OUn	Σ Amount in LC	L.cur	Reference
WE	101	5000000050	1	23.05.2014	20	PC	240.00	EUR	
WE	101	5000000028	1	12.04.2014	500	PC	6,000.00	EUR	
WE	101	5000000027	1	11.04.2014	10	PC	120.00	EUR	
WE	101	5000000026	1	11.04.2014	20	PC	240.00	EUR	
WE	101	5000000025	1	09.04.2014	10	PC	120.00	EUR	
Tr./Ev. Goods receipt					**560**	**PC**	**6,720.00**	**EUR**	
RE-L		5105608700	5	23.05.2014	20	PC	240.00	EUR	
RE-L		5105608685	3	10.05.2014	10	PC	116.40	EUR	
RE-L		5105608667	4	12.04.2014	500	PC	10,000.00	EUR	
RE-L		5105608666	2	11.04.2014	20	PC	400.00	EUR	
RE-L		5105608665	1	09.04.2014	10	PC	200.00	EUR	
Tr./Ev. Invoice receipt					**560**	**PC**	**10,956.40**	**EUR**	

4.1.18   Purchase Order Structure

In invoice entry transaction MIRO, or in invoice display transaction MIR4, display the purchase order structure by clicking   Show PO structure .

Display - PO structure	Qty	Amount	Posting date	Doc. No.
▽ 🖳 Müller KG				
▽ 🔃 4500017090				
▽ 🔃 10 Flat gasket	1,000.000 PC	12,000.00 EUR	09.04.2014	
▷ 🖨 Delivery note				
▷ 🖨 Delivery note				
▷ 🖨 Delivery note				
▷ 🖨 Delivery note				
▽ 🖨 Delivery note				
📄 WE	20.000 PC	240.00 EUR	23.05.2014	5000000050
📄 RE-L	20.000 PC	240.00 EUR	23.05.2014	5105608700

The purchase order structure displays the business transactions (goods receipts, posted invoices, parked invoices, etc.) for the purchase order items entered. Note that the purchase order structure is not a worklist.

4.1.19   Worklist

During invoice entry you can display the worklist by clicking   Show worklist .

Worklist	Doc. date	Reference no.	Vendor	Amount
🗀 Held documents				
▽ 🗁 Parked documents				
📄 5105608650 2014	30.03.2014		0000001002	1,000.00 EUR
📄 5105608657 2014	05.04.2014		0000001002	150.00 EUR
📄 5105608658 2014	05.04.2014		0000001002	270.00 EUR
📄 5105608672 2014	14.04.2014		0000001002	600.00 EUR
🗀 Docs complete for posting				

In the worklist, the system displays invoice documents that you have already processed, but which have not yet been posted. Documents that have been processed using transaction MIRA (Enter Invoice for Invoice Verification in Background) are not displayed in the worklist. In order to process these documents, use transaction MIR6 (Invoice Overview).

4.2   GOODS RECEIPT BASED INVOICE—STANDARD PRICE

Functional Consultant	User	Business Process Owner	Senior Management	My Rating	Understanding Level
A	A	A	B		

4.2.1   Scenario

Goods receipt based invoice verification

The vendor supplies material against a purchase order item. He may supply the entire quantity in one lot, or in several partial lots. When the vendor sends you an invoice, you may want him to invoice each goods receipt separately (one invoice item per goods receipt), or you may want him to club all goods receipts together. You specify this in the purchase order. For a purchase order item, you can specify ☑ GR-Bsd IV in the Invoice tab.

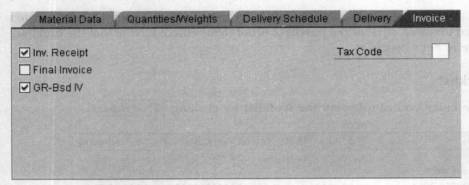

In goods receipt based invoice verification, an invoice contains information at goods receipt level. If an invoice is for multiple goods receipts, each goods receipt is an invoice item.

Standard price

In Accounting 1 tab of the material master, there is a field Price control   S. This field can have the following values:

Price control	Short text
S	Standard price
V	Moving average price/periodic unit price

If the price control of a material is the Moving average price., the total value of goods is debited to the Stock account and credited to the GR/IR account.

If the price control of a material is the Standard price, the value of goods determined at the standard price is debited to the Stock account. The total value is credited to the GR/IR account. The difference is debited or credited to the Price difference account.

4.2.2 Invoice

Enter the invoice using transaction MIRO.

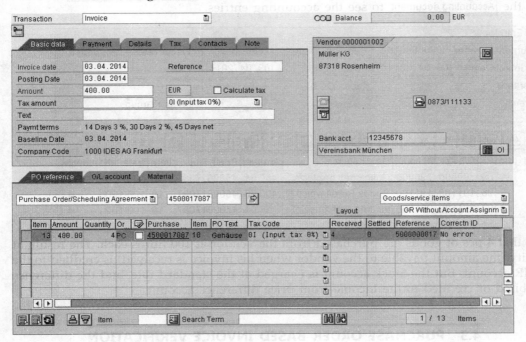

4.2.3 Accounting Entries

Display the invoice using transaction MIR4. Enter the Invoice Document No. and the Fiscal Year, Click 🔍 Display Document. The system displays the invoice. Click Follow-On Documents ... . The system displays the list of accounting documents. Double-click the Accounting document to see the accounting entries.

CoCd	Itm	PK	G/L Acc	Account	Description	Amount	Purch.Doc.	Item	Material	Quantity
1000	1	31	160000	1002	Müller KG	400.00-				
	2	86	191100	191100	Goods Rcvd/Invoice R	400.00	4500017087	10	100-100	4

The GR/IR account is debited and the vendor is credited.

4.2.4 Accounting Entries during Goods Receipt

In transaction MB02, display the goods receipt and click Accounting Documents... . Double-click the Accounting document to see the accounting entries.

Data Entry View							
Document Number	5000000016	Company Code	1000		Fiscal Year		2014
Document Date	03.04.2014	Posting Date	03.04.2014		Period		4
Reference		Cross-CC no.					
Currency	EUR	Texts exist	☐		Ledger Group		

CoCd	Itm	PK	G/L Acc	Account	Description	Amount	Purch.Doc.	Item	Material	Quantity
1000	1	89	790000	790000	Unfinished products	455.04	4500017087	10	100-100	4
	2	96	191100	191100	Goods Rcvd/Invoice R	400.00-	4500017087	10	100-100	4
	3	93	281500	281500	Income from price di	55.04-	4500017087	10	100-100	4

Note that 4 pcs of goods are purchased from the vendor at 100 Euros each. The resultant liability (the amount payable to the vendor when his invoice is received) is credited to the GR/IR account. But the Stock account is charged at the standard rate, and the difference is debited or credited to the Income from price difference account.

4.3 PURCHASE ORDER BASED INVOICE VERIFICATION

Functional Consultant	User	Business Process Owner	Senior Management	My Rating	Understanding Level
A	A	A	B		

4.3.1 Scenario

In goods receipt based invoice verification, there is an invoice item for each goods receipt. This offers excellent audit trail. But sometimes, particularly in Just-in-time scenario, goods receipts may be too numerous. In such cases, you may opt for purchase order based invoice verification. You specify this in the purchase order. For a purchase order item, you can specify ☐ GR-Bsd IV in the Invoice tab.

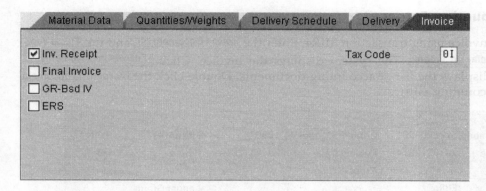

For these items, the system will use purchase order based invoice verification.

4.3.2 Invoice

Enter the invoice using transaction MIRO.

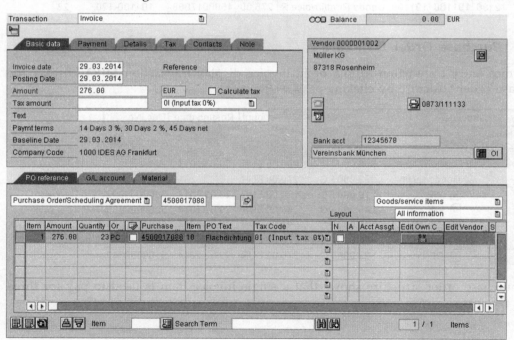

In purchase order based invoice verification, the system creates one invoice item for each purchase order item. In such an invoice item, the Ref. Doc. No. field is blank.

4.3.3   Accounting Entries

Display the invoice using transaction MIR4. Enter the Invoice Document No. and the Fiscal Year, Click Display Document. The system displays the invoice. Click Follow-On Documents ... The system displays the list of accounting documents. Double-click the Accounting document to see the accounting entries.

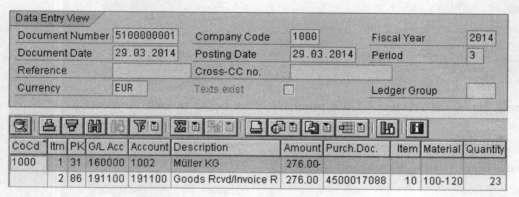

CoCd	Itm	PK	G/L Acc	Account	Description	Amount	Purch.Doc.	Item	Material	Quantity
1000	1	31	160000	1002	Müller KG	276.00-				
	2	86	191100	191100	Goods Rcvd/Invoice R	276.00	4500017088	10	100-120	23

4.3.4   Purchase Order Structure

In invoice entry transaction MIRO, or in invoice display transaction MIR4, display the purchase order structure by clicking Show PO structure.

Display - PO structure	Qty	Amount	Posting date	Doc. No.
Müller KG				
4500017088				
10 Flachdichtung	500.000 PC	6,000.00 EUR	29.03.2014	
Goods recpts	23.000 PC	276.00 EUR		
WE	10.000 PC	120.00 EUR	29.03.2014	5000000002
WE	5.000 PC	60.00 EUR	29.03.2014	5000000003
WE	8.000 PC	96.00 EUR	29.03.2014	5000000004
Invoices	23.000 PC	276.00 EUR		
RE-L	23.000 PC	276.00 EUR	29.03.2014	5105608643

This purchase order structure shows that a single invoice item is used to pay for three goods receipts.

4.4 DEDUCTIBLE INPUT TAX

Functional Consultant	User	Business Process Owner	Senior Management	My Rating	Understanding Level
A	A	A	A		

4.4.1 Scenario

Input tax

Each country specifies input taxes applicable on purchase of material. A material may attract one or more taxes, e.g. VAT and Surcharge. Different materials may have different tax rates. Also some input taxes may be deductible from the output tax you collect. All these are encapsulated in a tax code explained in section 4.4.2. The purchase department, the invoice verification department, and the vendor must have a common understanding of the taxes applicable on the purchase of a material.

The purchase department specifies the tax code for each item in the purchase order. When the vendor sends invoice, he specifies the taxes to be paid by your company. When the invoice verification clerk enters the invoice, he specifies the tax code for each invoice item. The system automatically computes the taxes payable.

Input tax deductible from output tax

This scenario illustrates the situation where input tax is payable and the tax is deductible from output tax, and hence posted to a separate G/L account; it does not increase the cost of the material.

4.4.2 Tax Code

Tax code

This scenario uses tax code VN.

Tax rate

You can see tax rate for tax code VN using transaction FTXP.

Country Key	DE	Germany
Tax Code	VN	16% domestic input tax
Procedure	TAXD	
Tax type	V	Input tax

Percentage rates					
Tax Type	Acct Key	Tax Percent. Rate	Level	From Lvl	Cond. Type
Base Amount			100	0	BASB
Output Tax	MWS		110	100	MWAS
Input Tax	VST	16.000	120	100	MWVS
Interest markdown	ZAS		125	100	ZAST
Travel Expenses (%)	VST		130	100	MWRK
Non-deduct.Input Tax	NAV		140	100	MWVN
Non-deduct.Input Tax	NVV		150	100	MWVZ
Acqu.Tax Outgoing	ESA		200	100	NLXA
Acquisition Tax Deb.	ESE		210	200	NLXV

Properties of account key

You can see the properties of account key VST in view V_T007B.

Process	VST

General details	
Description	Input tax
Tax type	2 Input tax
Not deductible	☐
Posting indic.	2 Separate line item
Not discnt rel.	☐

Not deductible ☐ indicates that this input tax is deductible.

Posting indic. 2 indicates that it is posted to a separate G/L account.

Although these two indicators are independent, usually deductible taxes are posted to separate G/L accounts, whereas non-deductible taxes are treated in the same way as the material cost and charged to Stock account or cost object.

Account determination

You can use transaction OMR0 to display/assign the G/L account to which this tax will be posted.

| Chart of Accounts | INT | Chart of accounts - international |
| Transaction | VST | Input tax |

Account assignment
Account
154000

4.4.3 Invoice

Enter the invoice using transaction MIRO.

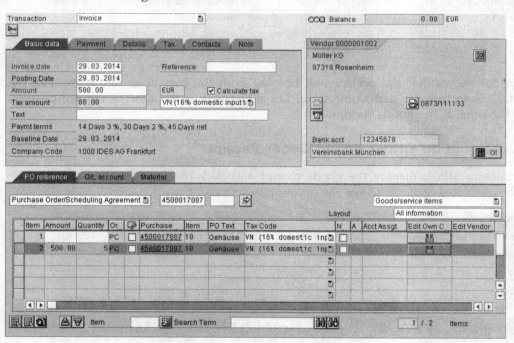

Enter the invoice date, posting date, and amount. Enter the purchase order number. The system gives the goods receipts. Select the goods receipt that has been invoiced, and select the appropriate Tax Code . Choose the ☑ Calculate tax checkbox in the Basic data tab. The system computes the tax amount. Post the invoice.

4.4.4 Accounting Entries

Display the invoice using transaction MIR4. Enter the Invoice Document No. and the Fiscal Year . Click &ᴏ Display Document . The system displays the invoice. Click Follow-On Documents ... . The system displays the list of accounting documents. Double-click the Accounting document to see the accounting entries.

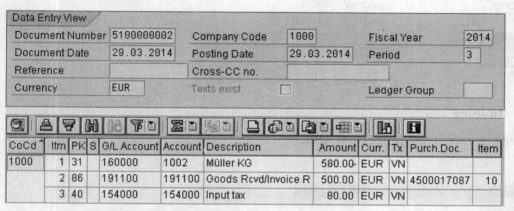

CoCd	Itm	PK	S	G/L Account	Account	Description	Amount	Curr.	Tx	Purch.Doc.	Item
1000	1	31		160000	1002	Müller KG	580.00-	EUR	VN		
	2	86		191100	191100	Goods Rcvd/Invoice R	500.00	EUR	VN	4500017087	10
	3	40		154000	154000	Input tax	80.00	EUR	VN		

The system shows that the vendor will be paid both the cost of goods, as well as the input tax. Note that the deductible input tax is charged at the time of invoice posting, not at the time of the goods receipt.

4.4.5 Accounting Entries during Goods Receipt

In transaction MB02, display the goods receipt and click Accounting Documents... . Double-click the Accounting document to see the accounting entries.

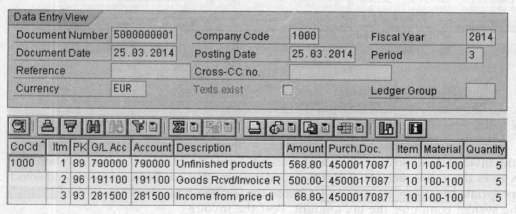

CoCd	Itm	PK	G/L Acc	Account	Description	Amount	Purch.Doc.	Item	Material	Quantity
1000	1	89	790000	790000	Unfinished products	568.80	4500017087	10	100-100	5
	2	96	191100	191100	Goods Rcvd/Invoice R	500.00-	4500017087	10	100-100	5
	3	93	281500	281500	Income from price di	68.80-	4500017087	10	100-100	5

Note that the deductible input tax is charged at the time of invoice posting, not at the time of the goods receipt.

4.5   NON-DEDUCTIBLE INPUT TAX

Functional Consultant	User	Business Process Owner	Senior Management	My Rating	Understanding Level
A	A	A	B		

4.5.1   Scenario

Each country specifies input taxes which are applicable on purchase of material. A material may attract one or more taxes, e.g. VAT and Surcharge. Different materials may have different tax rates. Also some input taxes may be deductible from the output tax you collect. All these are encapsulated in a tax code explained in Section 4.4.2. The purchase department, the invoice verification department, and the vendor must have a common understanding of the taxes applicable on the purchase of a material.

The purchase department specifies the tax code for each item in the purchase order. When the vendor sends invoice, he specifies the taxes to be paid by your company. When the invoice verification clerk enters the invoice, he specifies the tax code for each invoice item. The system automatically computes the taxes payable.

This scenario illustrates the situation where the input tax has two parts:

➤ One part of the input tax is deductible from the output tax, and hence posted to a separate G/L account; it does not increase the cost of the material.

➤ The other part of the input tax is not deductible from output tax, and is treated like the material cost.

4.5.2   Tax Code

Tax code

This scenario uses tax code NY.

Tax rate

You can see tax rate for tax code NY using transaction FTXP.

Country Key	DE	Germany
Tax Code	NY	
Procedure	TAXD	
Tax type	V	Input tax

Percentage rates

Tax Type	Acct. Key	Tax Percent. Rate	Level	From Lvl	Cond. Type
Base Amount			100	0	BASB
Output Tax	MWS		110	100	MWAS
Input Tax	VST	8.000	120	100	MWVS
Interest markdown	ZAS		125	100	ZAST
Travel Expenses (%)	VST		130	100	MWRK
Non-deduct.Input Tax	NAV		140	100	MWVN
Non-deduct.Input Tax	NVV	8.000	150	100	MWVZ
Acqu.Tax Outgoing	ESA		200	100	NLXA
Acquisition Tax Deb.	ESE		210	200	NLXV

Properties of account key VST

You can see the properties of account key VST in view V_T007B.

Process	VST

General details

Description	Input tax	
Tax type	2	Input tax
Not deductible	☐	
Posting indic.	2	Separate line item
Not discnt rel.	☐	

Not deductible ☐ indicates that this input tax is deductible.

Posting indic. 2 indicates that it is posted to a separate G/L account.

Although these two indicators are independent; usually deductible taxes are posted to separate G/L accounts, whereas non-deductible taxes are treated in the same way as the material cost and charged to Stock account or cost object.

Account determination for account key VST

You can use transaction OMR0 to display/assign the G/L account to which this tax will be posted.

Chart of Accounts	INT	Chart of accounts - international
Transaction	VST	Input tax

Account assignment

Account
154000

Properties of account key NVV

You can see the properties of account key NVV in view V_T007B.

Process	NVV

General details

Description	Non-d.input tax dist
Tax type	2 Input tax
Not deductible	☑
Posting indic.	3 Distribute to relevant expense/revenue items
Not discnt rel.	☐

Not deductible ☑ indicates that this input tax is not deductible.

Posting indic. 3 indicates that this input tax is charged to respective items and not posted to a separate G/L account.

Although these two indicators are independent; usually deductible taxes are posted to separate G/L accounts, whereas non-deductible taxes are treated in the same way as the material cost and charged to Stock account or cost object.

Account determination for account key NVV

You can use transaction OMR0 to display/assign the G/L account to which this tax will be posted. For account key NVV, the tax is not in a separate line item; it is posted in the same way as the material, hence there is no account determination.

4.5.3 Purchase Order

Purchase order is created using transaction ME21N.

🛒 NB Standard PO		4500017108	Vendor		1002 Müller KG				
Header									

S	Itm	A	I	Material	Short Text	PO Quantity	O	Net Price	Curre	Per	O
	10			100-100	Casing	10 PC		100.00 EUR		1	PC
	20			100-120	Flat gasket	10 PC		12.00 EUR		1	PC
	30	K		100-100	Casing	5 PC		100.00 EUR		1	PC

All three items have tax code NY (8% deductible tax and 8% non-deductible tax).

4.5.4 Goods Receipt

Goods receipt is performed using transaction MIGO.

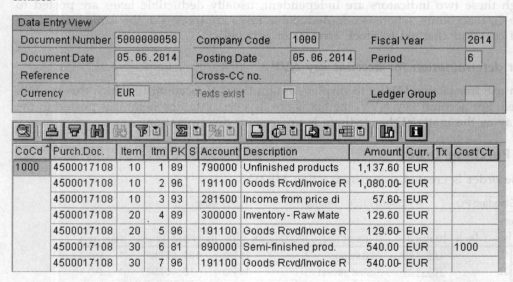

Change Material Document 5000000061 : Overview

| | | Details from Item | Material | Accounting Documents... |

| Posting Date | 05.06.2014 | | | | | | | Name | SAPUSER |

Items

Item	Quantity	EUn BUn	Material Material Description	Plnt	SLoc	PO Batch	Item R MvT	S S	DCI S
1	10	PC	100-100	1000	0001	4500017108	10	☑	
			Casing				101	+	
2	10	PC	100-120	1000	0001	4500017108	20	☑	
			Flat gasket				101	+	
3	5	PC	100-100	1000		4500017108	30	☑	
			Casing				101	+	

Accounting entries

Click | Accounting Documents... | and double-click the | Accounting document | to see the accounting entries.

Data Entry View

Document Number	5000000058	Company Code	1000	Fiscal Year	2014
Document Date	05.06.2014	Posting Date	05.06.2014	Period	6
Reference		Cross-CC no.			
Currency	EUR	Texts exist	☐	Ledger Group	

CoCd	Purch.Doc.	Item	Itm	PK	S	Account	Description	Amount	Curr.	Tx	Cost Ctr
1000	4500017108	10	1	89		790000	Unfinished products	1,137.60	EUR		
	4500017108	10	2	96		191100	Goods Rcvd/Invoice R	1,080.00-	EUR		
	4500017108	10	3	93		281500	Income from price di	57.60-	EUR		
	4500017108	20	4	89		300000	Inventory - Raw Mate	129.60	EUR		
	4500017108	20	5	96		191100	Goods Rcvd/Invoice R	129.60-	EUR		
	4500017108	30	6	81		890000	Semi-finished prod.	540.00	EUR		1000
	4500017108	30	7	96		191100	Goods Rcvd/Invoice R	540.00-	EUR		

Note that the non-deductible input tax is charged at the time of the goods receipt, not at the time of the invoice posting. The amount credited to the GR/IR account is inclusive of the non-deductible input tax.

Explanation of accounting entries

Item	Material	Price control	Account assignment	Debit/credit	Posting to account
10	100–100	Standard	None	Credit	GR/IR account including 8% non-deductible tax
				Debit	Stock account according to standard price
				Debit/credit	Price difference account for the difference
20	100–120	Moving average price	None	Credit	GR/IR account including 8% non-deductible tax
				Debit	Stock account
30	100–100	Standard	Cost centre	Credit	GR/IR account including 8% non-deductible tax
				Debit	Expense account of the cost centre

Note that there are no accounting entries for deductible tax.

4.5.5 Invoice

Enter the invoice using transaction MIRO.

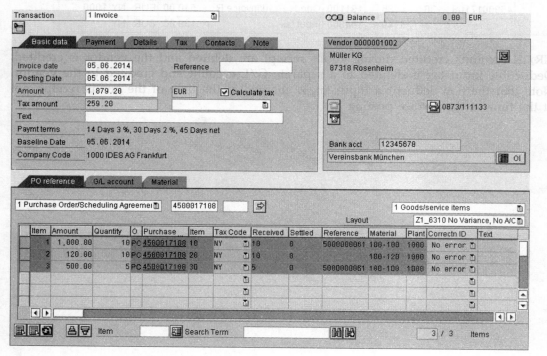

Enter the invoice date, posting date, and amount. Enter the purchase order number. The system gives the goods receipts. Select the goods receipt that has been invoiced, and select the appropriate `Tax Code`. Choose the ☑ `Calculate tax` checkbox in the `Basic data` tab. The system computes the tax amount. Post the invoice.

4.5.6   Accounting Entries

Display the invoice using transaction MIR4. Enter the `Invoice Document No.` and the `Fiscal Year`. Click `⚙ Display Document`. The system displays the invoice. Click `Follow-On Documents ...`. The system displays the list of accounting documents. Double-click the `Accounting document` to see the accounting entries.

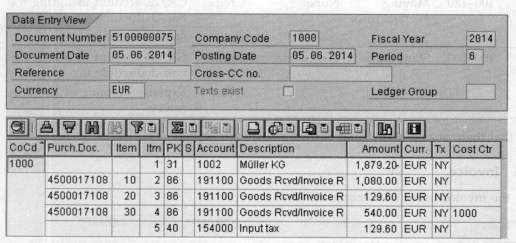

GR/IR accounts credited during goods receipt are debited and the vendor is credited. Deductible input tax is debited to a separate G/L account and credited to the vendor. Note that the non-deductible input tax is charged at the time of the goods receipt, not at the time of the invoice posting.

4.6 PLANNED DELIVERY COST

Functional Consultant	User	Business Process Owner	Senior Management	My Rating	Understanding Level
A	A	A	B		

4.6.1 Scenario

A purchase order item may include planned delivery costs. Planned delivery costs are automatically posted to clearing accounts at goods receipt. Each type of delivery cost has its own clearing account. When you post the invoice for these delivery costs, the corresponding clearing accounts are cleared and vendor credited. You can settle planned delivery costs separately, or along with material costs. In the former case choose `2 Planned delivery costs`; in the latter `3 Goods/service items + planned delivery costs`.

4.6.2 Invoice

Enter the invoice using transaction MIRO.

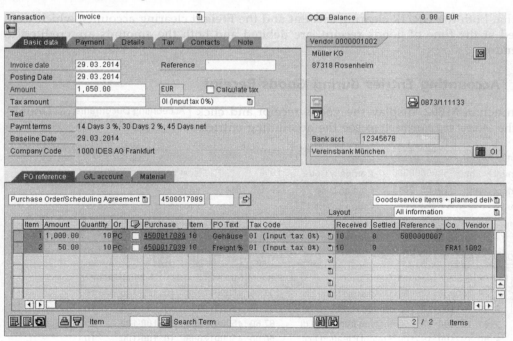

If a purchase order, and invoice, includes delivery cost, e.g. freight, select `3 Goods/service items + planned delivery costs`. You get two line items in the invoice; one for the material cost, and one for the freight. Post the invoice.

4.6.3 Accounting Entries

Display the invoice using transaction MIR4. Enter the Invoice Document No. and the Fiscal Year. Click 👓 Display Document. The system displays the invoice. Click Follow-On Documents ... . The system displays the list of accounting documents. Double-click the Accounting document to see the accounting entries.

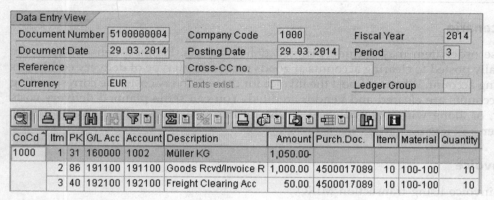

Note that both the GR/IR clearing account and the Freight clearing accounts, which were credited at the time of goods receipt, are debited and both the amounts are credited to the vendor.

4.6.4 Accounting Entries during Goods Receipt

In transaction MB02, display the goods receipt and click Accounting Documents... . Double-click the Accounting document to see the accounting entries.

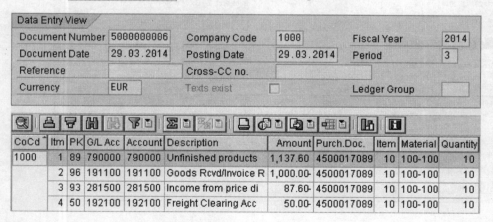

When goods receipt is posted, the material cost is credited to the GR/IR clearing account and the freight is credited to the Freight clearing account. Stock account is debited at standard price (since the price control of the material is Standard) and the difference is debited or credited to the Price difference account.

4.7 UNPLANNED DELIVERY COST

Functional Consultant	User	Business Process Owner	Senior Management	My Rating	Understanding Level
A	A	A	B		

4.7.1 Scenario

You can post an invoice received from the vendor that includes unplanned delivery costs. The price control of the material is Moving average price.

4.7.2 Basic Data

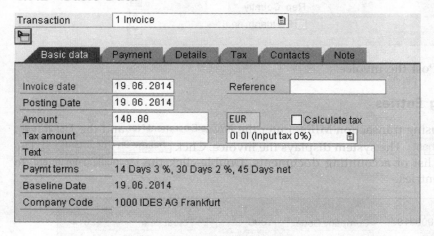

The Amount should include the unplanned delivery cost.

4.7.3 Items

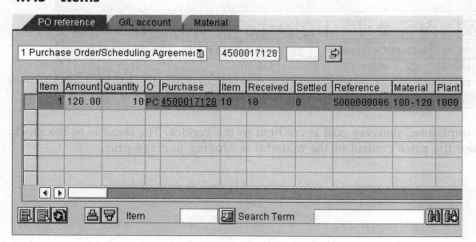

4.7.4 Details

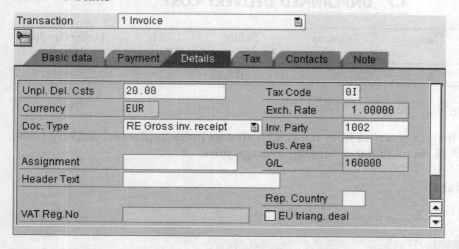

Enter Unpl. Del. Csts. Post the invoice.

4.7.5 Accounting Entries

Display the invoice using transaction MIR4. Enter the Invoice Document No. and the Fiscal Year. Click &❧ Display Document . The system displays the invoice. Click Follow-On Documents ... . The system displays the list of accounting documents. Double-click the Accounting document to see the accounting entries.

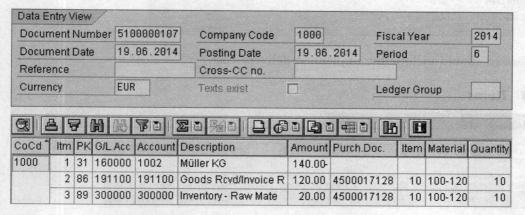

Note that the unplanned delivery cost is credited to the vendor. The debit is to the Stock account because the price control of the material is Moving average price.

4.7.6 Inventory Value

Inventory value before invoice posting

You can see the stock and the value of a material in the `Accounting 1` view of the material master using transaction MM02. The following image is a part of that view before the invoice was posted.

Total Stock	2,502	Total Value	35,000.16

Inventory value after invoice posting

The following image is a part of the `Accounting 1` view after the invoice was posted.

Total Stock	2,502	Total Value	35,020.16

Note that the total value of the material has gone up by 20.00 Euros on account of the unplanned delivery cost posted by the invoice.

4.7.7 Standard Price

If the price control of the material is Standard price, the stock account is charged at the standard rate, and the difference is debited or credited to the Price difference account. Therefore, the unplanned delivery cost is also debited to the Price difference account.

4.8 UNPLANNED DELIVERY COST POSTED TO A SPECIFIED G/L ACCOUNT

Functional Consultant	User	Business Process Owner	Senior Management	My Rating	Understanding Level
A	A	A		B	

4.8.1 Scenario

The invoice contains unplanned delivery cost, and you want to post it to a separate G/L account.

4.8.2 Unplanned Delivery Costs to a Specified G/L Account

In Section 4.7, you saw that unplanned delivery cost was credited to the vendor and debited to the Stock account (Moving average price material) or to the Price difference account (Standard price material). Some companies want to debit unplanned delivery costs to a separate G/L account. For each company code, in view V_169P_B, you can specify how unplanned delivery costs are to be posted.

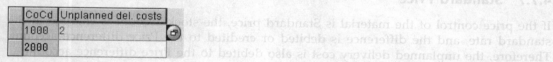

CoCd	Unplanned del. costs
1000	2
2000	

There are two options.

ID del. costs	Short text
	Distribute among invoice items
2	Different G/L line

In the first option, the system splits the unplanned delivery costs entered among the individual items, based on the amounts invoiced so far plus those in the invoice being entered and debits the Stock account or Price difference account depending on the price control of the material.

In the second option, unplanned delivery costs are posted in a separate posting line to a G/L account set up for this purpose.

4.8.3 Account Determination

You can use transaction OMR0 to see/set the G/L account to which the unplanned delivery cost will be posted.

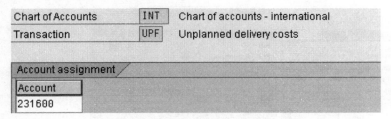

4.8.4 Invoice

Enter the invoice using transaction MIRO.

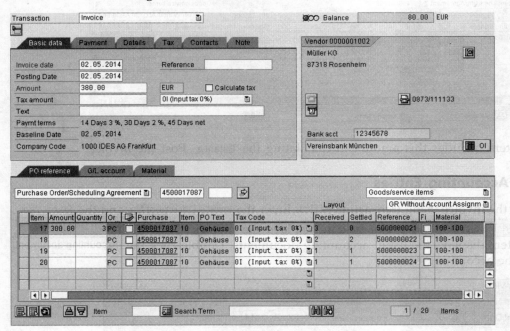

4.8.5 Unplanned Delivery Cost

Enter the unplanned delivery cost in the `Unpl. Del. Csts` field in the `Details` tab of the invoice header.

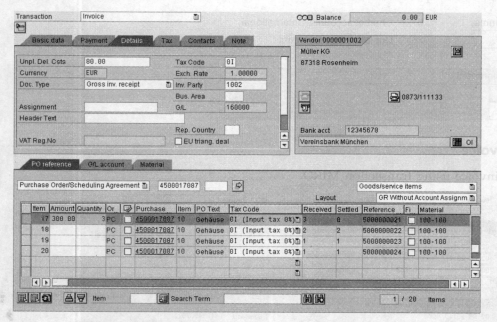

The system includes this amount in calculating the `Balance`. Post the invoice.

4.8.6 Accounting Entries

Display the invoice using transaction MIR4. Enter the `Invoice Document No.` and the `Fiscal Year`. Click `Display Document`. The system displays the invoice. Click `Follow-On Documents ...`. The system displays the list of accounting documents. Double-click the `Accounting document` to see the accounting entries.

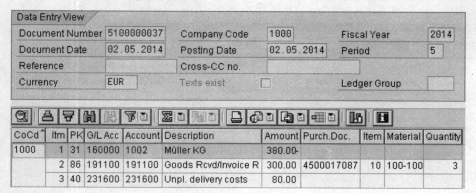

Note that the unplanned delivery costs are posted to a separate G/L account.

4.9   GOODS RECEIVED IN THE GR BLOCKED STOCK

Functional Consultant	User	Business Process Owner	Senior Management	My Rating	Understanding Level
A	A	B	C		

4.9.1   Scenario

You have received an invoice for the material received in the GR Blocked Stock.

4.9.2   Invoice for Goods in GR Blocked Stock

Enter the invoice using transaction MIRO.

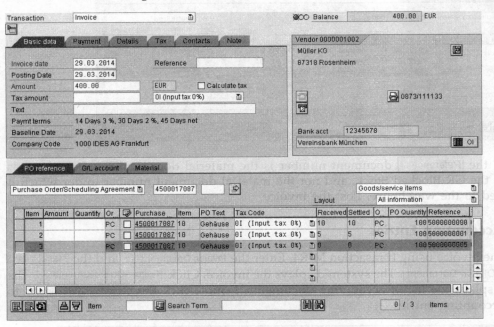

The system shows that the goods receipt has zero Received quantity. You cannot settle an invoice for material received in the GR Blocked Stock.

4.9.3 Invoice for Goods after Moving from GR Blocked Stock to Warehouse

After the goods are moved from GR Blocked Stock to warehouse using movement type 105, you can post the invoice.

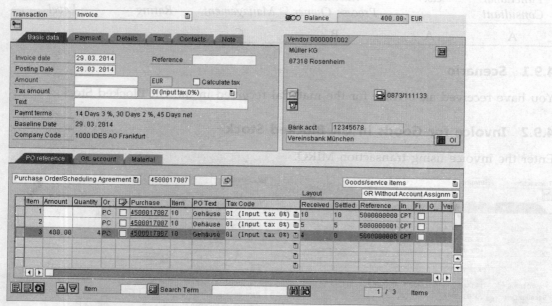

Note that the [Reference] document number is the material document number of goods receipt in the GR Blocked Stock, and not the material document number under which it was moved to the warehouse. Post the invoice.

4.9.4 Accounting Entries

Display the invoice using transaction MIR4. Enter the Invoice Document No. and the Fiscal Year. Click [&⅍ Display Document]. The system displays the invoice. Click [Follow-On Documents ...]. The system displays the list of accounting documents. Double-click the [Accounting document] to see the accounting entries.

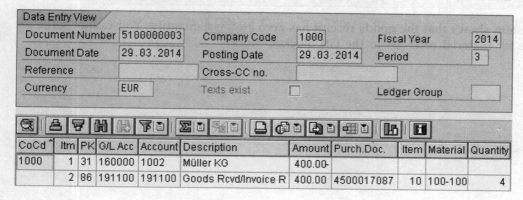

4.10   INVOICES REFERRING TO MULTIPLE PURCHASE ORDERS

Functional Consultant	User	Business Process Owner	Senior Management	My Rating	Understanding Level
A	A	B	C		

4.10.1   Scenario

You receive an invoice for multiple supplies that belong to different purchase orders.

4.10.2   Basic Data

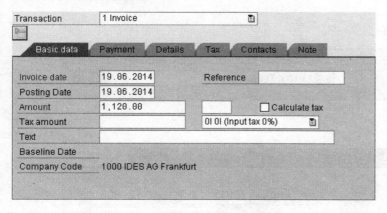

4.10.3   Items

Multiple allocation

In PO reference, click ⇨ and enter all purchase orders referred in the invoice.

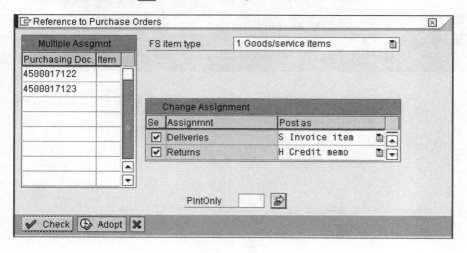

Proposed items

The system proposes all goods receipts for the specified purchase orders as invoice items.

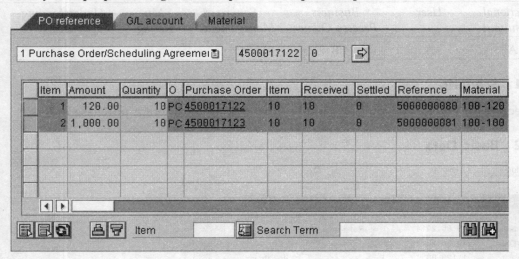

4.10.4 Payment

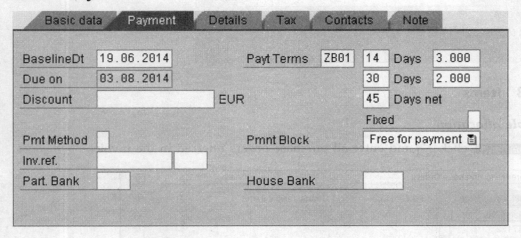

Payment terms

The buyer generally defines the terms of payment in the purchase order. The terms of payment are entered in the purchase order header, and therefore, apply to all items. These terms of payment are suggested in invoice verification, but can be overwritten. If an invoice refers to more than one purchase order, the terms of payment in the first purchase order are suggested.

Payment terms in purchase order 1

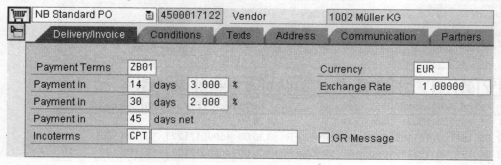

Payment terms in purchase order 1 are ZB01.

Payment terms in purchase order 2

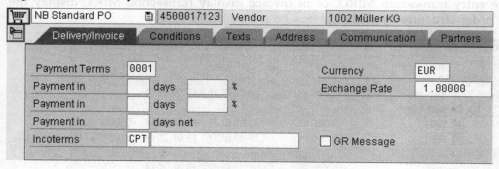

Payment terms in purchase order 2 are 0001.

Payment terms in invoice

Payment terms in invoice are ZB01, which are adopted from purchase order 1.

Posting

Post the invoice.

4.10.5   Accounting Entries

Display the invoice using transaction MIR4. Enter the Invoice Document No. and the Fiscal Year . Click Display Document . The system displays the invoice. Click Follow-On Documents ... . The system displays the list of accounting documents. Double-click the Accounting document to see the accounting entries.

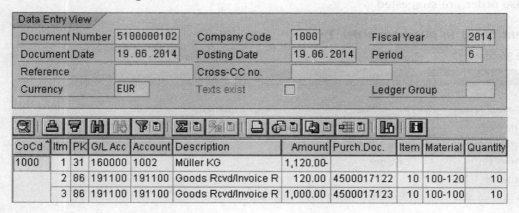

CoCd	Itm	PK	G/L Acc	Account	Description	Amount	Purch.Doc.	Item	Material	Quantity
1000	1	31	160000	1002	Müller KG	1,120.00-				
	2	86	191100	191100	Goods Rcvd/Invoice R	120.00	4500017122	10	100-120	10
	3	86	191100	191100	Goods Rcvd/Invoice R	1,000.00	4500017123	10	100-100	10

4.10.6   Purchase Order Structure

In invoice entry transaction MIRO, or in invoice display transaction MIR4, display the purchase order structure by clicking Show PO structure .

Display - PO structure	Qty	Amount	Posting date	Doc. No.
▽ 👤 Müller KG				
▽ 🔧 4500017122				
▽ 🔧 10 Flat gasket	10.000 PC	120.00 EUR	19.06.2014	
▽ 🚚 Delivery note				
📄 WE	10.000 PC	120.00 EUR	19.06.2014	5000000080
📄 RE-L	10.000 PC	120.00 EUR	19.06.2014	5105608743
▽ 🔧 4500017123				
▽ 🔧 10 Casing	10.000 PC	1,000.00 EUR	19.06.2014	
▽ 🚚 Delivery note				
📄 WE	10.000 PC	1,000.00 EUR	19.06.2014	5000000081
📄 RE-L	10.000 PC	1,000.00 EUR	19.06.2014	5105608743

Note that the purchase order structure shows both the purchase orders.

4.11 CASH DISCOUNT

Functional Consultant	User	Business Process Owner	Senior Management	My Rating	Understanding Level
A	A	A	B		

4.11.1 Scenario

Cash discount

The vendor may offer cash discount, if you pay him before the due date. Such discounts are usually specified in the payment terms in the purchase order.

Cash discount during payment runs

When invoice is posted, you may not take cognizance of cash discounts; it may be done when you run the program to make payment.

Cash discount during invoice verification

However, if you wish, you can post cash discounts at the time of invoice verification also. To do so, select | RN Net invoice receipt 📄 | in **Details** tab.

Price control

This scenario is for a material having Moving average price. Section 4.11.8 explains the difference for a material having Standard price.

4.11.2 Basic Data

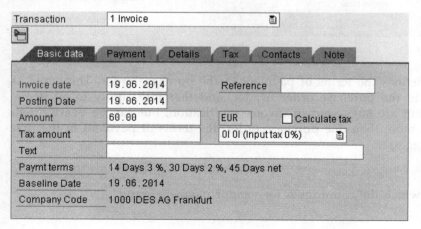

4.11.3 Items

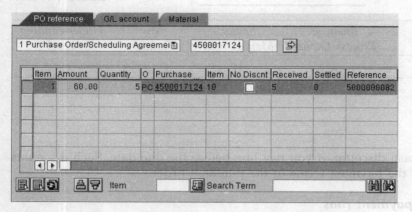

Enter the purchase order number. Select the items.

4.11.4 Payment

Payment terms

The buyer generally defines the terms of payment in the purchase order. The terms of payment are entered in the purchase order header, and therefore, apply to all items. These terms of payment are suggested in invoice verification, but can be overwritten. If an invoice refers to more than one purchase order, the terms of payment in the first purchase order are suggested.

Baseline date

This is the date from which the countdown for vendor payment starts.

Due on

This is the date on which payment to the vendor is due. It is computed by the system from the `BaselineDt` and `Days net` specified in the `Payt Terms`.

4.11.5 Details

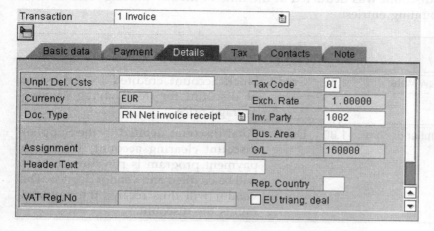

Document type

Choose from the following document types:

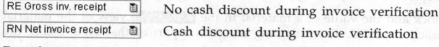

No cash discount during invoice verification

Cash discount during invoice verification

Post the invoice.

4.11.6 Accounting Entries

Display the invoice using transaction MIR4. Enter the Invoice Document No. and the Fiscal Year . Click Display Document . The system displays the invoice. Click Follow-On Documents ... . The system displays the list of accounting documents. Double-click the Accounting document to see the accounting entries.

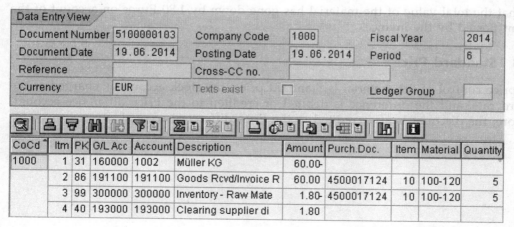

CoCd	Itm	PK	G/L Acc	Account	Description	Amount	Purch.Doc.	Item	Material	Quantity
1000	1	31	160000	1002	Müller KG	60.00-				
	2	86	191100	191100	Goods Rcvd/Invoice R	60.00	4500017124	10	100-120	5
	3	99	300000	300000	Inventory - Raw Mate	1.80-	4500017124	10	100-120	5
	4	40	193000	193000	Clearing supplier di	1.80				

In this invoice, cash discount was deducted at the time of invoice posting. This resulted in the following accounting entries:

Account		Amount	Debit/credit	Reason
300000	Inventory - Raw Mate	1.80-	Credit	Stock account credited to the extent of discount for item having Moving average price.
193000	Clearing supplier di	1.80	Debit	Total discount debited to the Supplier discount clearing account. When the payment program is run, this account will be credited and vendor debited. The vendor will thus receive the payment minus the discount.

4.11.7   Inventory Value

Inventory value before invoice posting

You can see the stock and the value of a material in the Accounting 1 view of the material master using transaction MM02. The following image is a part of that view before the invoice was posted.

Total Stock	2,462	Total Value	34,526.96

Inventory value after invoice posting

The following image is a part of the Accounting 1 view after the invoice was posted.

Total Stock	2,462	Total Value	34,525.16

Note that the total value of the material has gone down by 1.80 Euros on account of the discount posted by the invoice.

4.11.8   Standard Price

If the price control of the material is Standard price, the stock account is charged at the standard rate, and the difference is debited or credited to the Price difference account. Therefore, the discount is also credited to the Price difference account.

4.12   FIXED CASH DISCOUNT

Functional Consultant	User	Business Process Owner	Senior Management	My Rating	Understanding Level
A	A	B	C		

4.12.1   Scenario

The invoice contains a fixed cash discount.

4.12.2   Basic Data

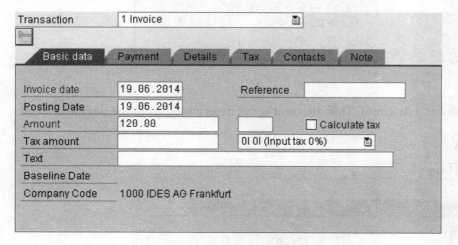

4.12.3   Items

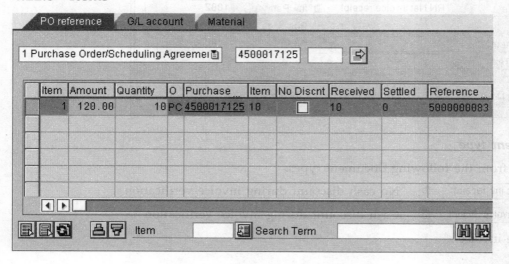

4.12.4 Payment

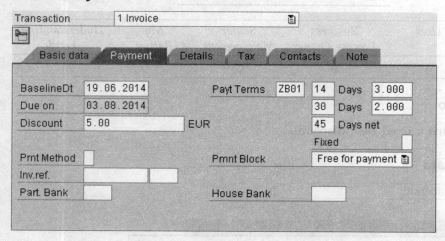

Discount

Here you enter the fixed discount. This discount is not determined from the payment terms.

4.12.5 Details

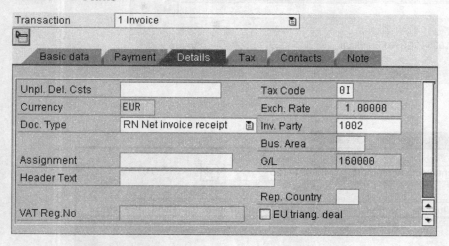

Document type

Choose from the following document types:

RE Gross inv. receipt   No cash discount during invoice verification

RN Net invoice receipt   Cash discount during invoice verification

Post the invoice.

4.12.6 Accounting Entries

Display the invoice using transaction MIR4. Enter the Invoice Document No. and the Fiscal Year. Click 👓 Display Document. The system displays the invoice. Click Follow-On Documents ... . The system displays the list of accounting documents. Double-click the Accounting document to see the accounting entries.

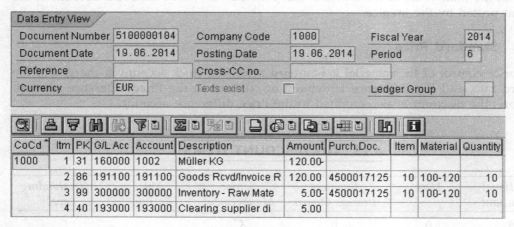

In this invoice cash discount was deducted at the time of invoice posting. This resulted in the following accounting entries.

Account		Amount	Debit/ credit	Reason
300000	Inventory - Raw Mate	5.00-	Credit	Stock account credited to the extent of discount for item having Moving average price.
193000	Clearing supplier di	5.00	Debit	Total discount debited to the Supplier discount clearing account. When the payment program is run, this account will be credited and vendor debited. The vendor will thus receive the payment minus the discount.

4.12.7 Inventory Value

Inventory value before invoice posting

You can see the stock and the value of a material in the Accounting 1 view of the material master using transaction MM02. The following image is a part of that view before the invoice was posted.

Total Stock	2,472	Total Value	34,645.16

Inventory value after invoice posting

The following image is a part of the `Accounting 1` view after the invoice was posted.

| Total Stock | 2,472 | Total Value | 34,640.16 |

Note that the total value of the material has gone down by 5.00 Euros on account of the discount posted by the invoice.

4.12.8   Standard Price

If the price control of the material is Standard price, the stock account is charged at the standard rate, and the difference is debited or credited to the Price difference account. Therefore, the discount is also credited to the Price difference account.

4.13   NO DISCOUNT ITEMS

Functional Consultant	User	Business Process Owner	Senior Management	My Rating	Understanding Level
A	A	B	C		

4.13.1   Scenario

Cash discount

The vendor may offer cash discount, if you pay him before the due date. Such discounts are usually specified in the payment terms in the purchase order.

Cash discount during payment runs

When invoice is posted, you may not take cognizance of cash discounts; it may be done when you run the program to make payment.

Cash discount during invoice verification

However, if you wish, you can post cash discounts at the time of invoice verification also. Select `RN Net invoice receipt` in `Details` tab.

No discount items

At item level you can select `No Discnt`. For these items, discount is not computed.

Invoice

The invoice contains some items on which there is no cash discount, and some items on which there is cash discount.

4.13.2 All Items with Cash Discount

Enter the invoice using transaction MIRO.

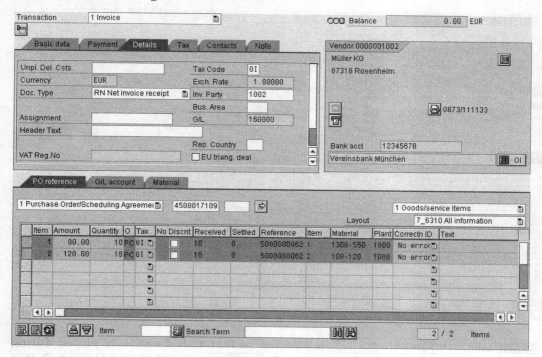

In **Details** tab RN Net invoice receipt is selected so that cash discount is posted during invoice verification. Also note that No Discnt is not selected for any item.

Simulation of accounting entries

P	A	G/L	Act/Mat/Ast/Vndr	Amount	Cur	Purchasing	Item	T	Vendor
1	K	160000	Müller KG / 87318 Rosenheim	200.00-	EUR			0I	1002
2	S	191100	Goods Rcvd/Invoice Rcvd (third party)	80.00	EUR	4500017109	10	0I	
3	M	300010	Sensor assembly	2.40-	EUR	4500017109	10	0I	
4	S	191100	Goods Rcvd/Invoice Rcvd (third party)	120.00	EUR	4500017109	20	0I	
5	M	300000	Flat gasket	3.60-	EUR	4500017109	20	0I	
6	S	193000	Clearing supplier discounts (Net meth	6.00	EUR			0I	

4.13.3 Some Items without Cash Discount

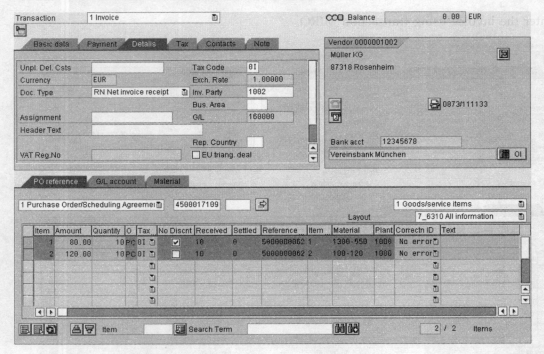

In **Details** tab RN Net invoice receipt 📋 is selected so that cash discount is posted during invoice verification. Also note that for item 1, No Discnt is selected, but for item 2, it is not selected.

Simulation of accounting entries

P	A	G/L	Act/Mat/Ast/Vndr	Amount	Cur	Purchasing	Item	T	Vendor
1	K	160000	Müller KG / 87318 Rosenheim	200.00-	EUR			OI	1002
2	S	191100	Goods Rcvd/Invoice Rcvd (third party)	80.00	EUR	4500017109	10	OI	
3	S	191100	Goods Rcvd/Invoice Rcvd (third party)	120.00	EUR	4500017109	20	OI	
4	M	300000	Flat gasket	3.60-	EUR	4500017109	20	OI	
5	S	193000	Clearing supplier discounts (Net meth	3.60	EUR			OI	

Note that the entry for discount on item 10 is not there because you selected No Discnt for that item. Post the invoice.

4.13.4 Accounting Entries

Display the invoice using transaction MIR4. Enter the Invoice Document No. and the Fiscal Year. Click 👓 Display Document. The system displays the invoice. Click Follow-On Documents ... . The system displays the list of accounting documents. Double-click the Accounting document to see the accounting entries.

Document Number	5100000076	Company Code	1000	Fiscal Year	2014
Document Date	05.06.2014	Posting Date	05.06.2014	Period	6
Reference		Cross-CC no.			
Currency	EUR	Texts exist	☐	Ledger Group	

Data Entry View

CoCd	Itm	PK	G/L Acc	Account	Description	Amount	W/o cash disc.	Disc.1	Disc.base
1000	1	31	160000	1002	Müller KG	200.00-		3.000	120.00
	2	86	191100	191100	Goods Rcvd/Invoice R	80.00	X	0.000	
	3	86	191100	191100	Goods Rcvd/Invoice R	120.00		0.000	
	4	99	300000	300000	Inventory - Raw Mate	3.60-		0.000	
	5	40	193000	193000	Clearing supplier di	3.60		0.000	

Note that W/o cash disc. is selected for item 2, and therefore, discount base excludes that item. Cash discount is computed on the discount base. Cash discount is credited to the stock account. At present, it is debited to a clearing account; when vendor will be paid, the clearing account will be credited and vendor will be debited.

4.14 PAYMENT IN INSTALLMENTS

Functional Consultant	User	Business Process Owner	Senior Management	My Rating	Understanding Level
A	A	A	B		

4.14.1 Scenario

You receive an invoice whose payment is to be made in installments.

4.14.2 Basic Data

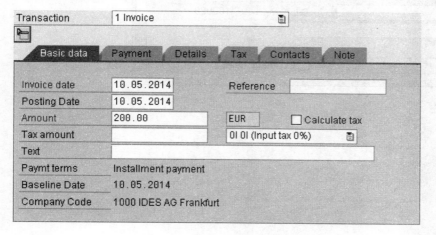

Transaction   1 Invoice

Basic data | Payment | Details | Tax | Contacts | Note

Invoice date	10.05.2014	Reference	
Posting Date	10.05.2014		
Amount	200.00	EUR ☐ Calculate tax	
Tax amount		0I 0I (Input tax 0%)	
Text			
Paymt terms	Installment payment		
Baseline Date	10.05.2014		
Company Code	1000 IDES AG Frankfurt		

4.14.3 Payment

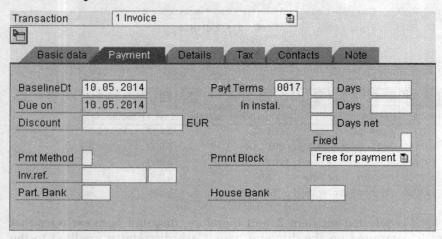

Payment terms

You can change the payment terms in invoice verification. Note that this payment term involves payment in installments.

4.14.4 Details

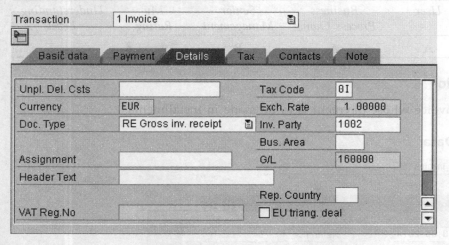

4.14.5 Items

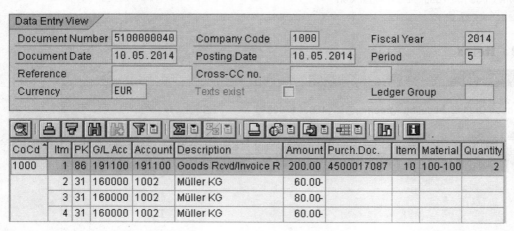

Select the items. Post the invoice.

4.14.6 Accounting Entries

Display the invoice using transaction MIR4. Enter the Invoice Document No. and the Fiscal Year. Click 𝒮 Display Document . The system displays the invoice. Click Follow-On Documents ... . The system displays the list of accounting documents. Double-click the Accounting document to see the accounting entries.

Data Entry View

Document Number	5100000040	Company Code	1000	Fiscal Year	2014
Document Date	10.05.2014	Posting Date	10.05.2014	Period	5
Reference		Cross-CC no.			
Currency	EUR	Texts exist	☐	Ledger Group	

CoCd	Itm	PK	G/L Acc	Account	Description	Amount	Purch.Doc.	Item	Material	Quantity
1000	1	86	191100	191100	Goods Rcvd/Invoice R	200.00	4500017087	10	100-100	2
	2	31	160000	1002	Müller KG	60.00-				
	3	31	160000	1002	Müller KG	80.00-				
	4	31	160000	1002	Müller KG	60.00-				

Installment

Note that the system has generated three entries for vendor credit; one for each installment.

4.15 FIXED ACCOUNT ASSIGNMENT

Functional Consultant	User	Business Process Owner	Senior Management	My Rating	Understanding Level
A	A	A	B		

4.15.1 Scenario

You receive an invoice for goods that were used on receipt.

4.15.2 Basic Data

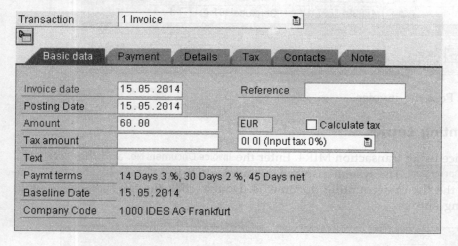

4.15.3 Items

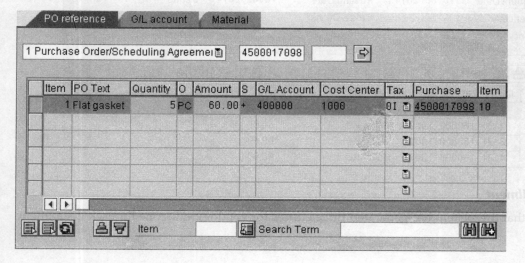

Select the items. Post the invoice.

4.15.4 Accounting Entries

Display the invoice using transaction MIR4. Enter the Invoice Document No. and the Fiscal Year. Click | ᇮ Display Document |. The system displays the invoice. Click | Follow-On Documents ... |. The system displays the list of accounting documents. Double-click the | Accounting document | to see the accounting entries.

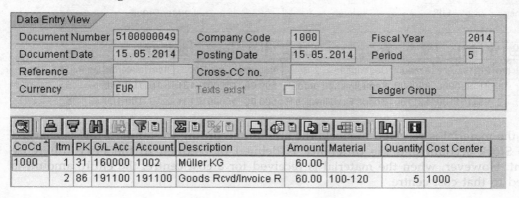

CoCd	Itm	PK	G/L Acc	Account	Description	Amount	Material	Quantity	Cost Center
1000	1	31	160000	1002	Müller KG	60.00-			
	2	86	191100	191100	Goods Rcvd/Invoice R	60.00	100-120	5	1000

4.15.5 Accounting Entries during Goods Receipt

In transaction MB02, display the goods receipt and click | Accounting Documents... |. Double-click the | Accounting document | to see the accounting entries.

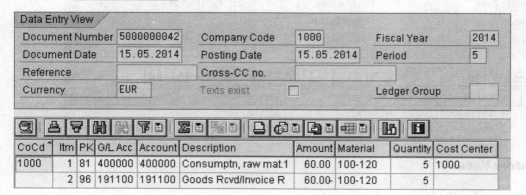

CoCd	Itm	PK	G/L Acc	Account	Description	Amount	Material	Quantity	Cost Center
1000	1	81	400000	400000	Consumptn, raw mat.1	60.00	100-120	5	1000
	2	96	191100	191100	Goods Rcvd/Invoice R	60.00-	100-120	5	

Note that during goods receipt the amount was debited to the Consumption account directly, and not to the Stock account.

4.15.6 Standard Price

Whether the price control of a material is Standard price or Moving average price, accounting entries are the same.

Accounting Entries for Goods Receipt

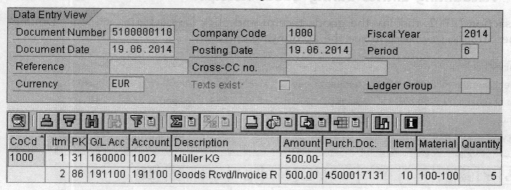

Data Entry View

Document Number	5000000086	Company Code	1000	Fiscal Year	2014
Document Date	19.06.2014	Posting Date	19.06.2014	Period	6
Reference		Cross-CC no.		
Currency	EUR	Texts exist	☐	Ledger Group	

CoCd	Itm	PK	G/L Acc	Account	Description	Amount	Purch.Doc.	Item	Material	Quantity
1000	1	81	890000	890000	Semi-finished prod.	500.00	4500017131	10	100-100	5
	2	96	191100	191100	Goods Rcvd/Invoice R	500.00-	4500017131	10	100-100	5

When the material is received in stock, the amount according to standard rate is charged to the Stock account and the difference is debited or credited to the Price difference account. However, when the material is received for a cost centre, the entire amount is charged to that cost centre.

Accounting Entries for Invoice Posting

Data Entry View

Document Number	5100000110	Company Code	1000	Fiscal Year	2014
Document Date	19.06.2014	Posting Date	19.06.2014	Period	6
Reference		Cross-CC no.		
Currency	EUR	Texts exist	☐	Ledger Group	

CoCd	Itm	PK	G/L Acc	Account	Description	Amount	Purch.Doc.	Item	Material	Quantity
1000	1	31	160000	1002	Müller KG	500.00-				
	2	86	191100	191100	Goods Rcvd/Invoice R	500.00	4500017131	10	100-100	5

Inventory Value

Inventory value before goods receipt

You can see the stock and the value of a material in the **Accounting 1** view of the material master using transaction MM02. The following image is a part of that view before the invoice was posted.

Total Stock	1,240	Total Value	141,062.40

Inventory value after goods receipt

The following image is a part of the **Accounting 1** view after goods receipt.

Total Stock	1,240	Total Value	141,062.40

Inventory value after invoice posting

The following image is a part of the `Accounting 1` view after the invoice was posted.

Total Stock	1,240	Total Value	141,062.40

Conclusion

Goods receipt and invoice verification of material with account assignment does not have any effect on the stock or the price of the material. This is true for materials having Standard price, as well as for materials having Moving average price.

4.16 CHANGEABLE ACCOUNT ASSIGNMENT

Functional Consultant	User	Business Process Owner	Senior Management	My Rating	Understanding Level
A	A	A	B		

4.16.1 Scenario

You receive invoice for a material for which no accounting entries were passed on goods receipt.

4.16.2 Purchase Order

You can change, or enter, account assignment in invoice verification only, if the following conditions are met:

Account Assignment

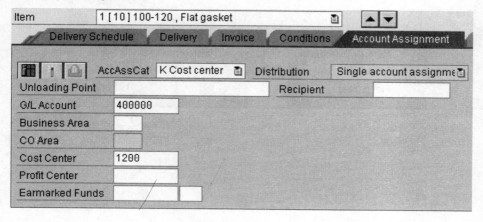

Account assignment category

The account assignment category you specify must have the property ☑ AA Chgable at IR in view V_T163K. This allows change of account assignment on invoice receipt.

Delivery

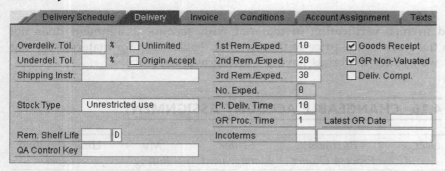

Goods receipt, goods receipt non-valuated

A non-valuated goods receipt or no goods receipt must be defined for the purchase order item. In the former case, goods are received, but no accounting entries are passed. In the latter case, you do not enter goods receipt, you directly post the invoice.

4.16.3 Goods Receipt

In transaction MB02, display the goods receipt.

Goods receipt

Accounting documents

Click Accounting Documents... .

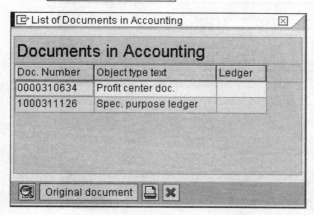

Since the goods receipt is non-valuated, no accounting entries are passed, and hence there is no accounting document.

4.16.4 Invoice

Enter the invoice using transaction MIRO.

Basic Data

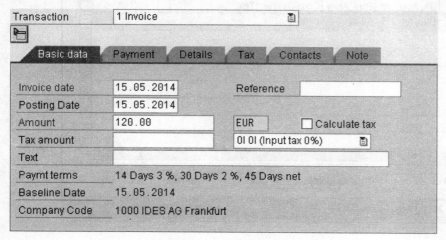

Items

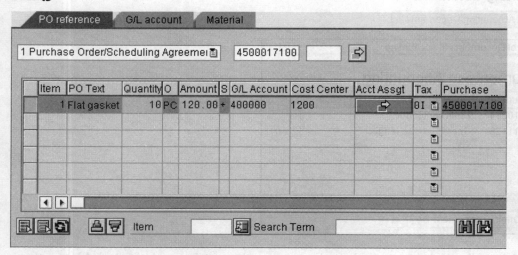

You can change the cost centre of the item, if you want.

Multiple account assignments

If you want to create multiple account assignment, click

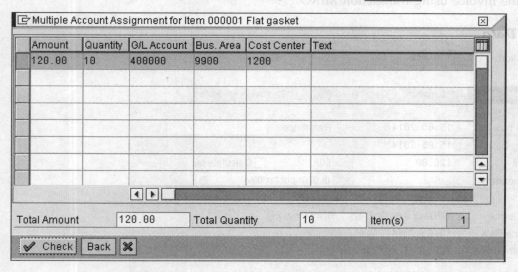

Change the account assignment as under.

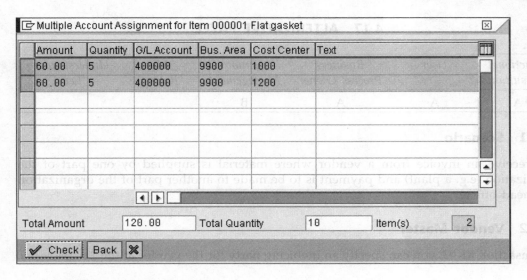

Click . ✓ Check and Back . Post the invoice.

4.16.5 Accounting Entries

Display the invoice using transaction MIR4. Enter the Invoice Document No. and the Fiscal Year . Click 👓 Display Document . The system displays the invoice. Click Follow-On Documents ... . The system displays the list of accounting documents. Double-click the Accounting document to see the accounting entries.

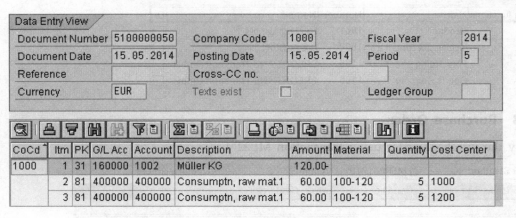

Note that the expense is debited to two different cost centres in the ratio specified during invoice entry.

4.17 ALTERNATIVE PAYEE

Functional Consultant	User	Business Process Owner	Senior Management	My Rating	Understanding Level
A	A	A	B		

4.17.1 Scenario

You receive an invoice from a vendor where material is supplied by one part of the organization (e.g. a plant) and payment is to be made to another part of the organization (e.g. head office).

4.17.2 Vendor Master

In transaction XK02, you can specify an invoicing party for the vendor at the Purchasing Org. level.

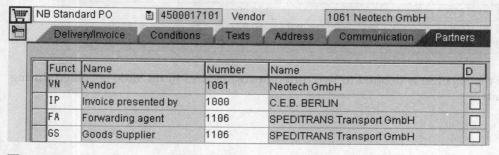

4.17.3 Purchase Order

Display the purchase order using transaction ME22N.

The partner functions are adopted from the vendor master. They can be changed in the purchase order.

4.17.4 Goods Receipt

Display the goods receipt using transaction MB02.

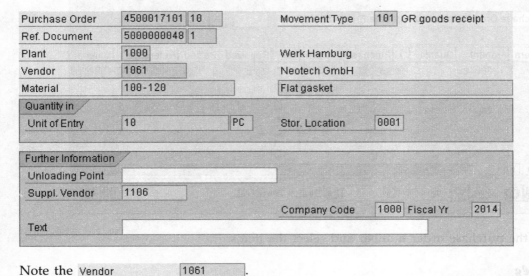

Note the Vendor 1061 .

4.17.5 Invoice

Basic Data

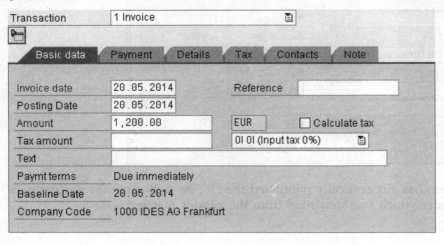

Items

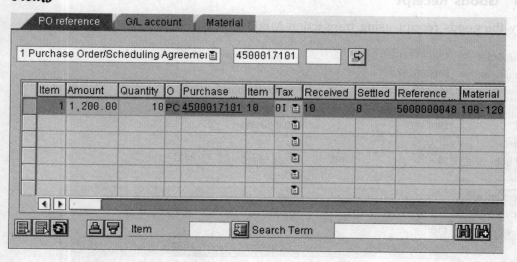

Enter the purchase order number and select the items.

Details

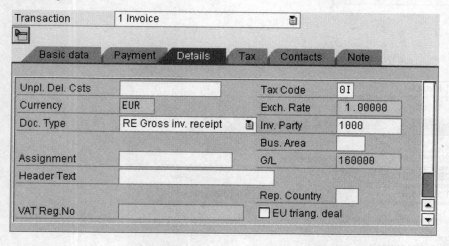

Note that the system has automatically populated the Inv. Party field from the partner data in the purchase order which was defaulted from the vendor master.

Vendor

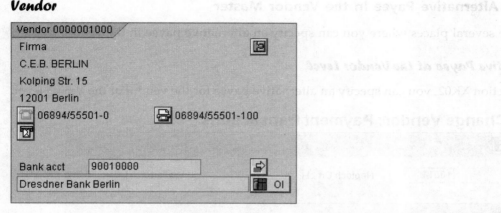

Note that the vendor is 1000, not 1061. This is because of the `Inv. Party` field in the `Details` tab.

4.17.6   Accounting Entries

Display the invoice using transaction MIR4. Enter the `Invoice Document No.` and the `Fiscal Year`. Click `Display Document`. The system displays the invoice. Click `Follow-On Documents ...`. The system displays the list of accounting documents. Double-click the `Accounting document` to see the accounting entries.

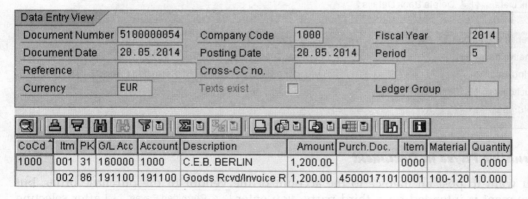

Note that the payment is credited to vendor 1000, although the purchase order was on vendor 1061.

4.17.7 Alternative Payee in the Vendor Master

There are several places where you can specify an alternative payee in the vendor master.

Alternative Payee at the Vendor Level

In transaction XK02, you can specify an alternative payee for the vendor at the Vendor level.

Change Vendor: Payment transactions

Vendor   1061   Neotech GmbH   Weilerbach

Bank details

Ctry	Bank Key	Bank Account	Acct holder	C	IBAN	BnkT	Reference details	C	Name of bank
DE	10020030	23453433	Neotecj GmbH		⇨			☐	Deutsche Bank
					⇨			☐	
					⇨			☐	
					⇨			☐	
					⇨			☐	

[Bank Data...] [🗐 Delete Bank Details]

Payment transactions

Alternative payee	
DME Indicator	
Instruction key	
ISR Number	

Alternative payee in document

☑ Individual spec.

☐ Spec. per reference

[Permitted Payee]

Alternative Payee in Document

If you want to post an invoice to the account of the vendor in the purchase order, but the payment is intended for a third party, you enter [Permitted Payee] after selecting ☑ Individual spec..

Individual specification

If this indicator is set, you can enter an address or bank details for automatic payment transactions in the document which differs from those in the vendor master record.

Permitted payee

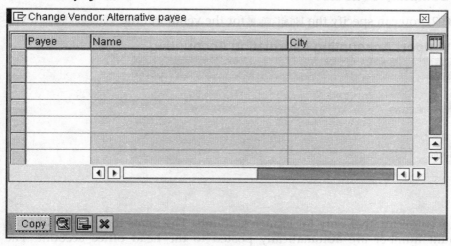

Alternative Payee at Company Code Level

In transaction XK02, you can specify an alternative payee for the vendor at the Company Code level.

Change Vendor: Payment transactions Accounting

Vendor	1061	Neotech GmbH	Weilerbach
Company Code	1000	IDES AG	

Payment data

Payt Terms		Tolerance group	
		Chk double inv. ☐	
Chk cashng time			

Automatic payment transactions

Payment methods		Payment block		Free for payment
Alternat.payee	1001	House Bank		
Individual pmnt ☐		Grouping key		
B/exch.limit		EUR		
Pmt adv. by EDI ☐				

Head Office at Company Code Level

In transaction XK02, you can specify the Head office for the vendor at the Company Code level.

Change Vendor: Accounting information Accounting

Vendor	1061	Neotech GmbH	Weilerbach
Company Code	1000	IDES AG	

Accounting information			
Recon. account	160000	Sort key	
Head office		Subsidy indic.	

Head office

You specify this account number only for branch accounts. The items that you post using the branch account number are automatically posted to the head office account. The system records the branch account number in the line items.

4.17.8   Crediting Invoice to Unauthorized Alternative Payee

Invoice

The following invoice was posted with an alternative payee, which was not authorized anywhere in the vendor master.

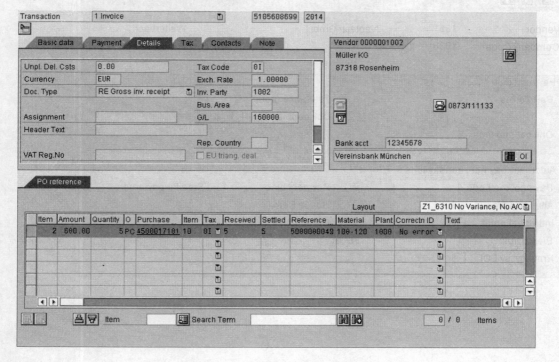

Accounting Entries

Display the invoice using transaction MIR4. Enter the `Invoice Document No.` and the `Fiscal Year`. Click `Display Document`. The system displays the invoice. Click `Follow-On Documents ...`. The system displays the list of accounting documents. Double-click the `Accounting document` to see the accounting entries.

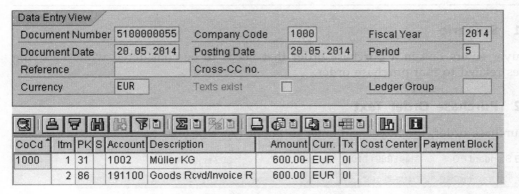

Caution

Note that an invoice can be posted to any alternative payee. It is not restricted by the entries in the vendor master. Even the payment is not blocked.

4.18 NOTIFICATION OF PURCHASE ORDER TEXT

Functional Consultant	User	Business Process Owner	Senior Management	My Rating	Understanding Level
A	A	B	C		

4.18.1 Scenario

The buyer enters text in a purchase order that needs to be considered while verifying invoices related to that purchase order.

4.18.2 Purchase Order Text

In a purchase order, the buyer can enter different types of text.

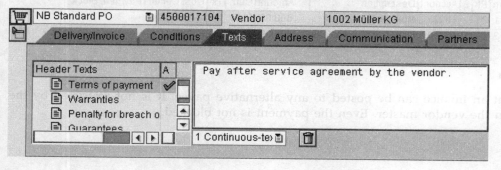

If such a text exists in a purchase order, it may be appropriate to draw the attention of the invoice processor to it when he is verifying an invoice referring to this purchase order.

4.18.3 Activation of Purchase Order Text Notification

In view V_169P_MB, you can activate purchase order text notification.

Co	Company Name	PO text
1000	IDES AG	☑
2000	IDES UK	☑
2200	IDES France	☑
2201	IDES France affiliate	☑

4.18.4 Text IDs Relevant for Purchase Order Text Notification

You can create different types of texts in a purchase order. Not all of them may be relevant for notification during invoice verification. In view V_T169B_ASSIGN, you specify the text ids for which the invoice processor should get a message.

CoCd	Company Name	ID	Meaning	Status
1000	IDES AG	F03	Pricing types	
1000	IDES AG	F07	Terms of payment	
2000	IDES UK	F03	Pricing types	
2000	IDES UK	F07	Terms of payment	

4.18.5   Notification during Invoice Processing

When you are entering an invoice using transaction MIRO, and specify the purchase order, the system gives the following message.

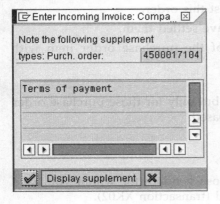

4.18.6   Displaying the Purchase Order Text

Click | Display supplement |. The system displays the purchase order texts relevant for invoice verification.

Purchasing Doc.	4500017104	Company Code	1000	Purchasing Group	000
		Document Type	NB	Purch. Organization	1000
Vendor	1002	Müller KG			

Header Texts

	TxtType Text	More Text	Status
☐	Pricing types		
		☐	
☐	Terms of payment		
	Pay after service agreement by the vendo		
		☑	

The system just notifies you. It is for you to take the necessary action manually. Click ⇦ to go back to invoice processing. You may cancel invoice entry, make changes in invoice data, or post the invoice as usual.

4.19   REVALUATION

Functional Consultant	User	Business Process Owner	Senior Management	My Rating	Understanding Level
A	A	A	B		

4.19.1   Scenario

➢ You have ordered an item on the vendor at certain price.

➢ The vendor has supplied you some material against this order.

➢ The vendor has raised invoice on you, and you have settled them.

➢ You and the vendor agree to change the rate of the purchase order item with retrospective effect.

➢ You now want to pay the difference.

➢ You can use the revaluation functionality to do so but only for those purchase order items where invoice verification is goods receipt based.

4.19.2   Activating Revaluation for a Vendor

You can use the revaluation functionality only for those vendors for whom you have selected ☑ Revaluation allowed in the vendor master record (transaction XK02).

Vendor	1002	Müller KG	Rosenheim
Purchasing Org.	1000	IDES Deutschland	

Control data

☑ GR-Based Inv. Verif.	ABC indicator	☐
☑ AutoEvalGRSetmt Del.	ModeOfTrnsprt-Border	☐
	Office of entry	☐
☑ Acknowledgment Reqd	Sort criterion	☐ By VSR sequence number
☑ Automatic purchase order		
☑ Subsequent settlement	☑ Revaluation allowed	
☐ Subseq. sett. index	☐ Grant discount in kind	

If you do not want to use the revaluation functionality for any vendor, you can suppress the New value method field using transaction OMSG.

4.19.3 Changing the Price of a Purchase Order Item

You can change the price of a purchase order item using transaction ME22N.

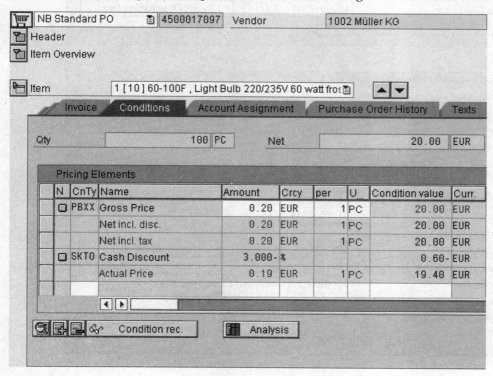

Save the changed prices.

4.19.4 Transaction

MRNB—Revaluation

4.19.5 Selection Screen

Purchasing Document Selection

| Purchasing Document | 4500017097 | Display Purchasing Doc. |
| Item | 10 | |

Date for GR Selection/Price Determination

Date of past period 01.03.2014 to 31.05.2014

- ◉ Posting date
- ○ Entry date
- ○ Delivery note date

Processing Options

Posting Date	31.05.2014	
Payment baseline dte		
Terms of payt, invoices	ZB01	Copy from Creditor
Trms of payt, cred. memos	ZB01	Copy from Creditor
Processing mode	0	Generate credit memos and invoices
Minimum value		EUR
Value Difference Check Active	☐	
Test Run	☑	

Display Options

| Variant | |

4.19.6 Test Run

Select Test Run ☑ and click . The system gives the following output:

Revaluation Results in Test Mode

Processing Mode:	Generate credit memos and invoices
Execution Time:	31.05.2014 / 13:30:59
User:	SAPUSER .
Vendor:	0000001002, Müller KG, DE 83204 Rosenheim
PO Number/Item:	4500017097 / 00010
Material/Short Text:	60-100F / Light Bulb 220/235V 60 watt frosted
Plant:	1000, Werk Hamburg
Company Code:	1000, IDES AG
Purchasing Org.:	1000, IDES Deutschland
Past Period:	01.03.2014 - 31.05.2014
Reference Date:	Posting Date
Terms of Payment:	ZB01
ToP Credit Memo:	ZB01
Settlement Currency:	EUR

	Deliv.Note	Material Doc.	Σ IR qty	BUn	Σ Old v	Σ New	Σ Diff.	Message text
		5000000040	10	PC	1.50	2.00	0.50	Invoice item can be generated
			▪ 10	PC	▪ 1.50	▪ 2.00	▪ 0.50	

4.19.7 Revaluation Run

Go back to the selection screen. Deselect Test Run ☐ and click . The system gives the following output:

Revaluation Log

Processing Mode:	Generate credit memos and invoices
Execution Time:	31.05.2014 / 13:35:00
User:	SAPUSER
Vendor:	0000001002, Müller KG, DE 83204 Rosenheim
PO Number/Item:	4500017097 / 00010
Material/Short Text:	60-100F / Light Bulb 220/235V 60 watt frosted
Plant:	1000, Werk Hamburg
Company Code:	1000, IDES AG
Purchasing Org.:	1000, IDES Deutschland
Past Period:	01.03.2014 - 31.05.2014
Reference Date:	Posting Date
Terms of Payment:	ZB01
ToP Credit Memo:	ZB01
Settlement Currency:	EUR

	Deliv.Note	Material Doc.	Σ IR qty	BUn	Σ Old v	Σ New	Σ Diff.	Message text
		5000000040	10	PC	1.50	2.00	0.50	Invoice posted: 5105608706/2014
			▪ 10	PC	▪ 1.50	▪ 2.00	▪ 0.50	

4.19.8 Invoice

Display the invoice using transaction MIR4. Enter the Invoice Document No. and the Fiscal Year . Click 🔍 Display Document . The system displays the invoice.

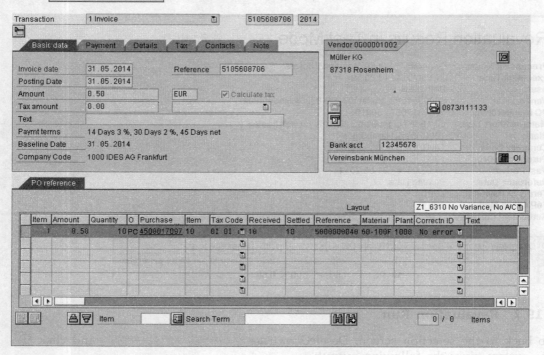

4.19.9 Accounting Entries

Click Follow-On Documents ... . The system displays the list of accounting documents. Double-click the Accounting document to see the accounting entries.

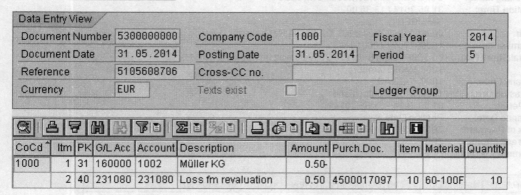

The system does not allocate the difference values determined during revaluation to the Stock accounts. Posting the revaluation does not change either the material stock value or the material valuation price (moving average price).

4.19.10 Credit Memo

Run transaction MR90 to see the messages generated. Select the invoice document and click 🖨 to see the message.

Müller KG
87318 Rosenheim

Credit memo

Page: 1 / 1

Document no. / Date	Currency
5105608706 / 31.05.2014	EUR
Your vendor number in our co.	Your tax ID number
1002	
Our customer no. in your co.	Our tax ID number
	DE123456789

Processed by

Your tax number

Mr. Agrawal

Telephone no.

Fax no.

E-mail address

The conditions have been retroactively changed for the purchase order or scheduling agreement items listed below. The deliveries and services settled in the specified period have been revaluated.
The difference amounts determined have been credited to your account in our company.

Period of review: 01.03.2014 - 31.05.2014
Purchasing doc. / Item: 4500017097 / 00010
Material number / EAN: 60-100F /
Material description: Light Bulb 220/235V 60 watt frosted

Item	Deliv. qty Un Old amount	DN/GR New amount	DN/GR date TaxC	Price date Difference/EUR
000001	10 PC 1,50	5000000040 2,00	14.05.2014 0I	14.05.2014 0,50
Totals:	10 PC			0,50

Total net value		0,50
Input tax 0% (0I)	0,50	0,00
Total		0,50

Terms of payment: Related to 31.05.2014:
Within 14 days 3 % cash discount
Within 30 days 2 % cash discount
Within 45 days Due net

Print this message and send it to the vendor.

4.20   PREPAYMENT BEFORE GOODS RECEIPT, GR BASED IV

Functional Consultant	User	Business Process Owner	Senior Management	My Rating	Understanding Level
A	A	B	C		

4.20.1   Prepayment

Usually the vendor is credited when an invoice is posted. However, sometimes the vendor needs to be paid in advance. This is called prepayment. You can do prepayment in the following ways:

➤ Prepayment before goods receipt
➤ Prepayment after goods receipt
➤ Prepayment on request

4.20.2   Scenario

This section deals with the following scenario:

➤ Prepayment before goods receipt
➤ The purchase order item has ☑ GR-Bsd IV.

4.20.3   Prerequisites

In order to use the prepayment functionality, it must be enabled at company code level as well as at vendor level as explained in sections 4.20.5 and 4.20.6.

4.20.4   Prepayment Process

Prepayment is done by entering the invoice and holding, parking, or saving it as completed. It has the following steps which are performed in the specified sequence:

1. Invoice prepayment
2. Goods receipt
3. Invoice posting

4.20.5   Enabling Prepayment at Company Code Level

Purpose

Here you specify whether prepayment is allowed for a company code or not.

IMG Node

SM30 ≻ V_WRF_PREPAYMENT

Screen

Company Code   `1000`

Prepayment Control at Company Code Level	
Doc. Type Prepayment	`RE`
Reversal Reason	
Field Stat.Grp Prep.	
☐ Distributed Systems	
Prepayment for	`A Held, Saved, and Fully Saved Documents` ▦
☐ Distribute ProfitCtr	

Primary Key

Company Code

Important Fields

Company code

You can activate prepayment at company code level.

Document type for prepayment

When an invoice is prepaid, an invoice document and an accounting document are created. Here you specify the document type of the accounting document.

Reversal reason

If the prepayment document is reversed—for instance, because a prepaid invoice is deleted—a reason for reversal has to be specified for the reversal in Financial Accounting. The reasons for reversal are defined in view T041C in G/L accounting.

Reason	Text
01	Reversal in current period
02	Reversal in closed period
03	Actual reversal in current period
04	Actual reversal in closed period
05	Accrual
06	Asset transaction reversal
07	Incorrect document date
RE	Reversal, incorrect original date

Field status group for prepayment

In prepayment scenario, first the invoice is entered at which time prepayment takes place, and then the invoice is posted. When you work on an invoice that has been entered and prepaid, before posting you may want to modify it. The system allows you to modify certain fields by default. If you want to allow modification of some other field, or prevent modification of a field that is allowed, you can specify a field status group here and define that field status group in view V_WRF_PREPAY_FCH.

Distributed systems

This indicator must be set, if you are using distributed systems.

Prepayment for

Here you specify the type of invoices that can be prepaid.

```
A  Held, Saved, and Fully Saved Documents
B  Saved and Fully Saved Documents
C  Only Fully Saved Documents
   No Prepayment of Parked Documents
```

Distribute prepayment clearing lines to profit centre

If this indicator is not set, the prepayment clearing item in the prepayment document is posted with a dummy profit centre. If the indicator is set, the system determines the profit centre from the purchase order items assigned to the invoice and the prepayment clearing amount, weighted by purchase order item amount, is posted in a distributed manner to this profit centre.

BAdI for Prepayment

SAP provides BAdI WRF_PREPAY_INVOICE to control the posting date of the prepayment document and the Prepayment Relevance field from the header of the current logistics invoice.

4.20.6 Enabling Prepayment at Vendor Level

Purpose

Even if your company uses the prepayment functionality, it may not do so for all vendors. You can enable prepayment for a vendor at company code level.

Transaction

FK01—Create Vendor (Accounting)
FK02—Change Vendor (Accounting)
XK01—Create Vendor (Centrally)
XK02—Change Vendor (Centrally)

Screen

Vendor	1002	Müller KG		Rosenheim
Company Code	1000	IDES AG		

Invoice verification	
Tolerance group	515
Prepayment	A

Important Fields

Prepayment

You can choose from the following options:

Prepayment Relevant	Short text
	Prepayment Not Allowed
A	Prepayment Requested
B	Prepayment Not Requested Before GR Effected (see Docu)
C	Prepayment Possible, but Not Planned

Prepayment relevant	Explanation
Blank	Prepayment not allowed
A	Prepayment in all cases
B	Prepayment in all cases where goods are received
C	Prepayment decided at the time of invoice entry

4.20.7 Purchase Order

Goods receipt based invoice verification

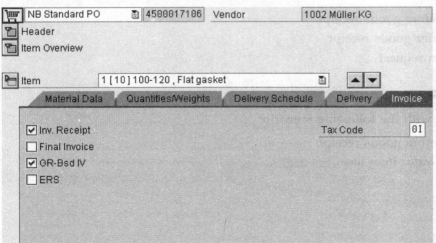

4.20.8 Prepaying the Invoice

After enabling prepayment both at company code level and at vendor level, use transaction MIR7 to enter and park an invoice. The system gives the following error:

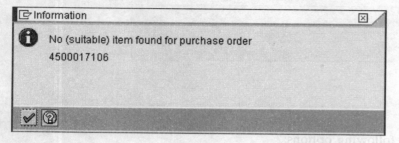

4.20.9 Conclusion

You cannot prepay an invoice before goods receipt, if the purchase order item has ☑ GR-Bsd IV.

4.21 PREPAYMENT BEFORE GOODS RECEIPT, PO BASED IV

Functional Consultant	User	Business Process Owner	Senior Management	My Rating	Understanding Level
A	A	A	B		

4.21.1 Prepayment

Usually the vendor is credited when an invoice is posted. However, sometimes the vendor needs to be paid in advance. This is called prepayment. You can do prepayment in the following ways:

➤ Prepayment before goods receipt
➤ Prepayment after goods receipt
➤ Prepayment on request

4.21.2 Scenario

This section deals with the following scenario:

➤ Prepayment before goods receipt
➤ The purchase order item has ☐ GR-Bsd IV.

4.21.3 Prerequisites

In order to use the prepayment functionality, it must be enabled at company code level as well as at vendor level as explained in sections 4.20.5 and 4.20.6.

4.21.4 Prepayment Process

Prepayment is done by entering the invoice and holding, parking, or saving it as completed. It has the following steps which are performed in the specified sequence:

1. Invoice prepayment
2. Goods receipt
3. Invoice posting

4.21.5 Purchase Order

Purchase order based invoice verification

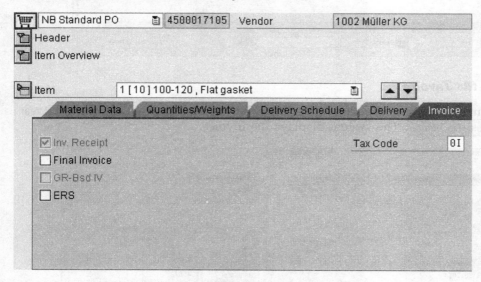

Note that the purchase order item has ☐ GR-Bsd IV.

4.21.6 Prepaying the Invoice

Parking the Invoice

After enabling prepayment both at company code level and at vendor level, use transaction MIR7 to enter and park an invoice.

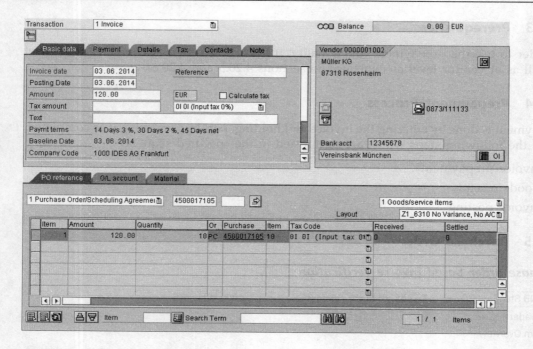

Displaying the Invoice

Display the invoice using transaction MIR4. Enter the Invoice Document No. and the Fiscal Year. Click 👓 Display Document. The system displays the invoice.

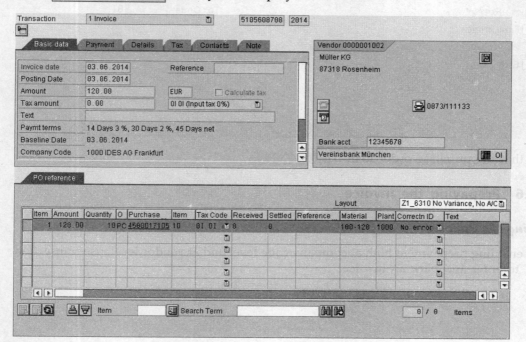

Accounting Entries

Click Follow-On Documents ... . The system displays the list of accounting documents. Double-click the Accounting document to see the accounting entries.

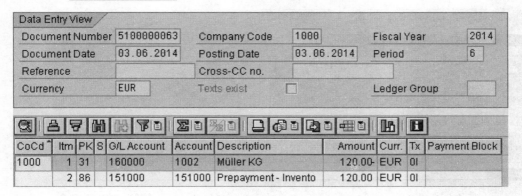

Note that the vendor is credited and the prepayment account is debited.

4.21.7 Posting Goods Receipt

Enter and post goods receipt using transaction MIGO. Display the material document using transaction MB02. Click Accounting Documents... . The system displays the list of accounting documents. Double-click the Accounting document to see the accounting entries.

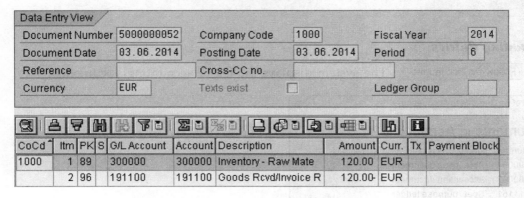

4.21.8 Posting the Invoice

Posting the Invoice

In transaction MIRO, click Show worklist . Double-click the prepaid invoice. Post it.

Displaying the Invoice

Display the invoice using transaction MIR4. Enter the Invoice Document No. and the Fiscal Year. Click ⚙ Display Document . The system displays the invoice.

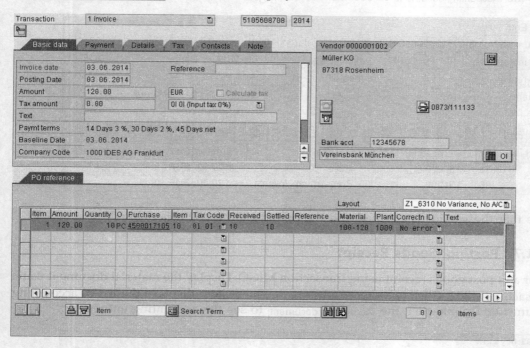

Accounting Entries

Click   Follow-On Documents ... . The system displays the list of accounting documents.

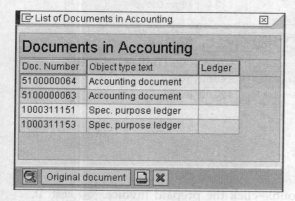

Note that there are two accounting documents. Document number 5100000063 was created when the invoice was prepaid. Document number 5100000064 is created at the time of posting the invoice. Double-click document number 5100000064 to see the accounting entries.

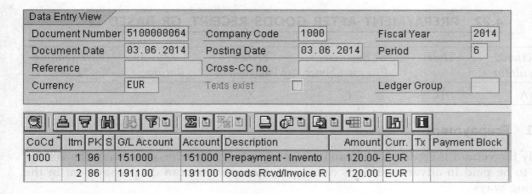

4.21.9 All Accounting Entries

Prepayment of the invoice

CoCd	Itm	PK	S	G/L Account	Account	Description	Amount	Curr.	Tx	Payment Block
1000	1	31		160000	1002	Müller KG	120.00-	EUR	0I	
	2	86		151000	151000	Prepayment - Invento	120.00	EUR	0I	

Goods receipt

CoCd	Itm	PK	S	G/L Account	Account	Description	Amount	Curr.	Tx	Payment Block
1000	1	89		300000	300000	Inventory - Raw Mate	120.00	EUR		
	2	96		191100	191100	Goods Rcvd/Invoice R	120.00-	EUR		

Posting of the invoice

CoCd	Itm	PK	S	G/L Account	Account	Description	Amount	Curr.	Tx	Payment Block
1000	1	96		151000	151000	Prepayment - Invento	120.00-	EUR		
	2	86		191100	191100	Goods Rcvd/Invoice R	120.00	EUR		

Net result

After all these transactions, the vendor is credited, and the stock account is debited. The GR/IR account and the prepayment account have no balance on account of these transactions.

Account	Net result
1002 Müller KG	Credited
300000 Inventory - Raw Mate	Debited
151000 Prepayment - Invento	No balance
191100 Goods Rcvd/Invoice R	No balance

4.22 PREPAYMENT AFTER GOODS RECEIPT, GR BASED IV

Functional Consultant	User	Business Process Owner	Senior Management	My Rating	Understanding Level
A	B	C	X		

4.22.1 Prepayment

Usually the vendor is credited when an invoice is posted. However, sometimes the vendor needs to be paid in advance. This is called prepayment. You can do prepayment in the following ways

➢ Prepayment before goods receipt

➢ Prepayment after goods receipt

➢ Prepayment on request

4.22.2 Scenario

This section deals with the following scenario:

➢ Prepayment after goods receipt

➢ The purchase order item has ☑ GR-Bsd IV.

4.22.3 Prerequisites

In order to use the prepayment functionality, it must be enabled at company code level as well as at vendor level as explained in sections 4.20.5 and 4.20.6.

4.22.4 Prepayment Process

Prepayment is done by entering the invoice and holding, parking, or saving it as completed. It has the following steps which are performed in the specified sequence:

1. Goods receipt
2. Invoice prepayment
3. Invoice posting

4.22.5 Purchase Order

Goods receipt based invoice verification

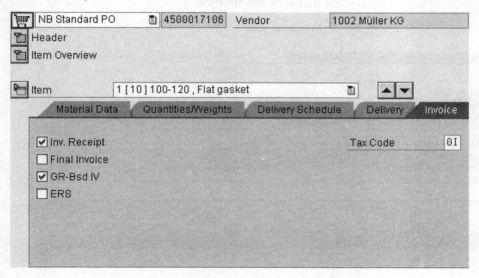

4.22.6 Posting Goods Receipt

Enter and post goods receipt using transaction MIGO. Display the material document using transaction MB02. Click Accounting Documents... . The system displays the list of accounting documents. Double-click the Accounting document to see the accounting entries.

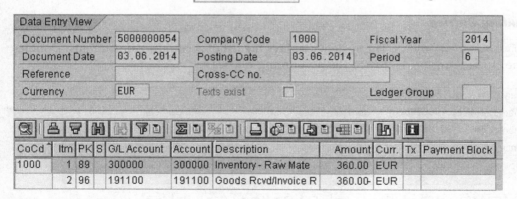

4.22.7 Prepaying the Invoice

Parking the Invoice

After enabling prepayment both at company code level and at vendor level, use transaction MIR7 to enter and park an invoice.

Displaying the Invoice

Display the invoice using transaction MIR4. Enter the Invoice Document No. and the Fiscal Year. Click 👓 Display Document . The system displays the invoice.

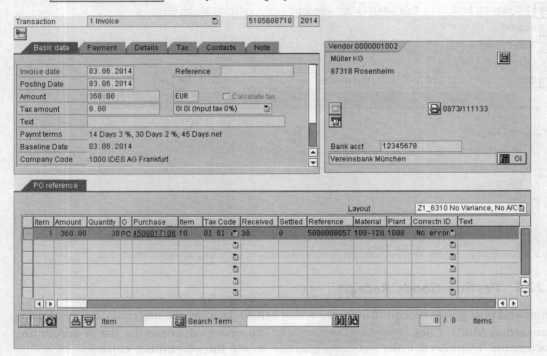

Accounting Entries

Click Follow-On Documents ... . The system displays the list of accounting documents. Double-click the Accounting document to see the accounting entries.

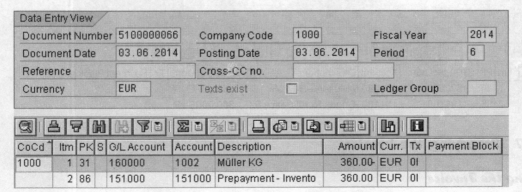

Note that the vendor is credited and the prepayment account is debited.

4.22.8 Posting the Invoice

Posting the Invoice

In transaction MIRO, click | Show worklist |. Double-click the prepaid invoice. | 🖫 Post | it.

Displaying the Invoice

Display the invoice using transaction MIR4. Enter the Invoice Document No. and the Fiscal Year. Click | 👓 Display Document |. The system displays the invoice.

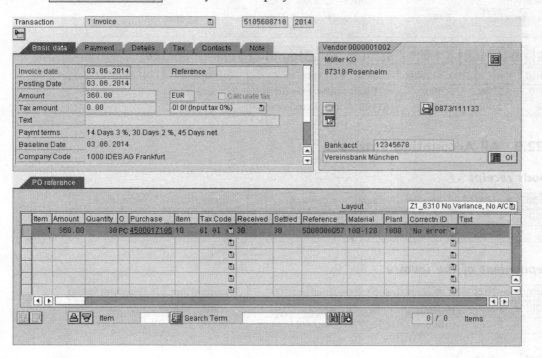

Accounting Entries

Click | Follow-On Documents ... |. The system displays the list of accounting documents.

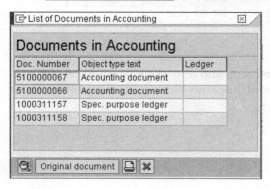

Doc. Number	Object type text	Ledger
5100000067	Accounting document	
5100000066	Accounting document	
1000311157	Spec. purpose ledger	
1000311158	Spec. purpose ledger	

Note that there are two accounting documents. Document number 5100000066 was created when the invoice was prepaid. Document number 5100000067 is created at the time of posting the invoice. Double-click document number 5100000067 to see the accounting entries.

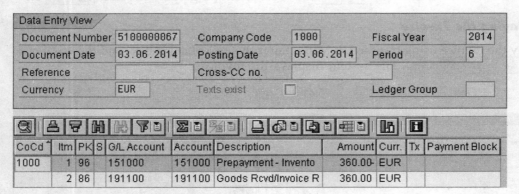

CoCd	Itm	PK	S	G/L Account	Account	Description	Amount	Curr.	Tx	Payment Block
1000	1	96		151000	151000	Prepayment - Invento	360.00-	EUR		
	2	86		191100	191100	Goods Rcvd/Invoice R	360.00	EUR		

4.22.9   All Accounting Entries

Goods receipt

CoCd	Itm	PK	S	G/L Account	Account	Description	Amount	Curr.	Tx	Payment Block
1000	1	89		300000	300000	Inventory - Raw Mate	360.00	EUR		
	2	96		191100	191100	Goods Rcvd/Invoice R	360.00-	EUR		

Prepayment of the invoice

CoCd	Itm	PK	S	G/L Account	Account	Description	Amount	Curr.	Tx	Payment Block
1000	1	31		160000	1002	Müller KG	360.00-	EUR	OI	
	2	86		151000	151000	Prepayment - Invento	360.00	EUR	OI	

Posting of the invoice

CoCd	Itm	PK	S	G/L Account	Account	Description	Amount	Curr.	Tx	Payment Block
1000	1	96		151000	151000	Prepayment - Invento	360.00-	EUR		
	2	86		191100	191100	Goods Rcvd/Invoice R	360.00	EUR		

Net result

After all these transactions, the vendor is credited, and the stock account is debited. The GR/IR account and the prepayment account have no balance on account of these transactions.

Account	Net result
1002 Müller KG	Credited
300000 Inventory - Raw Mate	Debited
151000 Prepayment - Invento	No balance
191100 Goods Rcvd/Invoice R	No balance

4.23 PREPAYMENT AFTER GOODS RECEIPT, PO BASED IV

Functional Consultant	User	Business Process Owner	Senior Management	My Rating	Understanding Level
A	B	C	X		

4.23.1 Prepayment

Usually the vendor is credited when an invoice is posted. However, sometimes the vendor needs to be paid in advance. This is called prepayment. You can do prepayment in the following ways:

➤ Prepayment before goods receipt
➤ Prepayment after goods receipt
➤ Prepayment on request

4.23.2 Scenario

This section deals with the following scenario:

➤ Prepayment after goods receipt
➤ The purchase order item has ☐ GR-Bsd IV.

4.23.3 Prerequisites

In order to use the prepayment functionality, it must be enabled at company code level as well as at vendor level as explained in sections 4.20.5 and 4.20.6.

4.23.4 Prepayment Process

Prepayment is done by entering the invoice and holding, parking, or saving it as completed. It has the following steps which are performed in the specified sequence:

1. Goods receipt
2. Invoice prepayment
3. Invoice posting

4.23.5 Purchase Order

Purchase order based invoice verification

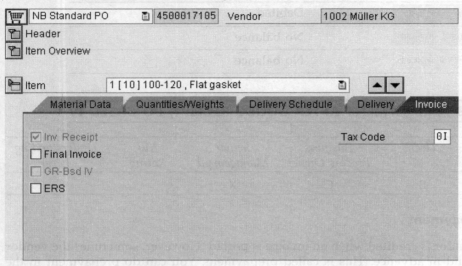

Note that the purchase order item has ☐ GR-Bsd IV.

4.23.6 Posting Goods Receipt

Enter and post goods receipt using transaction MIGO. Display the material document using transaction MB02. Click Accounting Documents... . The system displays the list of accounting documents. Double-click the Accounting document to see the accounting entries.

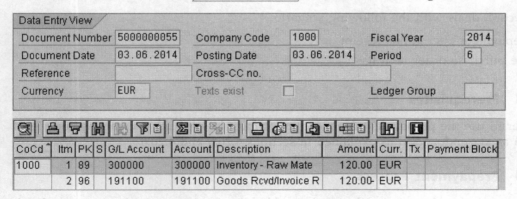

4.23.7 Prepaying the Invoice

Parking the Invoice

After enabling prepayment both at company code level and at vendor level, use transaction MIR7 to enter and park an invoice.

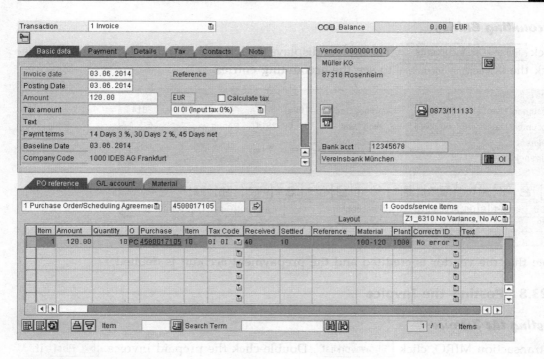

Displaying the Invoice

Display the invoice using transaction MIR4. Enter the Invoice Document No. and the Fiscal Year. Click 👓 Display Document . The system displays the invoice.

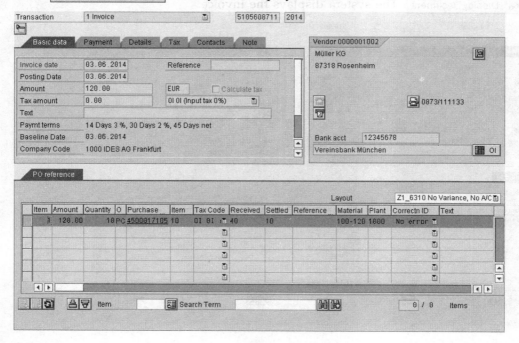

Accounting Entries

Click ⟦ Follow-On Documents ... ⟧. The system displays the list of accounting documents. Double-click the ⟦ Accounting document ⟧ to see the accounting entries.

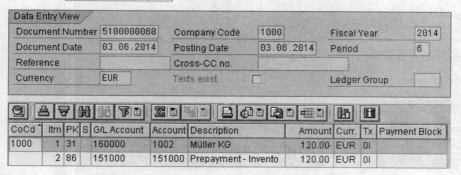

Note that the vendor is credited and the prepayment account is debited.

4.23.8   Posting the Invoice

Posting the Invoice

In transaction MIRO, click ⟦ Show worklist ⟧. Double-click the prepaid invoice. ⟦ 💾 Post ⟧ it.

Displaying the Invoice

Display the invoice using transaction MIR4. Enter the ⟦Invoice Document No.⟧ and the ⟦Fiscal Year⟧. Click ⟦ 👓 Display Document ⟧. The system displays the invoice.

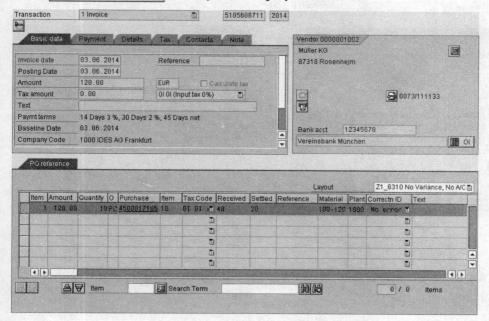

Accounting Entries

Click | Follow-On Documents ... |. The system displays the list of accounting documents.

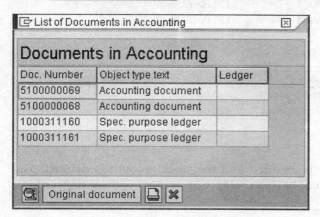

Note that there are two accounting documents. Document number 5100000068 was created when the invoice was prepaid. Document number 5100000069 is created at the time of posting the invoice. Double-click document number 5100000069 to see the accounting entries.

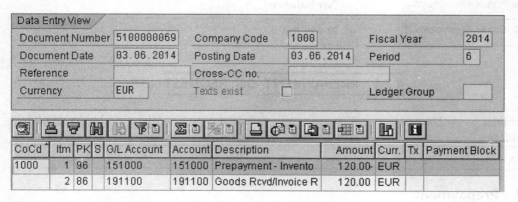

CoCd	Itm	PK	S	G/L Account	Account	Description	Amount	Curr.	Tx	Payment Block
1000	1	96		151000	151000	Prepayment - Invento	120.00-	EUR		
	2	86		191100	191100	Goods Rcvd/Invoice R	120.00	EUR		

4.23.9 All Accounting Entries

Goods receipt

CoCd	Itm	PK	S	G/L Account	Account	Description	Amount	Curr.	Tx	Payment Block
1000	1	89		300000	300000	Inventory - Raw Mate	120.00	EUR		
	2	96		191100	191100	Goods Rcvd/Invoice R	120.00-	EUR		

Prepayment of the invoice

CoCd	Itm	PK	S	G/L Account	Account	Description	Amount	Curr.	Tx	Payment Block
1000	1	31		160000	1002	Müller KG	120.00-	EUR	0I	
	2	86		151000	151000	Prepayment - Invento	120.00	EUR	0I	

Posting of the invoice

CoCd	Itm	PK	S	G/L Account	Account	Description	Amount	Curr.	Tx	Payment Block
1000	1	96		151000	151000	Prepayment - Invento	120.00-	EUR		
	2	86		191100	191100	Goods Rcvd/Invoice R	120.00	EUR		

Net result

After all these transactions, the vendor is credited and the stock account is debited. The GR/IR account and the prepayment account have no balance on account of these transactions.

Account		Net result
1002	Müller KG	Credited
300000	Inventory - Raw Mate	Debited
151000	Prepayment - Invento	No balance
191100	Goods Rcvd/Invoice R	No balance

4.24 PREPAYMENT ON REQUEST

Functional Consultant	User	Business Process Owner	Senior Management	My Rating	Understanding Level
A	A	A	B		

4.24.1 Prepayment

Usually the vendor is credited when an invoice is posted. However, sometimes the vendor needs to be paid in advance. This is called prepayment. You can do prepayment in the following ways:

➤ Prepayment before goods receipt
➤ Prepayment after goods receipt
➤ Prepayment on request

4.24.2 Scenario

Prepayment on request has four scenarios:

➤ Prepayment before or after goods receipt

➤ The purchase order item has ☑ GR-Bsd IV or ☐ GR-Bsd IV.

The key difference is that instead of the prepayment happening automatically when you park the invoice, you specify whether you want prepayment or not for each invoice. This section illustrates this process using the following scenario:

➤ Prepayment before goods receipt

➤ The purchase order item has ☐ GR-Bsd IV.

4.24.3 Prerequisites

In order to use the prepayment functionality, it must be enabled at company code level as well as at vendor level as explained in sections 4.20.5 and 4.20.6. Also, in the vendor master, you specify Prepayment ☐ C, Prepayment Possible, but Not Planned .

4.24.4 Prepayment Process

Prepayment is done by entering the invoice and holding, parking, or saving it as completed. It has the following steps which are performed in the specified sequence:

1. Invoice prepayment
2. Goods receipt
3. Invoice posting

4.24.5 Prepaying the Invoice

Parking the Invoice

After enabling prepayment both at company code level and at vendor level, use transaction MIR7 to enter an invoice.

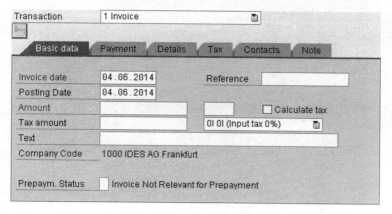

Prepayment status

Note the Prepaym. Status field. Here you specify whether you want the prepayment to take place or not. If you do not want to do prepayment, leave this field blank. To do prepayment, choose A.

Prepayment Status	Short text
	Invoice Not Relevant for Prepayment
A	Relevant, Invoice Not Saved Yet
B	Relevant; No Prepayment Document due to Error
C	Relevant; Prepayment Document under Conditions
D	Prepayment Document Was Posted

Parking the invoice

After entering the remaining data of the invoice, park it.

Displaying the Invoice

Display the invoice using transaction MIR4. Enter the Invoice Document No. and the Fiscal Year. Click Display Document. The system displays the invoice.

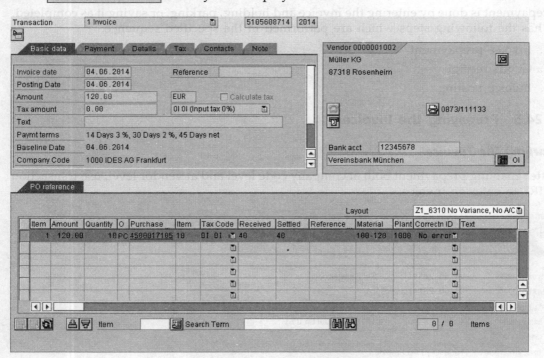

Accounting Entries

Click Follow-On Documents ... . The system displays the list of accounting documents. Double-click the Accounting document to see the accounting entries.

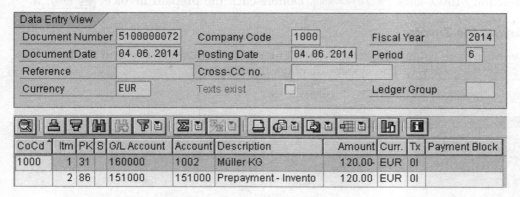

Note that the vendor is credited and prepayment account is debited. The GR/IR account remains unaffected.

4.24.6 Posting Goods Receipt

Enter and post goods receipt using transaction MIGO. Display the material document using transaction MB02. Click Accounting Documents... . The system displays the list of accounting documents. Double-click the Accounting document to see the accounting entries.

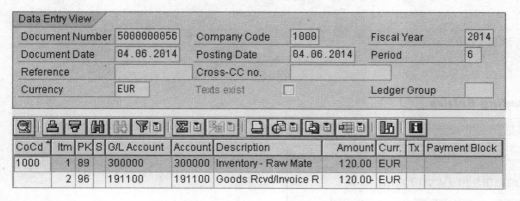

4.24.7   Posting the Invoice

Posting the Invoice

In transaction MIRO, click `Show worklist`. Double-click the prepaid invoice. `Post` it.

Displaying the Invoice

Display the invoice using transaction MIR4. Enter the Invoice Document No. and the Fiscal Year. Click `Display Document`. The system displays the invoice.

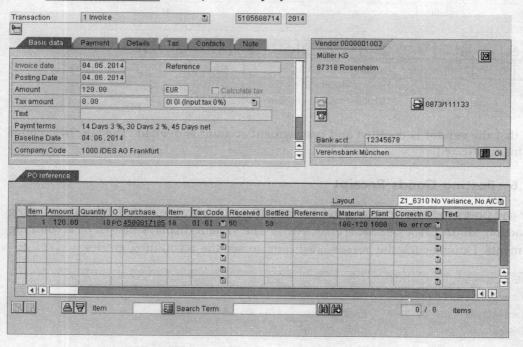

Accounting Entries

Click `Follow-On Documents ...`. The system displays the list of accounting documents.

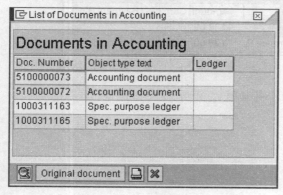

Note that there are two accounting documents. Document number 5100000072 was created when the invoice was prepaid. Document number 5100000073 is created at the time of posting the invoice. Double-click document number 5100000073 to see the accounting entries.

Data Entry View						
Document Number	5100000073	Company Code	1000	Fiscal Year		2014
Document Date	04.06.2014	Posting Date	04.06.2014	Period		6
Reference		Cross-CC no.				
Currency	EUR	Texts exist	☐	Ledger Group		

CoCd	Itm	PK	S	G/L Account	Account	Description	Amount	Curr.	Tx	Payment Block
1000	1	96		151000	151000	Prepayment - Invento	120.00-	EUR		
	2	86		191100	191100	Goods Rcvd/Invoice R	120.00	EUR		

4.24.8 All Accounting Entries

Prepayment of the invoice

CoCd	Itm	PK	S	G/L Account	Account	Description	Amount	Curr.	Tx	Payment Block
1000	1	31		160000	1002	Müller KG	120.00-	EUR	0I	
	2	86		151000	151000	Prepayment - Invento	120.00	EUR	0I	

Goods receipt

CoCd	Itm	PK	S	G/L Account	Account	Description	Amount	Curr.	Tx	Payment Block
1000	1	89		300000	300000	Inventory - Raw Mate	120.00	EUR		
	2	96		191100	191100	Goods Rcvd/Invoice R	120.00-	EUR		

Posting of the invoice

CoCd	Itm	PK	S	G/L Account	Account	Description	Amount	Curr.	Tx	Payment Block
1000	1	96		151000	151000	Prepayment - Invento	120.00-	EUR		
	2	86		191100	191100	Goods Rcvd/Invoice R	120.00	EUR		

Net result

After all these transactions, the vendor is credited and the stock account is debited. The GR/IR account and the prepayment account have no balance on account of these transactions.

Account		Net result
1002	Müller KG	Credited
300000	Inventory - Raw Mate	Debited
151000	Prepayment - Invento	No balance
191100	Goods Rcvd/Invoice R	No balance

4.25 INVOICE TEXTS

Functional Consultant	User	Business Process Owner	Senior Management	My Rating	Understanding Level
A	A	B	C		

4.25.1 Scenario

You enter texts in the invoice document at header and item level. These are not only stored in the invoice for further reference, but also transferred to the accounting document.

4.25.2 Basic Data

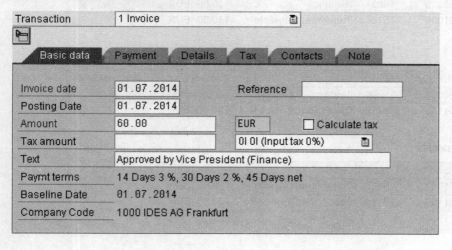

4.25.3 Note

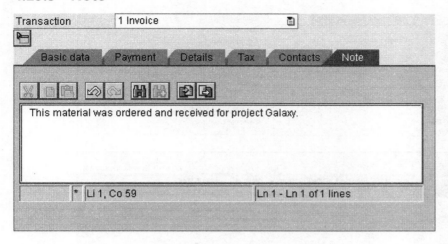

4.25.4 Items

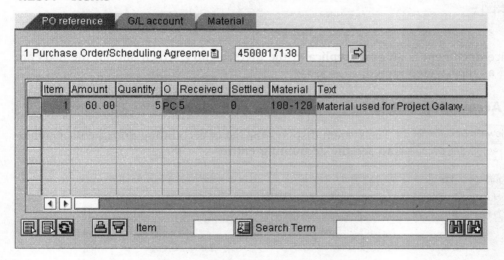

4.25.5 Invoice Display

Display the invoice using transaction MIR4. Enter the Invoice Document No. and the Fiscal Year. Click &° Display Document . The system displays the invoice.

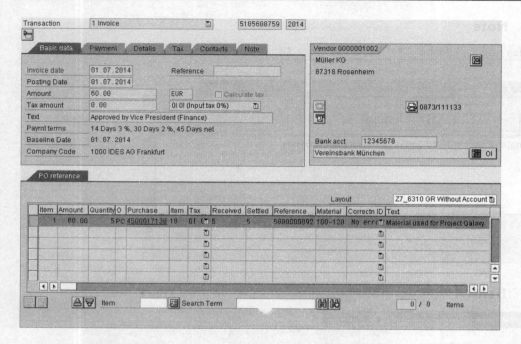

The invoice document is an exact replica of the invoice entry screen and all the texts are displayed as they were entered.

4.25.6   Accounting Entries

Click Follow-On Documents ... . The system displays the list of accounting documents. Double-click the Accounting document to see the accounting entries.

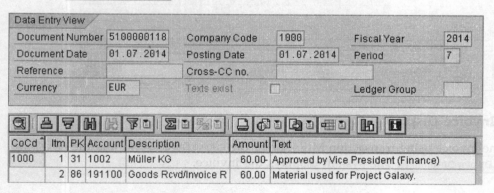

4.25.7   Texts Transferred in the Accounting Document

Note that the text in the Basic data tab is transferred to the accounting document line crediting the vendor, and the text entered in the item is transferred to the accounting document line debiting the GR/IR account.

CHAPTER 5

Invoices having System Price more than Vendor Price

5.1 NEGATIVE DIFFERENCE AND TOLERANCE

Functional Consultant	User	Business Process Owner	Senior Management	My Rating	Understanding Level
A	A	A	A		

5.1.1 Differences

Difference

The system determines the difference between the net invoice amount (= gross invoice amount less taxes and unplanned delivery costs) and the net total of the items.

Negative difference

If the vendor's invoice amount is smaller than your amount, then the difference is negative.

Automatic acceptance of negative difference

If you do not change the amount in items, there is a non-zero Balance. You may still be able to post the invoice. This is called automatic acceptance of negative difference.

Manual acceptance of negative difference

If you change the amount in items, you are manually accepting the negative difference.

Non-acceptance of negative difference

Even though the vendor's claim is for a smaller amount, it is not prudent to accept invoices with large differences; the vendor may have made a mistake, or you may not have selected the right set of goods receipts. Instead of resolving the problem later, it is better to reconcile the difference before settling the invoice.

Small difference

Sometimes the difference may be so small that it is not worth investigating. Therefore, many companies have a policy of accepting the amount in the vendor's invoice and posting the difference to a small difference account.

Small difference tolerance

You can specify the amount below which you would consider a difference to be small. You can also group your vendors and specify small difference tolerance for each group.

Small difference account

If the difference is within the tolerance range, the system automatically generates a difference line on a G/L account for small differences when posting the invoice. If the system creates a small difference, it posts this difference to the account specified in account determination for transaction DIF.

Treatment of negative differences

The system pays the invoice amount unless you decide not to pay and park the invoice.

5.1.2 Small Difference Tolerance at Company Code Level

Purpose

You can specify the amount below which you would consider a difference to be small. This is specified here. You can also group your vendors and specify small difference tolerance for each group as explained in section 5.1.3. If no tolerance group is assigned to a vendor or if no tolerances have been specified for the assigned tolerance group, the system takes the tolerances from here. This tolerance is for both negative and positive small differences.

IMG Node

SM30 ➣ V_169G, Tolerance key BD

Screen

Tolerance key	BD	Form small differences automatically
Company Code	1000	IDES AG
Amounts in	EUR	Euro (EMU currency as of 01/01/1999)

Upper limit

   Absolute

     ○ Do not check

     ◉ Check limit

      Val.   2.50

5.1.3 Negative Difference Tolerance at Vendor Group Level

Purpose

Apart from small differences, SAP lets you specify negative differences that can be accepted.

JMG Node

SM30 ➤ V_169L

Screen

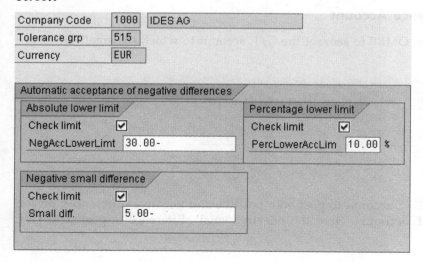

Company Code	1000	IDES AG
Tolerance grp	515	
Currency	EUR	

Automatic acceptance of negative differences

   Absolute lower limit

    Check limit ☑

    NegAccLowerLimt   30.00-

   Percentage lower limit

    Check limit ☑

    PercLowerAccLim   10.00 %

   Negative small difference

    Check limit ☑

    Small diff.   5.00-

Tolerance Group

You can specify different tolerances for different vendors. For this purpose you group the vendors in tolerance groups. In transaction XK02, in `Company code data`, select ☑`Payment transactions` and specify the tolerance group of the vendor.

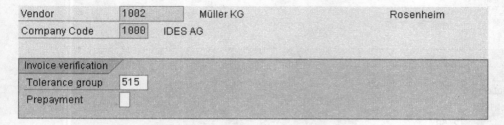

Negative Small Difference

If you want the limit of negative small difference to be different for different groups of vendors, you can specify it here. If no tolerance group is assigned to a vendor or if no tolerances have been specified for the assigned tolerance group, the system takes the tolerances from view V_169G, tolerance key BD.

Automatic Acceptance of Negative Differences

If the difference is more than the limit of the negative small difference, you can still accept an invoice, if it satisfies the criteria defined here. You can specify an absolute value and a percentage value. You can specify one or both limits. If both limits are specified, both limits are applied. If an invoice satisfies the negative difference criteria, it is accepted.

5.1.4   Small Difference Account

You can use transaction OMR0 to see/set the G/L account to which the small difference will be posted.

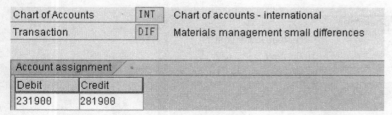

You may use a single G/L account to post both positive and negative differences, or you may use different G/L accounts. Here the negative small difference is posted to G/L account 281900.

5.2　AUTOMATIC ACCEPTANCE OF NEGATIVE SMALL DIFFERENCE

Functional Consultant	User	Business Process Owner	Senior Management	My Rating	Understanding Level
A	A	A	A		

5.2.1　Scenario

You receive an invoice with small negative difference.

5.2.2　Invoice

Enter the invoice using transaction MIRO.

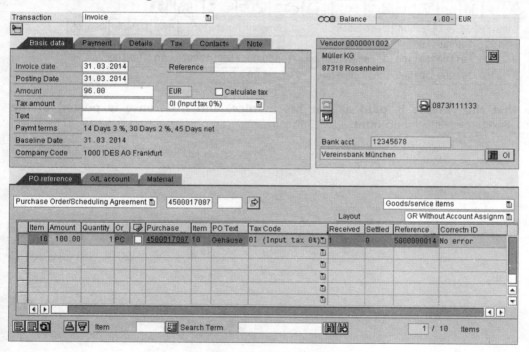

Note that the traffic light ⬤⬤⬤ Balance [　　4.00-] EUR is green despite there being a negative difference of 4 Euros. Post the invoice.

5.2.3 Accounting Entries

Display the invoice using transaction MIR4. Enter the Invoice Document No. and the Fiscal Year. Click &ø Display Document. The system displays the invoice. Click Follow-On Documents ... . The system displays the list of accounting documents. Double-click the Accounting document to see the accounting entries.

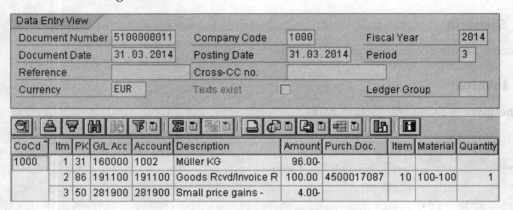

Note that the vendor is paid as per his invoice, and difference is posted to the 281900 Small price gains - account.

5.3 AUTOMATIC ACCEPTANCE OF NEGATIVE DIFFERENCE

Functional Consultant	User	Business Process Owner	Senior Management	My Rating	Understanding Level
A	A	A	A		

5.3.1 Scenario

You can accept an invoice where the difference is larger than the limit of the small negative difference, but which satisfies the criteria for automatic acceptance of negative differences.

5.3.2 Tolerance for Automatic Acceptance of Negative Difference

Purpose

Apart from small differences, SAP lets you specify negative differences that can be accepted. If the difference is more than the limit of the negative small difference, you can still accept an invoice, if it satisfies the criteria defined in view V_169L. You can specify an absolute value and a percentage value. You can specify one or both limits. If both limits are specified, both limits are applied. If an invoice satisfies the negative difference criteria, it is accepted.

Screen

Company Code	1000	IDES AG
Tolerance grp	515	
Currency	EUR	

Automatic acceptance of negative differences

Absolute lower limit		Percentage lower limit	
Check limit	☑	Check limit	☑
NegAccLowerLimt	30.00-	PercLowerAccLim	10.00 %

Tolerance Group

You can specify different tolerances for different vendors. For this purpose, you group the vendors in tolerance groups. In transaction XK02, in Company code data, select ☑ Payment transactions and specify the tolerance group of the vendor.

Vendor	1002	Müller KG	Rosenheim
Company Code	1000	IDES AG	

Invoice verification

Tolerance group	515

5.3.3 Invoice

Enter the invoice using transaction MIRO.

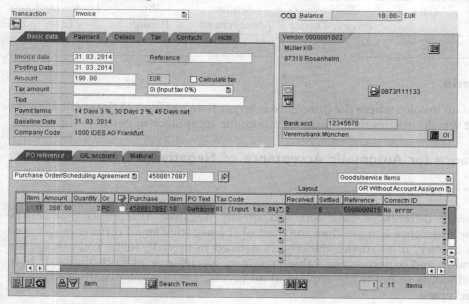

Post the invoice.

5.3.4 Accounting Entries

Display the invoice using transaction MIR4. Enter the Invoice Document No. and the Fiscal Year . Click Display Document . The system displays the invoice. Click Follow-On Documents ... . The system displays the list of accounting documents. Double-click the Accounting document to see the accounting entries.

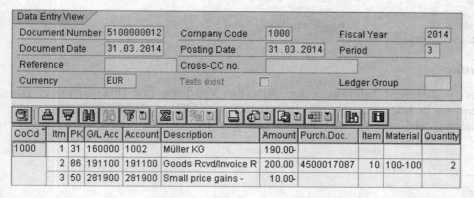

Note that the vendor is paid as per his invoice, and difference is posted to the 281900 Small price gains - account. Thus, both the negative small difference and automatic acceptance of negative difference are credited to the same G/L account.

5.4 MANUAL ACCEPTANCE OF NEGATIVE DIFFERENCE

Functional Consultant	User	Business Process Owner	Senior Management	My Rating	Understanding Level
A	A	A	A		

5.4.1 Scenario

You receive an invoice where the price is lower than the purchase order price. If the negative difference is more than the criteria specified in Automatic acceptance of negative differences (see section 5.1.3), you cannot post the invoice unless you manually accept the lower price given in the invoice.

5.4.2 Basic Data

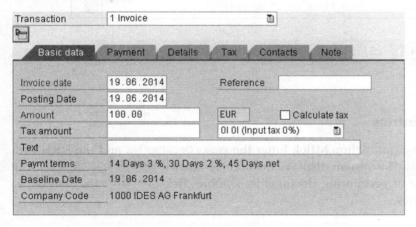

5.4.3 Items

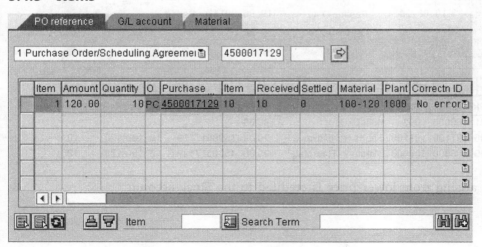

Amount

If you think that the vendor's invoice for 100 Euros is correct, change the `Amount` field.

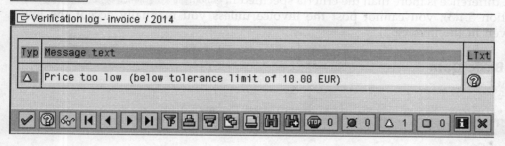

Item	Amount	Quantity	O	Purchase	Item	Received	Settled	Material	Plant	Correctn ID
1	100.00	10	PC	4500017129	10	10	0	100-120	1000	No error

Messages

The system allows the change, but gives you a warning that you can see by clicking
△ Messages .

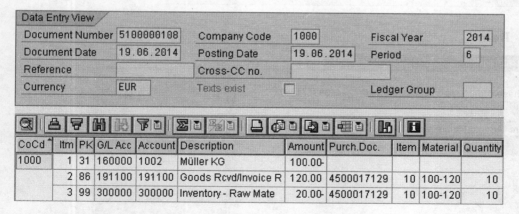

Post the invoice.

5.4.4 Accounting Entries

Display the invoice using transaction MIR4. Enter the `Invoice Document No.` and the `Fiscal Year` .
Click `Display Document` . The system displays the invoice. Click `Follow-On Documents ...` . The
system displays the list of accounting documents. Double-click the `Accounting document` to
see the accounting entries.

CoCd	Itm	PK	G/L Acc	Account	Description	Amount	Purch.Doc.	Item	Material	Quantity
1000	1	31	160000	1002	Müller KG	100.00-				
	2	86	191100	191100	Goods Rcvd/Invoice R	120.00	4500017129	10	100-120	10
	3	99	300000	300000	Inventory - Raw Mate	20.00-	4500017129	10	100-120	10

The benefit arising from lower price is credited to the Stock account.

5.4.5 Inventory Value

Inventory value before invoice posting

You can see the stock and the value of a material in the `Accounting 1` view of the material master using transaction MM02. The following image is a part of that view before the invoice was posted.

Total Stock	2,512	Total Value	35,140.16

Inventory value after invoice posting

The following image is a part of the `Accounting 1` view after the invoice was posted:

Total Stock	2,512	Total Value	35,120.16

Note that the total value of the material has gone down by 20.00 Euros on account of the lower price posted by the invoice.

5.4.6 Standard Price

If the price control of the material is Standard price, the stock account is charged at the standard rate, and the difference is debited or credited to the Price difference account. Therefore, the benefit on account of lower price is also credited to the Price difference account.

5.4.7 Account Assignment

If a material is procured for a specific purpose, it is automatically issued on goods receipt. For such material, Stock account is not debited; the cost object to which it is issued is debited. Any differences at the time of invoice receipt are also charged to the same cost object regardless of the price control of the material. For positive price variance this is illustrated in Section 6.6.

5.5 MANUAL NON-ACCEPTANCE OF NEGATIVE DIFFERENCE

Functional Consultant	User	Business Process Owner	Senior Management	My Rating	Understanding Level
A	A	A	A		

5.5.1 Scenario

You receive an invoice from a vendor claiming amount significantly smaller than that calculated by your system. You want to seek clarification from the vendor before settling this invoice.

5.5.2 Invoice

Enter the invoice using transaction MIRO.

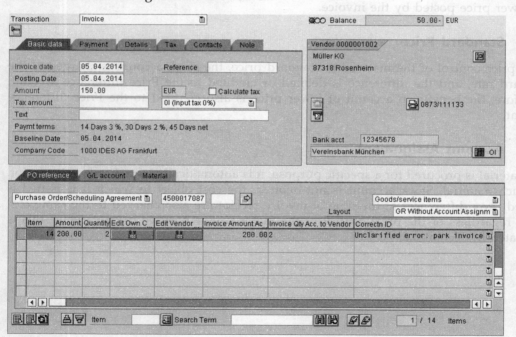

Correction id

If you cannot accept an invoice item because you suspect that it may be in error, select `Unclarified error: park invoice 🗒` in this field.

Invoice quantity according to vendor

If you select `Correctn ID` `Unclarified error: park invoice 🗒`, you can enter the quantity specified by the vendor in the invoice in this field.

Invoice amount according to vendor

If you select `Correctn ID` `Unclarified error: park invoice 🗒`, you can enter the amount specified by the vendor in the invoice in this field. Alternatively, the system can compute it from `Edit Vendor Conditions` and `Invoice Qty Acc. to Vendor`.

Edit own conditions

If you select `Correctn ID` `Unclarified error: park invoice 🗒`, but think that your own data may also not be correct, you can edit your own conditions.

Edit vendor conditions

If you select `Correctn ID` `Unclarified error: park invoice 🗒`, you can also edit vendor conditions. The new conditions are used to calculate the `Invoice Amount Acc. to Vendor`, and Balance.

5.5.3 Parking the Invoice

Click `Edit` ➤ `Switch to Document Parking` and 🖫. If you know from the beginning that an invoice is to be parked, you can also use transaction MIR7. Parked documents show in the worklist in transaction MIRO.

Worklist	Doc. date	Reference no.	Vendor	Amount
🗀 Held documents				
▽ 🗀 Parked documents				
📄 5105608650 2014	30.03.2014		0000001002	1,000.00 EUR
📄 5105608657 2014	05.04.2014		0000001002	150.00 EUR
🗀 Docs complete for posting				

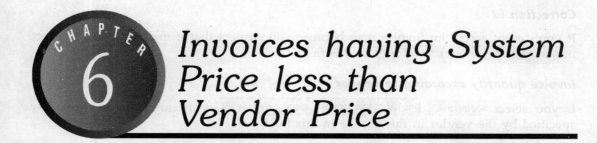

Invoices having System Price less than Vendor Price

6.1 POSITIVE DIFFERENCE AND TOLERANCE

Functional Consultant	User	Business Process Owner	Senior Management	My Rating	Understanding Level
A	A	A	A		

6.1.1 Differences

Difference

The system determines the difference between the net invoice amount (= gross invoice amount less taxes and unplanned delivery costs) and the net total of the items.

Positive difference

If the vendor's invoice amount is greater than your amount, then the difference is positive.

Automatic acceptance of positive difference

If you do not change the amount in items, there is a non-zero `Balance`. You may still be able to post the invoice. This is called automatic acceptance of positive difference.

Manual acceptance of positive difference

If you change the amount in items, you are manually accepting the positive difference.

Non-acceptance of positive difference

If the vendor's invoice amount is greater than your amount, then the difference is positive. You do not want to pay the vendor what he claims unless you have reconciled your calculation with the vendor's invoice, understood the difference, and arrived at an action plan acceptable both to your company and the vendor.

Small difference

Sometimes the difference may be so small that it is not worth investigating. Therefore, many companies have a policy of accepting the amount in the vendor's invoice and posting the difference to a small difference account.

Small difference tolerance

You can specify the amount below which you would consider a difference to be small. You can also group your vendors and specify small difference tolerance for each group.

Small difference account

If the difference is within the tolerance range, the system automatically generates a difference line on a G/L account for small differences when posting the invoice. If the system creates a small difference, it posts this difference to the account specified in account determination for transaction DIF.

Treatment of positive differences

The system does not pay more than the system computed amount unless manually accepted. The system can automatically pay a higher amount, if the difference meets the criteria of small difference.

6.1.2 Small Difference Tolerance at Company Code Level

Purpose

You can specify the amount below which you would consider a difference to be small. This is specified here. You can also group your vendors and specify small difference tolerance for each group as explained in section 6.1.3. If no tolerance group is assigned to a vendor or if no tolerances have been specified for the assigned tolerance group, the system takes the tolerances from here. This tolerance is for both negative and positive small differences.

JMG Node

SM30 ➤ V_169G, Tolerance key BD

Screen

Tolerance key	BD	Form small differences automatically
Company Code	1000	IDES AG
Amounts in	EUR	Euro (EMU currency as of 01/01/1999)

Upper limit

Absolute
- ○ Do not check
- ◉ Check limit
  - Val. `2.50`

6.1.3   Positive Difference Tolerance at Vendor Group Level

Purpose

Apart from small differences, SAP lets you specify positive differences that can be accepted. You can also specify the upper limit of invoice reduction; invoices where the positive difference is beyond this limit cannot be posted.

IMG Node

SM30 ➢ V_169L

Screen

Company Code	1000	IDES AG
Tolerance grp	515	
Currency	EUR	

Automatic acceptance of positive differences

Positive small difference
- Check limit ☑
- Small diff. `5.00`

Absolute upper limit	**Percentage upper limit**
Check limit ☑	Check limit ☑
PosAccUpperLimt `30.00`	PercUpperAccLim `1.00` %

Automatic invoice reduction

Absolute upper limit	**Percentage upper limit**
Check limit ☑	Check limit ☐
Inv.Red.Tol.Amn `50.00`	Per.Inv.Red.Tol `____` %

Tolerance Group

You can specify different tolerances for different vendors. For this purpose, you group the vendors in tolerance groups. In transaction XK02, in `Company code data`, select `☑ Payment transactions`. Specify the tolerance group of the vendor.

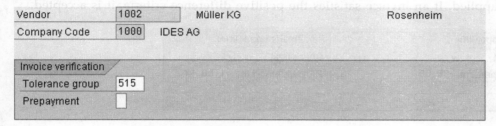

Difference below Positive Small Difference

If you want the limit of positive small difference to be different for different groups of vendors, you can specify it here. If no tolerance group is assigned to a vendor or if no tolerances have been specified for the assigned tolerance group, the system takes the tolerances from view V_169G, tolerance key BD.

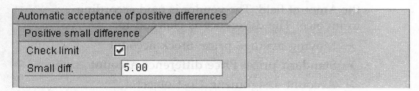

If the difference is below this limit, you have the following options:

Correction id	Action	Section
`No error`, Automatic acceptance of invoice amount.	The difference is treated as small difference and posted to `Small price loss - i` account.	6.2
`No error`, Manual acceptance of invoice amount.	You accept the vendor's amount and change it in the Amount field. The vendor is paid according to invoice. The difference is charged to: ➤ Moving average price: Stock account ➤ Standard price: Price difference account ➤ Account assignment: Cost object	
1 Unclarified error: park invoice	The invoice is not posted; it is parked.	
2 Vendor error: reduce invoice	The invoice is reduced. The vendor is paid as per your calculation.	

Difference below Automatic Acceptance of Positive Differences

If the difference is more than the limit of positive small difference, you can still accept an invoice, if it satisfies the criteria defined here. You can specify an absolute value and a percentage value. You can specify one or both limits. If both limits are specified, both limits are applied. If an invoice satisfies the positive difference criteria, it is accepted.

Absolute upper limit		Percentage upper limit	
Check limit ☑		Check limit ☑	
PosAccUpperLimt 30.00		PercUpperAccLim 1.00 %	

If the difference is below this limit, you have the following options:

Correction id	Action	Section
No error , Automatic acceptance of invoice amount.	The invoice is reduced. The vendor is paid as per your calculation.	6.3
No error , Manual acceptance of invoice amount.	You accept the vendor's amount and change it in the Amount field. The vendor is paid according to invoice. The difference is charged to: ➤ Moving average price: Stock account ➤ Standard price: Price difference account ➤ Account assignment: Cost object	
1 Unclarified error: park invoice	The invoice is not posted; it is parked.	
2 Vendor error: reduce invoice	The invoice is reduced. The vendor is paid as per your calculation.	

Difference below Automatic Invoice Reduction

Here you can set the upper limit of automatic invoice reduction.

Automatic invoice reduction			
Absolute upper limit		Percentage upper limit	
Check limit ☑		Check limit ☐	
Inv.Red.Tol.Amn 50.00		Per.Inv.Red.Tol %	

If the difference is below this limit, you have the following options:

Correction id	Action	Section
No error, Automatic acceptance of invoice amount.	The invoice cannot be posted, if the difference is above Automatic acceptance of positive differences	
No error, Manual acceptance of invoice amount.	You accept the vendor's amount and change it in the Amount field. The vendor is paid according to invoice. The difference is charged to: ➤ Moving average price: Stock account ➤ Standard price: Price difference account ➤ Account assignment: Cost object	6.4
1 Unclarified error: park invoice	The invoice is not posted; it is parked.	
2 Vendor error: reduce invoice	The invoice is reduced. The vendor is paid as per your calculation.	6.7

Difference above Automatic Invoice Reduction

If the difference is more than the limit above, you have the following options:

Correction id	Action	Section
No error, Automatic acceptance of invoice amount.	The invoice cannot be posted, if the difference is above Automatic acceptance of positive differences	
No error, Manual acceptance of invoice amount.	You accept the vendor's amount and change it in the Amount field. The vendor is paid according to invoice. The difference is charged to: ➤ Moving average price: Stock account ➤ Standard price: Price difference account ➤ Account assignment: Cost object	
1 Unclarified error: park invoice	The invoice is not posted; it is parked.	6.9
2 Vendor error: reduce invoice	The invoice is not posted; it may be parked.	6.8

6.1.4 Small Difference Account

You can use transaction OMR0 to see/set the G/L account to which the small difference will be posted.

Chart of Accounts	INT	Chart of accounts - international
Transaction	DIF	Materials management small differences

Account assignment	
Debit	Credit
231900	281900

You may use a single G/L account to post both positive and negative differences, or you may use different G/L accounts. Here the positive small difference is posted to G/L account 231900.

6.2   AUTOMATIC ACCEPTANCE—POSITIVE SMALL DIFFERENCE

Functional Consultant	User	Business Process Owner	Senior Management	My Rating	Understanding Level
A	A	A	A		

6.2.1   Scenario

You receive an invoice with small positive difference.

6.2.2   Invoice

Enter the invoice using transaction MIRO.

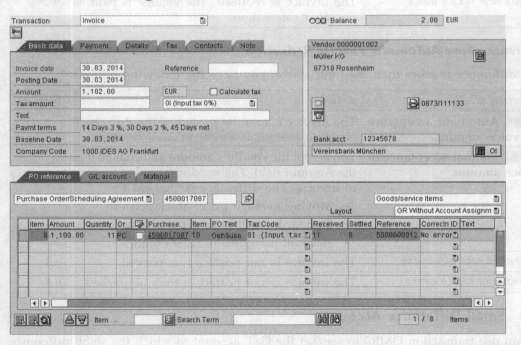

Note that despite a non-zero balance the traffic light is green ◯◯◻ Balance　2.00 EUR .
Post the invoice.

6.2.3 Accounting Entries

Display the invoice using transaction MIR4. Enter the Invoice Document No. and the Fiscal Year. Click &° Display Document. The system displays the invoice. Click Follow-On Documents ... . The system displays the list of accounting documents. Double-click the Accounting document to see the accounting entries.

Data Entry View									
Document Number	5100000009		Company Code	1000			Fiscal Year		2014
Document Date	30.03.2014		Posting Date	30.03.2014			Period		3
Reference			Cross-CC no.						
Currency	EUR		Texts exist	☐			Ledger Group		

CoCd	Itm	PK	G/L Acc	Account	Description	Amount	Purch.Doc.	Item	Material	Quantity
1000	1	31	160000	1002	Müller KG	1,102.00-				
	2	86	191100	191100	Goods Rcvd/Invoice R	1,100.00	4500017087	10	100-100	11
	3	40	231900	231900	Small price loss - i	2.00				

Note that the vendor is paid as per his invoice, and difference is posted to the 231900 Small price loss - i account, which is different from the 281900 Small price gains - account.

6.3 AUTOMATIC ACCEPTANCE—INVOICE REDUCTION

Functional Consultant	User	Business Process Owner	Senior Management	My Rating	Understanding Level
A	A	A	A		

6.3.1 Scenario

You get an invoice where the difference is larger than the limit of the small positive difference, but which satisfies the criteria specified in Automatic acceptance of positive differences. The system automatically reduces the invoice (no warning is given). The vendor is paid the amount computed by the system, not the invoice amount.

6.3.2 Invoice

Enter the invoice using transaction MIRO.

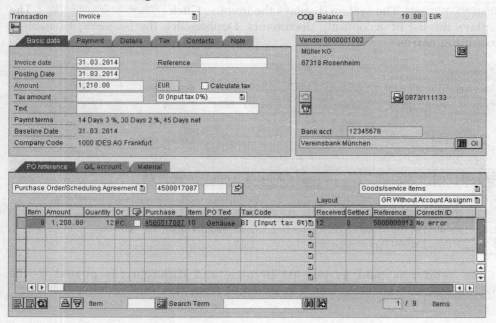

Post the invoice.

6.3.3 Accounting Documents

Display the invoice using transaction MIR4. Enter the Invoice Document No. and the Fiscal Year. Click 🔍 Display Document. The system displays the invoice. Click Follow-On Documents ... The system displays the list of accounting documents.

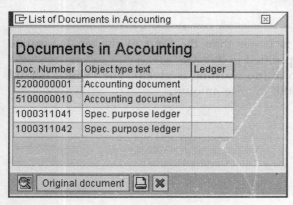

Note that there are two accounting documents.

6.3.4 Accounting Entries

Double-click the Accounting document to see the accounting entries.

Invoice document

Data Entry View			
Document Number 5100000010	Company Code 1000	Fiscal Year	2014
Document Date 31.03.2014	Posting Date 31.03.2014	Period	3
Reference	Cross-CC no.		
Currency EUR	Texts exist ☐	Ledger Group	

CoCd	Itm	PK	G/L Acc	Account	Description	Amount	Purch.Doc.	Item	Material	Quantity
1000	1	31	160000	1002	Müller KG	1,210.00-				
	2	86	191100	191100	Goods Rcvd/Invoice R	1,200.00	4500017087	10	100-100	12
	3	40	191120	191120	Clrg-invoice reduct.	10.00				

Invoice reduction document

Data Entry View			
Document Number 5200000001	Company Code 1000	Fiscal Year	2014
Document Date 31.03.2014	Posting Date 31.03.2014	Period	3
Reference	Cross-CC no.		
Currency EUR	Texts exist ☐	Ledger Group	

CoCd	Itm	PK	G/L Acc	Account	Description	Amount	Purch.Doc.	Item	Material	Quantity
1000	1	21	160000	1002	Müller KG	10.00				
	2	50	191120	191120	Clrg-invoice reduct.	10.00-				

Net effect of the two documents

Account	Explanation
191100 Goods Rcvd/Invoice R	1,200.00 debited by invoice posting nullifies the same amount credited by goods receipt posting.
191120 Clrg-invoice reduct.	The amount debited by one document is credited by the other.
1002 Müller KG	1,210.00- credited to vendor in invoice document. 10.00 debited to vendor in invoice reduction document. Thus the vendor is paid as per your calculation.

6.3.5 Complaint Letter

Run transaction MR90 to see the messages generated. Select the invoice document and click 🗐 to see the message.

```
Müller KG
87318 Rosenheim
```

```
***********************************
***********************************
**
Complaint Display

Complaint number, date
5105608652, 31.03.2014
With reference to your invoice from
31.03.2014
Your vendor number , Your tax ID no.
1002,
Our customer number , Our tax ID number
      , DE123456789
Contact person, Tel. no, Fax no.
Prem Agrawal

Currency
```

```
We reduced your invoice to the amount calculated by our system, based
on the purchase orders and deliveries to which your invoice refers. No
item check was made.
```

```
Net total                                                            10.00
plus tax at                       0.000 %         10.00               0.00
```

```
Amount of complaint incl. tax                                         EUR
10.00
```

6.4 MANUAL ACCEPTANCE—POSITIVE DIFFERENCE

Functional Consultant	User	Business Process Owner	Senior Management	My Rating	Understanding Level
A	A	A	A		

6.4.1 Scenario

You receive an invoice where the price is higher than the purchase order price. If the positive difference is more than the criteria specified in Automatic acceptance of positive differences (see section 6.1.3), you cannot post the invoice unless you manually accept the higher price given in the invoice.

6.4.2 Basic Data

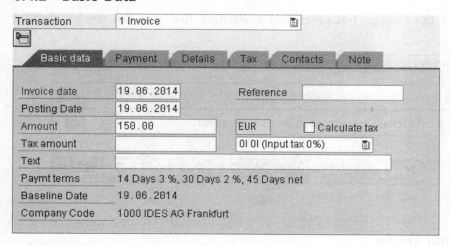

6.4.3 Items

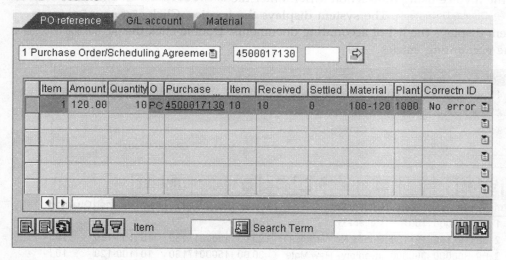

Amount

If you think that the vendor's invoice for 150 Euros is correct, change the Amount field.

Item	Amount	Quantity	O	Purchase	Item	Received	Settled	Material	Plant	Correctn ID
1	150.00	10	PC	4500017130	10	10	0	100-120	1000	No error

Messages

The system allows the change, but gives you a warning that you can see by clicking △ Messages .

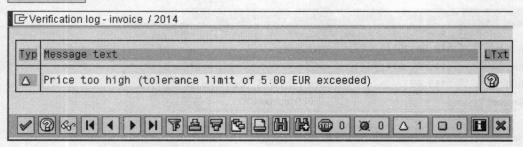

Post the invoice.

6.4.4 Accounting Entries

Display the invoice using transaction MIR4. Enter the Invoice Document No. and the Fiscal Year . Click Display Document . The system displays the invoice. Click Follow-On Documents ... . The system displays the list of accounting documents. Double-click the Accounting document to see the accounting entries.

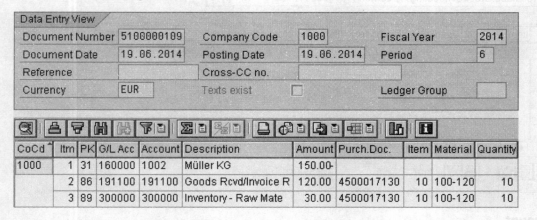

The extra cost arising from higher price is debited to the Stock account.

6.4.5 Inventory Value

Inventory value before invoice posting

You can see the stock and the value of a material in the `Accounting 1` view of the material master using transaction MM02. The following image is a part of that view before the invoice was posted:

Total Stock	2,522	Total Value	35,240.16

Inventory value after invoice posting

The following image is a part of the `Accounting 1` view after the invoice was posted:

Total Stock	2,522	Total Value	35,270.16

Note that the total value of the material has gone up by 30.00 Euros on account of the higher price posted by the invoice.

6.4.6 Standard Price

If the price control of the material is Standard price, the stock account is charged at the standard rate, and the difference is debited or credited to the Price difference account. Therefore, the extra cost on account of higher price is also debited to the Price difference account.

6.5 MANUAL ACCEPTANCE—INADEQUATE COVERAGE

Functional Consultant	User	Business Process Owner	Senior Management	My Rating	Understanding Level
B	C	X	X		

6.5.1 Scenario

You receive an invoice where the amount is more than the system calculation. After investigation you decide to accept it. The material is valuated at moving average price. The difference is charged to stock account. But at the time of invoice receipt, the quantity in stock is less than the invoice quantity. This will result in steep increase in the price of remaining material. If the stock is zero, it will result in stock value without stock quantity. Therefore, SAP charges part of the difference to the stock account (stock x rate difference), and the balance to the price difference account.

6.5.2 Invoice

Enter the invoice using transaction MIRO.

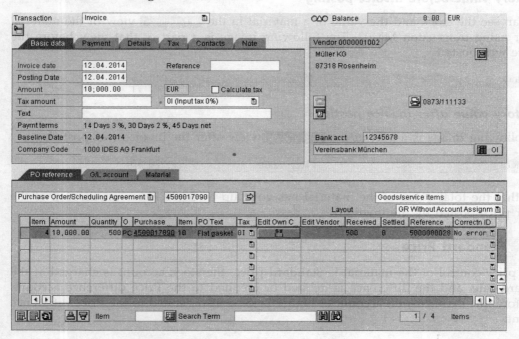

Amount

You can either change the Amount field directly, or change it by doing Edit Own Conditions.

Post

Post the invoice.

6.5.3 Accounting Entries

Display the invoice using transaction MIR4. Enter the Invoice Document No. and the Fiscal Year. Click 🔍 Display Document. The system displays the invoice. Click Follow-On Documents .... The system displays the list of accounting documents. Double-click the Accounting document to see the accounting entries.

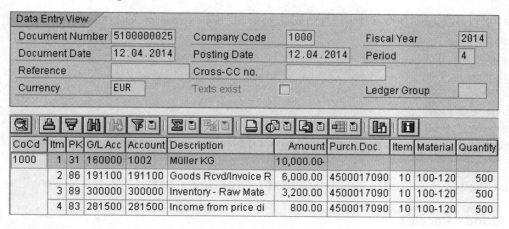

CoCd	Itm	PK	G/L Acc	Account	Description	Amount	Purch.Doc.	Item	Material	Quantity
1000	1	31	160000	1002	Müller KG	10,000.00-				
	2	86	191100	191100	Goods Rcvd/Invoice R	6,000.00	4500017090	10	100-120	500
	3	89	300000	300000	Inventory - Raw Mate	3,200.00	4500017090	10	100-120	500
	4	83	281500	281500	Income from price di	800.00	4500017090	10	100-120	500

The goods receipt was 500 pcs. Subsequently some material was issued and only 400 pcs were left in stock. When the invoice was settled at a higher price, the difference for 400 pcs was charged to the Stock account, while that for 100 pcs was charged to the Income from price difference account.

6.6 MANUAL ACCEPTANCE—COST ASSIGNMENT

Functional Consultant	User	Business Process Owner	Senior Management	My Rating	Understanding Level
A	A	A	B		

6.6.1 Scenario

You receive an invoice where the amount is more than the system calculation. After investigation you decide to accept it. The material is valuated at moving average price. The purchase order had an account assignment and goods were issued and charged to a cost centre on receipt. In this scenario, the difference is charged to the same cost centre.

6.6.2 Purchase Order

After saving the purchase order, run transaction ME23N to display the account assignment.

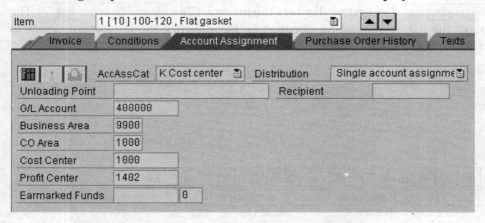

Note that the purchase order item is assigned to cost centre 1000.

6.6.3 Goods Receipt

After goods receipt run transaction MB02. Enter material document number and year. Display document. Click Accounting Documents... . Double-click the Accounting document .

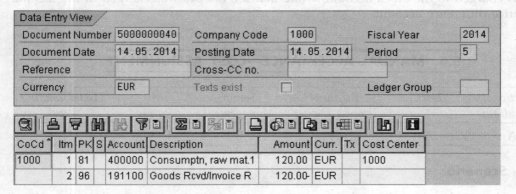

Note that the goods are debited to cost centre 1000.

6.6.4 Invoice

Enter the invoice using transaction MIRO.

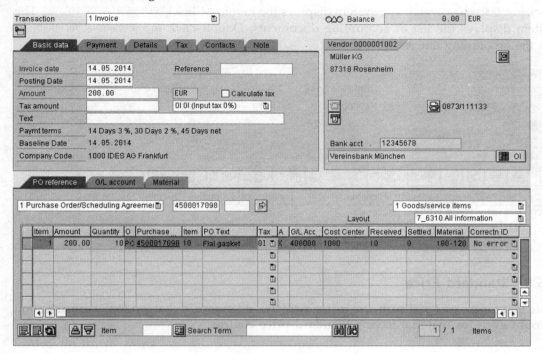

Amount

You can either change the `Amount` field directly, or change it by doing `Edit Own Conditions`.

Cost centre

Note that the invoice item shows cost centre 1000.

Post

Post the invoice.

6.6.5 Accounting Entries

Display the invoice using transaction MIR4. Enter the Invoice Document No. and the Fiscal Year. Click &ϸ Display Document. The system displays the invoice. Click Follow-On Documents .... The system displays the list of accounting documents. Double-click the Accounting document to see the accounting entries.

CoCd	Itm	PK	G/L Acc	Account	Description	Amount	Material	Quantity	Cost Center
1000	1	31	160000	1002	Müller KG	200.00-			
	2	86	191100	191100	Goods Rcvd/Invoice R	120.00	100-120	10	1000
	3	81	400000	400000	Consumptn, raw mat.1	80.00	100-120	10	1000

Data Entry View

Document Number	5100000047	Company Code	1000	Fiscal Year	2014

Document Number 5100000047 Company Code 1000 Fiscal Year 2014
Document Date 14.05.2014 Posting Date 14.05.2014 Period 5
Reference Cross-CC no.
Currency EUR Texts exist ☐ Ledger Group

6.6.6 Standard Price

Note that for the material with cost assignment, the difference is charged to the consumption account even for material having Standard price control.

6.7 MANUAL ACCEPTANCE—INVOICE REDUCTION

Functional Consultant	User	Business Process Owner	Senior Management	My Rating	Understanding Level
A	A	A	B		

6.7.1 Scenario

You get an invoice where the difference is larger than the criteria specified in Automatic acceptance of positive differences. You can ask the system to reduce the invoice. The system gives warning and reduces the invoice. The vendor is paid the amount computed by the system, not the invoice amount.

6.7.2 Invoice

Enter the invoice using transaction MIRO.

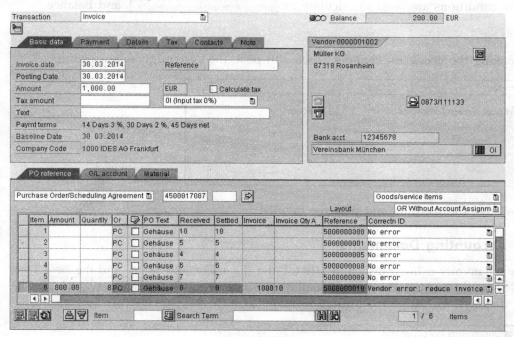

Correction id

If you cannot accept an invoice item because you think that the vendor made an error and want to settle the invoice as per your calculations, select `2 Vendor error: reduce invoice` in this field.

Invoice quantity according to vendor

If you select `Correctn ID` `2 Vendor error: reduce invoice`, you can enter the quantity specified by the vendor in the invoice in this field.

Invoice amount according to vendor

If you select `Correctn ID` `2 Vendor error: reduce invoice`, you can enter the amount specified by the vendor in the invoice in this field. Alternatively, the system can compute it from vendor conditions (which you can edit) and invoice quantity according to vendor.

Edit own conditions

If you select `Correctn ID` `2 Vendor error: reduce invoice`, but think that your own data may also not be correct, you can edit your own conditions.

Edit vendor conditions

If you select `Correctn ID` `2 Vendor error: reduce invoice ☰`, you can also edit vendor conditions. The new conditions are used to calculate the `Invoice Amount Acc. to Vendor`, and Balance.

Post

After making the necessary changes when you post, the system gives a warning.

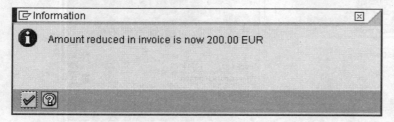

Acknowledge the warning and post the invoice.

6.7.3   Accounting Documents

Display the invoice using transaction MIR4. Enter the `Invoice Document No.` and the `Fiscal Year`. Click `🔍 Display Document`. The system displays the invoice. Click `Follow-On Documents ...`. The system displays the list of accounting documents.

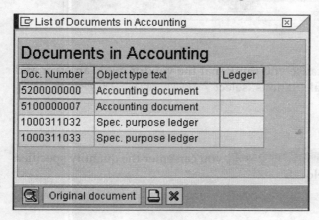

Note that there are two accounting documents.

6.7.4   Accounting Entries

Double-click the `Accounting document` to see the accounting entries.

Invoice document

Data Entry View

Document Number	5100000007	Company Code	1000	Fiscal Year	2014
Document Date	30.03.2014	Posting Date	30.03.2014	Period	3
Reference		Cross-CC no.			
Currency	EUR	Texts exist	☐	Ledger Group	

CoCd	Itm	PK	G/L Acc	Account	Description	Amount	Purch.Doc.	Item	Material	Quantity
1000	1	31	160000	1002	Müller KG	1,000.00-				
	2	86	191100	191100	Goods Rcvd/Invoice R	800.00	4500017087	10	100-100	8
	3	40	191120	191120	Clrg-invoice reduct.	200.00				

Invoice reduction document

Data Entry View

Document Number	5200000000	Company Code	1000	Fiscal Year	2014
Document Date	30.03.2014	Posting Date	30.03.2014	Period	3
Reference		Cross-CC no.			
Currency	EUR	Texts exist	☐	Ledger Group	

CoCd	Itm	PK	G/L Acc	Account	Description	Amount	Purch.Doc.	Item	Material	Quantity
1000	1	21	160000	1002	Müller KG	200.00				
	2	50	191120	191120	Clrg-invoice reduct.	200.00-				

Net effect of the two documents

Account	Explanation
191100 Goods Rcvd/Invoice R	**800.00** debited by invoice posting nullifies the same amount credited by goods receipt posting.
191120 Clrg-invoice reduct.	The amount debited by one document is credited by the other.
1002 Müller KG	**1,000.00-** credited to vendor in invoice document. **200.00** debited to vendor in invoice reduction document. Thus the vendor is paid as per your calculation.

6.7.5 Complaint Letter

Run transaction MR90 to see the messages generated. Select the invoice document and click 🖷 to see the message.

Müller KG
87318 Rosenheim

Reklamationsanzeige

Reklamationsnummer, Datum
5105608649, 30.03.2014

In Bezug auf Ihre Rechnung vom
30.03.2014

Ihre Lieferantennummer bei uns , Ihre USt.-Id. Nr.
1002,

Unsere Kundennummer bei Ihnen , Unsere USt.-Id. Nr.
, DE123456789

Ansprechpartner/in, Telefon, Telefax
Prem Agrawal

Währung
EUR

Ihre Rechnung wurde in folgenden Positionen gekürzt.

Material	Menge geliefert	Menge Einheit berechnet	Preis vereinbart	Preis berechnet	reklamierter Nettowarenwert

Positionen zu Werk 1000, Werk Hamburg,
22299 Hamburg, Alsterdorfer Strasse 13

unsere Nummer: 100-100,

	8	10 ST	100.00	100.00	200.00

Summe netto					200.00
zzgl. Steuern zu			0.000 %	200.00	0.00

Reklamationsbetrag inkl. Steuern   EUR
200.00

6.8 MANUAL ACCEPTANCE—INVOICE REDUCTION NOT ALLOWED

Functional Consultant	User	Business Process Owner	Senior Management	My Rating	Understanding Level
A	A	A	B		

6.8.1 Scenario

Sometimes you may receive an invoice where the difference in the vendor's claim and your calculation is too large. Your company may not want to settle such invoices using the method of invoice reduction.

6.8.2 Upper Limit of Invoice Reduction

Purpose

You can specify the limit of invoice reduction.

IMG Node

SM30 ➢ V_169L

Screen

Company Code	1000	IDES AG
Tolerance grp	515	
Currency	EUR	

Automatic acceptance of positive differences

Positive small difference

Check limit	☑
Small diff.	5.00

Absolute upper limit		Percentage upper limit	
Check limit	☑	Check limit	☑
PosAccUpperLimt	30.00	PercUpperAccLim	1.00 %

Automatic invoice reduction

Absolute upper limit		Percentage upper limit	
Check limit	☑	Check limit	☐
Inv.Red.Tol.Amn	50.00	Per.Inv.Red.Tol	%

Tolerance Group

You can specify different tolerances for different vendors. For this purpose, you group the vendors in tolerance groups. In transaction XK02, in `Company code data` , select ☑ `Payment transactions` . Specify the tolerance group of the vendor.

Vendor	1002	Müller KG	Rosenheim
Company Code	1000	IDES AG	

Invoice verification

Tolerance group	

If no tolerance group is assigned to a vendor or if no tolerances have been specified for the assigned tolerance group, the system takes the tolerances from view V_169G, tolerance key BD.

Upper Limit of Automatic Invoice Reduction

If the difference is more than the limit of Automatic acceptance of positive differences, the system gives a warning, but you can still accept the invoice. However, if the difference is more than the limit of Automatic invoice reduction, you cannot post the invoice. You can specify an absolute value and a percentage value. You can specify one or both limits. If both limits are specified, both limits are applied.

6.8.3   Invoice

Enter the invoice using transaction MIRO.

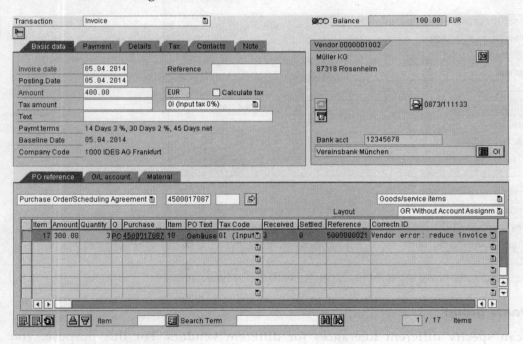

Correction id

If you cannot accept an invoice item because you think that the vendor made an error and want to settle the invoice as per your calculations, select 2 Vendor error: reduce invoice in this field.

Invoice quantity according to vendor

If you select Correctn ID 2 Vendor error: reduce invoice , you can enter the quantity specified by the vendor in the invoice in this field.

Invoice amount according to vendor

If you select Correctn ID 2 Vendor error: reduce invoice ▤ , you can enter the amount specified by the vendor in the invoice in this field. Alternatively, the system can compute it from vendor conditions (which you can edit) and invoice quantity according to vendor.

Edit own conditions

If you select Correctn ID 2 Vendor error: reduce invoice ▤ , but think that your own data may also not be correct, you can edit your own conditions.

Edit vendor conditions

If you select Correctn ID 2 Vendor error: reduce invoice ▤ , you can also edit vendor conditions. The new conditions are used to calculate the S̲witch to Document Parking , and Balance.

Message

Click ▣ Messages . The system shows the following message:

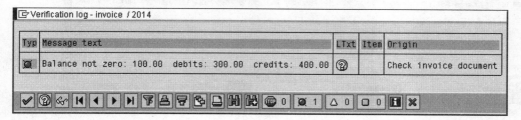

If you try to save the invoice, the system does not do so as the ✅ Invoice document still contains messages .

6.8.4 Parking the Invoice

Click Edit ➤ S̲witch to Document Parking and 🖫. If you know from the beginning that an invoice is to be parked, you can also use transaction MIR7. Parked documents show in the worklist in transaction MIRO.

6.9 MANUAL NON-ACCEPTANCE—INVOICE PARKING

Functional Consultant	User	Business Process Owner	Senior Management	My Rating	Understanding Level
A	A	A	B		

6.9.1 Scenario

You may receive an invoice where the vendor's claim is more than the amount as per you, and his claim is not acceptable. You can enter and park such an invoice and post it later after resolving the difference with the vendor.

6.9.2   Invoice

Enter the invoice using transaction MIRO.

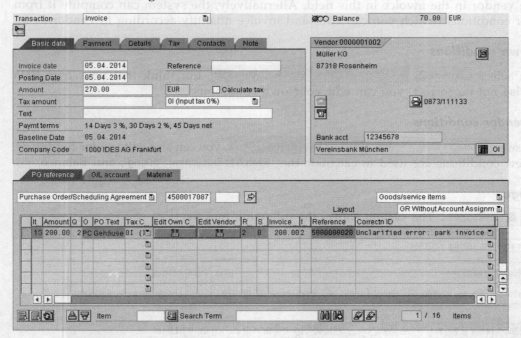

Correction id

If you cannot accept an invoice item because you suspect that it may be in error, select `Unclarified error: park invoice ▤` in this field.

Invoice quantity according to vendor

If you select `Correctn ID` `Unclarified error: park invoice ▤`, you can enter the quantity specified by the vendor in the invoice in this field.

Invoice amount according to vendor

If you select `Correctn ID` `Unclarified error: park invoice ▤`, you can enter the amount specified by the vendor in the invoice in this field. Alternatively, the system can compute it from vendor conditions (which you can edit) and invoice quantity according to vendor.

Edit own conditions

If you select `Correctn ID` `Unclarified error: park invoice ▤`, but think that your own data may also not be correct, you can edit your own conditions.

Edit vendor conditions

If you select `Correctn ID` `Unclarified error: park invoice ▣` , you can also edit vendor conditions. The new conditions are used to calculate the `Invoice Amount Acc. to Vendor` , and Balance.

6.9.3 Parking the Invoice

Click `Edit` ➤ `Switch to Document Parking` and ▣ . If you know from the beginning that an invoice is to be parked, you can also use transaction MIR7. Parked documents show in the worklist in transaction MIRO.

Worklist	Doc. date	Reference no.	Vendor	Amount
🗀 Held documents				
▽ 🗁 Parked documents				
📄 5105608650 2014	30.03.2014		0000001002	1,000.00 EUR
📄 5105608657 2014	05.04.2014		0000001002	150.00 EUR
📄 5105608658 2014	05.04.2014		0000001002	270.00 EUR
🗀 Docs complete for posting				

6.10 INVOICE REDUCTION—TAX REDUCTION IN ORIGINAL DOCUMENT

Functional Consultant	User	Business Process Owner	Senior Management	My Rating	Understanding Level
A	B	C	X		

6.10.1 Scenario

The vendor's invoice is erroneous. You choose to reduce the invoice. The system generates two documents: the original document settles the invoice in full, and the complaint document debits the vendor for the difference. Thus, the vendor is paid the amount computed by the system, not the invoice amount. Taxes are also paid as per your amount. In this scenario, in the original document, you pay the tax as per your calculation.

6.10.2 Tax Treatment in Invoice Reduction

When you receive an over-valued invoice, you do invoice reduction. In invoice reduction, two documents are created: an invoice document and an invoice reduction document. The invoice reduction document contains the difference between the vendor invoice and your calculation.

A complication arises when the invoice contains taxes. In the invoice document should the tax be computed based on your amount or on vendor amount? SAP lets you choose. In view V_169P_IRTAX, you can specify that.

CoCode	Name	Tax for invoice reduction
1000	IDES AG	Tax reduction in original document ▣

For each company code, you select one of the following options:

Tax reduction in complaint document
1 Tax reduction in original document

Tax reduction in complaint document

You do not choose this option in which the tax is computed on vendor's amount.

Tax reduction in original document

You choose this option in which the tax is computed on your amount.

6.10.3 Invoice

Enter the invoice using transaction MIRO.

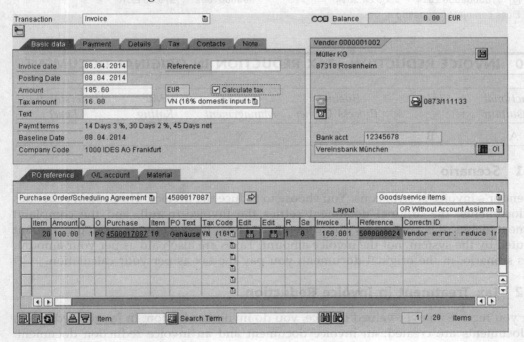

Post the invoice.

6.10.4 Accounting Documents

Display the invoice using transaction MIR4. Enter the Invoice Document No. and the Fiscal Year.
Click &ℛ Display Document. The system displays the invoice. Click Follow-On Documents ....
The system displays the list of accounting documents.

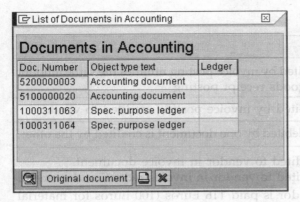

Note that there are two accounting documents.

6.10.5 Accounting Entries

Double-click the Accounting document to see the accounting entries.

Invoice document

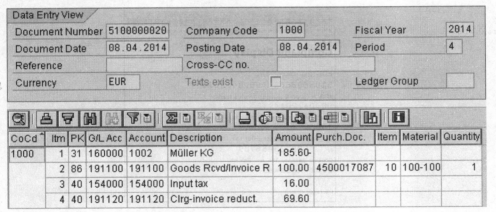

CoCd	Itm	PK	G/L Acc	Account	Description	Amount	Purch.Doc.	Item	Material	Quantity
1000	1	31	160000	1002	Müller KG	185.60-				
	2	86	191100	191100	Goods Rcvd/Invoice R	100.00	4500017087	10	100-100	1
	3	40	154000	154000	Input tax	16.00				
	4	40	191120	191120	Clrg-invoice reduct.	69.60				

Invoice reduction document

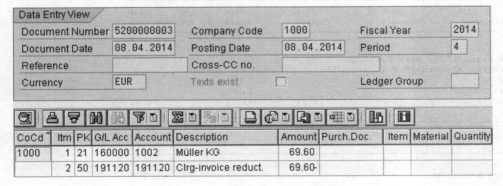

CoCd	Itm	PK	G/L Acc	Account	Description	Amount	Purch.Doc.	Item	Material	Quantity
1000	1	21	160000	1002	Müller KG	69.60				
	2	50	191120	191120	Clrg-invoice reduct.	69.60-				

Net effect of the two documents

Account	Explanation
191100 Goods Rcvd/Invoice R	**100.00** debited by invoice posting nullifies the same amount credited by goods receipt posting.
154000 Input tax	**16.00** debited by invoice posting credited to vendor.
191120 Clrg-invoice reduct.	The amount debited by one document is credited by the other.
1002 Müller KG	**185.60** credited to vendor in invoice document. **69.60** debited to vendor in invoice reduction document. Thus the vendor is paid 116 Euros (100 Euros for material and 16 Euros for tax). Thus, the tax is computed on the material value determined by you.

6.10.6 Complaint Letter

Run transaction MR90 to see the messages generated. Select the invoice document and click  to see the message.

```
Müller KG
87318 Rosenheim
```

****
****
**
Complaint Display

Complaint number, date
5105608661, 08.04.2014
With reference to your invoice from
08.04.2014
Your vendor number , Your tax ID no.
1002,
Our customer number , Our tax ID number
, DE123456789
Contact person, Tel. no, Fax no.
Prem Agrawal

Currency

```
The following items in your invoice were reduced:
```

Material	Qty Delivered	Qty Invoiced	Qty Unit	Price Agreed	Price Invoiced	At Issue Net value/goods

```
Items for plant 1000, Werk Hamburg,
22299 Hamburg, Alsterdorfer Strasse 13
```

Material	Qty Delivered	Qty Invoiced	Qty Unit	Price Agreed	Price Invoiced	At Issue Net value/goods
Our number: 100-100,	1		1 PC	100.00	160.00	60.00

Net total						60.00
plus tax at			16.000 %		60.00	9.60

```
Amount of complaint incl. tax
69.60
```
                                                                                    EUR

6.11 INVOICE REDUCTION—TAX REDUCTION IN COMPLAINT DOCUMENT

Functional Consultant	*User*	*Business Process Owner*	*Senior Management*	*My Rating*	*Understanding Level*
A	B	C	X		

6.11.1 Scenario

The vendor's invoice is erroneous. You choose to reduce the invoice. The system generates two documents: the original document settles the invoice in full, and the complaint document debits the vendor for the difference. Thus, the vendor is paid the amount computed by the system, not the invoice amount. Taxes are also paid as per your amount. In this scenario, in the original document, you pay the material cost as well as tax in full; in the complaint document, you recover both extra material cost as well as extra tax.

6.11.2 Tax Treatment in Invoice Reduction

When you receive an over-valued invoice, you do invoice reduction. In invoice reduction, two documents are created: an invoice document and an invoice reduction document. The invoice reduction document contains the difference between the vendor invoice and your calculation.

A complication arises when the invoice contains taxes. In the invoice document should the tax be computed based on your amount or on vendor amount? SAP lets you choose. In view V_169P_IRTAX, you can specify that.

CoCode	Name	Tax for invoice reduction
1000	IDES AG	Tax reduction in complaint document 📄

For each company code, you select one of the following options:

	Tax reduction in complaint document
1	Tax reduction in original document

Tax reduction in complaint document

You choose this option in which the tax is computed on vendor's amount.

Tax reduction in original document

You do not choose this option in which the tax is computed on your amount.

6.11.3 Invoice

Enter the invoice using transaction MIRO.

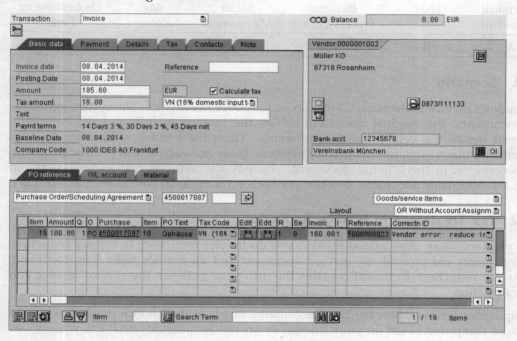

Post the invoice.

6.11.4 Accounting Documents

Display the invoice using transaction MIR4. Enter the Invoice Document No. and the Fiscal Year. Click `&▽ Display Document`. The system displays the invoice. Click `Follow-On Documents ...`. The system displays the list of accounting documents.

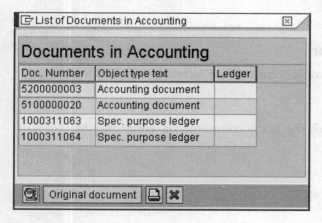

Note that there are two accounting documents.

6.11.5 Accounting Entries

Double-click the `Accounting document` to see the accounting entries.

Invoice document

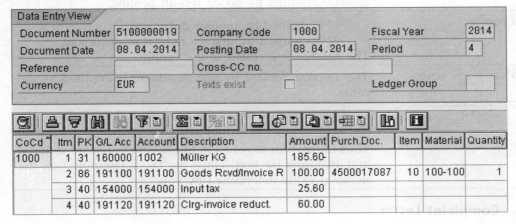

CoCd	Itm	PK	G/L Acc	Account	Description	Amount	Purch.Doc.	Item	Material	Quantity
1000	1	31	160000	1002	Müller KG	185.60-				
	2	86	191100	191100	Goods Rcvd/Invoice R	100.00	4500017087	10	100-100	1
	3	40	154000	154000	Input tax	25.60				
	4	40	191120	191120	Clrg-invoice reduct.	60.00				

Invoice reduction document

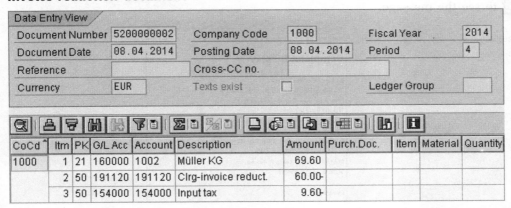

CoCd	Itm	PK	G/L Acc	Account	Description	Amount	Purch.Doc.	Item	Material	Quantity
1000	1	21	160000	1002	Müller KG	69.60				
	2	50	191120	191120	Clrg-invoice reduct.	60.00-				
	3	50	154000	154000	Input tax	9.60-				

Both excess value of material and excess value of tax are recovered in the complaint letter.

Net effect of the two documents

Account	Explanation
191100 Goods Rcvd/Invoice R	100.00 debited by invoice posting nullifies the same amount credited by goods receipt posting.
154000 Input tax	25.60 debited by invoice document. 9.60- credited by invoice reduction document. The balance is credited to the vendor.
191120 Clrg-invoice reduct.	The amount debited by one document is credited by the other.
1002 Müller KG	185.60- credited to vendor in invoice document. 69.60 debited to vendor in invoice reduction document. Thus the vendor is paid 116 Euros (100 Euros for material and 16 Euros for tax). Thus, the tax is computed on the material value determined by you.

6.11.6 Complaint Letter

Run transaction MR90 to see the messages generated. Select the invoice document and click  to see the message.

Müller KG
87318 Rosenheim

```
*********************************
*********************************
**
Complaint Display

Complaint number, date
5105608660, 08.04.2014
With reference to your invoice from
08.04.2014
Your vendor number  , Your tax ID no.
1002,
Our customer number , Our tax ID number
      , DE123456789
Contact person, Tel. no. Fax no.
Prem Agrawal

Currency
```

The following items in your invoice were reduced:

Material	Qty Delivered	Qty Unit Invoiced	Price Agreed	Price Invoiced	At Issue Net value/goods

Items for plant 1000, Werk Hamburg,
22299 Hamburg, Alsterdorfer Strasse 13

Our number:	100-100,				
	1	1 PC	100.00	160.00	60.00

Net total					60.00
plus tax at			16.000 %	60.00	9.60

Amount of complaint incl. tax
69.60   EUR

7

CHAPTER

Invoices having System Quantity more than Vendor Quantity

7.1 MANUAL ACCEPTANCE OF A PARTIAL INVOICE

Functional Consultant	User	Business Process Owner	Senior Management	My Rating	Understanding Level
A	A	B	C		

7.1.1 Scenario

You receive invoice for partial quantity of a goods receipt. Subsequently you receive invoice for remaining quantity of the goods receipt.

7.1.2 Invoice

Enter the invoice using transaction MIRO.

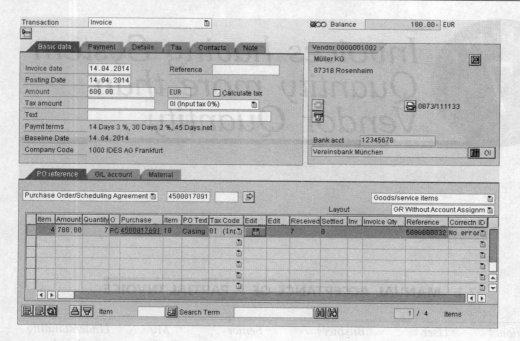

Amount and quantity

You cannot post this invoice because of non-zero Balance. You can post this invoice only if you change the Amount and the Quantity fields thereby indicating to the system that you are accepting the invoice for partial quantity.

Post the invoice.

7.1.3 Accounting Entries

Display the invoice using transaction MIR4. Enter the Invoice Document No. and the Fiscal Year. Click ‎ Display Document. The system displays the invoice. Click Follow-On Documents ... The system displays the list of accounting documents. Double-click the Accounting document to see the accounting entries.

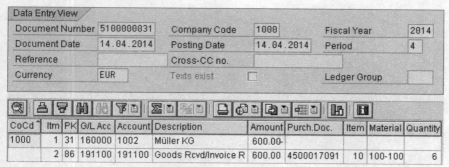

7.1.4 Purchase Order Structure

In invoice entry transaction MIRO, or in invoice display transaction MIR4, display the purchase order structure by clicking `Show PO structure`.

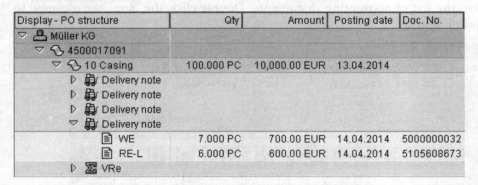

Display - PO structure	Qty	Amount	Posting date	Doc. No.
▽ 🙎 Müller KG				
▽ 🕓 4500017091				
▽ 🕓 10 Casing	100.000 PC	10,000.00 EUR	13.04.2014	
▷ 🖨 Delivery note				
▷ 🖨 Delivery note				
▷ 🖨 Delivery note				
▽ 🖨 Delivery note				
📄 WE	7.000 PC	700.00 EUR	14.04.2014	5000000032
📄 RE-L	6.000 PC	600.00 EUR	14.04.2014	5105608673
▷ Σ VRe				

Note the difference in quantity between the goods receipt and the invoice.

7.1.5 Subsequent Invoice

You may receive and enter an invoice for the balance quantity using transaction MIRO.

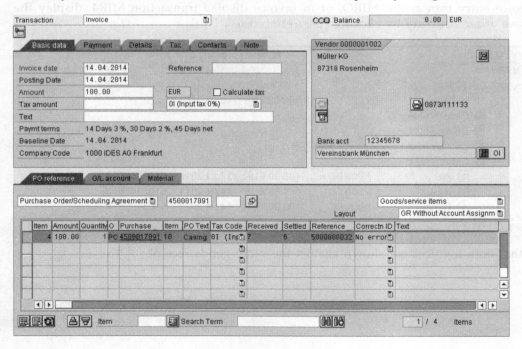

Post the invoice.

7.1.6 Accounting Entries

Display the invoice using transaction MIR4. Enter the Invoice Document No. and the Fiscal Year. Click 𝒮 Display Document . The system displays the invoice. Click Follow-On Documents ... . The system displays the list of accounting documents. Double-click the Accounting document to see the accounting entries.

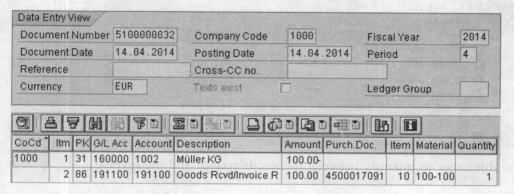

7.1.7 Purchase Order Structure

In invoice entry transaction MIRO, or in invoice display transaction MIR4, display the purchase order structure by clicking Show PO structure .

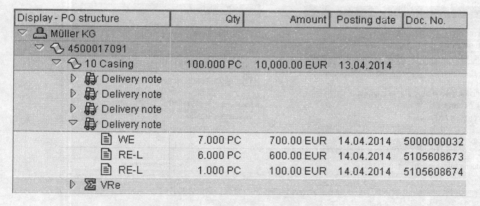

Note that both invoices are shown against the same goods receipt.

7.2   NON-ACCEPTANCE OF A PARTIAL INVOICE

Functional Consultant	User	Business Process Owner	Senior Management	My Rating	Understanding Level
A	A	B	C		

7.2.1   Scenario

You receive an invoice. When you start entering it, you find a mismatch between invoice quantity and goods receipt quantity. You decide to park the invoice and wait for corrected invoice from the vendor.

7.2.2   Invoice

Enter the invoice using transaction MIRO.

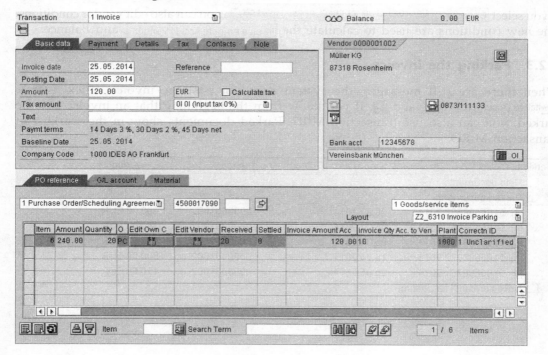

Correction id

If you cannot accept an invoice item because you suspect that it may be in error, select Unclarified error: park invoice 🔲 in this field.

Invoice quantity according to vendor

If you select Correctn ID Unclarified error: park invoice ⊟ , you can enter the quantity specified by the vendor in the invoice in this field.

Invoice amount according to vendor

If you select Correctn ID Unclarified error: park invoice ⊟ , you can enter the amount specified by the vendor in the invoice in this field. Alternatively, the system can compute it from vendor conditions (which you can edit) and invoice quantity according to vendor.

Edit own conditions

If you select Correctn ID Unclarified error: park invoice ⊟ , but think that your own data may also not be correct, you can edit your own conditions.

Edit vendor conditions

If you select Correctn ID Unclarified error: park invoice ⊟ , you can also edit vendor conditions. The new conditions are used to calculate the Invoice Amount Acc. to Vendor , and Balance.

7.2.3 Parking the Invoice

When there are still messages, the system does not post the invoice. Click Edit ➢ Switch to Document Parking and 🖫. If you know from the beginning that an invoice is to be parked, you can also use transaction MIR7. Parked documents show in the worklist in transaction MIRO.

Worklist	Doc. date	Reference no.	Vendor	Amount
🗀 Held documents				
▽ 🗁 Parked documents				
📄 5105608650 2014	30.03.2014		0000001002	1,000.00 EUR
📄 5105608657 2014	05.04.2014		0000001002	150.00 EUR
📄 5105608658 2014	05.04.2014		0000001002	270.00 EUR
📄 5105608672 2014	14.04.2014		0000001002	600.00 EUR
📄 5105608701 2014	25.05.2014		0000001002	120.00 EUR
🗀 Docs complete for posting				

CHAPTER 8

Invoices having System Quantity less than Vendor Quantity

8.1 INVOICE REDUCTION

Functional Consultant	User	Business Process Owner	Senior Management	My Rating	Understanding Level
A	A	B	C		

8.1.1 Scenario

You receive invoice having larger quantity than the goods receipt. You instruct the system to settle the invoice as per your data by doing invoice reduction.

8.1.2 Invoice

Enter the invoice using transaction MIRO.

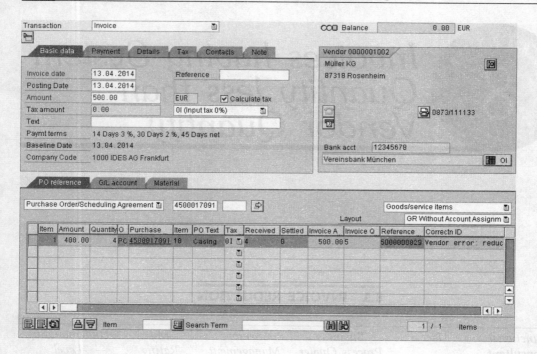

Correction id

If you cannot accept an invoice item because you suspect that it may be in error, select
2 Vendor error: reduce invoice 🖻 in this field.

Invoice quantity according to vendor

If you select Correctn ID 2 Vendor error: reduce invoice 🖻 , you can enter the quantity specified
by the vendor in the invoice in this field.

Invoice amount according to vendor

If you select Correctn ID 2 Vendor error: reduce invoice 🖻 , you can enter the amount specified
by the vendor in the invoice in this field. Alternatively, the system can compute it from
Edit Vendor Conditions and Invoice Qty Acc. to Vendor .

Edit own conditions

If you select Correctn ID 2 Vendor error: reduce invoice 🖻 , but think that your own data
may also not be correct, you can edit your own conditions.

Edit vendor conditions

If you select Correctn ID 2 Vendor error: reduce invoice ☷ , you can also edit vendor conditions. The new conditions are used to calculate the Invoice Amount Acc. to Vendor , and Balance.

Post

Post the invoice.

8.1.3 Accounting Documents

Display the invoice using transaction MIR4. Enter the Invoice Document No. and the Fiscal Year . Click &ᐟ Display Document . The system displays the invoice. Click Follow-On Documents ... . The system displays the list of accounting documents.

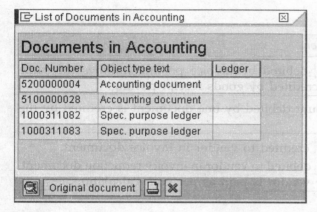

Note that there are two accounting documents.

8.1.4 Accounting Entries

Double-click the Accounting document to see the accounting entries.

Invoice document

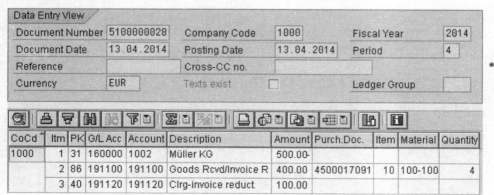

Invoice reduction document

Data Entry View				
Document Number	5200000004	Company Code	1000	Fiscal Year 2014
Document Date	13.04.2014	Posting Date	13.04.2014	Period 4
Reference		Cross-CC no.		
Currency	EUR	Texts exist ☐		Ledger Group

CoCd	Itm	PK	G/L Acc	Account	Description	Amount	Purch.Doc.	Item	Material	Quantity
1000	1	21	160000	1002	Müller KG	100.00				
	2	50	191120	191120	Clrg-invoice reduct.	100.00-				

Net effect of the two documents

Account	Explanation
191100 Goods Rcvd/Invoice R	400.00 debited by invoice posting nullifies the same amount credited by goods receipt posting.
191120 Clrg-invoice reduct.	The amount debited by one document is credited by the other.
1002 Müller KG	500.00- credited to vendor in invoice document. 100.00 debited to vendor in invoice reduction document. Thus the vendor is paid as per your calculation.

8.1.5 Complaint Letter

Run transaction MR90 to see the messages generated. Select the invoice document and click 📧 to see the message.

Müller KG
87318 Rosenheim

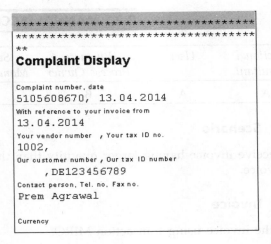

```
******************************************
******************************************
**
Complaint Display

Complaint number, date
5105608670, 13.04.2014
With reference to your invoice from
13.04.2014
Your vendor number  , Your tax ID no.
1002,
Our customer number , Our tax ID number
     , DE123456789
Contact person, Tel. no, Fax no.
Prem Agrawal


Currency
```

The following items in your invoice were reduced:

Material	Qty Delivered	Qty Invoiced	Qty Unit	Price Agreed	Price Invoiced	At Issue Net value/goods

Items for plant 1000, Werk Hamburg,
22299 Hamburg, Alsterdorfer Strasse 13

Our number: 100-100,

	4	5 PC		100.00	100.00	100.00

						100.00
Net total						
plus tax at				0.000 %	100.00	0.00

Amount of complaint incl. tax   EUR
100.00

8.1.6 Purchase Order Structure

In invoice entry transaction MIRO, or in invoice display transaction MIR4, display the purchase order structure by clicking Show PO structure .

Display - PO structure	Qty	Amount	Posting date	Doc. No.
👤 Müller KG				
� 4500017091				
🔧 10 Casing	100.000 PC	10,000.00 EUR	13.04.2014	
🚚 Delivery note				
📄 WE	4.000 PC	400.00 EUR	13.04.2014	5000000029
📄 RE-L	4.000 PC	400.00 EUR	13.04.2014	5105608670

8.2 MANUAL ACCEPTANCE

Functional Consultant	User	Business Process Owner	Senior Management	My Rating	Understanding Level
A	A	B	C		

8.2.1 Scenario

You receive invoice having larger quantity than the goods receipt. You decide to accept the invoice.

8.2.2 Invoice

Enter the invoice using transaction MIRO.

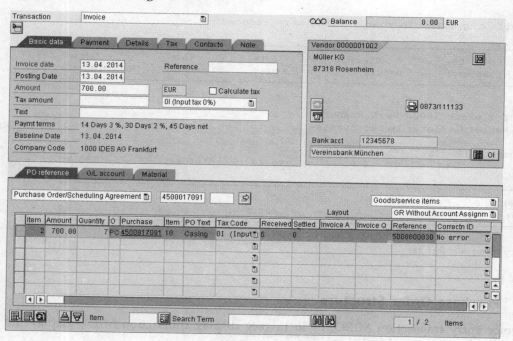

Amount and quantity

You cannot post this invoice because of non-zero Balance. You can post this invoice only if you change the Amount and the Quantity fields thereby indicating to the system that you are accepting the invoice for partial quantity.

Post

Post the invoice.

8.2.3 Accounting Entries

Display the invoice using transaction MIR4. Enter the Invoice Document No. and the Fiscal Year. Click 🗇 Display Document. The system displays the invoice. Click Follow-On Documents ... . The system displays the list of accounting documents. Double-click the Accounting document to see the accounting entries.

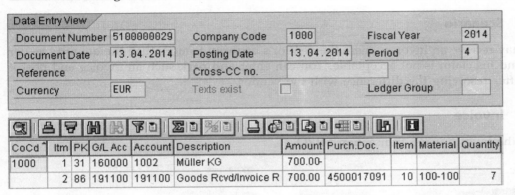

GR/IR account

This posting will create a mismatch in the GR/IR account.

8.2.4 Purchase Order Structure

In invoice entry transaction MIRO, or in invoice display transaction MIR4, display the purchase order structure by clicking Show PO structure.

Display - PO structure	Qty	Amount	Posting date	Doc. No.
👤 Müller KG				
🔾 4500017091				
🔾 10 Casing	100.000 PC	10,000.00 EUR	13.04.2014	
▷ 📥 Delivery note				
▽ 📥 Delivery note				
📄 WE	6.000 PC	600.00 EUR	13.04.2014	5000000030
📄 RE-L	7.000 PC	700.00 EUR	13.04.2014	5105608671

Note that the invoice posting does not change the stock.

8.3   NON-ACCEPTANCE—INVOICE PARKING

Functional Consultant	User	Business Process Owner	Senior Management	My Rating	Understanding Level
A	A	B	C		

8.3.1   Scenario

You may receive an invoice where the vendor's quantity is more than the quantity as per you, and his claim is not acceptable. You can enter and park such an invoice and post it later after resolving the difference with the vendor.

8.3.2   Invoice

Enter the invoice using transaction MIRO.

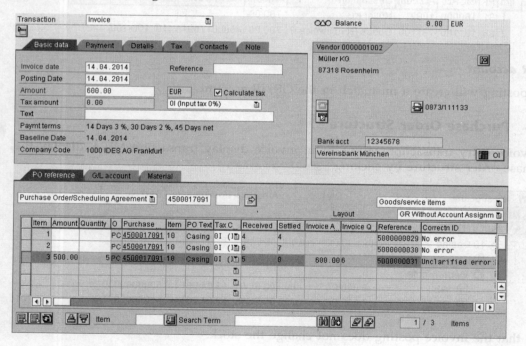

Correction id

If you cannot accept an invoice item because you suspect that it may be in error, select `Unclarified error: park invoice` in this field.

Invoice quantity according to vendor

If you select Correctn ID Unclarified error: park invoice 🗒 , you can enter the quantity specified by the vendor in the invoice in this field.

Invoice amount according to vendor

If you select Correctn ID Unclarified error: park invoice 🗒 , you can enter the amount specified by the vendor in the invoice in this field. Alternatively, the system can compute it from vendor conditions (which you can edit) and invoice quantity according to vendor.

Edit own conditions

If you select Correctn ID Unclarified error: park invoice 🗒 , but think that your own data may also not be correct, you can edit your own conditions.

Edit vendor conditions

If you select Correctn ID Unclarified error: park invoice 🗒 , you can also edit vendor conditions. The new conditions are used to calculate the Invoice Amount Acc. to Vendor , and Balance.

8.3.3 Parking the Invoice

When you post the invoice, the system gives the following message:

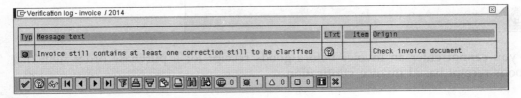

Since you cannot post the invoice, click Edit ➤ Switch to Document Parking and 🖳. If you know from the beginning that an invoice is to be parked, you can also use transaction MIR7. Parked documents show in the worklist in transaction MIRO.

Worklist	Doc. date	Reference no.	Vendor	Amount
🗀 Held documents				
▽ 🗁 Parked documents				
📄 5105608650 2014	30.03.2014		0000001002	1,000.00 EUR
📄 5105608657 2014	05.04.2014		0000001002	150.00 EUR
📄 5105608658 2014	05.04.2014		0000001002	270.00 EUR
📄 5105608672 2014	14.04.2014		0000001002	600.00 EUR
🗀 Docs complete for posting				

8.4 INVOICE BEFORE GOODS RECEIPT—GR BASED IV

Functional Consultant	User	Business Process Owner	Senior Management	My Rating	Understanding Level
A	A	B	C		

8.4.1 Scenario

The vendor sends an invoice for a delivery that the goods receipt has not yet been posted for. The purchase order item has goods receipt based invoice verification.

8.4.2 Invoice

In invoice entry transaction MIRO when you enter the purchase order number and press Enter, the system gives the following message:

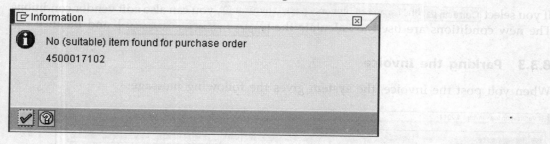

Thus, you cannot enter an invoice before goods receipt for a purchase order item that has goods receipt based invoice verification.

8.5 INVOICE BEFORE GOODS RECEIPT—PO BASED IV

Functional Consultant	User	Business Process Owner	Senior Management	My Rating	Understanding Level
A	A	B	C		

8.5.1 Scenario

The vendor sends an invoice for a delivery that the goods receipt has not yet been posted for. The purchase order item has purchase order based invoice verification.

8.5.2 Invoice

Enter the invoice using transaction MIRO.

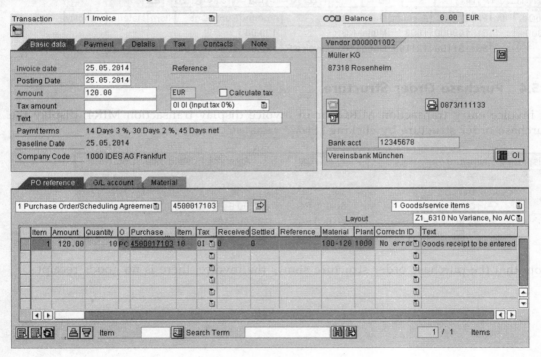

Note that the received quantity is zero. Post the invoice.

8.5.3   Accounting Entries

Display the invoice using transaction MIR4. Enter the Invoice Document No. and the Fiscal Year . Click 𝒞 Display Document . The system displays the invoice. Click Follow-On Documents ... . The system displays the list of accounting documents. Double-click the Accounting document to see the accounting entries.

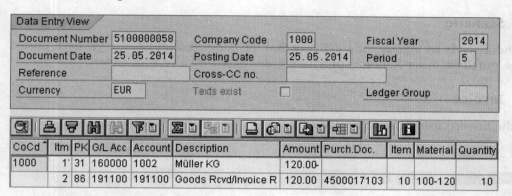

8.5.4   Purchase Order Structure

In invoice entry transaction MIRO, or in invoice display transaction MIR4, display the purchase order structure by clicking Show PO structure .

Display - PO structure	Qty	Amount	Posting date	Doc. No.
👤 Müller KG				
🔗 4500017103				
🔗 10 Flat gasket	50.000 PC	600.00 EUR	25.05.2014	
Σ Invoices	10.000 PC	120.00 EUR		
📄 RE-L	10.000 PC	120.00 EUR	25.05.2014	5105608703

Note that the purchase order structure shows the invoice; there is no goods receipt.

CHAPTER 9

Invoices without Purchase Order Reference

9.1 DIRECT POSTING TO G/L ACCOUNT

Functional Consultant	User	Business Process Owner	Senior Management	My Rating	Understanding Level
A	B	C	C		

9.1.1 Scenario

SAP also lets you post invoices that do not refer to a purchase order or a delivery. A typical example of this is a bill for expenses. In contrast to invoices with a reference, the system does not display any proposed values for the invoice items, since it cannot determine any purchase order items and posted goods receipts for this invoice. As a result, the system does not know which accounts are affected by the offsetting entry for the vendor line item. Therefore, you must specify which accounts the amounts are to be posted to. You may do direct posting to a G/L account either along with an invoice, or independently.

9.1.2 Activation

There are three tabs for entering invoice line items: `PO reference` `G/L account` `Material`. Invoice line items are entered primarily in the `PO reference` tab during invoice entry. The other two tabs `G/L account` and `Material` are for direct posting. Some companies do not want to use the feature of direct posting. Therefore, SAP lets you activate, or deactivate, direct posting to `G/L account` and direct posting to `Material` in view TCULIV.

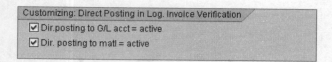

If direct posting to G/L account or direct posting to Material is not active, the corresponding tab does not appear in the invoice entry screen.

9.1.3 Basic Data

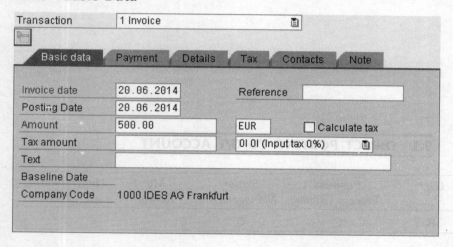

In this tab of the header, you enter mandatory information, e.g. Invoice date, Posting date, Amount, and Currency.

9.1.4 Payment

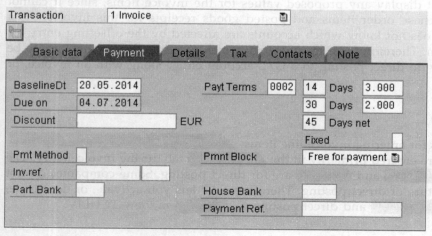

In this tab, enter the Baseline date, Payment terms, etc.

9.1.5   Details

Transaction	1 Invoice

| Basic data | Payment | Details | Tax | Contacts | Note |

Unpl. Del. Csts				
Currency	EUR		Exch. Rate	1.00000
Doc. Type	RE Gross inv. receipt		Inv. Party	1002
			Bus. Area	
Assignment			G/L	160000
Header Text				
			Rep. Country	
VAT Reg.No			☐ EU triang. deal	

In this tab, enter the invoicing party. Since this invoice does not refer to a purchase order, the vendor must be entered here.

9.1.6   Vendor

When you enter the invoicing party, the system shows the vendor details.

Vendor 0000001002

Müller KG

87318 Rosenheim

0873/111133

Bank acct   12345678

Vereinsbank München   OI

9.1.7 G/L Account

	St	G/L acct	Short Text	D/C	Amount	Loc.curr.	Company	Cost center	Controlling area
	✔	416300	Water	Debit	500.00	500.00	1000	1000	1000
				Debit		0.00	1000		
				Debit		0.00	1000		
				Debit		0.00	1000		
				Debit		0.00	1000		
				Debit		0.00	1000		

Enter details of invoice items in the G/L account tab. After entering the invoice, check that the Balance is zero; then post the invoice. The system gives the document number of the invoice created.

Document no. 5105608752 created

9.1.8 Accounting Entries

Display the invoice using transaction MIR4. Enter the Invoice Document No. and the Fiscal Year. Click Display Document . The system displays the invoice. Click Follow-On Documents ... . The system displays the list of accounting documents. Double-click the Accounting document to see the accounting entries.

Data Entry View

Document Number	5100000111	Company Code	1000	Fiscal Year	2014
Document Date	20.06.2014	Posting Date	20.06.2014	Period	6
Reference		Cross-CC no.			
Currency	EUR	Texts exist	☐	Ledger Group	

CoCd	Itm	PK	G/L Acc	Account	Description	Amount	Curr.	Cost Center
1000	1	31	160000	1002	Müller KG	500.00-	EUR	
	2	40	416300	416300	Water	500.00	EUR	1000

The account specified in the invoice item is debited, and the vendor is credited.

9.2 DIRECT POSTING TO MATERIAL ACCOUNT

Functional Consultant	User	Business Process Owner	Senior Management	My Rating	Understanding Level
A	B	C	C		

9.2.1 Scenario

Sometimes you may debit or credit a certain amount to a vendor for various reasons. For example, you may receive a consignment which you segregate in defective and acceptable goods. Apart from returning the defective part of the consignment, you may want to charge the cost of sorting to the vendor. You may do so using direct posting to material account. You may do direct posting to a material account either along with an invoice, or independently.

9.2.2 Activation

There are three tabs for entering invoice line items: **PO reference** **G/L account** **Material** . Invoice line items are entered primarily in the **PO reference** tab during invoice entry. The other two tabs **G/L account** and **Material** are for direct posting. Some companies do not want to use the feature of direct posting. Therefore, SAP lets you activate, or deactivate, direct posting to **G/L account** and direct posting to **Material** in view TCULIV.

> Customizing: Direct Posting in Log. Invoice Verification
> ☑ Dir.posting to G/L acct = active
> ☑ Dir. posting to matl = active

If direct posting to **G/L account** or direct posting to **Material** is not active, the corresponding tab does not appear in the invoice entry screen.

9.2.3 Basic Data

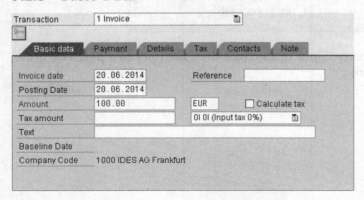

In this tab, enter mandatory information, e.g. Invoice date, Posting date, Amount, and Currency.

9.2.4 Payment

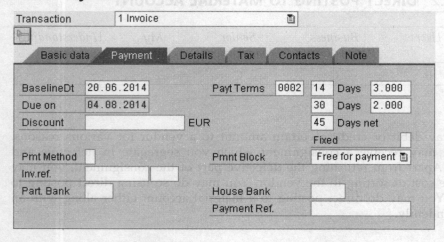

In this tab, enter the Baseline date, Payment terms, etc.

9.2.5 Details

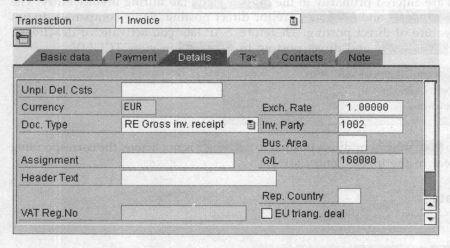

In this tab, enter the invoicing party. Since this invoice does not refer to a purchase order, the vendor must be entered here.

9.2.6 Vendor

When you enter the invoicing party, the system shows the vendor details.

9.2.7 Material

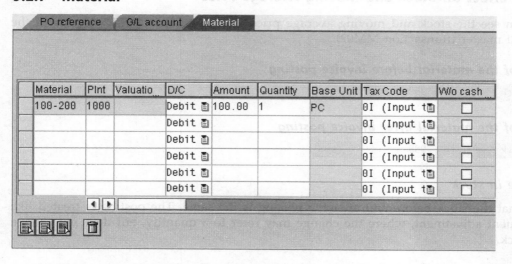

Enter details of invoice items in this tab. After entering the invoice, check that the Balance is zero; then post the invoice. The system gives the document number of the invoice created.

9.2.8 Accounting Entries

Display the invoice using transaction MIR4. Enter the Invoice Document No. and the Fiscal Year. Click &✗ Display Document . The system displays the invoice. Click Follow-On Documents ... . The system displays the list of accounting documents. Double-click the Accounting document to see the accounting entries.

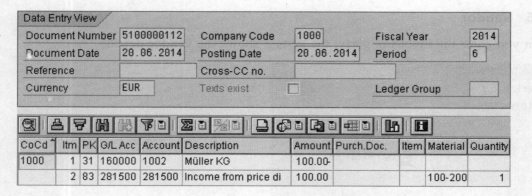

The vendor is credited. The debit is posted to the income from price difference account because the price control of the material has Standard price. If the price control of the material is Moving average price, the debit will be posted to the stock account.

9.2.9   Effect on Stock and Moving Average Price

You can see the stock and moving average price of a material in Accounting 1 tab of the material master (transaction MM02).

Stock of the material before invoice posting

Total Stock	900

Stock of the material after invoice posting

Total Stock	900

Change in stock

Note that the stock before and after the posting is the same. The posting is treated like subsequent adjustment, where the change may refer to a quantity, but does not change the stock.

Moving average price of the material before invoice posting

Moving price	108.07

Moving average price of the material after invoice posting

Moving price	108.19

Change in moving average price

Note the change in the moving average price of the material. This is expected given that an additional amount has been paid for the material.

Invoice Payment Block

10.1 MANUAL PAYMENT BLOCK OF AN INVOICE ITEM

Functional Consultant	User	Business Process Owner	Senior Management	My Rating	Understanding Level
A	A	A	B		

10.1.1 Scenario

You want to block payment for an invoice item manually because of some problems. Invoice gets posted, but payment to the vendor is blocked.

10.1.2 Invoice Entry

Enter the invoice using transaction MIRO.

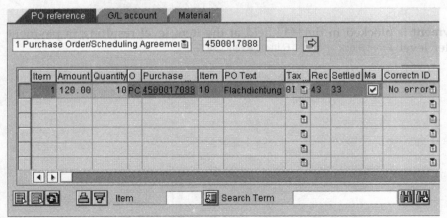

Set manual block indicator [Ma] for the invoice item. Note that the traffic light of
∞ Balance [0.00] EUR is yellow even though the balance is zero. Post the
invoice. The system gives the message that the invoice is blocked for payment.

⊘ Document no. 5105608689 created (Blocked for payment)

10.1.3 Invoice Display

Display the invoice using transaction MIR4. Enter the Invoice Document No. and the Fiscal Year.
Click ✧ Display Document . The system displays the invoice.

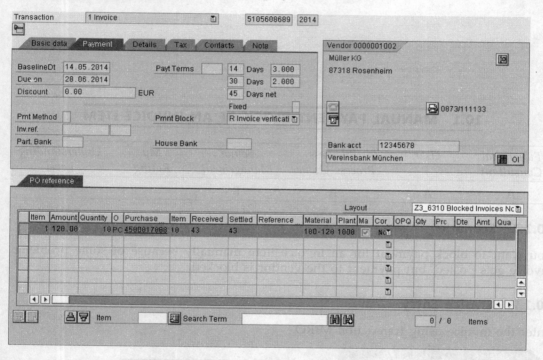

Note that the payment is blocked in the [Ma] field at the item level resulting in payment
block at the header level Pmnt Block [R Invoice verificati ▤].

10.1.4 Accounting Entries

Click Follow-On Documents ... . The system displays the list of accounting documents. Double-click the Accounting document to see the accounting entries.

Data Entry View							
Document Number	5100000045	Company Code	1000	Fiscal Year		2014	
Document Date	14.05.2014	Posting Date	14.05.2014	Period		5	
Reference		Cross-CC no.					
Currency	EUR	Texts exist	☐	Ledger Group			

CoCd	Item	PK	G/L Account	Account	Description	Amount	Curr.	Payment Block
1000	1	31	160000	1002	Müller KG	120.00-	EUR	R
	2	86	191100	191100	Goods Rcvd/Invoice R	120.00	EUR	

Note that the vendor is credited, but payment is blocked. Payment block indicator R indicates that the payment is blocked by invoice verification.

10.2 MANUAL PAYMENT BLOCK OF AN INVOICE

Functional Consultant	User	Business Process Owner	Senior Management	My Rating	Understanding Level
A	A	A	B		

10.2.1 Scenario

You want to block payment of an invoice for a specific reason, e.g. clearance from end users. You can define your own payment block keys and use them for blocking payment manually.

10.2.2 Payment Block Keys

SAP has predefined payment block keys in view V_008. You should not delete them because they are used by various processes of SAP. However, you can define your own keys so that you can assign them manually.

Payment block	Description
	Free for payment
*	Skip account
A	Blocked for payment
B	Blocked for payment
N	IP postprocessing
P	Payment request
R	Invoice verification
V	Payment clearing
Z	Clear. reqd end user

Payment block key Z   Clear. reqd end user   has been added to meet customer requirement.

10.2.3 Invoice Entry

Enter the invoice using transaction MIRO.

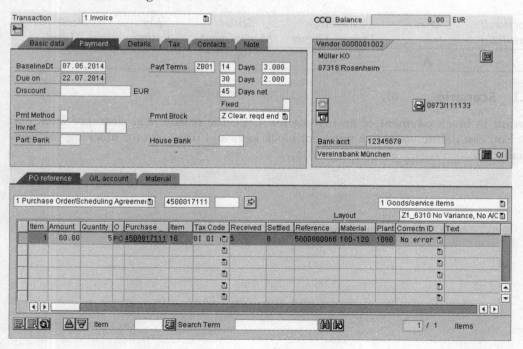

Block the payment using Pmnt Block   Z Clear. reqd end 📋. Post the invoice.

10.2.4 Invoice Display

Display the invoice using transaction MIR4. Enter the Invoice Document No. and the Fiscal Year.
Click 👓 Display Document. The system displays the invoice.

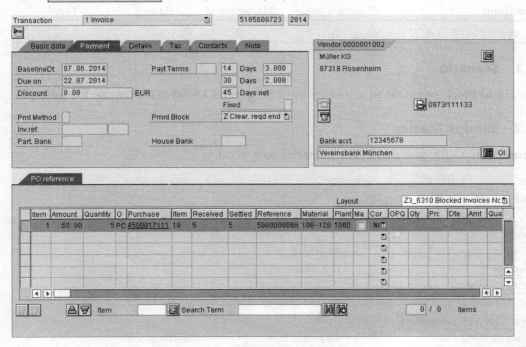

Note that there is a payment block at header level, but no payment block at item level.

10.2.5 Accounting Entries

Click Follow-On Documents ... . The system displays the list of accounting documents. Double-click the Accounting document to see the accounting entries.

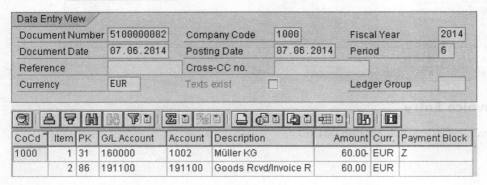

Note that the payment block indicator Z was manually assigned.

10.3   MANUAL PAYMENT BLOCK OF A VENDOR

Functional Consultant	User	Business Process Owner	Senior Management	My Rating	Understanding Level
A	A	A	B		

10.3.1   Scenario

You want to block payment to a vendor until he gets ISO 9000 certification, for example.

10.3.2   Vendor Master

In transaction XK02, you can block payment to a vendor.

Vendor	1002	Müller KG	Rosenheim
Company Code	1000	IDES AG	

Payment data

Payt Terms	ZB01	Tolerance group	1000
Cr memo terms		Chk double inv.	☑
Chk cashng time			

Automatic payment transactions

Payment methods	SU	Payment block	A	Blocked for payment
Alternat.payee		House Bank		
Individual pmnt	☐	Grouping key		
B/exch.limit		EUR		
Pmt adv. by EDI	☐	Alt.payee(doc.)	☐	Permitted Payee

Invoice verification

Tolerance group	515
Prepayment	

Set Payment block   A   Blocked for payment .

10.3.3   Invoice Entry

Enter the invoice using transaction MIRO.

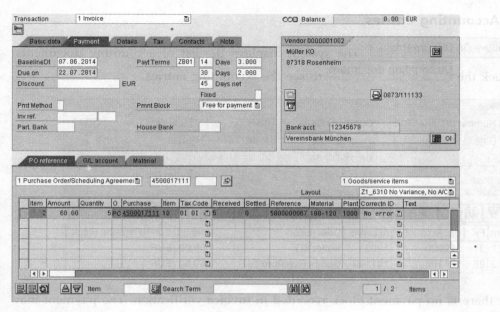

Post the invoice.

10.3.4 Invoice Display

Display the invoice using transaction MIR4. Enter the Invoice Document No. and the Fiscal Year. Click 𝒢 Display Document. The system displays the invoice.

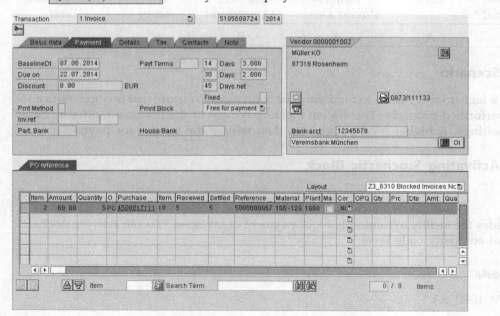

Note that there is no payment block either at header level or at item level.

10.3.5 Accounting Entries

Click Follow-On Documents ... . The system displays the list of accounting documents. Double-click the Accounting document to see the accounting entries.

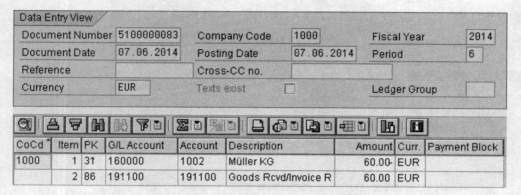

Note that there is no payment block recorded in invoice verification. The payment may be blocked during payment run.

10.4 RANDOM SELECTION

Functional Consultant	User	Business Process Owner	Senior Management	My Rating	Understanding Level
A	A	A	B		

10.4.1 Scenario

You want a higher level person to randomly check invoices to ensure that invoice verification is being performed properly. The system blocks payment of the invoices randomly based on your settings. A higher level person can then release the invoice for payment.

10.4.2 Activating Stochastic Block

Purpose

SAP provides the facility to randomly block payment of invoices. You can activate stochastic blocking at company code level.

IMG Node

SM30 ➤ V_169P_SA

Screen

CoCd	Company Name	Stochastic block
1000	IDES AG	☑
2000	IDES UK	☐
2200	IDES France	☐
2201	IDES France affiliate	☐

10.4.3 Setting Probability of Stochastic Block

Purpose

You can set the probability of stochastic block for a company code. If the stochastic block is active and you post an invoice that is not subject to any other blocking reason, it can be randomly selected for blocking of payment. A stochastic block is not set at item level, but for the whole invoice. If a stochastic block is set when you post the invoice, the system automatically sets Pmnt Block R Invoice verificati in the Payment tab of the invoice header. There is no blocking indicator in the individual items.

IMG Node

SM30 ➤ V_169P_S

Screen

CoCd	Company Name	Threshold value	Currency	Percentage
1000	IDES AG	4,000.00	EUR	50.00
2000	IDES UK		GBP	
2200	IDES France		EUR	
2201	IDES France affiliate		EUR	

Probability of Stochastic Block

Probability of an invoice getting stochastically blocked depends on its value and is computed as Invoice value / Threshold value × Percentage .

Company code	Invoice value in Euros	Probability of stochastic block	Percentage
1000	5000	50	Full percentage
1000	4000	50	Full percentage
1000	3000	37.5	Reduced percentage
1000	2000	25	Reduced percentage
1000	1000	12.5	Reduced percentage

10.4.4 Invoice Entry

Enter the invoice using transaction MIRO.

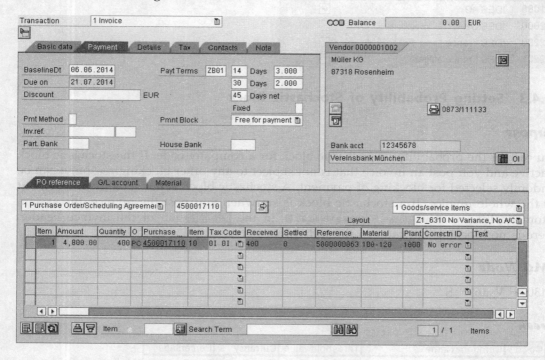

Note the Pmnt Block   Free for payment 🗓. Post the invoice.

10.4.5 Invoice Display

Display the invoice using transaction MIR4. Enter the Invoice Document No. and the Fiscal Year.
Click 👓 Display Document. The system displays the invoice.

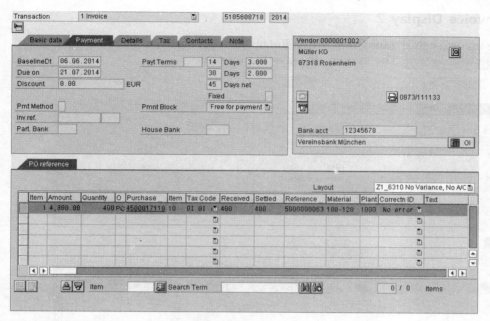

Note that the invoice was not blocked.

10.4.6 Invoice Entry 2

Enter the invoice using transaction MIRO.

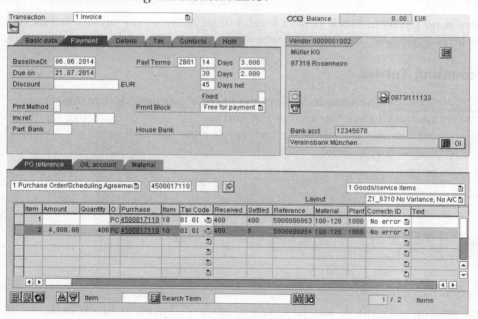

Note the Pmnt Block   Free for payment 📋. Post the invoice.

10.4.7 Invoice Display 2

Display the invoice using transaction MIR4. Enter the Invoice Document No. and the Fiscal Year .
Click 👓 Display Document . The system displays the invoice.

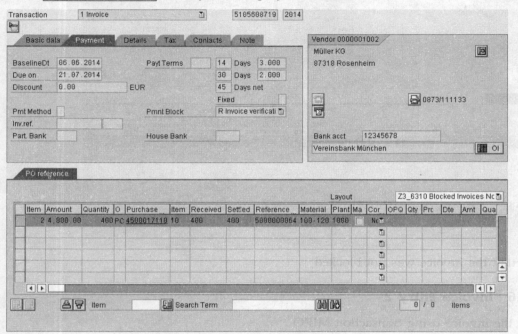

Note that there is no payment block at item level, but payment of the invoice is blocked
at the header level Pmnt Block   R Invoice verificati 🗐 .

10.4.8 Accounting Entries

Click Follow-On Documents ... . The system displays the list of accounting documents. Double-
click the Accounting document to see the accounting entries.

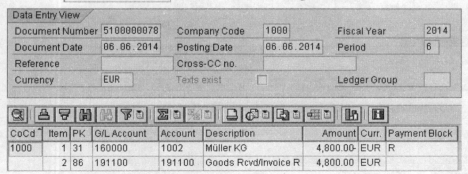

CoCd	Item	PK	G/L Account	Account	Description	Amount	Curr.	Payment Block
1000	1	31	160000	1002	Müller KG	4,800.00-	EUR	R
	2	86	191100	191100	Goods Rcvd/Invoice R	4,800.00	EUR	

Note that the vendor is credited, but payment is blocked. Payment block indicator R
indicates that the payment is blocked by invoice verification.

10.5 HIGH VALUE ITEM

Functional Consultant	User	Business Process Owner	Senior Management	My Rating	Understanding Level
A	A	A	B		

10.5.1 Scenario

You want payment of invoice items above certain value to be blocked. A higher level person can then release the invoice for payment.

10.5.2 Item Amount Check

Overview

Item amount check is configured as under.

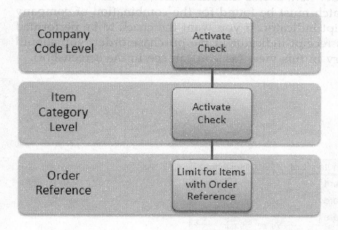

Activating Item Amount Check at Company Code Level

Purpose

SAP can automatically block payment of an invoice item that exceeds a specified value limit during invoice posting. You can activate item amount check at company code level.

IMG node

SM30 ➤ V_169P_PA

Screen

CoCd	Company Name	Check item amount
1000	IDES AG	☑
2000	IDES UK	☐
2200	IDES France	☐
2201	IDES France affiliate	☐

Activating Item Amount Check at Item Category Level

Purpose

If the item amount check is activated for a company code, you can restrict it to only certain item categories. If an item category exists in this view, the check is on; if it does not, the check is off. You can further restrict the check based on the goods receipt indicator specified in the `Delivery` tab of a purchase order item. For a purchase order item, the goods receipt indicator may be ☑ Goods Receipt or ☐ Goods Receipt. The value of the goods receipt indicator for the purchase order item is also matched when this view is searched. For the check to be performed, a match must be found for the combination of company code, item category, and goods receipt indicator. If you want the check to be performed regardless of the value of the goods receipt indicator in the purchase order, you should have two lines for each item category in this view (as you can see in the screenshot).

IMG node

SM30 ➢ V_169D

Screen

CoCd	Company Name	I	Text for Item Cat.	Goods Receipt
1000	IDES AG		Standard	☐
1000	IDES AG		Standard	☑
2700	IDES Schweiz		Standard	☐
2700	IDES Schweiz		Standard	☑

Amount Check for Items with Order Reference

Purpose

Here you can specify the amount above which invoice items with order reference are blocked automatically.

IMG node

SM30 ➢ V_169G, Tolerance key AP

Screen

Tolerance key	AP	Amount for item with order reference
Company Code	1000	IDES AG
Amounts in	EUR	Euro (EMU currency as of 01/01/1999)

Upper limit

  Absolute

    ○ Do not check

    ◉ Check limit

      Val.   5000

10.5.3   Invoice Entry

Enter the invoice using transaction MIRO.

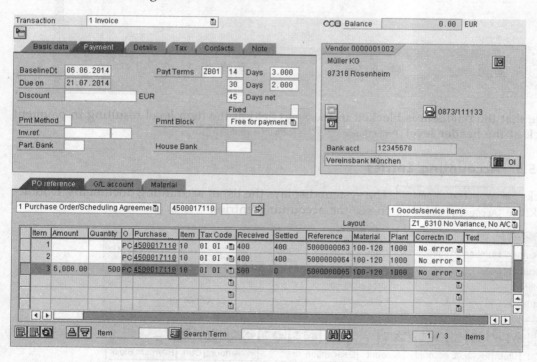

Note the Pmnt Block   Free for payment 🗒 . Post the invoice.

10.5.4   Invoice Display

Display the invoice using transaction MIR4. Enter the Invoice Document No. and the Fiscal Year.
Click   Display Document . The system displays the invoice.

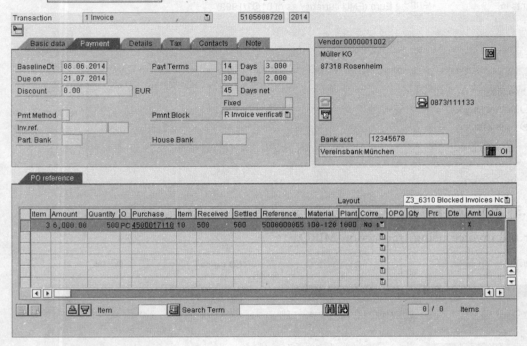

Note that the payment is blocked in the Amt field at the item level resulting in payment
block at the header level Pmnt Block   R Invoice verificati .

10.5.5   Accounting Entries

Click Follow-On Documents ... . The system displays the list of accounting documents. Double-
click the Accounting document to see the accounting entries.

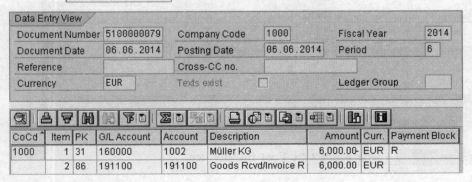

Note that the vendor is credited, but payment is blocked. Payment block indicator R
indicates that the payment is blocked by invoice verification.

10.6 HIGH VALUE ITEM WITHOUT ORDER REFERENCE

Functional Consultant	User	Business Process Owner	Senior Management	My Rating	Understanding Level
A	B	C		C	

10.6.1 Scenario

SAP also lets you post invoices that do not refer to a purchase order or a delivery. However, you may want their payment to be blocked, if the invoice item is above the value you specify. The payment is then released by a senior person having the necessary authorization.

10.6.2 Activation

There are three tabs for entering invoice line items: 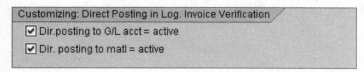. Invoice line items are entered primarily in the PO reference tab during invoice entry. The other two tabs G/L account and Material are for direct posting. Some companies do not want to use the feature of direct posting. Therefore, SAP lets you activate, or deactivate, direct posting to G/L account and direct posting to Material in view TCULIV.

> Customizing: Direct Posting in Log. Invoice Verification
> ☑ Dir.posting to G/L acct = active
> ☑ Dir. posting to matl = active

If direct posting to G/L account or direct posting to Material is not active, the corresponding tab does not appear in the invoice entry screen.

10.6.3 Item Amount Check

Overview

Item amount check is configured as under.

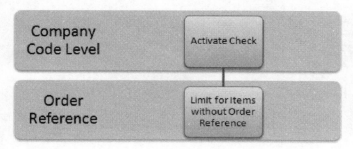

Activating Item Amount Check at Company Code Level

Purpose

SAP can automatically block payment of an invoice item that exceeds a specified value limit during invoice posting. You can activate item amount check at company code level.

IMG node

SM30 ≻ V_169P_PA

Screen

CoCd	Company Name	Check item amount
1000	IDES AG	☑
2000	IDES UK	☐
2200	IDES France	☐
2201	IDES France affiliate	☐

Amount Check for Items without Order Reference

Purpose

Here you can specify the amount above which invoice items without order reference are blocked automatically.

IMG node

SM30 ≻ V_169G, Tolerance key AN

Screen

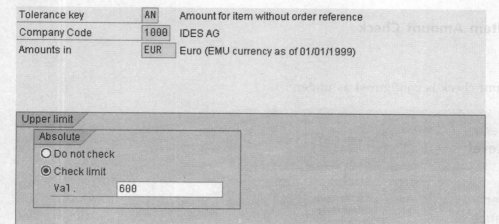

Tolerance key	AN	Amount for item without order reference
Company Code	1000	IDES AG
Amounts in	EUR	Euro (EMU currency as of 01/01/1999)

Upper limit

Absolute

○ Do not check

◉ Check limit

Val. 600

10.6.4 Invoice Entry

Enter the invoice using transaction MIRO.

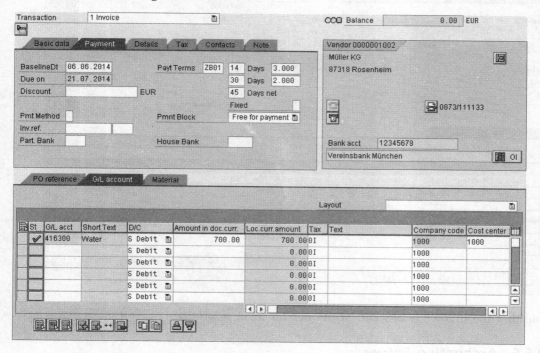

Note the Pmnt Block   Free for payment 🖫. Post the invoice.

10.6.5 Invoice Display

Display the invoice using transaction MIR4. Enter the Invoice Document No. and the Fiscal Year. Click 𝒢 Display Document. The system displays the invoice.

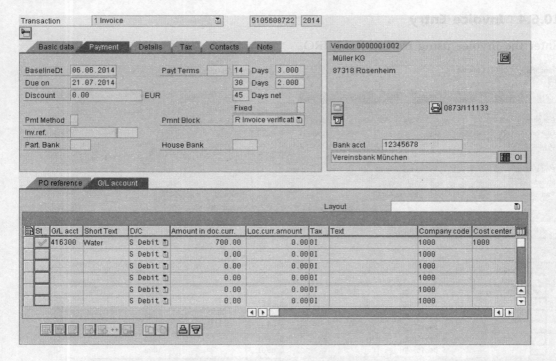

Note that the invoice is blocked at the header level Pmnt Block   R Invoice verificati ☑.

10.6.6 Accounting Entries

Click Follow-On Documents ... . The system displays the list of accounting documents. Double-click the Accounting document to see the accounting entries.

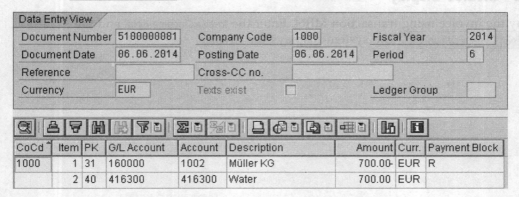

Note that the vendor is credited, but payment is blocked. Payment block indicator R indicates that the payment is blocked by invoice verification.

10.7   PRICE VARIANCE

Functional Consultant	User	Business Process Owner	Senior Management	My Rating	Understanding Level
A	A	A	B		

10.7.1   Scenario

If the price per unit quantity in the invoice is different from the price in the purchase order, you want the invoice item to be blocked.

10.7.2   Tolerance for Price Variance

In view V_169G, tolerance key PP, you can set up tolerance for price variance.

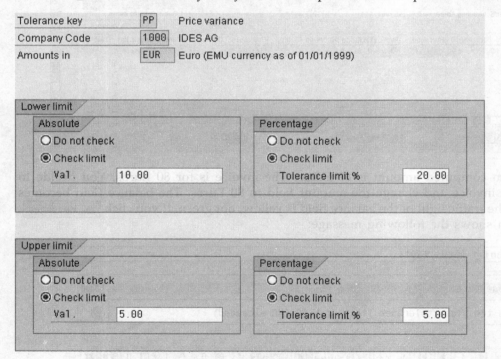

You can switch off the check, set zero tolerance for variation, or allow specified tolerance. In the case of absolute value check, the total material cost (of this and previous invoices) cannot exceed the material cost of supplied quantity by the specified amount.

10.7.3 Invoice Entry

Enter the invoice using transaction MIRO.

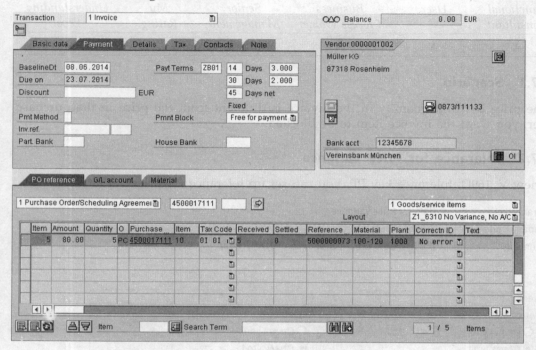

The system computed amount is 60 Euros. The invoice is for 80 Euros. You decide to accept the invoice and change the amount field to 80 Euros. The balance field becomes zero, but the traffic light of the balance field is yellow, not green. If you click △ Messages , the system shows the following message:

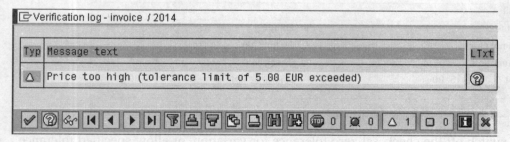

Post the invoice.

10.7.4 Invoice Display

Display the invoice using transaction MIR4. Enter the Invoice Document No. and the Fiscal Year . Click &v Display Document . The system displays the invoice.

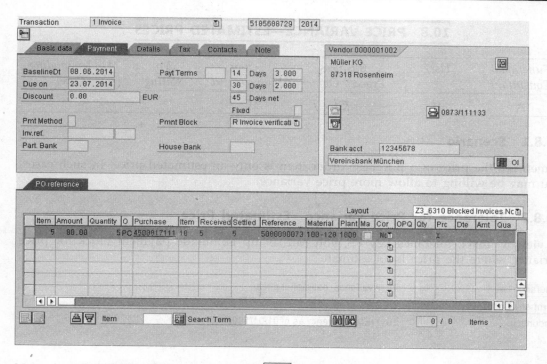

Note that the payment is blocked in the Prc field at the item level resulting in payment block at the header level Pmnt Block R Invoice verificati.

10.7.5 Accounting Entries

Click Follow-On Documents ... . The system displays the list of accounting documents. Double-click the Accounting document to see the accounting entries.

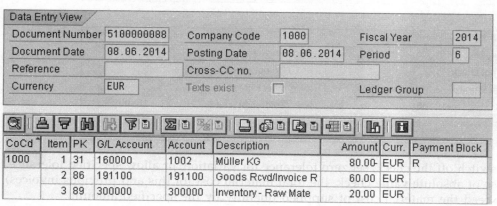

Note that the payment is blocked automatically. The price difference is charged to the stock account.

10.8 PRICE VARIANCE—ESTIMATED PRICES

Functional Consultant	User	Business Process Owner	Senior Management	My Rating	Understanding Level
A	B	C	C		

10.8.1 Scenario

Sometimes the price of a purchase order item is only an estimated price. In such cases, you may be willing to allow more price variance.

10.8.2 Tolerance for Price Variance—Estimated Price

In view V_169G, tolerance key PS, you can set up automatic payment block for price variance where the price is an estimate.

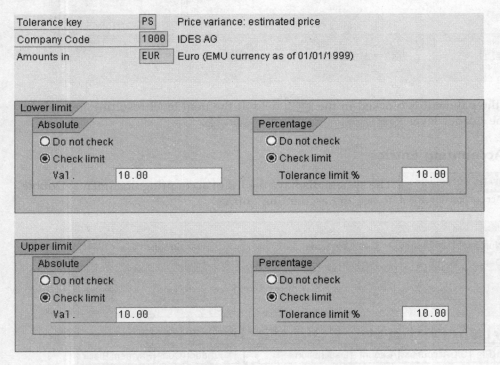

You can switch off the check, set zero tolerance for variation, or allow specified tolerance. In the case of absolute value check, the total material cost (of this and previous invoices) cannot exceed the material cost of supplied quantity by the specified amount.

10.8.3 Purchase Order

In the purchase order, you specify that the item has an estimated price.

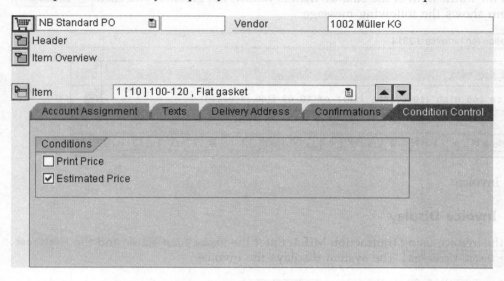

10.8.4 Invoice Entry

After goods receipt, enter the invoice using transaction MIRO.

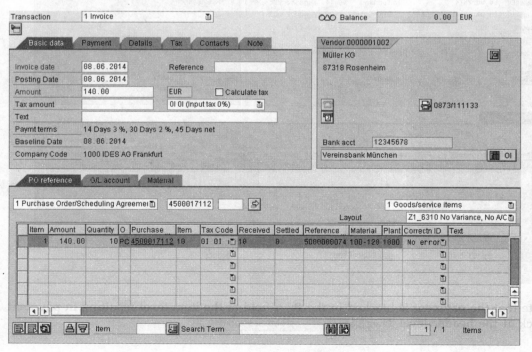

The system computed amount is 120 Euros. The invoice is for 140 Euros. You decide to accept the invoice and change the amount field to 140 Euros. The balance field becomes zero, but the traffic light of the balance field is yellow, not green. If you click △ Messages , the system shows the following message:

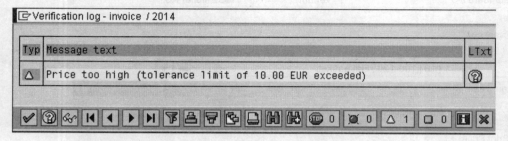

Post the invoice.

10.8.5 Invoice Display

Display the invoice using transaction MIR4. Enter the Invoice Document No. and the Fiscal Year . Click Display Document . The system displays the invoice.

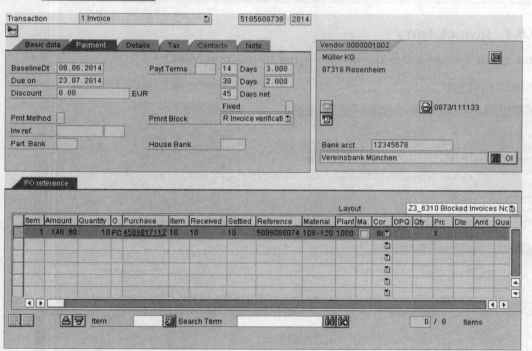

Note that the payment is blocked in the Prc field at the item level resulting in payment block at the header level Pmnt Block R Invoice verificati .

10.8.6 Accounting Entries

Click Follow-On Documents ... . The system displays the list of accounting documents. Double-click the Accounting document to see the accounting entries.

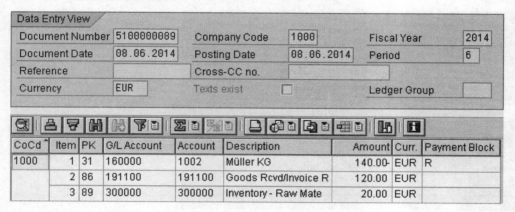

Note that the payment is blocked automatically. The price difference is charged to the stock account.

10.9 DELIVERY COST VARIANCE

Functional Consultant	User	Business Process Owner	Senior Management	My Rating	Understanding Level
A	B	C	C		

10.9.1 Scenario

You receive an invoice where the delivery cost is more than the planned delivery cost. You manually accept the delivery cost, but want the payment to be blocked, so that a senior person can review and endorse your decision.

10.9.2 Tolerance for Delivery Cost Variance

In view V_169G, tolerance key KW, you can set up automatic payment block for variance in delivery cost.

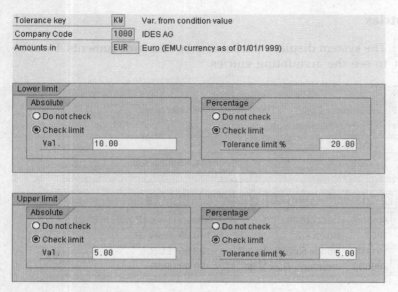

You can switch off the check, set zero tolerance for variation, or allow specified tolerance. In the case of absolute value check, the total delivery cost (of this and previous invoices) cannot exceed the planned delivery cost of supplied quantity by the specified amount.

10.9.3 Invoice Entry

Enter the invoice using transaction MIRO.

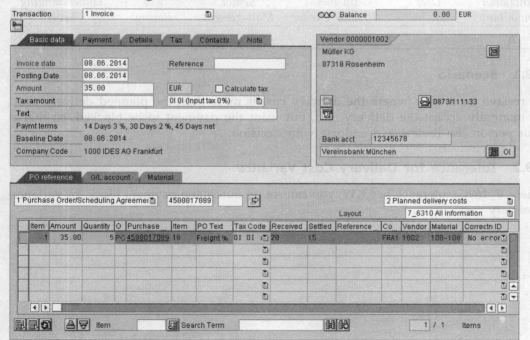

Note that only delivery cost is being settled, not the material cost. As per the purchase order, the delivery cost should have been 25 Euro. The invoice is for 35 Euro. The amount field is changed to indicate acceptance of the invoice value. The balance field becomes zero, but the traffic light of the balance field is yellow, not green. If you click △ Messages , the system shows the following message:

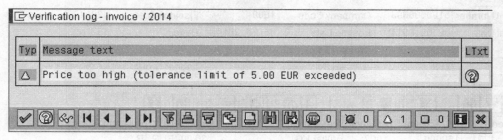

Post the invoice.

10.9.4 Invoice Display

Display the invoice using transaction MIR4. Enter the Invoice Document No. and the Fiscal Year . Click ⟨⟨⟩ Display Document . The system displays the invoice.

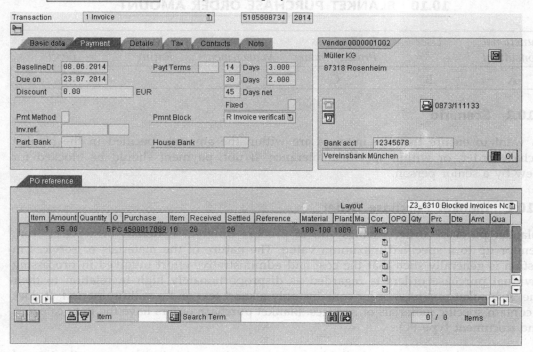

Note that the payment is blocked in the Prc field at the item level resulting in payment block at the header level Pmnt Block   R Invoice verificati ⬚ .

10.9.5 Accounting Entries

Click Follow-On Documents ... . The system displays the list of accounting documents. Double-click the Accounting document to see the accounting entries.

Data Entry View						
Document Number	5100000093	Company Code	1000	Fiscal Year		2014
Document Date	08.06.2014	Posting Date	08.06.2014	Period		6
Reference		Cross-CC no.				
Currency	EUR	Texts exist	☐	Ledger Group		

CoCd	Item	PK	G/L Account	Account	Description	Amount	Curr.	Payment Block
1000	1	31	160000	1002	Müller KG	35.00-	EUR	R
	2	40	192100	192100	Freight Clearing Acc	25.00	EUR	
	3	83	281500	281500	Income from price di	10.00	EUR	

Note that the payment is blocked.

10.10 BLANKET PURCHASE ORDER AMOUNT

Functional Consultant	User	Business Process Owner	Senior Management	My Rating	Understanding Level
A	B	C	C		

10.10.1 Scenario

You want to ensure that the invoices are within the amount specified in the blanket purchase order, or within specified tolerance. If not, payment should be blocked for review by a senior person.

10.10.2 Blanket Purchase Order

A blanket purchase order enables you to procure different materials or services from a vendor up to a specified maximum value. The nature of the materials or services in question is generally such that the cost and administrative effort involved in processing individual purchase orders is regarded as disproportionately high in relation to their value. A blanket purchase order contains only a short text and a validity period. It does not contain specific materials or services. Blanket purchase orders have the item category B and document type FO.

The account assignment of the individual requirements need not be known at the time of ordering. It can be entered during the invoice verification process. If account assignment data was maintained in the purchase order, it can be changed at the time of invoice verification (for example, single account assignment can be changed to multiple account assignment).

Neither a goods receipt nor the entry and acceptance of services performed are necessary with regard to blanket purchase orders. Instead, invoices can be posted directly with reference to the PO provided that the value limit is not exceeded.

10.10.3 Amount Check for Blanket Purchase Order

In view V_169G, tolerance key LA, you can specify that the system ensure that invoices for blanket purchase order are within specified value.

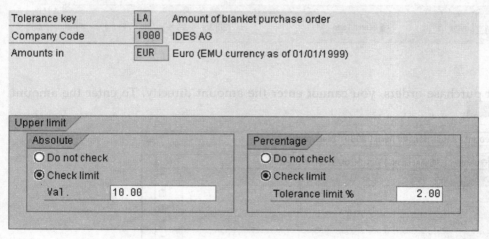

You can switch off the check, set zero tolerance for variation, or allow specified tolerance in absolute value and percentage. If the tolerance is exceeded, payment for the invoice item is blocked.

10.10.4 Invoice Entry

Enter the invoice using transaction MIRO.

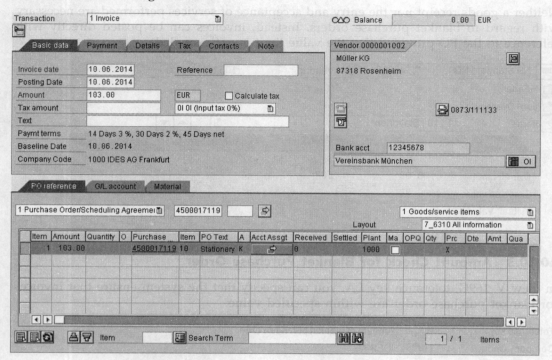

Amount

For blanket purchase orders, you cannot enter the amount directly. To enter the amount click [➡].

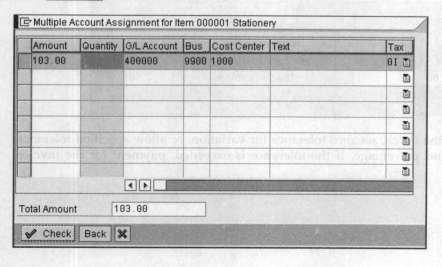

Enter the amount. If the amount is outside the tolerance, the system gives the following message:

Post the invoice.

10.10.5 Invoice Display

Display the invoice using transaction MIR4. Enter the Invoice Document No. and the Fiscal Year. Click ⟨⟨ Display Document ⟩. The system displays the invoice.

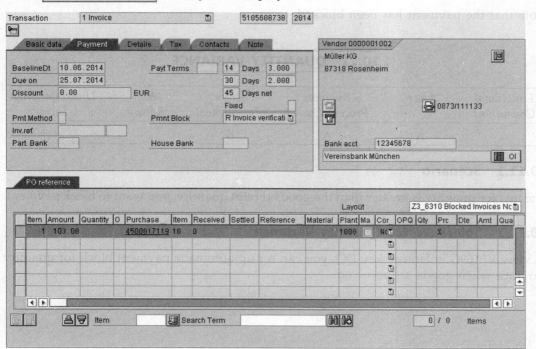

Note that the payment is blocked in the Prc field at the item level resulting in payment block at the header level Pmnt Block   R Invoice verificati ⬚.

10.10.6 Accounting Entries

Click | Follow-On Documents ... |. The system displays the list of accounting documents. Double-click the | Accounting document | to see the accounting entries.

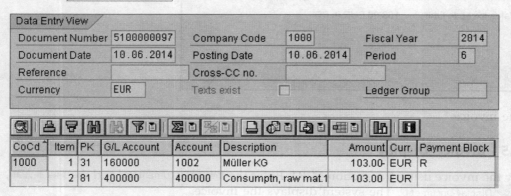

Note that the payment has been blocked.

10.11 QUANTITY VARIANCE

Functional Consultant	User	Business Process Owner	Senior Management	My Rating	Understanding Level
A	A	A	B		

10.11.1 Scenario

The invoice quantity is greater than the goods receipt quantity; you want to block payment.

10.11.2 Tolerance for Quantity Variance

In view V_169G, tolerance key DQ, you can set up automatic payment block for quantity variance when goods are received.

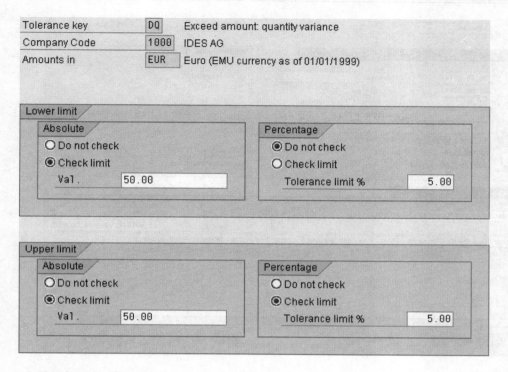

Percentage limits

You can specify zero tolerance, or you may specify a percentage of quantity that is allowed.

Absolute limits

You can also specify a tolerance on absolute value. If the invoice value exceeds the goods receipt value by this amount, payment is blocked.

Lower and upper limits

You can set the tolerance both on the upper side as well as on the lower side. You should be careful about setting tolerance on the lower side because it will block payment of partial invoices.

10.11.3 Invoice Entry

Enter the invoice using transaction MIRO.

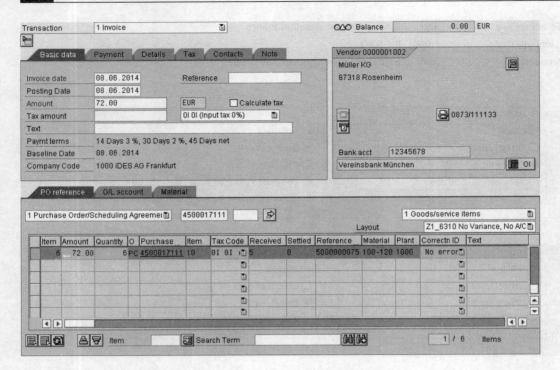

The system defaulted the goods receipt quantity 5 and value 60 Euros. The invoice is for quantity 6 and value 72 Euros. You decide to accept the invoice and change the amount and quantity fields in line with the invoice. The balance field becomes zero, but the traffic light of the balance field is yellow, not green. If you click △ Messages , the system shows the following message:

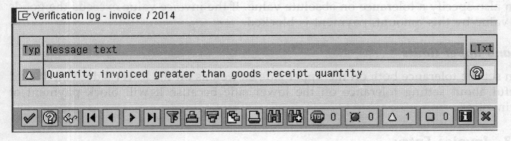

Post the invoice.

10.11.4   Invoice Display

Display the invoice using transaction MIR4. Enter the Invoice Document No. and the Fiscal Year . Click Display Document . The system displays the invoice.

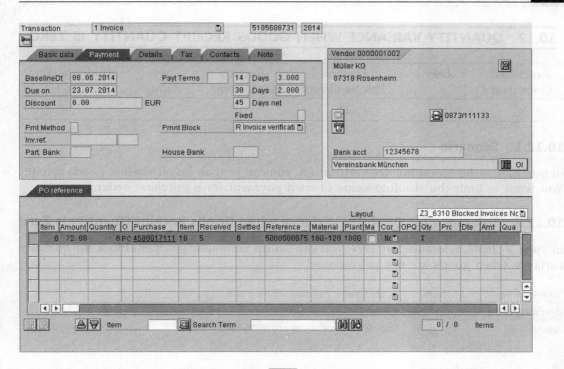

Note that the payment is blocked in the Qty field at the item level resulting in payment block at the header level Pmnt Block   R Invoice verificati 📋 .

10.11.5 Accounting Entries

Click Follow-On Documents ... . The system displays the list of accounting documents. Double-click the Accounting document to see the accounting entries.

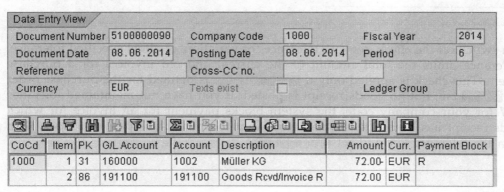

Note that the payment is blocked automatically. The difference is charged to the GR/IR account because more goods are expected to be received.

10.12 QUANTITY VARIANCE WHEN GOODS RECEIPT QUANTITY IS ZERO

Functional Consultant	User	Business Process Owner	Senior Management	My Rating	Understanding Level
A	B	C	C		

10.12.1 Scenario

In purchase order based invoice verification, you can post an invoice before goods receipt. You want to limit the absolute value of such payment for a purchase order item.

10.12.2 Tolerance for Quantity Variance when Goods Receipt Quantity is Zero

In view V_169G, tolerance key DW, you can set up automatic payment block for quantity variance when goods are not yet received.

Tolerance key	DW	Quantity variance when GR qty = zero
Company Code	1000	IDES AG
Amounts in	EUR	Euro (EMU currency as of 01/01/1999)

Upper limit
Absolute
○ Do not check
◉ Check limit
Val.   100.00

You can switch off the check, set zero tolerance for variation, or allow specified tolerance. This tolerance limits the total amount of the current and old invoices for a purchase order item. This check is applied only if ☑ Goods Receipt is defined for the purchase order item in Delivery tab, but no goods receipt is posted. If you have not maintained tolerance key DW for your company code, the system blocks payment for an invoice for which no goods receipt has been posted yet. If you want to prevent this payment block, then maintain the tolerance key and set ◉ Do not check.

10.12.3 Invoice Entry

Enter the invoice using transaction MIRO.

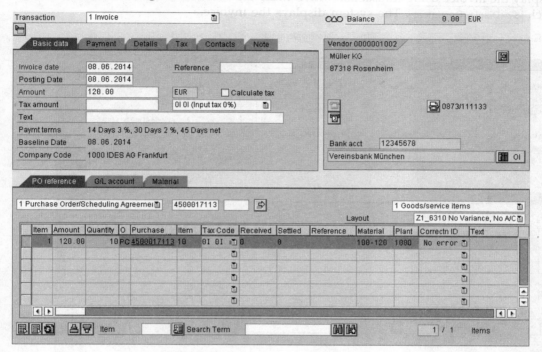

Since there is no goods receipt, the system did not propose the amount and the quantity. They were entered as per the invoice. The balance field becomes zero, but the traffic light of the balance field is yellow, not green. If you click ◁ Messages , the system shows the following message:

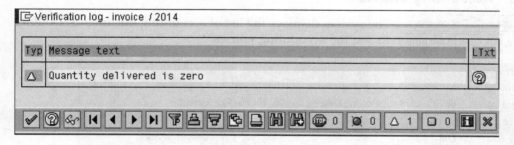

Post the invoice.

10.12.4 Invoice Display

Display the invoice using transaction MIR4. Enter the Invoice Document No. and the Fiscal Year.
Click ✏ Display Document. The system displays the invoice.

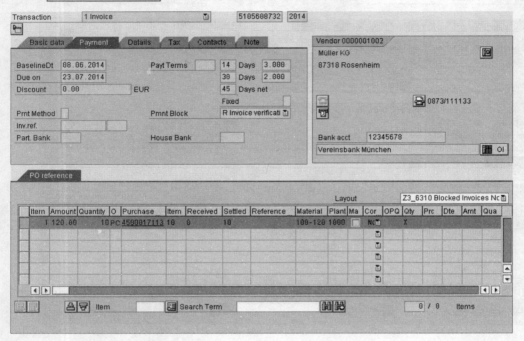

Note that the payment is blocked in the Qty field at the item level resulting in payment
block at the header level Pmnt Block R Invoice verificati ▣.

10.12.5 Accounting Entries

Click Follow-On Documents ... . The system displays the list of accounting documents. Double-
click the Accounting document to see the accounting entries.

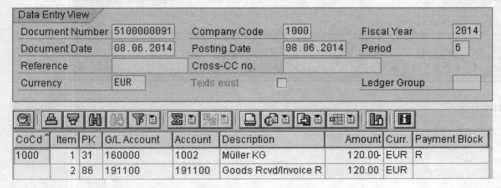

Note that the payment is blocked automatically.

10.13 ORDER PRICE QUANTITY VARIANCE

Functional Consultant	User	Business Process Owner	Senior Management	My Rating	Understanding Level
A	B	C	C		

10.13.1 Scenario

Sometimes order unit may be different from order price unit. For example, you may order 10 steel bars of 100-mm diameter and 1-me length (order unit pcs), but the payment will be on the basis of weight in kg (order price unit kg). In such cases, the following information is recorded:

Document	Quantity in order price unit	Quantity in order unit	Ratio of quantity in order price quantity to quantity in order unit
Purchase order	kg	Pcs	kg/Pc
Goods receipt	kg	Pcs	kg/Pc
Invoice receipt	kg	Pcs	kg/Pc

Ideally the ratios at the time of goods receipt and invoice receipt should be the same. If they are different, the variance is compared with the lower and upper limits, and if it is outside any limit, the invoice item is blocked for payment.

10.13.2 Materials Master

Descriptions	Units of measure	Additional EANs	Document data	Basic data

Material | 1157 | 170DS55001C-184M

Units of measure grp

Units of measure/EANs/dimensions

X	AUn	Measur	<=>	Y	BUn	Measur	EAN/UPC	Ct	Au	A	Length	Width	Height
1	EA	Each	<=>	1	EA	Each							
500	KG	Kilogram	<=>	1	EA	Each							

10.13.3 Purchase Order

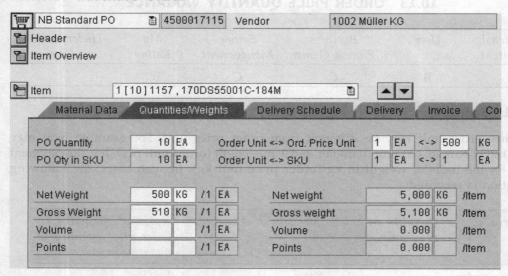

10.13.4 Goods Receipt

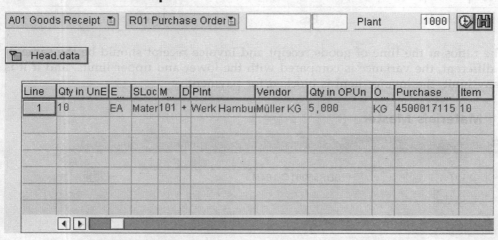

10.13.5   Tolerance for Order Price Unit Variance

In view V_169G, tolerance key BW, you specify the tolerance.

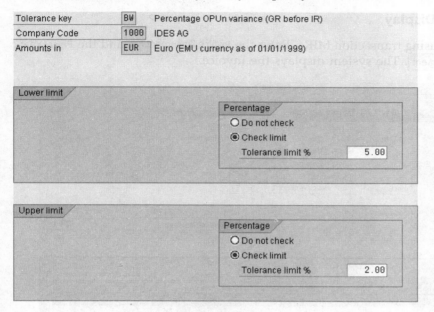

10.13.6   Invoice Entry

Enter the invoice using transaction MIRO.

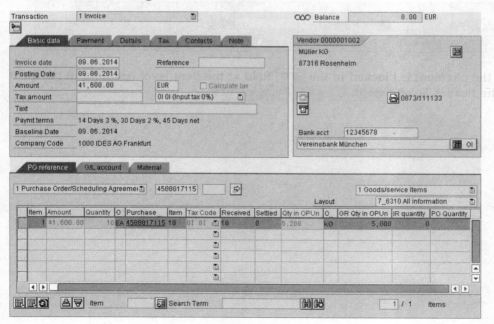

When you change the $\boxed{\text{Qty in OPUn}}$, the system gives message: $\boxed{① \text{ Order price quantity exceeded by more than 2.00 \%}}$. Post the invoice.

10.13.7   Invoice Display

Display the invoice using transaction MIR4. Enter the Invoice Document No. and the Fiscal Year . Click $\boxed{\text{&}\text{ Display Document}}$. The system displays the invoice.

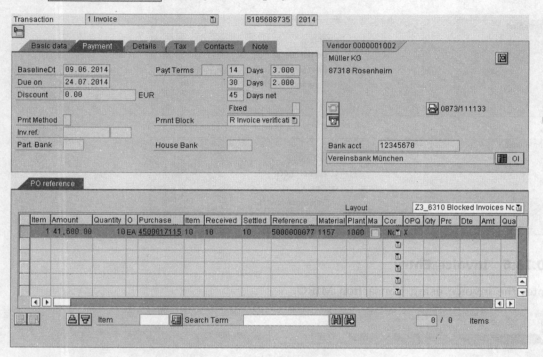

Note that the payment is blocked in the $\boxed{\text{OPQ}}$ field at the item level resulting in payment block at the header level $\boxed{\text{Pmnt Block}}$ $\boxed{\text{R Invoice verificati} \boxed{\text{▣}}}$.

10.13.8 Accounting Entries

Click | Follow-On Documents ... |. The system displays the list of accounting documents. Double-click the | Accounting document | to see the accounting entries.

Data Entry View					
Document Number	5100000094	Company Code	1000	Fiscal Year	2014
Document Date	09.06.2014	Posting Date	09.06.2014	Period	6
Reference		Cross-CC no.			
Currency	EUR	Texts exist	☐	Ledger Group	

CoCd	Item	PK	G/L Account	Account	Description	Amount	Curr.	Payment Block
1000	1	31	160000	1002	Müller KG	41,600.00-	EUR	R
	2	86	191100	191100	Goods Rcvd/Invoice R	40,000.00	EUR	
	3	89	790000	790000	Unfinished products	1,600.00	EUR	

Note that the invoice is blocked for payment.

10.14 ORDER PRICE QUANTITY VARIANCE (IR BEFORE GR)

Functional Consultant	User	Business Process Owner	Senior Management	My Rating	Understanding Level
A	B	C	C		

10.14.1 Scenario

Sometimes order unit may be different from order price unit. For example, you may order 10 steel bars of 100 mm diameter and 1 m length (order unit pcs), but the payment will be on the basis of weight in kg (order price unit kg). In such cases, the following information is recorded:

Document	Quantity in order price unit	Quantity in order unit	Ratio of quantity in order price quantity to quantity in order unit
Purchase order	kg	Pcs	kg/Pc
Invoice receipt	kg	Pcs	kg/Pc

Ideally the ratios at the time of purchase order and invoice receipt should be the same. If they are different, the variance is compared with the lower and upper limits and if it is outside any limit, the invoice item is blocked for payment.

10.14.2 Materials Master

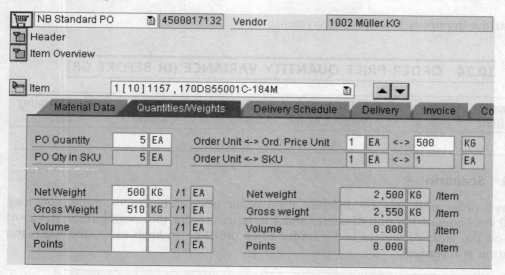

	Descriptions	Units of measure	Additional EANs	Document data	Basic data

Material 1157   170DS55001C-184M

Units of measure grp

Units of measure/EANs/dimensions

X	AUn	Measur	<=>	Y	BUn	Measur	EAN/UPC	Ct	Au	A	Length	Width	Height
1	EA	Each	<=>	1	EA	Each			☐	☐			
500	KG	Kilogram	<=>	1	EA	Each			☐	☐			

10.14.3 Purchase Order

Quantities/weights

NB Standard PO   4500017132   Vendor   1002 Müller KG

Header
Item Overview

Item   1 [10] 1157 , 170DS55001C-184M

	Material Data	Quantities/Weights	Delivery Schedule	Delivery	Invoice	Co

PO Quantity	5 EA	Order Unit <-> Ord. Price Unit	1 EA <-> 500 KG
PO Qty in SKU	5 EA	Order Unit <-> SKU	1 EA <-> 1 EA

Net Weight	500 KG	/1 EA	Net weight	2,500 KG	/Item
Gross Weight	510 KG	/1 EA	Gross weight	2,550 KG	/Item
Volume		/1 EA	Volume	0.000	/Item
Points		/1 EA	Points	0.000	/Item

Invoice

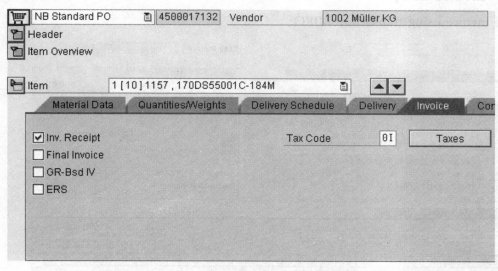

Note that the invoice can be received before goods receipt only for purchase order based invoice verification ☐ GR-Bsd IV.

10.14.4 Tolerance for Order Price Quantity Variance (IR before GR)

In view V_169G, tolerance key BR, you specify the tolerance.

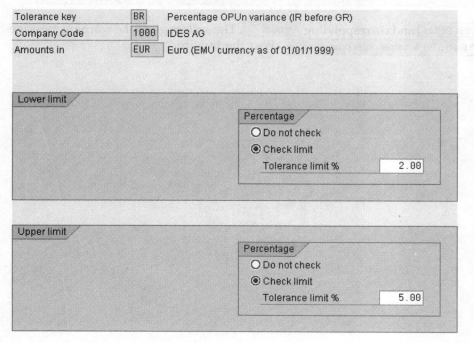

10.14.5 Invoice Entry

Enter the invoice using transaction MIRO.

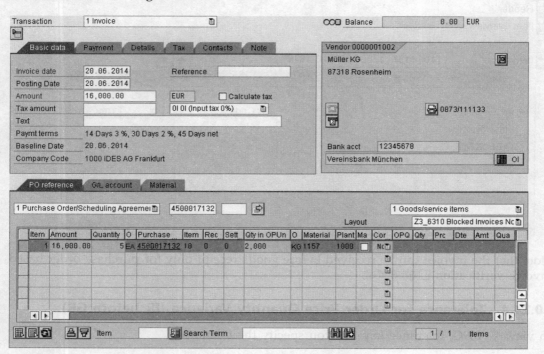

Enter lower Qty in OPUn and corresponding Amount . The system gives the warning message
① Quantity more than 5.00 % below order price quantity . Post the invoice.

10.14.6 Invoice Display

Display the invoice using transaction MIR4. Enter the Invoice Document No. and the Fiscal Year.
Click ⚙ Display Document. The system displays the invoice.

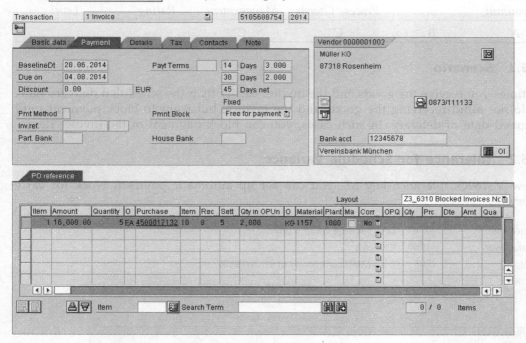

Note that the invoice is not blocked for payment.

10.14.7 Accounting Entries

Click Follow-On Documents .... The system displays the list of accounting documents. Double-
click the Accounting document to see the accounting entries.

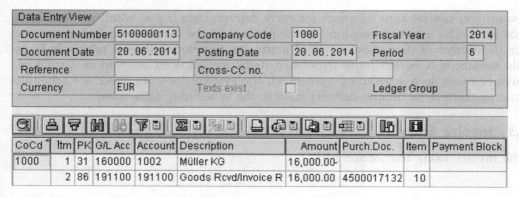

Note that there is no payment block.

10.15 SCHEDULE VARIANCE

Functional Consultant	User	Business Process Owner	Senior Management	My Rating	Understanding Level
A	B	C	C		

10.15.1 Scenario

Sometimes you receive the goods and the invoice earlier than the scheduled delivery date. You do not mind receiving the goods and the invoice, but want to block payment until the agreed date of delivery. In such cases, you can block payment of the invoice item.

10.15.2 Tolerance for Schedule Variance

In view V_169G, tolerance key ST, you can set up automatic payment block for early delivery.

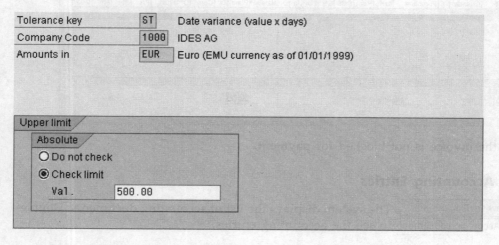

If you want you can set zero tolerance for early delivery; but if you want, you can set a tolerance limit. The quantity you limit is the product of the invoice item value and the variance in number of days. Lower priced items are, therefore, allowed relatively large schedule variances, whereas more expensive items are allowed only small variances. If an invoice refers to a scheduling agreement, the system does not check for schedule variances, as there is no unique delivery date in the scheduling agreement.

10.15.3 Invoice Entry

Enter the invoice using transaction MIRO.

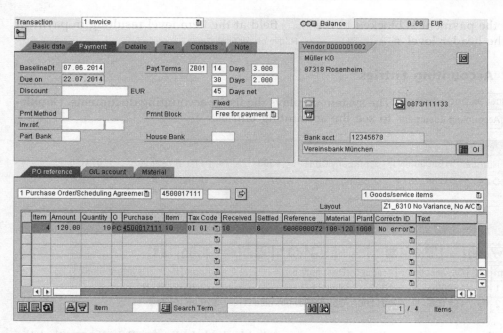

Note the Pmnt Block [Free for payment ▣]. Post the invoice.

10.15.4 Invoice Display

Display the invoice using transaction MIR4. Enter the Invoice Document No. and the Fiscal Year. Click [⚙ Display Document]. The system displays the invoice.

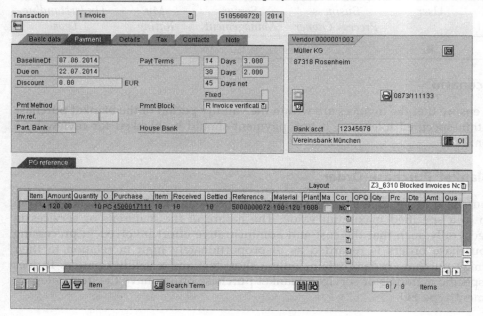

Note that the payment is blocked in the `Dte` field at the item level resulting in payment block at the header level `Pmnt Block` `R Invoice verificati ▣`.

10.15.5 Accounting Entries

Click `Follow-On Documents ...`. The system displays the list of accounting documents. Double-click the `Accounting document` to see the accounting entries.

Data Entry View					
Document Number	5100000087	Company Code	1000	Fiscal Year	2014
Document Date	07.06.2014	Posting Date	07.06.2014	Period	6
Reference		Cross-CC no.			
Currency	EUR	Texts exist	☐	Ledger Group	

CoCd	Item	PK	G/L Account	Account	Description	Amount	Curr.	Payment Block
1000	1	31	160000	1002	Müller KG	120.00-	EUR	R
	2	86	191100	191100	Goods Rcvd/Invoice R	120.00	EUR	

Note that the vendor is credited, but payment is blocked. Indicator R indicates that the payment is blocked by invoice verification.

10.16 BLANKET PURCHASE ORDER VALIDITY PERIOD

Functional Consultant	User	Business Process Owner	Senior Management	My Rating	Understanding Level
A	B	C	C		

10.16.1 Scenario

You want to ensure that the invoices are within the validity period of the blanket purchase order, or within specified tolerance. If not, payment should be blocked for review by a senior person.

10.16.2 Blanket Purchase Order

A blanket purchase order enables you to procure different materials or services from a vendor up to a specified maximum value. The nature of the materials or services in question is generally such that the cost and administrative effort involved in processing individual purchase orders is regarded as disproportionately high in relation to their value. A blanket purchase order contains only a short text and a validity period. It does not contain specific materials or services. Blanket purchase orders have the item category B and document type FO.

The account assignment of the individual requirements need not be known at the time of ordering. It can be entered during the invoice verification process. If account assignment data was maintained in the purchase order, it can be changed at the time of invoice verification (for example, single account assignment can be changed to multiple account assignment).

Neither a goods receipt nor the entry and acceptance of services performed are necessary with regard to blanket purchase orders. Instead, invoices can be posted directly with reference to the PO provided that the value limit is not exceeded.

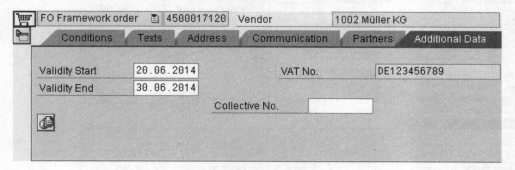

10.16.3   Tolerance for Blanket Purchase Order Validity Period

In view V_169G, tolerance key LD, you can specify that the system ensures that invoices for blanket purchase order are within specified validity period.

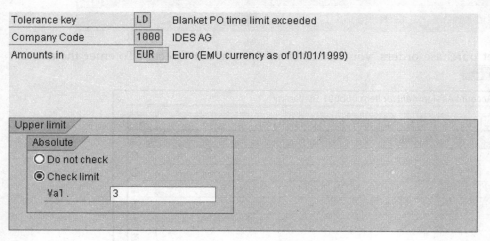

You can switch off the check, set zero tolerance for variation, or allow specified tolerance. The system determines the number of days by which the invoice is outside the planned time interval. If the posting date of the invoice is before the validity period, the system calculates the number of days between the posting date and the start of the validity period. If the posting date of the invoice is after the validity period, the system calculates the number of days between the posting date and the end of the validity period. The system compares the number of days with the absolute upper limit defined. If the variance exceeds the limit, the invoice item is blocked for payment.

10.16.4 Invoice Entry

Enter the invoice using transaction MIRO.

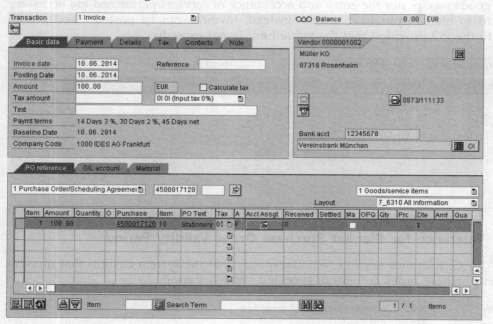

For blanket purchase orders, you cannot enter the amount directly. To enter the amount click [🠖].

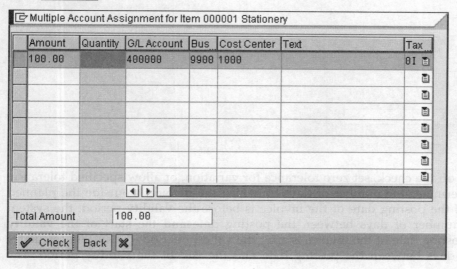

Enter the amount. Click △ Messages.

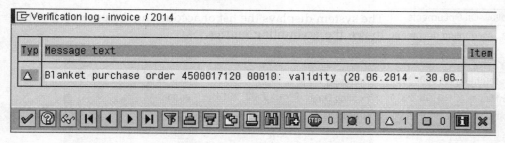

Post the invoice.

10.16.5 Invoice Display

Display the invoice using transaction MIR4. Enter the Invoice Document No. and the Fiscal Year. Click 👓 Display Document. The system displays the invoice.

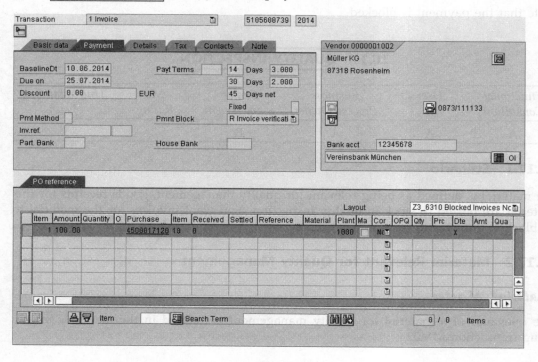

Note that the payment is blocked in the Dte field at the item level resulting in payment block at the header level Pmnt Block R Invoice verificati 🗐.

10.16.6   Accounting Entries

Click `Follow-On Documents ...`. The system displays the list of accounting documents. Double-click the `Accounting document` to see the accounting entries.

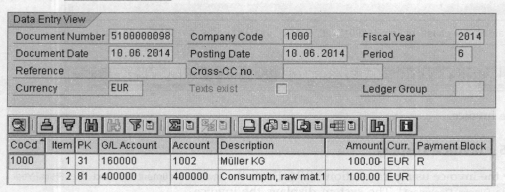

Data Entry View

Document Number	5100000098	Company Code	1000	Fiscal Year	2014
Document Date	10.06.2014	Posting Date	10.06.2014	Period	6
Reference		Cross-CC no.			
Currency	EUR	Texts exist	☐	Ledger Group	

CoCd	Item	PK	G/L Account	Account	Description	Amount	Curr.	Payment Block
1000	1	31	160000	1002	Müller KG	100.00-	EUR	R
	2	81	400000	400000	Consumptn, raw mat.1	100.00	EUR	

Note that the payment is blocked.

10.17   QUALITY INSPECTION

Functional Consultant	User	Business Process Owner	Senior Management	My Rating	Understanding Level
A	A	A	B		

10.17.1   Scenario

If a material is defined as being relevant for quality management, goods receipts for this material are posted to stock in quality inspection. You want invoices for the material to be blocked until the inspection has been successfully completed.

10.17.2   Material Relevant for Quality Management

Material Master

The relevance of a material for quality management is defined in the materials master using transaction MM02.

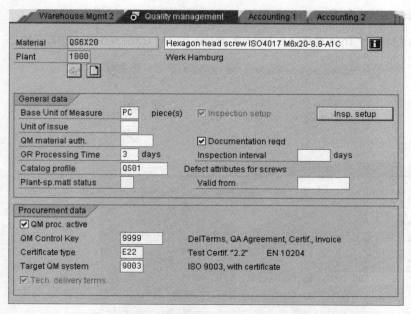

Note the QM Control Key   9999   .

QM Control Keys

QM control keys are defined in view V_TQ08.

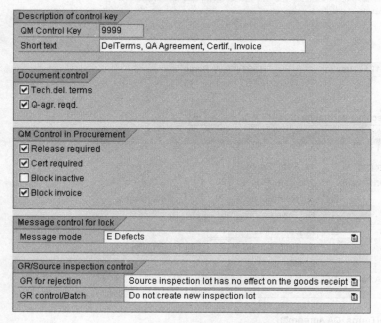

You should use a QM control key where ☑ Block invoice is selected.

10.17.3 Quality Info Record: Procurement

You need to maintain a Quality Info Record: Procurement using transaction QI01/QI02.

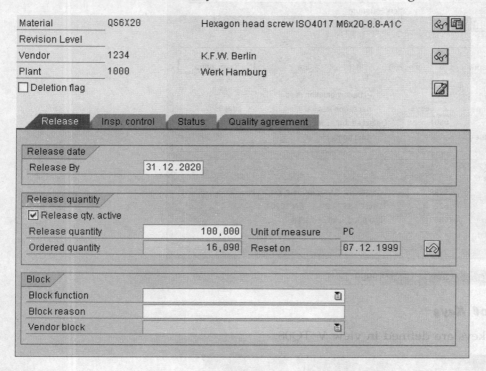

10.17.4 Purchase Order

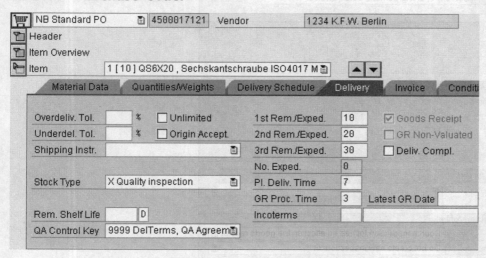

Note the QA Control Key 9999 DelTerms, QA Agreem .

10.17.5   Goods Receipt

After goods receipt, display the material document using transaction MB02.

Purchase Order	4500017121	10		Movement Type	101	GR goods receipt
Ref. Document	5000000078	1				
Plant	1000			Werk Hamburg		
Vendor	1234			K.F.W. Berlin		
Incoterms	EXW					
Material	QS6X20			Hexagon head screw ISO4017 M6x20-8.8-A1C		

Quantity in

Unit of Entry	10		PC	Stor. Location	0001		Stock Type	X

Further Information

Unloading Point							
						GR Status	1
			Company Code	1000	Fiscal Yr	2014	
Text							

Stock type.

Note the 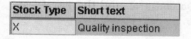 Stock Type   X , which indicates that the material is received in quality inspection.

Stock Type	Short text
X	Quality inspection

Goods receipt status

Also note the GR Status   1 , which indicates that inspection is active.

Status GR Doc.	Short text
1	Inspection active (insp. lot created)

10.17.6   Invoice Entry

Enter the invoice using transaction MIRO.

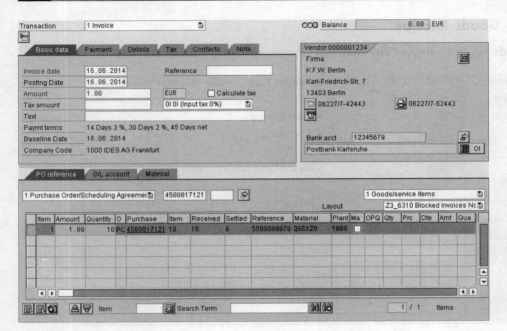

Post the invoice.

10.17.7 Invoice Display

Display the invoice using transaction MIR4. Enter the Invoice Document No. and the Fiscal Year. Click 🔗 Display Document. The system displays the invoice.

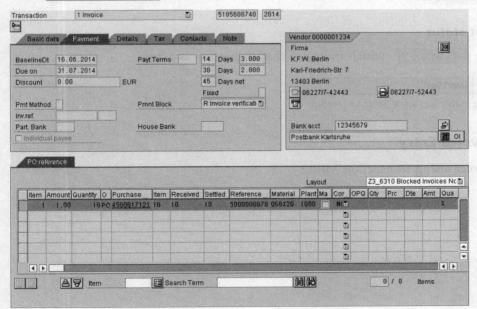

Note that the payment is blocked in the Qua field at the item level resulting in payment block at the header level Pmnt Block   R Invoice verificati .

10.17.8   Accounting Entries

Click Follow-On Documents ... . The system displays the list of accounting documents. Double-click the Accounting document to see the accounting entries.

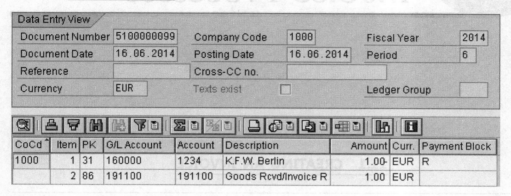

Note that the payment is blocked.

Invoice Processes

11.1 CREATING AN INVOICE

Functional Consultant	User	Business Process Owner	Senior Management	My Rating	Understanding Level
A	A	A	A		

You can create an invoice using transaction MIRO as explained in Section 4.1.

11.2 CHANGING AN INVOICE

Functional Consultant	User	Business Process Owner	Senior Management	My Rating	Understanding Level
A	A	A	A		

You cannot change a posted invoice. If an invoice is held, parked, or saved as completed, you can open it from the worklist in transaction MIRO and change it. You can then post it or save it in an intermediate state.

11.3 DISPLAYING AN INVOICE

Functional Consultant	User	Business Process Owner	Senior Management	My Rating	Understanding Level
A	A	A	A		

You can display an invoice document using transaction MIR4.

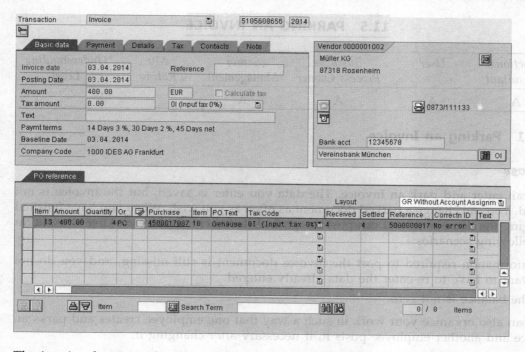

The invoice document has the same format as the invoice entry, except that it cannot be changed and it has a document number and a financial year of posting.

11.4 HOLDING AN INVOICE

Functional Consultant	User	Business Process Owner	Senior Management	My Rating	Understanding Level
A	A	A	A		

You can enter data for an invoice using transaction MIRO and save it by clicking [Hold]. The system saves the data even if there are errors. No updates take place in the system. Held invoices are displayed in the worklist.

Worklist	Doc. date	Reference no.	Vendor	Amount
☐ Held documents				
▷ ☐ Parked documents				
☐ Docs complete for posting				

If an invoice is held, parked, or saved as completed, you can open it from the worklist in transaction MIRO and change it. You can then post it or save it in an intermediate state.

11.5 PARKING AN INVOICE

Functional Consultant	User	Business Process Owner	Senior Management	My Rating	Understanding Level
A	A	A	A		

11.5.1 Parking an Invoice

Purpose

You can enter and park an invoice. The data you enter is saved, but the invoice is not posted. You can change a parked document as often as you wish. When you have finished changing the document, you can post the parked document. Invoice parking is useful in the following scenarios:

> ➢ Information required to post the invoice document is still missing, and you do not want to have to re-enter the data already entered.

> ➢ The balance is not zero.

You can also organize your work in such a way that one employee creates and parks an invoice and another employee posts it, if necessary after changing it.

Transaction

MIR7—Park Invoice
MIRO—Enter Invoice. During invoice entry, click Edit ➤ Switch to Document Parking .

Invoice parking also becomes necessary when you assign Correctn ID Unclarified error: park invoice ☷ to an invoice item.

Data Entry

You enter data in invoice parking in the same way as in transaction MIRO.

Parking an Invoice

You can enter data for an invoice in transaction MIR7 and park it by clicking 💾. The document being parked may still contain errors.

Updates

When you park a document, following updates take place in the system to show that an invoice is under processing:

> ➢ Purchase order history
> ➢ Data for advance tax returns
> ➢ Index for duplicate invoice check

> Open vendor items in parked documents
> Log of document changes

11.5.2   Parked Invoice

Displaying a Parked Invoice

When you park an invoice, the invoice document is created. You can display it using transaction MIR4.

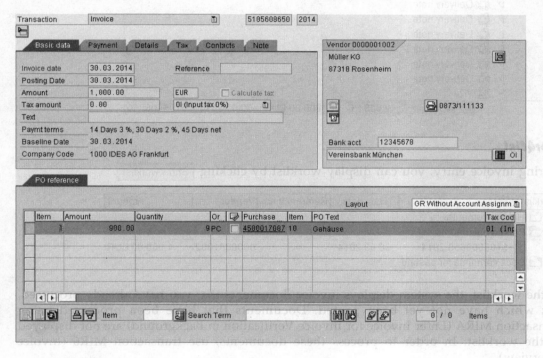

Follow-on Documents

In the invoice document, click   Follow-On Documents ... .

```
Doc.Type : RE ( Gross inv. receipt ) Parked document
Doc. Number   5100000008       Company code   1000          Fiscal year   2014
Doc. date     30.03.2014       Posting date   30.03.2014     Period        03
Calculate Tax   ☐
Doc.currency   EUR
```

Itm	PK	Account	Account short text	Assignment	Tx	Amount
1	31	1002	Müller KG			1,000.00-

This shows that when you park an invoice, credit to the vendor is created.

Purchase Order Structure

In invoice entry transaction MIRO, or in invoice display transaction MIR4, display the purchase order structure by clicking **Show PO structure**.

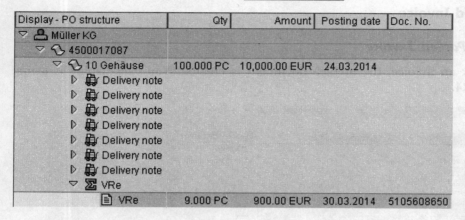

Display - PO structure	Qty	Amount	Posting date	Doc. No.
▽ 👤 Müller KG				
▽ 🔗 4500017087				
▽ 🔗 10 Gehäuse	100.000 PC	10,000.00 EUR	24.03.2014	
▷ 🏠 Delivery note				
▷ 🏠 Delivery note				
▷ 🏠 Delivery note				
▷ 🏠 Delivery note				
▷ 🏠 Delivery note				
▷ 🏠 Delivery note				
▷ 🏠 Delivery note				
▽ Σ VRe				
📄 VRe	9.000 PC	900.00 EUR	30.03.2014	5105608650

Worklist

During invoice entry, you can display worklist by clicking **Show worklist**.

Worklist	Doc. date	Reference no.	Vendor	Amount
☐ Held documents				
▽ 🗀 Parked documents				
📄 5105608650 2014	30.03.2014		0000001002	1,000.00 EUR
☐ Docs complete for posting				

In the worklist, the system displays invoice documents that you have already processed, but which have not yet been posted. Documents that have been processed using transaction MIRA (Enter Invoice for Invoice Verification in Background) are not displayed in the worklist. In order to process these documents, use transaction MIR6 (Invoice Overview).

Purchase Order History

You can display a purchase order using transaction ME23N and see its history.

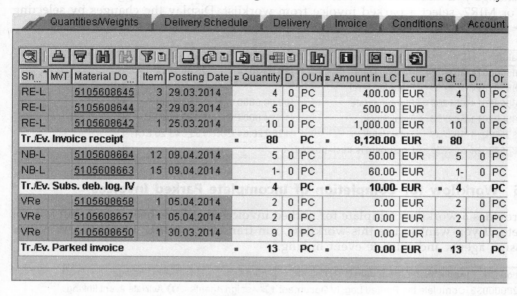

Sh...	MvT	Material Do...	Item	Posting Date	Σ Quantity	D	OUn	Σ Amount in LC	L.cur	Σ Qt	D...	Or...
RE-L		5105608645	3	29.03.2014	4	0	PC	400.00	EUR	4	0	PC
RE-L		5105608644	2	29.03.2014	5	0	PC	500.00	EUR	5	0	PC
RE-L		5105608642	1	25.03.2014	10	0	PC	1,000.00	EUR	10	0	PC
Tr./Ev. Invoice receipt					■ 80		PC ■	■ 8,120.00	EUR	■ 80		PC
NB-L		5105608664	12	09.04.2014	5	0	PC	50.00	EUR	5	0	PC
NB-L		5105608663	15	09.04.2014	1-	0	PC	60.00-	EUR	1-	0	PC
Tr./Ev. Subs. deb. log. IV					■ 4		PC ■	■ 10.00-	EUR	■ 4		PC
VRe		5105608658	1	05.04.2014	2	0	PC	0.00	EUR	2	0	PC
VRe		5105608657	1	05.04.2014	2	0	PC	0.00	EUR	2	0	PC
VRe		5105608650	1	30.03.2014	9	0	PC	0.00	EUR	9	0	PC
Tr./Ev. Parked invoice					■ 13		PC ■	■ 0.00	EUR	■ 13		PC

Note that the invoice number 5105608650 is included in Tr./Ev. Parked invoice .

11.5.3 Changing a Parked Invoice

In transaction MIRO or MIR7 you can select a parked invoice from the worklist, or by clicking 🔲 and specifying the number of the parked invoice. Once the invoice is fetched, you can change it, post it, park it again, save as completed, or delete it.

11.5.4 Deleting a Parked Invoice

In transaction MIRO or MIR7, click Show worklist .

Worklist	Doc. date	Reference no.	Vendor	Amount
🗀 Held documents				
▽ 🗁 Parked documents				
📄 5105608650 2014	30.03.2014		0000001002	1,000.00 EUR
📄 5105608657 2014	05.04.2014		0000001002	150.00 EUR
📄 5105608658 2014	05.04.2014		0000001002	270.00 EUR
📄 5105608672 2014	14.04.2014		0000001002	600.00 EUR
📄 5105608701 2014	25.05.2014		0000001002	120.00 EUR
🗀 Docs complete for posting				

Double-click the parked invoice you want to delete. Delete the selected parked invoice by choosing Invoice Document ➤ Delete .

11.5.5 Displaying Invoice Change Document

Every change you make to an invoice document after it is created is logged. In transaction MIRO or MIR7, select a parked invoice from worklist. Display the changes by selecting `Goto` ➤ `Display Change Documents`.

Object value	Doc. no.	Long Field Label	Old value	New value	Change ID
51056086502014	563738	Posting Date	30.03.2014	25.05.2014	U
51056086502014	563738	Planning level		F1	U
51056086502014	563738	Planning date	00.00.0000	13.04.2014	U
51056086502014	563738	Total Stock	1,114.000 PC	1,195.000 PC	U
51056086502014	563738	Total Value	126,728.64 EUR	135,943.20 EUR	U
51056086502014	563738	Document is back-posted	X		U

11.5.6 Workflow for Completion of Incomplete Parked Invoices

SAP provides a workflow template for parked invoices that have been saved, but are not complete. If you want to use this workflow, run transaction MIRU_WORKFLOW_VERV and assign agents and activate event linking.

Application Co...	Application Component Description	Agent Assignment	Event Linkage
Σ 20000039	Complete the Parked Log. IV Document	Assign Agents	Activate event linking

11.6 SAVING AN INVOICE AS COMPLETED

Functional Consultant	User	Business Process Owner	Senior Management	My Rating	Understanding Level
A	A	A	A		

11.6.1 Invoice Posting in Two Steps

You can organize your work in such a way that one employee enters the invoice and another posts it.

11.6.2 Saving an Invoice as Completed

The first employee enters the invoice using transaction MIRO, ensures that the invoice is complete and error free and clicks `Save as Completed`. The system performs all the checks as if the invoice is being posted. When you save an invoice as completed, the following updates take place in the system to show that an invoice is under processing:

➤ Purchase order history

➤ Data for advance tax returns

➤ Index for duplicate invoice check

> ➤ Open vendor items in parked documents
> ➤ Purchase order commitments
> ➤ Funds management documents
> ➤ Log of document changes

11.6.3 Workflow for Releasing Completed Invoices

You can use transaction MIRU_WORKFLOW_FREIG to activate the workflow for releasing completed documents. You need to assign agents and activate event linking.

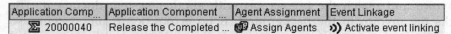

Application Comp...	Application Component ...	Agent Assignment	Event Linkage
∑ 20000040	Release the Completed ... 🔍 Assign Agents	⟫ Activate event linking

You also need to define the releasing authority. In view T169WF01, you can specify that certain invoices and credit memos need to be released. If a document satisfies any line in this view, a workflow is started to release the document.

CoCode	Rel. group	D/C indic.	Rel.St >=	Curr	Obj. type	ID
1000	1000	S Debit 📄	5,000.00	EUR	US	SAPUSER
1000	1000	S Debit 📄	20,000.00	EUR	US	BURKEJ
1000	1000	S Debit 📄	50,000.00	EUR	S	50010676

The releasing authority `Obj. type` `ID` is determined based on the invoice amount. In `D/C indic.` debit means invoice and credit means credit memo. `Rel. group` is determined from the `☑ Accounting info` of the vendor master. Master list of release groups is defined in view V_VBWF08.

AGrp	Name
0001	Vendor A
0002	vendor B
0003	Vendor C
0004	G/L accounts
0100	New internet customer ok
1000	CoCd 1000, Vendor 2200
3000	CoCd 3000, Vendor 2210

11.6.4 Processing Invoices Saved as Completed

If the workflow is not implemented or does not determine a releasing authority, you can post a completed invoice using transaction MIRO. Click `Show worklist`.

Worklist	Doc. date	Reference no.	Vendor	Amount
☐ Held documents				
▷ ☐ Parked documents				
☐ Docs complete for posting				

Double-click an invoice under ☐ Docs complete for posting. Change it, if required. Post it.

11.7   PROCESSING INVOICES IN BACKGROUND

Functional Consultant	User	Business Process Owner	Senior Management	My Rating	Understanding Level
A	A	B	C		

11.7.1   Purpose

You can also enter invoices for processing in the background. You only enter the total amount of the invoice and match the invoice up with another system document. The system then checks the invoice in the background. If no errors occur, the system also posts the invoice in the background. If errors do occur, the system saves the invoice and you then have to process it in a separate step.

11.7.2   Invoice Entry

Enter the invoice for background processing using transaction MIRA.

Transaction	1 Invoice	

Basic data   Payment   Details   Tax   Contacts   Note

Invoice date	21.06.2014	Reference	
Posting Date	21.06.2014		
Amount	120.00		☐ Calculate tax
Tax amount		0I 0I (Input tax 0%)	
Text			
Company Code	1000 IDES AG Frankfurt		
Prepaym. Status		Invoice Not Relevant for Prepayment	

1 Purchase Order/Scheduling Agreemei

Multiple Assgmnt		FS item type	1 Goods/service items
Purchasing Doc.	Item		
4500017133			

Change Assignment		
Se	Assignmnt	Post as
☑	Deliveries	S Invoice item
☑	Returns	H Credit memo

PlntOnly

The fields on this screen are the same as in invoice entry transaction MIRO. In this screen, you can specify multiple allocations (assignment) simultaneously. Save the invoices. The system gives appropriate message ⊘ Invoice document 5105608690 / 2014 saved .

11.7.3 Invoice Document

You can display the invoice document using transaction MIR4.

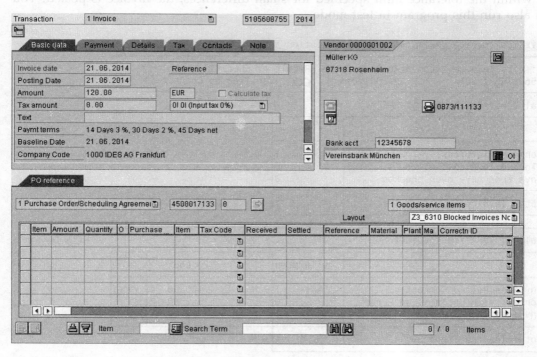

Note that the invoice document does not contain any items.

11.7.4 Invoice Status

Run transaction MIR6 to see the status of the invoice.

Status	Doc. no.	Ite	Invo	Name of	Gross	Invoice status
	5105608755 ✎	1	002	Müller KG	120.00	1 Defined for background verification ▤

11.7.5 Invoice Processing in Background

Invoice verification in the background is run using program RMBABG00, transaction MRBP. Usually you schedule this job so that it runs during lean hours. When this job runs, the system verifies the invoice in the background using the allocation criteria you entered to determine the item list. It then calculates the net total from the item list and compares with the gross invoice amount you entered in the header. If the two match, or are within the tolerance limit specified for small differences, the invoice is posted. You can also run this program in test mode.

```
Logistics Invoice Verification - Verification in Background

Logistics Invoice Document  Posting Date    Result of Check
5105608755 / 2014              21.06.2014     OCO  Verified as Correct
```

Total Verification Result:

	Number
Verified Invoices:	1
Blocked Invoices:	0
Invs that have been checked	0
Total Invoices	1

Result of Verified Invoices:

	Number	Percent	
Invoices Posted Correctly	1	100.00 %	OCO
Correct with Unclarified Error	0	0.00 %	OAO
Invoices with Errors	0	0.00 %	OCO
Total Invoice Items	1		

Runtime Anal.:

Start Time	08:04:51
End Time	08:04:57
Runtime in Microseconds	5,484,000
Runtime in hh:mm:ss	00:00:05
Milliseconds per Invoice	5,484
Microseconds per Item	5,484,000

With invoice verification in the background, the system does not check for any quantity or price differences at item level. Since you do not enter any actual invoice item data, the system uses the default data for comparison.

11.7.6   Invoice Overview

You can use transaction MIR6 (Invoice Overview) to generate the following lists:

➤ Invoices posted in the background

➤ Invoices that could not be posted in the background, and therefore, require manual processing

Status	Doc. no.	Ite	Invo	Name of	Gross	Invoice status	D	Document	Posting Date
∞	5105608755	🐾	1002	Müller KG	120.00	5 Posted 📄	RE	21.06.2014	21.06.2014

You can change an unposted invoice by selecting it and clicking [🖉]; correct the data and save the invoice. The system shows the updated status.

11.7.7   Manual Supervision

Purpose

The background processing of invoices described above is fully automated. You may want that the invoices processed by the system in the background are subjected to manual supervision.

Setting up Manual Supervision

You can set up manual supervision for background processing on invoices.

Fully automatic background processing

When the background processing is fully automatic, view V_169P_K has the following setting:

CoCd	Company Name	Set correct invoice to "co
1000	IDES AG	☑

Under this setting, the invoices processed in background have [Invoice status] [5 Posted 📄].

Background processing with manual supervision

When the background processing has manual supervision, view V_169P_K has the following setting:

CoCd	Company Name	Set correct invoice to "co
1000	IDES AG	☐

Under this setting, the invoices processed in background have [Invoice status] [4 Correct (posted, not completed)📄]. The status is changed to [5 Posted 📄] for each invoice manually.

Invoice Entry

The invoice is entered using transaction MIRA.

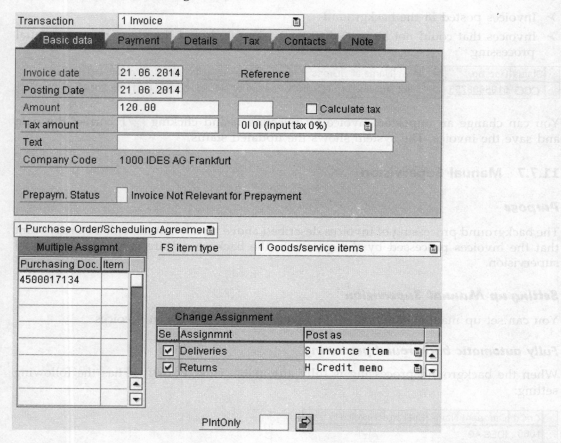

Invoice Status

Run transaction MIR6 to see the status of the invoice.

Status	Doc. no.	Ite	Invo	Name of	Gross	Invoice status	
	5105608756	✐	1002	Müller KG	120.00	1 Defined for background verification	🗎

Invoice Processing in Background

The invoice is processed in background using transaction MRBP.

```
Logistics Invoice Verification - Verification in Background

Logistics Invoice DocumentPosting Date   Result of Check
5105608756 / 2014        21.06.2014      OOO   Verified as Correct
```

Total Verification Result:

	Number
Verified Invoices:	1
Blocked Invoices:	0
Invs that have been checked	0
Total Invoices	1

Result of Verified Invoices:

	Number	Percent	
Invoices Posted Correctly	1	100.00 %	OOO
Correct with Unclarified Error	0	0.00 %	OOO
Invoices with Errors	0	0.00 %	OOO
Total Invoice Items	1		

Runtime Anal.:

Start Time	08:30:23
End Time	08:30:29
Runtime in Microseconds	5,156,000
Runtime in hh:mm:ss	00:00:05
Milliseconds per Invoice	5,156
Microseconds per Item	5,156,000

Invoice Overview

Run transaction MIR6 to see the status of the invoice.

Status	Doc. no.	I	Controlled	Invo	Name of	Gross	Invoice status
OOO	5105608756			1002	Müller KG	120.00	4 Correct (posted, not completed)

Note that the invoice status is not 5 Posted.

Display the Invoice

You can display the invoice by clicking.

Confirm the Invoice

If you are satisfied with the background processing of the invoice, click [🖉].

Status	Doc. no.	Ite	Invo	Name of	Gross	Invoice status	D	Document	Posting Date
◯◯◻	5105608756	⟨⟩	1002	Müller KG	120.00	5 Posted ▣	RE	21.06.2014	21.06.2014

Note that the status changes to 5 Posted ▣. If you are not satisfied with the invoice, you may cancel the invoice.

11.7.8 Assignment Test

Purpose

The assignment test is a background process step that precedes invoice verification. You use this function to ensure that the system only starts invoice verification, if open goods receipts exist for an invoice. Using the assignment test has the following advantages:

➢ Even an unsuccessful assignment test is quicker than a complete invoice check in the background, as the system is required to process less data from the database (for example, no article data is required) and perform fewer checks and reports. Moreover, instead of completely assigning open goods receipts, as in the background process, the system performs only rudimentary assignment for these.

➢ An error in a background check always requires a manual response, but this is only required for an assignment test, if the assignment test period is exceeded.

To allow the system to carry out an assignment test, invoices must be related to a Purchase order, or a Delivery note, or a Bill of lading.

Methodology

The system uses the assignment test to check whether a goods receipt exists for an invoice that has already been entered, and only performs the relevant invoice verification in the background, if a goods receipt does exist.

You can customize the assignment test so that all invoices that have been in the system for so long that it is safe to assume they contain errors (for example, invoice with a delivery note number that does not exist) are included in the background check. After the check has been completed, invoices that still contain errors must be processed manually by the invoice verification clerk.

Invoices are not included in the assignment test immediately after they have been created, but rather only after the waiting time that the system determines using the settings in view V_WRF_ASSIGN_GRP.

CoCd	Assignm.	Wait Time	Add to Deliv	Duration to	Interval Btw	Max. Assig

The first assignment test takes place after the waiting time expires. If a goods receipt was found during the assignment test, the invoice can then be checked in the background. If the system was unable to find a goods receipt that it could assign to an invoice, it repeats the assignment test after a waiting period defined in view V_WRF_ASSIGN_GRP. In this view, you specify how often this assignment test is to be performed, based on your vendor settings. You can combine waiting periods into assignment groups and then assign one such group to each vendor in the vendor master at company code level (database table LFB1).

You can use BAdI WRF_MRM_ASSIGN_TEST to override the assignment date and the end of the assignment test period in a customer-specific manner.

11.8 CANCELLING AN INVOICE

Functional Consultant	User	Business Process Owner	Senior Management	My Rating	Understanding Level
A	A	A	A		

11.8.1 Purpose

If you have made a mistake in an invoice and posted it, you can cancel it. Accounting movements are reversed and goods receipts settled through the invoice become available for allocation again.

11.8.2 Transaction

MR8M—Cancel Invoice Document

11.8.3 Initial Screen

Invoice Document No.	5105608669
Fiscal Year	2014

Details Re Reversal Posting	
Reversal Reason	01
Posting Date	12.04.2014

Invoice document number and fiscal year

Enter the details of the invoice to be reversed.

Reversal reason

Here you can specify the reason for reversing the invoice. Master list of reversal reasons is maintained in view T041C.

Reason	Text	Neg.postng	Alt.pos.dt
01	Reversal in current period	☐	☐
02	Reversal in closed period	☐	☑
03	Actual reversal in current period	☑	☐
04	Actual reversal in closed period	☑	☑
05	Accrual	☑	☑
06	Asset transaction reversal	☑	☑
07	Incorrect document date	☑	☐
RE	Reversal, incorrect original date	☑	☐

For a reversal reason, you can specify whether negative posting is to be generated or not, and whether alternative posting date can be entered.

Posting date

Posting date for cancellation of an invoice could be the same as the posting date of the original invoice. However, that posting period may be closed, or you may not want to post the cancellation on that date. In such cases, you specify posting date here. Only certain reversal reasons permit you to enter an alternative posting date.

11.8.4 Document Display

You should click 🔍 Display Document before cancelling it.

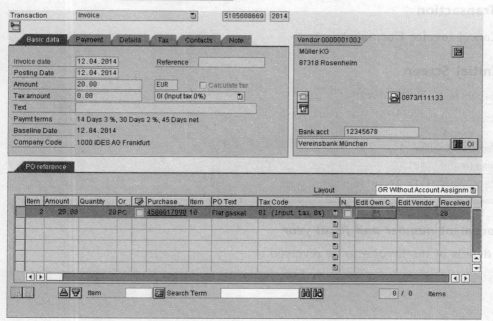

It is important to ensure that you are cancelling the right invoice.

11.8.5 Reversing the Invoice Document

Go back to the initial screen and select `Invoice Document` ➤ `Reverse` . The system reverses the invoice document by creating a new reversal document.

> ✅ Document reversed with no. 5105608680: Please manually clear FI documents

When you cancel documents in invoice verification, the document line items are not automatically cleared in Financial Accounting. You should periodically clear such items.

11.8.6 Reversal Document

You can display the reversal document using transaction MIR4.

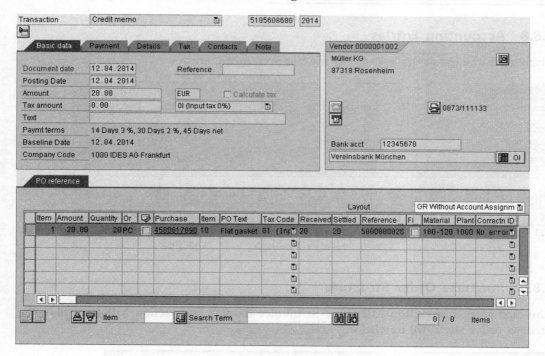

Note that the reversal document of an invoice is a credit memo. If you reverse a credit memo, the reversal document is an invoice. Also note that the reference document of both the invoice receipt and invoice receipt reversal is the same goods receipt document.

11.8.7 Accounting Documents

Display the invoice using transaction MIR4. Enter the `Invoice Document No.` and the `Fiscal Year` . Click `Display Document` . The system displays the invoice. Click `Follow-On Documents ...` . The system displays the list of accounting documents.

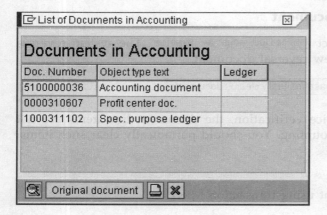

11.8.8 Accounting Entries

Double-click the `Accounting document` to see the accounting entries.

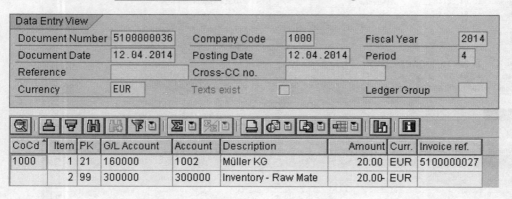

11.8.9 Purchase Order Structure

In invoice entry transaction MIRO, or in invoice display transaction MIR4, display the purchase order structure by clicking `Show PO structure`.

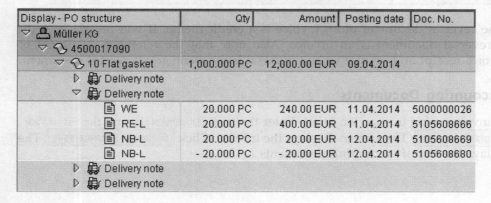

Note that the entry 📄 NB-L   - 20.000 PC   - 20.00 EUR   12.04.2014   5105608680 is due to invoice cancellation.

11.8.10   Purchase Order History

You can also display the purchase order document using transaction ME23N and see purchase order history.

Sh...	MvT	Material Do...	Item	Posting Date	Σ Quantity	D	OUn	Σ Amount in LC	L.cur	Σ Qty in OPUn
WE	101	5000000026	1	11.04.2014	20	0	PC	240.00	EUR	20
WE	101	5000000025	1	09.04.2014	10	0	PC	120.00	EUR	10
Tr./Ev. Goods receipt				■	540		PC ■	6,480.00	EUR ■	540
RE-L		5105608667	4	12.04.2014	500	0	PC	10,000.00	EUR	500
RE-L		5105608666	2	11.04.2014	20	0	PC	400.00	EUR	20
RE-L		5105608665	1	09.04.2014	10	0	PC	200.00	EUR	10
Tr./Ev. Invoice receipt				■	530		PC ■	10,600.00	EUR ■	530
NB-L		5105608680	1	12.04.2014	20-	0	PC	20.00-	EUR	20-
NB-L		5105608669	2	12.04.2014	20	0	PC	20.00	EUR	20
NB-L		5105608668	1	12.04.2014	10-	0	PC	10.00-	EUR	10-
Tr./Ev. Subs. deb. log. IV				■	10-		PC ■	10.00-	EUR ■	10-

The invoice cancellation document 5105608680 is included in Tr./Ev. Subs. deb. log. IV .

11.9   BLOCKING PAYMENT OF AN INVOICE

Functional Consultant	User	Business Process Owner	Senior Management	My Rating	Understanding Level
A	A	A	A		

11.9.1   Blocking Payment

The payment of an invoice may be blocked manually or automatically. Various scenarios of blocking payment of invoices are illustrated in Chapter 10.

11.9.2   Types of Payment Block

When you post an invoice, there may be reasons to block payment to the vendor. An invoice may be blocked for payment manually, or the system may do so automatically when conditions for doing so arise. Note that the invoice is posted; only payment is blocked.

Variance

If there is a difference between your calculation and vendor's claim, you may not post the invoice. If you do, the payment may be blocked as per the policy of the company. There are three types of variances:

➢ Quantity variance

➢ Price variance

➢ Order price unit variance

➢ Schedule variance

Amount

Your company may have a policy of double-checking invoice items of high value. Such invoice items may be blocked for payment on posting and released by another person after the necessary check.

Stochastic block

Your company may want to randomly check the invoices being posted. The system can block payment of randomly selected invoices.

Manual block

You may manually block an invoice item.

Quality block

If a material is defined as being relevant for quality management, goods receipts for this material are posted to stock in quality inspection. You want invoices for the material to be blocked until the inspection has been successfully completed.

11.9.3   Level of Payment Block

Even if you block payment of only one item in an invoice, the payment of the entire invoice is blocked.

11.9.4   Workflow for Invoices whose Payment is Blocked for Price

SAP provides a workflow template for invoices whose payment is blocked for price. If you want to use this workflow, assign agents and activate event linking in transaction MIRO_WORKFLOW.

Application Com.	Application Component Description	Agent Assignment	Event Linkage
Σ 20000030	Treatment of inv. blkd for price, Log.IV	🞉 Assign Agents	») Activate event linking

11.10   RELEASING INVOICES WITH BLOCKED PAYMENT

Functional Consultant	User	Business Process Owner	Senior Management	My Rating	Understanding Level
A	A	B	C		

11.10.1   Purpose

If an invoice is blocked due to any reason (manual, variances, stochastic), you can release it.

11.10.2   Transaction

MRBR—Release Blocked Invoices

11.10.3   Initial Screen

Selection of Blocked Invoices

Company Code		to	
Invoice Document		to	
Fiscal Year		to	
Vendor		to	
Posting Date		to	
Due Date		to	
Purchasing Group		to	
User		to	

Processing

◉ Release Manually   ○ Release Automatically
☐ Move Cash Disc. Date

Blocking Procedure

◉ Blocked Due to Variances
○ Manual Payment Block
○ Stochastically Blocked

Display options

Variant

Move cash discount date

Sometimes delay in payment is on account of problems at the vendor's end, and he agrees to give cash discount despite delay in payment due to blocking of the invoice. If you select this field, the system determines the difference between the current date and the baseline date for payment. If this difference is positive, that is, the baseline date for payment is in the past, the system adds this difference to the cash discount days.

Release automatically

Invoices that are blocked automatically by the system remain blocked even when the reason for blocking them is no longer valid. This can be the case for invoices blocked due to quantity, price, or schedule variances, or due to quality inspection. You can choose this option to release them automatically.

11.10.4 List

	Status	Doc. No.	Year	Posting Date	Inv. Pty	Amount	Crcy	OP	Qty	Prc	Qua	ItA	Dte	Man
		5105608659	2014	08.04.2014	1002	260.00	EUR			✖				
		5105608665	2014	09.04.2014	1002	200.00	EUR			✖				
		5105608666	2014	11.04.2014	1002	400.00	EUR			✖				
		5105608667	2014	12.04.2014	1002	10,000.00	EUR			✖				
		5105608671	2014	13.04.2014	1002	700.00	EUR		✖					
		5105608689	2014	14.05.2014	1002	120.00	EUR							✖

11.10.5 Deleting Blocking Reason

An invoice may contain several blocking reasons. The time required to investigate each reason can differ. If a particular blocking reason is no longer valid, you can remove it, without affecting the other blocking reasons. To delete a blocking reason, place the cursor on the blocking reason that you want to delete and click 🗑 Blocking Reason . After removing the blocking reason, you need to save the changes. When all blocking reasons are removed, the invoice is released.

11.10.6 Releasing a Blocked Invoice

Select a line and click 📲. The background colour of the entire line becomes green. When you save, the invoice is released. The released invoice disappears from the list.

	Status	Doc. No.	Year	Posting Date	Inv. Pty	Amount	Crcy	OP	Qty	Prc	Qua	ItA	Dte	Man
		5105608665	2014	09.04.2014	1002	200.00	EUR			✖				
		5105608666	2014	11.04.2014	1002	400.00	EUR			✖				
		5105608667	2014	12.04.2014	1002	10,000.00	EUR			✖				
		5105608671	2014	13.04.2014	1002	700.00	EUR		✖					
		5105608689	2014	14.05.2014	1002	120.00	EUR							✖

11.10.7 Invoice Document

You can display the invoice document using transaction MIR4. Note that the payment block is now lifted Pmnt Block   Free for payment 🖹 .

11.10.8 Accounting Entries after Invoice Release

Display the invoice using transaction MIR4. Enter the Invoice Document No. and the Fiscal Year. Click 👓 Display Document . The system displays the invoice. Click Follow-On Documents ... . The system displays the list of accounting documents. Double-click the Accounting document to see the accounting entries.

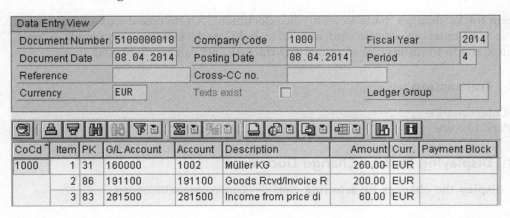

Note that there is no payment block.

11.10.9 Accounting Entries before Invoice Release

Before releasing the invoice, there was a payment block.

Data Entry View					
Document Number	5100000018	Company Code	1000	Fiscal Year	2014
Document Date	08.04.2014	Posting Date	08.04.2014	Period	4
Reference		Cross-CC no.			
Currency	EUR	Texts exist ☐		Ledger Group	

CoCd	Item	PK	G/L Account	Account	Description	Amount	Curr.	Payment Block
1000	1	31	160000	1002	Müller KG	260.00-	EUR	R
	2	86	191100	191100	Goods Rcvd/Invoice R	200.00	EUR	
	3	83	281500	281500	Income from price di	60.00	EUR	

11.11 DISPLAYING INVOICE CHANGE DOCUMENT

Functional Consultant	User	Business Process Owner	Senior Management	My Rating	Understanding Level
A	A	B	C		

11.11.1 Purpose

The system tracks changes made to an invoice document. An invoice document is created as soon as you enter an invoice and save it to hold, park, save as completed, or post. Any change made to an invoice document is tracked and can be displayed.

11.11.2 Transaction

MIRO—Enter Invoice
MIR7—Park Invoice

11.11.3 Displaying Invoice Change Document

You can display the changes by selecting Goto ➤ Display Change Documents.

11.11.4 Screen

Object value	Doc. no.	Long Field Label	Old value	New value	Change ID
51056086502014	563738	Posting Date	30.03.2014	25.05.2014	U
51056086502014	563738	Planning level		F1	U
51056086502014	563738	Planning date	00.00.0000	13.04.2014	U
51056086502014	563738	Total Stock	1,114.000 PC	1,195.000 PC	U
51056086502014	563738	Total Value	126,728.64 EUR	135,943.20 EUR	U
51056086502014	563738	Document is back-posted	X		U

11.12 DISPLAYING LIST OF INVOICES

Functional Consultant	User	Business Process Owner	Senior Management	My Rating	Understanding Level
A	A	B	C		

11.12.1 Purpose

You can display list of invoices as per your selection criteria.

11.12.2 Transaction

MIR5—Display List of Invoice Documents

11.12.3 Selection Screen

The selection screen offers a large number of parameters that can be used to find invoices of your choice.

11.12.4 List of Invoices

	Doc. No.	Year	T...	Doc. Date	Posting Date	Entered on	Tr...	CoCd	Inv. ...	Crcy	Gross amnt
	5105608677	2014	KR	01.05.2014	01.05.2014	01.05.2014	RD	1000	1002	EUR	500.00
	5105608678	2014	VI	01.05.2014	01.05.2014	01.05.2014	RD	1000	1002	EUR	200.00
	5105608679	2014	VI	02.05.2014	02.05.2014	02.05.2014	RD	1000	1002	EUR	100.00

11.12.5 Individual Invoice Display

You can click a document number in the list to display it. You can also display an invoice document to view its contents using transaction MIR4—Display Invoice Document. The invoice document has the same format as invoice entry, except that it cannot be changed, and it has a document number and financial year of posting.

11.12.6 Follow-on Documents

You can select a line and click Follow-On Documents ... to display them.

11.13   DISPLAYING ACCOUNTING DOCUMENT

Functional Consultant	User	Business Process Owner	Senior Management	My Rating	Understanding Level
A	A	B	C		

11.13.1   Purpose

You can display accounting documents created by posting of invoices or by other processes.

11.13.2   Transaction

FB03—Display Accounting Document

11.13.3   Selection Screen

```
Keys for Entry View
Document Number      [          ]
Company Code         [    ]
Fiscal Year          [    ]
```

11.13.4   More Selection Criteria

You can get more selection criteria by clicking [Document List]

```
Company code        ▣ [    ]        to [        ]  ⇨
Document Number       [       ]      to [       ]  ⇨
Fiscal Year           [     ]        to [    ]     ⇨
Ledger                [  ]

General selections
Document type         [ ]           to [ ]         ⇨
Posting date          [       ]     to [       ]   ⇨
Entry date            [       ]     to [       ]   ⇨
Reference number      [         ]   to [          ] ⇨
Reference Transaction [    ]        to [          ] ⇨
Reference key         [          ]  to [          ] ⇨
Logical system        [       ]     to [       ]   ⇨

Also display noted items
☐ Display noted items

Search for own documents
☐ Own documents only
```

Reference key

You can display the accounting documents for an invoice by specifying the invoice number followed by the fiscal year in the reference key.

11.13.5 List of Accounting Documents

Click 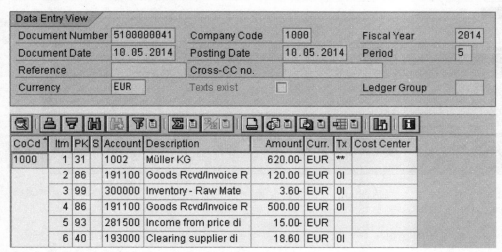 to display the list of accounting documents.

	CoCd	DocumentNo	Year	Type	Doc. Date	Posting Date
	1000	5100000041	2014	RN	10.05.2014	10.05.2014

11.13.6 Accounting Document

Double-click to open a document.

Data Entry View							
Document Number	5100000041	Company Code	1000		Fiscal Year		2014
Document Date	10.05.2014	Posting Date	10.05.2014		Period		5
Reference		Cross-CC no.					
Currency	EUR	Texts exist	☐		Ledger Group		

CoCd	Itm	PK	S	Account	Description	Amount	Curr.	Tx	Cost Center
1000	1	31		1002	Müller KG	620.00-	EUR	**	
	2	86		191100	Goods Rcvd/Invoice R	120.00	EUR	0I	
	3	99		300000	Inventory - Raw Mate	3.60-	EUR	0I	
	4	86		191100	Goods Rcvd/Invoice R	500.00	EUR	0I	
	5	93		281500	Income from price di	15.00-	EUR		
	6	40		193000	Clearing supplier di	18.60	EUR	0I	

11.13.7 Original Document

You can display the original document for an accounting document by clicking Environment ➤ Document Environment ➤ Original Document .

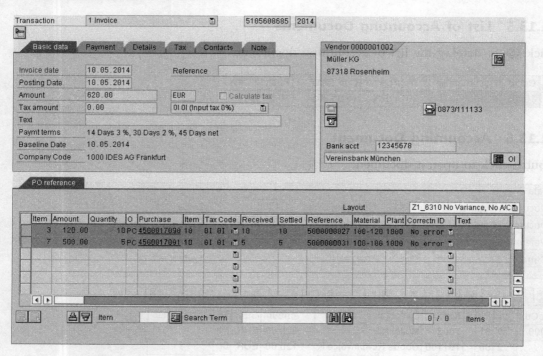

Invoice Customizing

12.1 ITEM LIST VARIANTS

Functional Consultant	User	Business Process Owner	Senior Management	My Rating	Understanding Level
A	C	X	X		

12.1.1 Item List Variants

Business requirement

SAP has many fields for invoice items. A user will like to see only the fields he needs. Also, his needs may vary depending on the function he is performing.

Item list variants

SAP lets you group item list fields in item list variants. SAP provides predefined item list variants which you can modify, delete, or add to. In invoice entry, a user can select an item list variant in the field Layout. He can also switch to another Layout any time.

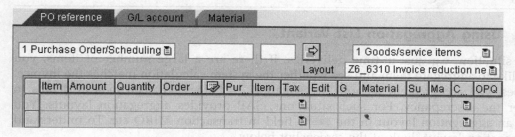

12.1.2 Maintaining Item List Variants

SAP provides predefined item list variants which you can modify, delete, or add to using transaction OLMRLIST.

```
Screen variants for transaction        MIRO


 Screen values     6310 Program  SAPLMR1M

 ☑ Copy settings                    Name of screen variant:  7_6310
                                    Screen variant short txt  All information
 ☐ Do not display screen

 Field                              Contents        W. content   Output only
 ▣         (Pushbutton)                                ☐            ☐
 Layout                                                ☐            ☐

 TC_MR1M          (Table Ctrl)  ☑ Adopt column sequence  ☑ Adopt column

 DRSEG-SELKZ     (Check box)  1                          ☐            ☐
 Item                         1                          ☐            ☐
 Amount                       1                          ☐            ☐
 Quantity                     1                          ☐            ☐
 Order Unit                   1                          ☐            ☐
 ▣               (Check box)  1                          ☐            ☐
 Purchase Order               1                          ☐            ☐
 @\QItem Number Purch         1                          ☐            ☐
 Procurement Doc.             1                          ☐            ☐
 PO Text                      1                          ☐            ☐
 Tax Code                     1                          ☐            ☐
 No Di           (Check box)  1                          ☐            ☐
```

12.2 AGGREGATION LIST VARIANTS

Functional Consultant	User	Business Process Owner	Senior Management	My Rating	Understanding Level
B	C	X	X		

12.2.1 Using Aggregation List Variant

In any situation, e.g. just-in-time deliveries, if there are a large number of items, you would like to aggregate them and see whether the system calculation matches the invoice. If it does, you accept them without investigation. If it does not, you look at details to discover the discrepancy. For such situations, SAP provides aggregation layouts. You choose an aggregation layout in the Layout field in transaction MIRO etc. To understand an aggregation layout, look at the screenshot below.

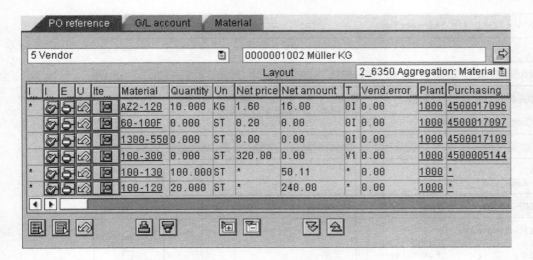

Aggregation

In the screenshot above, in several fields, you see a `*`. The `*` indicates that the field does not have a single value. For example, a `*` in the Purchasing field means that the line contains items from multiple purchasing documents.

Inclusion indicator, include, exclude

Inclusion indicator is the first field in the list, and it indicates whether the line is included or not. If a line is included, its value is taken in calculating the Balance field. When you click the icon, the inclusion indicator is set. It is unset by clicking the other icon.

Items

If you click the icon, the system displays items in the aggregation line.

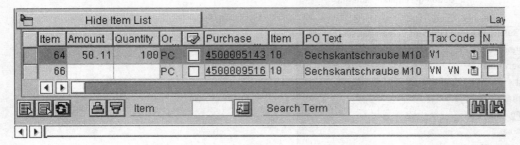

12.2.2   Maintaining Aggregation List Variants

SAP provides predefined aggregation list variants which you can modify, delete, or add to using transaction OLMRVERDLIST.

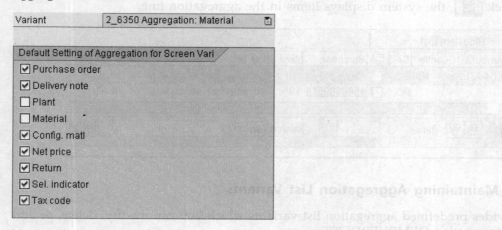

```
Screen variants for transaction          MIRO

Screen values    6350 Program  SAPLMR1M

☑ Copy settings                    Name of screen variant:  1_6350
                                   Screen variant short txt Aggregation: Plant
☐ Do not display screen

Field                              Contents        W. content  Output only

Layout                                                 ☐           ☐
RM08M-AGGR_LIST_VERS                                   ☐           ☐

TC_AGGREGATION    (Table Ctrl)   ☑ Adopt column sequence   ☑ Adopt column

Inclusion indicator       1                            ☐           ☐
Include         (Pushbutton 1                          ☐           ☐
Exclude         (Pushbutton 1                          ☐           ☐
Undo            (Pushbutton 1                          ☐           ☐
Items           (Pushbutton 1                          ☐           ☐
Purchasing Doc.           1                            ☐           ☐
Plant                     1                            ☐           ☐
Net amount in doc. c      1                            ☐           ☐
Returns item              1                            ☐           ☐
Tax codes                 1                            ☐           ☐
Material                  1                            ☐           ☐
Quantity                  1                            ☐           ☐
Un                        1                            ☐           ☐
```

12.2.3 Aggregation Criteria

In view T169Y, you can define the criteria by which aggregation takes place for each aggregation variant.

```
Variant          2_6350 Aggregation: Material    ▣

Default Setting of Aggregation for Screen Vari
☑ Purchase order
☑ Delivery note
☐ Plant
☐ Material
☑ Config. matl
☑ Net price
☑ Return
☑ Sel. indicator
☑ Tax code
```

All the fields that are selected are aggregated. According to the above screenshot, you will get an aggregate line for each combination of material and plant.

12.3 NUMBER ASSIGNMENT FOR INVOICE DOCUMENTS

Functional Consultant	User	Business Process Owner	Senior Management	My Rating	Understanding Level
B	C	X	X		

12.3.1 Determining Transaction from Transaction Code

The transactions are determined from transaction code in table T169. This table is SAP maintained; do not change it.

Transaction Code	TTyp	Transact.	Tr.	FunCls	Transaction Code
MIR6	B	RD	RMRP		MIR6
MIR7	H	RD	RMRP		MIR7
MIRA	H	RD	RMRP		MIRA
MIRH	H	RD	RMRP		MIRU
MIRO	H	RD	RMRP		MR1M

Logistics invoice verification contains two transactions.

Transaction Type	Short text
RD	Logistics invoice
RS	Logistics invoice, cancel

12.3.2 Assignment of Number Ranges to Transactions

In view VV_T003R_01, you assign a number range to a transaction.

Transactn	No. range
RD	01
RS	01

For transaction RS, you must not set up a number range for which external number assignment has been defined.

12.3.3 Number Ranges for Invoice Documents

In transaction OMRJ, you maintain number ranges for invoice documents.

NR Object	Update document

Intervals

	No	Year	From number	To number	Current number	Ext
	01	1995	5200000000	5299999999	5200000057	☐
	01	1996	5200000000	5299999999	5200000199	☐
	01	9999	5105600101	5105699999	5105608651	☐

If year does not exist, the number is taken from year 9999.

12.4 NUMBER ASSIGNMENTS FOR ACCOUNTING DOCUMENTS

Functional Consultant	User	Business Process Owner	Senior Management	My Rating	Understanding Level
A	C	X	X		

12.4.1 Accounting Document Types used in Invoice Verification

In view V_169F, you specify the default accounting document type that will get defaulted/generated in invoice verification.

Transaction Code	MIRO
Transaction Text	Enter Incoming Invoice

Default Value

Document Type	RE	Gross inv. receipt
Doc. type reval.	RE	Gross inv. receipt
Doc. type add. doc.		
DocType invoice reduction	RK	Gross inv. receipt

For the financial accounting document only internal number assignment is possible. Therefore, choose only the document type for which the number range is set to internal number assignment.

12.4.2   Number Range Assignment to Accounting Document Type

In view V_T003, you specify the number range interval for an accounting document type.

Document Type	RE	Gross inv. receipt

Properties		
Number range	51	Number range information

12.4.3   Number Range Definition

In transaction MRM4, you define the number ranges for each interval and year.

NR Object	Accounting document
Subobject	1000

Intervals

	No	Year	From number	To number	Current number		Ext
	51	2014	5100000000	5199999999	5100000059		☐

12.5   INPUT TAX

Functional Consultant	User	Business Process Owner	Senior Management	My Rating	Understanding Level
A	C	X	X		

12.5.1   Tax Procedure for a Country

Invoice verification takes place in a company code. The company code, in turn belongs to a country. To each country, a tax procedure is assigned in view V_005_E (transaction OBBG).

	Cty	Name	Proc.
	DE	Germany	TAXD

12.5.2   Tax Codes for a Country

When you buy material, you pay taxes. Taxes on different materials may be different, and may have multiple components. Tax codes are usually predefined by SAP for each country in table T007A. If you have to report tax-exempt or non-taxable sales to the tax authorities, you need to define a tax rate with the value 0.

Procedure	TAXD

Maintain Tax Codes		
Tax Code	Description	Tax type
0I	Input tax 0%	V Input tax 🖹
1I	Input tax 10%	V Input tax 🖹
5I	Input tax 5%	V Input tax 🖹

12.5.3 Tax Code for a Purchase Order Item

When you raise a purchase order, you specify a tax code for each item.

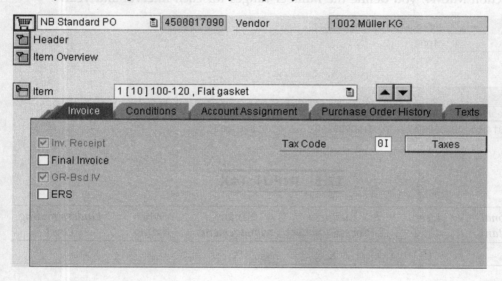

12.5.4 Tax Code for an Invoice Item

When you receive an invoice from the vendor, the vendor specifies the taxes. When you enter the invoice, the system copies the tax code from the purchase order item which you can change. The system computes taxes on the basis of this tax code and the tax rates maintained in the system.

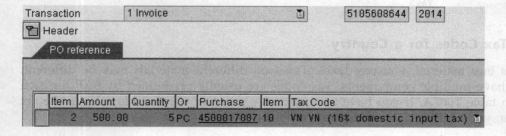

12.5.5 Tax Rates

You can see and maintain tax rates using transaction FTXP. A tax code may have multiple components, e.g. VAT, surcharge on VAT, etc. Each component of tax is identified by a tax type. You specify a rate for each tax type.

Country Key	DE	Germany
Tax Code	1I	Input tax 10%
Procedure	TAXD	
Tax type	V	Input tax

Percentage rates						
Tax Type	Acct Key	Tax Percent. Rate	Level	From Lvl	Cond. Type
Base Amount			100	0	BASB
Output Tax	MWS		110	100	MWAS
Input Tax	VST	10.000	120	100	MWVS
Interest markdown	ZAS		125	100	ZAST
Travel Expenses (%)	VST		130	100	MWRK
Non-deduct.Input Tax	NAV	0.000	140	100	MWVN
Non-deduct.Input Tax	NVV	0.000	150	100	MWVZ
Acqu.Tax Outgoing	ESA		200	100	NLXA
Acquisition Tax Deb.	ESE		210	200	NLXV

12.5.6 Account Determination

Purpose

After determining tax amount, the system needs to determine the G/L account to which these taxes are to be posted. There may be different G/L accounts for different taxes. SAP determines G/L accounts for taxes automatically through the account determination process. Account determination is linked to account keys. Consequently, you need to assign accounts to all account keys given in the screenshot above that post to a separate G/L account. Account keys that do not post to a separate G/L account do not need account determination.

IMG Node

Transaction OMR0—Automatic Posting

Screen

Description	Transaction	Account determ.
Input tax	VST	☑

Account

Select a transaction and click 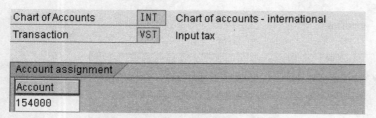 to assign accounts.

Chart of Accounts	INT	Chart of accounts - international
Transaction	VST	Input tax

Account assignment
Account
154000

Posting Key

Click **Posting Key** to display the debit and credit posting keys.

Transaction	VST	Input tax

Posting Key	
Debit	40
Credit	50

Rules

Click **Rules**.

Chart of Accounts	INT	Chart of accounts - international
Transaction	VST	Input tax

Accounts are determined based on		
Debit/Credit	☐	Not changeable
Tax code	☐	

If you want to maintain different G/L accounts for different tax codes, select the `Tax code ☑`.

12.5.7 Account Key

Purpose

Account keys have important properties that determine whether the tax is deductible or not, and how it is posted, etc.

JMG Node

SM30 ➤ V_T007B

Screen

Process	VST

General details

Description	Input tax
Tax type	2	Input tax
Not deductible	☐
Posting indic.	2	Separate line item
Not discnt rel.	☐

Primary Key

Internal processing key

Important Fields

Processing key and description

Processing keys are used by the system to determine accounts or posting keys for line items which are created automatically. The processing keys are predefined by SAP and cannot be changed. You can, however, change the description.

Tax type

You can have different types of taxes, e.g. input tax, output tax, etc.

Tax type	Short text
1	Output tax
2	Input tax
3	Additional tax
4	Not relevant to tax

Posting of input tax can only be done to a G/L account that accepts input tax.

Not deductible

Value Added Tax (VAT) allows deduction of input tax from output tax, and only the balance is paid to the tax authorities. This indicator specifies whether a tax is deductible or not. If a tax is partly deductible, you create one account key for the deductible part, and one for the non-deductible part. Both account keys can be linked to a tax code.

Posting indicator

Posting indicator	Short text
1	No posting required
2	Separate line item
3	Distribute to relevant expense/revenue items

Posting indicator	Description	Explanation
1	No posting required	You use a tax code even if the tax rate is zero. This facilitates tax reporting. These tax codes do not require posting to Financial Accounting.
2	Separate line item	In the case of VAT, input tax paid is deducted from output tax collected. Therefore, the input tax does not increase the cost of material. In order to know how much input tax was paid, this tax is debited to a separate G/L account.
3	Distribute to relevant expense/revenue items	If a tax is not deductible, usually you would charge it to the cost of material.

Not discount relevant

If you select this checkbox, the tax portion which is assigned to the corresponding transaction key is not taken into account in determining the cash discount base. This option is only necessary for Canadian sales tax at the federal level (GST).

12.5.8 Default Values for Tax Codes

Purpose

Here you can specify tax codes that are defaulted in the header of invoice verification.

JMG Node

SM30 ➤ V_169V_ST

Screen

Company Code	1000	IDES AG

Defaults, domestic

Tax Code	VN	16% domestic input tax

Default value unplanned delivery costs

Tax code	VN	16% domestic input tax
Jurisdiction code		

Primary Key

Company Code

Important Fields

Company code

Default tax codes can be different for different company codes.

Default tax code for domestic invoices

When you enter a domestic invoice, the system proposes this tax code by default.

Default tax code for unplanned delivery costs

In this field, you enter the tax code for unplanned delivery costs, if they are posted to a separate G/L account.

Default jurisdiction code

In some countries, tax rates are based on tax jurisdiction areas. For these countries, the jurisdiction code defined here is defaulted for unplanned delivery costs.

12.5.9 Message Control for Taxes

Some of the messages are configurable, i.e. you can specify whether they will be error, warning, or information in your company. You can do this for messages in tax area; application areas for tax are FF and FS. Message control is explained in Section 12.6.

12.6   ATTRIBUTES OF SYSTEM MESSAGES

Functional Consultant	User	Business Process Owner	Senior Management	My Rating	Understanding Level
A	C	X	X		

12.6.1   Messages

When you work, the system gives you error/warning/information messages. These messages are defined in table T100.

	Language	Area	Message	Message text
☐	E	M8	000	You do not have authorization for plant & and activity &
☐	E	M8	001	G/L account & only postable automatically
☐	E	M8	002	Vendor & does not exist
☐	E	M8	003	Material & does not exist
☐	E	M8	004	Select only one option
☐	E	M8	005	Select only one option
☐	E	M8	006	No more items exist
☐	E	M8	007	G/L account & blocked/flagged for deletion
☐	E	M8	008	SYSTEM ERROR: error in routine &
☐	E	M8	009	Posting key & not defined for account type 'K'

Application area

Application area for invoice verification is M8. Application area for taxes is FF and FS.

12.6.2   Configurable System Messages

Some of the messages are configurable, i.e. you can specify whether they will be error, warning, or information in your company. Master list of these messages is maintained in view T100S.

	Application Area	MsgNo	Allowed	Standard	Switch off
☐	M8	010	IWE	E	☐
☐	M8	039	IWE	W	☑
☐	M8	051	E	E	☑
☐	M8	060	IS	S	☐
☐	M8	070	IWE	W	☑
☐	M8	075	IS	S	☐

Application area

Application area M8 is invoice verification.

Message number

Each message is given a unique message number in an application area.

Allowed

Here you specify the ways in which a message may be output: S, I, W, E or A.

Standard

Here you specify the output mode of a message. This mode is used unless changed in view V_T100C.

Switch off

If you do not want to use a message, you can switch it off, instead of deleting it.

12.6.3 Configuration of System Messages

You can set the properties of messages as per your requirement in view V_T100C. These properties can be user dependent. If properties of messages are not defined here, they are taken from view T100S.

Area	M8	Invoice Verification/Valuation

Message Control by User

	Msg	Message text	User Name	Online	Batchl	Standard
	155	Standard cost estimate exists in period & &		E	E	E
	155	Standard cost estimate exists in period & &	SCHAFFT	I	E	E
	298	Value exceeds limit & & in PO		I	I	I

Message number and text

For some messages, SAP allows you to change their properties. You can select one of these messages by clicking 🖉 in this field.

MsgNo	Message text
010	Purchase order & does not exist
039	Terms of payment in PO & differ from those entered
051	An error has occurred during transmission of an automatic message
060	Document no. & created

User name

If you want to create user specific setting, specify the user name here. Message properties are selected in the following priority:

Priority	Setting	Implementation
1	User specific	An entry in this table with user name specified.
2	Client specific	An entry in this table with user name field blank.
3	SAP standard	No entry in this table.

Online

Here you specify the property of a message for online operation.

MsgTyp	Description	TEXT2
I	Note in window	
W	Warning	Standard
E	Errors	
-	Switch off message	

Batch input

Here you specify the property of a message for batch input.

MsgTyp	Description	TEXT2
I	Note in window	
W	Warning	Standard
E	Errors	
-	Switch off message	

Standard

Here the system displays the standard property of a message from view T100S which is applicable both to online entry and batch input.

12.7 INVOICES RECEIVED VIA EDI

Functional Consultant	User	Business Process Owner	Senior Management	My Rating	Understanding Level
B	C	X	X		

12.7.1 Processing IDocs

Data transfer

Information can be transferred between different companies using EDI. This enables a vendor to transfer invoice information electronically instead of in the form of a printed paper invoice.

Data conversion

The data in the IDocs is interpreted to determine the company code, the invoicing party, and the tax code. These are determined using customizing tables explained in this section. If you want to do it differently, you can use customer exit EXIT_SAPLMRMH_011 (enhancement MRMH0002).

Match up

When processing EDI invoices, the system tries to post an invoice document. It uses the purchase order history to determine the quantity to be invoiced and the value to be invoiced for the purchase order item received (proposed quantity and proposed value). If the proposed values match, the invoice is posted.

Handling mismatches

What the system should do in the case of variances is specified in view V_076S_M. If the system cannot post the invoice, it gives the IDoc the appropriate error status. You must then process the IDoc manually using invoice overview transaction MIR6.

12.7.2   Determining the Company Code

Purpose

The EDI data is received as an IDoc. In the IDoc, the vendor specifies the invoice recipient, which is used to determine the company code using this table.

JMG Node

SM30 ➢ V_T076B

Screen

Partn.Type	PartnerNo	Comp.code name in the invoice	CoCd
KU	2009	2009	4500
KU	30099	0000010099	3000
KU	30099	10099	3000
KU	30099	30099	3000

Primary Key

Partner Type
Partner number
Company Code Name in the Invoice

Logic

Invoice recipient in IDoc

The EDI data is received as an IDoc. The system first determines an IDoc segment of type E1EDKA1 using the qualifier (E1EDKA1-PARVW) RE (invoice recipient). This segment has two fields: PARTN and NAME1. These fields contain data that is used to determine the company code for which the invoice is received.

Determining company code from partner number

The system matches the content of the field Partner number (E1EDKA1-PARTN) with the field PartnerNo in the table above, where Partn.Type is KU . If a match is found, the CoCd is picked up.

Determining company code from description

If no match is found, the system matches the content of the field Description (E1EDKA1-NAME1) with the field Comp.code name in the invoice in the table above, where Partn.Type is KU . If a match is found, the CoCd is picked up. If no match is found still, the CoCd is not determined.

12.7.3   Determining the Invoicing Party

Purpose

The EDI data is received as an IDoc. In the IDoc, the vendor may directly specify the vendor number (invoicing party). Alternatively, he may specify your company's account number with the vendor, from which you determine the vendor number (invoicing party).

Logic

Invoice recipient in IDoc

The EDI data is received as an IDoc. The system first determines an IDoc segment of type E1EDKA1 using the qualifier (E1EDKA1-PARVW) LF (vendor) or RS (invoicing party). This segment has two fields: PARTN and LIFNR. These fields contain data that is used to determine the invoicing party from table LFB1 (Vendor Master - Company Code). This table can be accessed only after determining the company code.

Determining the invoicing party from the partner number

The vendor directly specifies the vendor number, i.e. the number used for the vendor's company within your company. The invoicing party specified in the field Partner number (E1EDKA1-PARTN) must be present in table LFB1 for the company code on which the invoice is raised.

Determining the invoicing party from your account number with the vendor

The vendor specifies the number used for your company within the vendor's company in the field E1EDKA1-LIFNR. The system matches this with the field EIKTO (Your account number with the vendor) in table LFB1 (Vendor Master - Company Code). More than one vendor could have maintained the same number for your company, so the vendor number is only adopted here when the system can clearly determine it.

12.7.4 Determining the Tax Code

Purpose

The IDoc you receive does not contain tax code, as it is your company-specific information. Instead it contains the partner number, tax type, and tax rate. The tax type and tax rate are specified in the IDoc segment of type E1EDK04 (header) and type E1EDP04 (items). The country is determined from the company code. The system uses the following order of priority to determine the IDoc data:

1. Tax type and tax rate in the IDoc, country of the company code
2. Tax type is 'VAT', tax rate in the IDoc, country of the company code
3. Tax type and tax rate in the IDoc, country not defined
4. Tax type is 'VAT', tax rate in the IDoc, country not defined

IMG Node

SM30 ➢ T076M

Screen

Partn.Type	PartnerNo	Tax type	Tax rate	Cty	Tx
LI	603	S0	0		I0
LI	603	VAT	0		I0
LI	604	S0	0		I0

Primary Key

Partner Type
Partner number
External Name of Tax Type
Tax Rate Determined Externally
Country Key

12.7.5 Determining Program Parameters

Purpose

Here you specify the document types of the invoice and credit memo documents created by EDI invoice posting. You also specify how the system should react, if the invoice quantity is larger than the proposed quantity or the invoice value is greater than the proposed value.

JMG Node

SM30 ➢ V_076S_M

Screen

Partn.Type	LI
Partner No.	3333
Company Code	1000	IDES AG	Frankfurt

Posting details

| Invoice doc.type | KR |
| Cred.memo doc.type | KG |

Conventional Invoice Verification only

| Park document | ☐ |

Logistics Invoice Verification only

Processing	☐
Check negative variances	☐
Check material no.	☐
Check unit of measure	☐

Primary Key

| Partner Type |
| Partner number |
| Company Code |

Important Fields

Partner type

Partner type ⬚LI indicates that the partner is a vendor.

Partner number

The parameters for creating an IDoc can be different for different vendors.

Company code

The parameters for creating an IDoc can be different for different company codes.

Invoice document type

This document type is used, if an invoice is transferred by EDI.

Credit memo document type

This document type is used, if a credit memo is transferred by EDI.

Park document

If you are using conventional invoice verification, not logistics invoice verification; you can activate this switch, if the invoice is not to be posted immediately, but is to be entered in the Preliminary Posting system. In program version 2.2A, this function is only possible within invoice verification.

Processing

You can use this indicator to determine how the system reacts when there are variances between the data in the invoice and the data the system expects to receive.

Processing	Short text
	No error
1	Unclarified error: park invoice
2	Vendor error: reduce invoice
3	Vendor-specific tolerances: either " " or "1"
4	Tolerances correspond to those for online processing

Indicator	Description
Blank	The system posts the invoice document using the data in the EDI invoice. If the invoice contains quantity or price variances, the system blocks it for payment.
1	The proposed values that the system determined and the values in the EDI invoice are saved. The items that contain variances are saved as unclarified errors. The invoice document is parked. You have to process it manually using transaction MIR6.
2	The invoice document is posted using the proposed values that the system determined. The EDI invoice is reduced by the total of the variances.
3	Depending on the small differences limit in the vendor-specific tolerances, the invoice document is created as follows: If the total of the positive differences in the invoice items is smaller than the positive small difference tolerance limit, the invoice is posted with price variances, but the system blocks it for payment. If the total of the positive differences in the invoice items is greater than the positive small difference tolerance limit, the invoice is parked as containing unclarified errors and must be processed manually.
4	The system verifies the invoice according to the tolerances used in online processing. You maintain the tolerance keys on a company code-specific basis and use them to determine which variances are checked.

Check negative variances

If you set this indicator for a partner, the system checks the invoice for negative variances and rejects it, if the negative variance exceeds the specified limit. If you do not tick this checkbox, the invoice is accepted in the case of negative variances.

Check material number

If you set this indicator for a partner, and the invoice item contains a material number, it must be found in the manufacturer part number or the material number of the purchase order item. If there are inconsistencies, you cannot post the invoice.

Check unit of measure

If you set this indicator for a partner, the units of measure in the EDI invoice are compared with those in the purchase order items. If there are variances, the invoice cannot be posted.

12.8 TREATMENT OF EXCHANGE RATE DIFFERENCES

Functional Consultant	User	Business Process Owner	Senior Management	My Rating	Understanding Level
B	C		X	X	

12.8.1 Purpose

In this view, you set how exchange rate differences should be calculated for invoices in foreign currencies.

12.8.2 IMG Node

SM30 ➢ V_169P_PK

12.8.3 Screen

CoCd	Act.	ERT
0100		
0110		
1000		

12.8.4 Primary Key

Company Code

12.8.5 Important Fields

Company code

The method of treating exchange rate difference can differ from company to company.

Activate exchange rate difference

The specification in this field controls how exchange rate differences will be handled for invoices in foreign currencies. You have the following options:

Activate Exch. Rt. Diff.	Short text
	Exchange rate differences between GR and IR
X	Exch. rate differences between IR and assumed exch. rate
N	No exchange rate differences, only price differences

Indicator	Explanation
Blank	The exchange rate differences will be calculated from the difference between the exchange rate at the time of the goods receipt and the exchange rate at the time of the invoice receipt.
X	The exchange rate differences will be calculated from the difference between the exchange rate at the time of the invoice receipt and an assumed exchange rate that is valid for a specific amount of time, such as a year or a season.
N	No exchange rate differences will be calculated. Instead, differences from exchange rate variations will be considered as price differences and posted to a price difference account.

Exchange rate type

If you specify X in the previous column, here you can specify the exchange rate type which is used for calculating the exchange rate differences.

ExRt	Usage
0021	Current exchange rate
0022	Average exchange rate

12.9   DOCUMENT TYPE FOR BAR CODE ENTRY

Functional Consultant	User	Business Process Owner	Senior Management	My Rating	Understanding Level
B	C	X	X		

12.9.1   Purpose

Here you use the company code and the accounting document type to determine the document type for bar code entry. This allows you to control whether the additional window for entering the bar code appears when you enter documents. The system accesses this table to find a record in the following priority:

Priority	Company code	Accounting document type
1	Present	Present
2	Present	Blank
3	Blank	Present
4	Blank	Blank

The first entry found determines the document type for bar code entry. In the step 'Activate bar code storing', you use the transaction 'Settings for Bar Code Entry' to enter information on the bar code for object type BUS2081 and your document type. You can do this for all users or individual users. You have to choose the setting 'Bar code active' so that the additional window for entering the bar code appears when you post a document.

12.9.2 IMG Node

SM30 ➤ T003S

12.9.3 Screen

CoCd	Type	Doc. type
2000	RE	
2000	RN	
2200	RE	

12.9.4 Primary Key

Company Code
Document Type

12.10 START LOGO

Functional Consultant	User	Business Process Owner	Senior Management	My Rating	Understanding Level
B	C	X	X		

12.10.1 Purpose

For each company code, you can specify the start logo that appears on the invoice verification screen. You can enable or disable display of the start logo and specify its URL.

12.10.2 IMG Node

SM30 ➤ V_169P_LOGO

12.10.3 Screen

Co	Name	Dis	URL
1000	IDES AG	☐	
2000	IDES UK	☐	
2200	IDES France	☐	

12.10.4 Primary Key

Company Code

12.11 CHECK FOR DUPLICATE INVOICES

Functional Consultant	User	Business Process Owner	Senior Management	My Rating	Understanding Level
B	C	X	X		

12.11.1 Purpose

The check for duplication of invoice entry aims to avoid invoices being accidentally created and paid twice. When an invoice is entered, the system checks for duplicate invoices by matching the current invoice data with the data of invoices in the system.

12.11.2 Duplication Check

Current invoice has a reference document

If the current invoice has a reference document then the system checks for previously posted invoices or credit memos in Financial Accounting that match all the following attributes:

➢ Company code
➢ Vendor
➢ Currency
➢ Document date
➢ Reference document number

Current invoice does not have a reference document

If the current invoice does not have a reference document then the system checks for previously posted invoices or credit memos in Financial Accounting that match all the following attributes:

➢ Company code
➢ Vendor
➢ Currency
➢ Document date
➢ Amount in document currency

12.11.3 Message

If all the attributes of the current invoice match with a stored invoice, the system gives a message. Unless all the fields match, no message is given.

Area	M8	Invoice Verification/Valuation

Message Control by User					
M	Message text	U	Online	Batch	Standard
108	Check if invoice already entered under accounting doc. no. & &	E	E	I
462	Check if invoice already entered as logistics inv. doc. number & &	W	W	W

Whether the message is a warning or an error is specified in view V_T100C (see Section 12.6). The messages relevant for duplicate invoices are 108 and 462 in application area M8.

12.11.4 Customizing the Duplicate Invoices Check

Full match check

If the duplicate invoice check is to be based on full match of all the criteria listed above, all fields should be selected in this view V_169P_DC. The check can be different for different company codes.

Broadening the check

In view V_169P_DC, you can specify if some attribute is not to be checked. For example, if you specify that the company code is not to be matched then an invoice in another company code which matches the current invoice in remaining parameters will be considered to be a duplicate.

CoCode	Name	Check co. code	Check reference	Check inv. date
1000	IDES AG	☐	☐	☐
2000	IDES UK	☐	☐	☐
2200	IDES France	☐	☐	☐

12.11.5 Vendor Master

In vendor master at company code level, you can specify Chk double inv. ☑ to indicate that the check for duplicate invoice is to be carried out.

Vendor	1002	Müller KG		Rosenheim
Company Code	1000	IDES AG		

Payment data				
Payt Terms	ZB01		Tolerance group	1000
			Chk double inv.	☑
Chk cashng time				

12.12 VARIANCE TYPES

Functional Consultant	User	Business Process Owner	Senior Management	My Rating	Understanding Level
B	C	X	X		

12.12.1 Creating New Variance Types

The variance type field at item level of an invoice is only filled with the values Blank, A, and B in the standard SAP system. If you need additional values for the variance type, you can use view V169VARIANCETYP to create them.

Var. Type	Variance Type
A	Difference Between GR and IR (PO-Based IR)
B	Difference Between GR and IR (GR-Based IR)

12.12.2 Filling Variance Type Field

You can use BAdI MRM_VARIANCE_TYPE to control how the variance type field is filled.

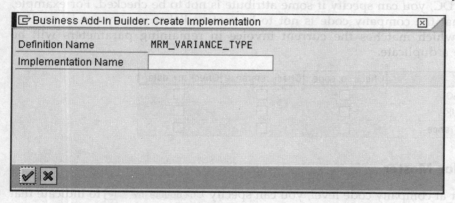

12.13 CUSTOMER EXITS

Functional Consultant	User	Business Process Owner	Senior Management	My Rating	Understanding Level
B	C	X	X		

You may use transaction CMOD for maintaining the following customer exits in invoice verification:

Customer exit	Description
MM08R001	ERS (conventional Invoice Verification)
MM08R002	Tolerance checks
LMR1M001	Transfer of document header and item data, account assignment proposal for invoices for blanket POs
LMR1M002	Account grouping for GR/IR account determination
LMR1M003	Number assignment in Logistics Invoice Verification
LMR1M004	Item text in follow-on documents
LMR1M005	Change criteria for releasing parked documents for posting
LMR1M006	Change XML data for BAPI call CreateFromData
RMVKON00	Consignment/pipeline settlement
MRMH0001	ERS (Logistics Invoice Verification)
MRMH0002	EDI invoice receipt (Logistics Invoice Verification)
MRMH0003	Revaluation (Logistics Invoice Verification)
MRMN0001	Message output for Invoice Verification

12.14 BUSINESS ADD-INS

Functional Consultant	User	Business Process Owner	Senior Management	My Rating	Understanding Level
B	C	X	X		

You may use transaction SE19 to maintain the following Business Add-Ins (BAdIs):

BAdI	Description
INVOICE_UPDATE	BAdI before updating, during updating, and saving an invoice document
MRM_HEADER_DEFAULT	BAdI to prepopulate various header fields
MRM_PAYMENT_TERMS	BAdI to set terms of payment
MRM_UDC_DISTRIBUTE	BAdI to distribute unplanned delivery costs
MRM_TRANSACT_DEFAULT	BAdI to prepopulate various transaction fields
MRM_WT_SPLIT_UPDATE	BAdI to change the withholding tax data and the data during a vendor split
MRM_TOLERANCE_GROUP	BAdI to set vendor-specific tolerance groups
MRM_RELEASE_CHECK	BAdI for additional checks before invoices are released
MRM_MRIS_HDAT_MODIFY	BAdI to change document header data in invoicing plans
MRM_MRKO_HDAT_MODIFY	BAdI to change document header data in consignment settlement
MRM_ITEM_CUSTFIELDS	BAdI to Change Customer's Own Fields

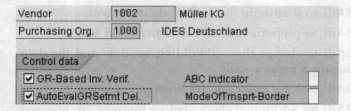

CHAPTER 13

Evaluated Receipt Settlement

13.1 EVALUATED RECEIPT SETTLEMENT (ERS)

Functional Consultant	User	Business Process Owner	Senior Management	My Rating	Understanding Level
A	A	B	C		

13.1.1 Evaluated Receipt Settlement

In evaluated receipt settlement, you settle goods receipts directly without receiving an invoice from the vendor. The system generates the corresponding invoices and posts them. The settlement documents are automatically created. You can print them and send to the vendor.

13.1.2 Evaluated Receipt Settlement for a Vendor

In order to use evaluated receipt settlement, it must be enabled for a vendor.

Vendor	1002	Müller KG
Purchasing Org.	1000	IDES Deutschland

Control data

☑ GR-Based Inv. Verif. ☐ ABC indicator
☑ AutoEvalGRSetmt Del. ☐ ModeOfTrnsprt-Border

13.1.3   Purchase Order

Item	[10] 100-100 , Casing		▲ ▼

| Material Data | Quantities/Weights | Delivery Schedule | Delivery | Invoice |

☑ Inv. Receipt   Tax Code   01
☐ Final Invoice
☑ GR-Bsd IV
☑ ERS

In the Invoice tab of the purchase order item, ☑ERS must be selected, ☑GR-Bsd IV must be selected and Tax Code must be specified. Also, in the Condition Control tab of the purchase order item, ☐Estimated Price must not be selected.

13.1.4   Goods Receipt

The material is received using transaction MIGO with reference to the purchase order.

13.1.5   BAdIs

You can use the following BAdIs to change the header and lines of the invoice document created by ERS:

BAdI	Purpose
MRM_ERS_HDAT_MODIFY	BAdI to change document header data in ERS
MRM_ERS_IDAT_MODIFY	BAdI to change document lines in ERS

13.2   SETTLEMENT OF MATERIAL COST

Functional Consultant	User	Business Process Owner	Senior Management	My Rating	Understanding Level
A	A	B	C		

13.2.1   Purpose

You can automatically create and settle invoices for goods receipt without waiting for invoice from the vendor using the Evaluated Receipt Settlement process. You can also settle planned delivery cost using this process.

13.2.2　Transaction

MRRL—Evaluated Receipt Settlement (ERS)

13.2.3　Initial Screen

Document Selection		
Company Code	1000	to
Plant	1000	to
Posting Date of Goods Receip		to
Goods Receipt Document		to
Fiscal Year of Goods Receipt	2014	to
Vendor	1002	to
Purchasing Document		to
Item		to

Processing Options		
Doc. selection	3	Document selection per order item
Test Run	☑	
☐ Settle Goods Items + Planned Delivery Costs		

Display Options	
Layout	

13.2.4　Test Run

	Pst	Vendor	Ref. Doc.	FYrRef	Rflt	Purch.Doc.	Item	Ref	Doc	Year	Info	FI	DC	B/L	P
	X	1002	5000000034	2014	1	4500017092	10							

If you do not want to settle a goods receipt, deselect ⬜ Pst and save. The deselected goods receipt will not be selected when you execute this transaction again.

13.2.5　Settlement Run

Go back to the initial screen. Deselect Test Run and execute.

	Pst	Vendor	Ref. Doc.	FYrRef	Rflt	Purch.Doc.	Item	Ref	Doc. No.	Year	Info	FI Doc.	DC	B/L	Pr.
	X	1002	5000000034	2014	1	4500017092	10		5105608676	2014		5100000034			

13.2.6 Invoice

You can view the invoice created by the evaluated receipt settlement program by clicking <u>5105608676</u>, or by using transaction MIR4 and specifying the invoice number.

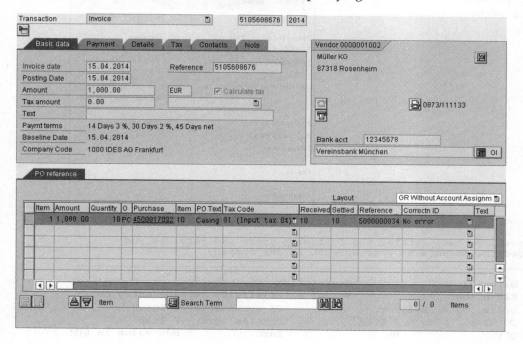

13.2.7 Accounting Entries

You can display the accounting document by clicking <u>5100000034</u>. Alternatively, you display the invoice using transaction MIR4. Enter the Invoice Document No. and the Fiscal Year . Click ⏎ Display Document . The system displays the invoice. Click ┌ Follow-On Documents ... ┐. The system displays the list of accounting documents. Double-click the ┌ Accounting document ┐ to see the accounting entries.

Data Entry View

Document Number	5100000034		Company Code	1000		Fiscal Year	2014			
Document Date	15.04.2014		Posting Date	15.04.2014		Period	4			
Reference	5105608676		Cross-CC no.							
Currency	EUR		Texts exist	☐		Ledger Group				

CoCd	Itm	PK	G/L Acc	Account	Description	Amount	Purch.Doc.	Item	Material	Quantity
1000	1	31	160000	1002	Müller KG	1,000.00-				
	2	86	191100	191100	Goods Rcvd/Invoice R	1,000.00	4500017092	10	100-100	10

13.2.8 Message to Vendor

You can see the message generated for the vendor using transaction MR90.

Müller KG
87318 Rosenheim

Credit memo	
	Page: 1 / 1
Document no. / Date	Currency
5105608676 / 15.04.2014	EUR
Your vendor number in our co.	Your tax ID number
1002	
Our customer no. in your co.	Our tax ID number
	DE123456789
Processed by	Your tax number
Mr. Agrawal	
Telephone no.	
Fax no.	
E-mail address	

As agreed, we have settled the following goods and services and
credited the amounts to your account in our company:

Item	Material		Description	
	EAN number		Vendor material/ext. service entry no.	
	Deliv. note /Ref./ of		GR doc./SEnt. / Item	
	PO (SA) / Item		Outline agrmt / Item	
	Qty	Un	TaxC	Net value in EUR

Settlement items for plant: 1000, Werk Hamburg,
                             22299 Hamburg, Alsterdorfer Strasse 13

00001	100-100		Casing	
	5000000034 / 15.04.2014		5000000034 / 0001	
	4500017092 / 00010			
	10	PC	0I	1.000,00

Total net value			1.000,00
Input tax 0% (0I)		1.000,00	0,00
Total			**1.000,00**

Terms of payment: Related to 15.04.2014:
                       Within 14 days 3 % cash discount
                       Within 30 days 2 % cash discount
                       Within 45 days Due net

You can print and send it.

13.3 SETTLEMENT OF PLANNED DELIVERY COST

Functional Consultant	User	Business Process Owner	Senior Management	My Rating	Understanding Level
A	A	B	C		

13.3.1 Purpose

You can use this program to effect automatic settlement of planned delivery costs. If you enter several goods receipts against a purchase order item, the system generates one invoice item per condition type for the total quantity delivered.

13.3.2 Activation

If you also want to settle planned delivery cost automatically, you can specify that in view V_T169DC_ERS.

Comp.	Purch.	Freight Vendor	Activate Autom.
1000	1000	1002	☑

13.3.3 Transaction

MRDC—Automatic Delivery Cost Settlement

13.3.4 Initial Screen

Document Selection

Company Code		to	⇨
Freight Vendor		to	⇨
Purchasing Document		to	⇨
Item		to	⇨
Bill of Lading		to	⇨

Processing Options

Document Selection	3	Document Selection per Order Item
Test Run	☑	

Display Options

Layout	

13.3.5   Test Run

	Postable	Vendor	Purch.Doc.	Item	Doc. No.	Year	Info. Text	FI Doc.	B/Lading	Proc. Doc.
	X	1002	4500017089	10						

If you do not want to settle a goods receipt, deselect [Pst] and save. The deselected goods receipt will not be selected when you execute this transaction again.

13.3.6   Settlement Run

Go back to the initial screen. Deselect Test Run and execute.

	Postable	Vendor	Purch.Doc.	Item	Doc. No.	Year	Info. Text	FI Doc.	B/Lading	Proc. Doc.
	X	1002	4500017089	10	5105608704	2014		5100000059		

13.3.7   Invoice

You can view the invoice created by the evaluated receipt settlement program by clicking <u>5105608704</u>, or by using transaction MIR4 and specifying the invoice number.

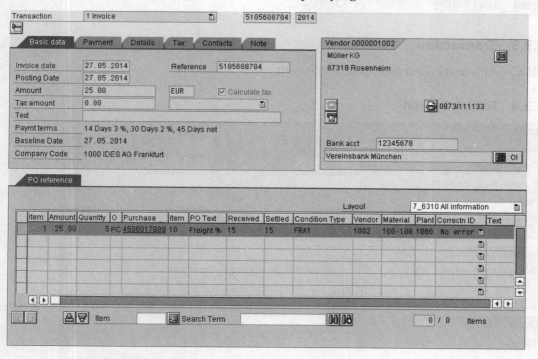

Note the | Condition Type / FRA1 | and | PO Text / Freight % |.

13.3.8 Accounting Entries

You can display the accounting document by clicking 5100000059. Alternatively, you display the invoice using transaction MIR4. Enter the Invoice Document No. and the Fiscal Year . Click 𝒢 Display Document . The system displays the invoice. Click Follow-On Documents ... . The system displays the list of accounting documents. Double-click the Accounting document to see the accounting entries.

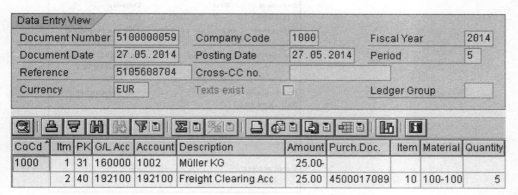

CoCd	Itm	PK	G/L Acc	Account	Description	Amount	Purch.Doc.	Item	Material	Quantity
1000	1	31	160000	1002	Müller KG	25.00-				
	2	40	192100	192100	Freight Clearing Acc	25.00	4500017089	10	100-100	5

13.3.9 Message to Vendor

You can see the message generated for the vendor using transaction MR90.

Müller KG
87318 Rosenheim

```
Credit memo
                                          Page: 1 / 1

Document no. / Date                Currency
5105608704 / 27.05.2014            EUR
Your vendor number in our co.      Your tax ID number
1002
Our customer no. in your co.       Our tax ID number
                                   DE123456789


Processed by                       Your tax number
Mr. Agrawal
Telephone no.


Fax no.


E-mail address
```

As agreed, we have settled the following goods and services and
credited the amounts to your account in our company:

Item	Material		Description	
	EAN number		Vendor material/ext. service entry no.	
	Deliv. note /Ref./ of		GR doc./SEnt. / Item	
	PO (SA)	/ Item	Outline agrmt / Item	
	Qty	Un	TaxC	Net value in EUR

Settlement items for plant: 1000, Werk Hamburg,
                               22299 Hamburg, Alsterdorfer Strasse 13

Delivery costs

00001 100-100			Freight %	
4500017089		/ 00010		
	5	PC	0I	25,00

Total net value			25,00
Input tax 0% (0I)		25,00	0,00
Total			**25,00**

Terms of payment: Related to 27.05.2014:
                       Within 14 days 3 % cash discount
                       Within 30 days 2 % cash discount
                       Within 45 days Due net

You can print and send it.

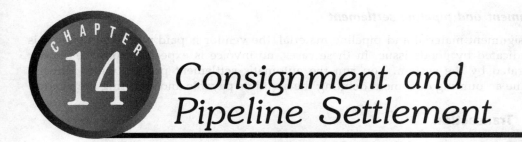

Consignment and Pipeline Settlement

14.1 CONSIGNMENT AND PIPELINE SETTLEMENT

Functional Consultant	User	Business Process Owner	Senior Management	My Rating	Understanding Level
A	A	B	C		

14.1.1 Purpose

Goods receipt for consignment material

You receive consignment material in your store. The quantity of material in stock increases, but the value does not because the material still belongs to the vendor.

Goods issue for consignment material

You issue consignment material for use. The quantity of material in stock decreases, but the value is not affected. The customer now has to pay for the material to the vendor.

Goods receipt for pipeline material

There is no receipt of pipeline material.

Goods issue for pipeline material

The pipeline material is directly issued for use and the customer is liable to pay for the material to the vendor.

405

Consignment and pipeline settlement

For consignment material and pipeline material, the vendor is paid when the material is used, indicated by goods issue. In these cases, no invoice is expected from the vendor or generated by the system. You run the automatic settlement process which directly creates the accounting document debiting the accounts payable and crediting the vendor.

14.1.2 Transaction

MRKO—Consignment and Pipeline Settlement

14.1.3 Initial Screen

Selection				
Company Code	☑	to		➪
Vendor		to		➪
Plant		to		➪
Material		to		➪
Document Date		to		➪
Posting Date		to		➪
Material Document		to		➪

☑ Consignment
☑ Pipeline

Processing
◉ Display
○ Settle

Display Options
☑ Withdrawals not settled
☐ Settled withdrawals
Document Number [ ] to [ ] ➪
Layout [ ]

Consignment and pipeline material

You can use this program for both consignment and pipeline material.

Display/settle

You should first choose the ◉ Display option and check the list. Return to the initial screen, choose the ◉ Settle option and Execute. You cannot settle the consignment and pipeline material from the display list.

Withdrawals not settled

Tick this checkbox to display withdrawals that are not yet settled. If you want to see only settled withdrawals, leave this checkbox blank.

Settled withdrawals

You can use this report to display settled withdrawals as well. For settled withdrawals, the system displays the details of settlement document.

Layout

If you have saved any layouts for this report, you can specify the one you want to use.

14.1.4   Displaying the List

You should first select the ⊙ Display option.

CoCd	Vendor	Mat. Doc.	MatYr	Item	Doc. Date	Plant	Material	Qty Withdr	Un	Amount	Crcy	DocumentNo	Year	Item	Info
1000	1000	4900000007	2014	1	02.05.2014	1000	1300-550	10	PC	67.00	EUR				Not settled
1000	1000	4900000008	2014	1	02.05.2014	1000	1300-550	5	PC	33.50	EUR				Not settled
1000	1050	4900000005	2014	1	02.05.2014	1000	1300-800	100	L	72.00	EUR				Not settled
1000	1050	4900000006	2014	1	02.05.2014	1000	1300-800	50	L	36.00	EUR				Not settled

The system shows the list of consignment and pipeline withdrawals that will be settled. For settled withdrawals, the system displays the details of settlement document.

14.1.5   Crediting the Vendor for Goods Used

You cannot settle an item from the list display. You must select the ⊙ Settle option in the initial screen. When you execute, the system creates accounting documents for the selected documents.

CoCd	Vendor	Mat. Doc.	MatYr	Item	Doc. Date	Plant	Material	Qty Withdr	Un	Amount	Crcy	DocumentNo	Year	Item	Information text
1000	1050	4900000005	2014	1	02.05.2014	1000	1300-800	100	L	72.00	EUR	5100000035	2014	2	Document created
1000	1050	4900000006	2014	1	02.05.2014	1000	1300-800	50	L	36.00	EUR	5100000035	2014	3	Document created

14.1.6   Invoice

In the case of consignment and pipeline settlement, no invoice is generated. Accounting documents are generated directly.

14.1.7   Accounting Entries

You may click the document number 5100000035 to open it or use transaction FB03.

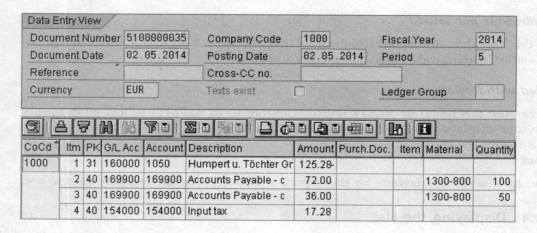

CoCd	Itm	PK	G/L Acc	Account	Description	Amount	Purch.Doc.	Item	Material	Quantity
1000	1	31	160000	1050	Humpert u. Töchter Gr	125.28-				
	2	40	169900	169900	Accounts Payable - c	72.00			1300-800	100
	3	40	169900	169900	Accounts Payable - c	36.00			1300-800	50
	4	40	154000	154000	Input tax	17.28				

14.1.8 Purchasing Info Record

For consignment and pipeline material, there is no invoice. These materials are settled based on prices stored in the purchasing info record. You can select a line in the list and display the purchasing info record by clicking `Info Record`. In the purchasing info record, you can click `Conditions` to see prices.

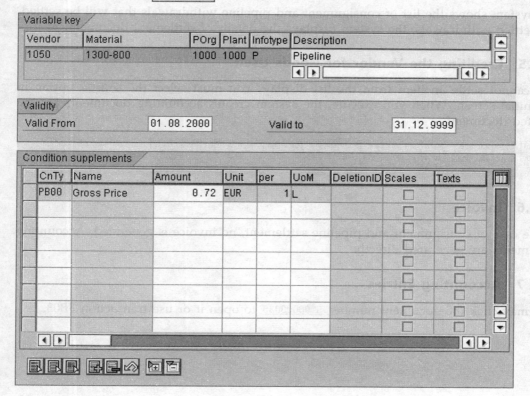

14.1.9 Messages

You can select a line in the list and click 📇 Messages to process messages. The system calls transaction MR91 with selection screen having details of the line.

Selection Screen

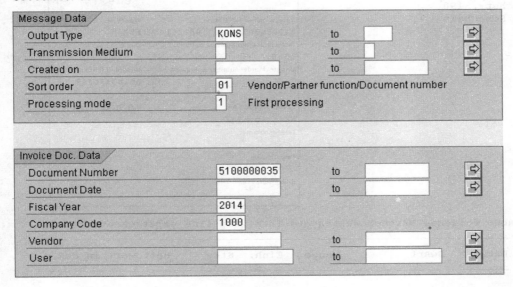

Message Data			
Output Type	KONS	to	
Transmission Medium		to	
Created on		to	
Sort order	01	Vendor/Partner function/Document number	
Processing mode	1	First processing	

Invoice Doc. Data			
Document Number	5100000035	to	
Document Date		to	
Fiscal Year	2014		
Company Code	1000		
Vendor		to	
User		to	

List of Messages

Click 🔄.

	Inv. Doc. No.	Item	CoCd	Vendor	Role	Name 1	Out.	Created on	Med	St.	User
	5100000035		1000	1050	LF	Humpert u. Töchter	KONS	02.05.2014	1	0	SAPUSER

Message

Select the message and click 🖼 to display it.

Company
Humpert u. Töchter GmbH
Mosbachstr. 190
83026 Rosenheim

Pipelineabrechnung

	Seite: 1 / 1
Belegnummer / Datum	Währung
5100000035 / 02.05.2014	EUR
Ihre Lieferantennummer bei uns	Ihre USt.-Id. Nr.
1050	
Unsere Kundennummer bei Ihnen	Unsere USt.-Id. Nr.
	DE123456789
Sachbearbeiter/in	Ihre Steuernummer
Herr Agrawal	
Telefonnummer	
Faxnummer	
E-Mail-Adresse	

Wir haben folgende Warenentnahmen aus Ihrer Pipeline abgerechnet:

Datum	BwArt	Menge	Einh.	StKz	Nettowert in EUR
Abrechnungspositionen Werk:		**1000, Werk Hamburg,**			
		22299 Hamburg, Alsterdorfer Strasse 13			
Material: 1300-800		Benzin 95 Oktan			
02.05.2014	201	100	L	VN	72,00
02.05.2014	201	50	L	VN	36,00
		150	L		108,00

Summe Nettowert		108,00
Vorsteuer Inland 16% (VN)	108,00	17,28
Endbetrag		**125,28**

Zahlungsbedingungen: Bezogen auf den 02.05.2014:
                             14 Tage 3%, 30/2%, 45 netto

Note that the message is in the language of the vendor.

Invoicing Plan Settlement

15.1 PERIODIC INVOICING PLAN

Functional Consultant	User	Business Process Owner	Senior Management	My Rating	Understanding Level
B	C	X	X		

15.1.1 Periodic Invoicing Plan

An invoicing plan enables you to schedule invoice creation over a series of future due dates independently of individual procurement transactions and the actual receipt of goods or services. You do not wait for the vendor invoice for goods supplied or services performed every time. Instead you create invoices based on the dates scheduled in the purchase order and these trigger the payment to the vendor. You can inform the vendor when the invoice documents are created. In periodic invoicing plan, same amount is paid at fixed interval.

411

15.1.2   Purchase Order

For using invoicing plan, you need to ensure the following for a purchase order item:

Services

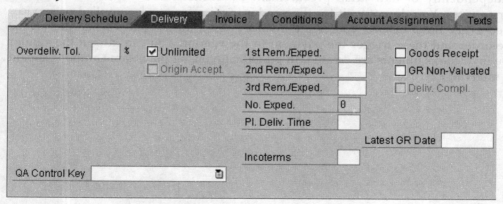

Invoicing plans are generally used for services. If you select item category 'Service', specify the details of services here.

Delivery

Goods receipt

☐ Goods Receipt must not be selected

Account Assignment

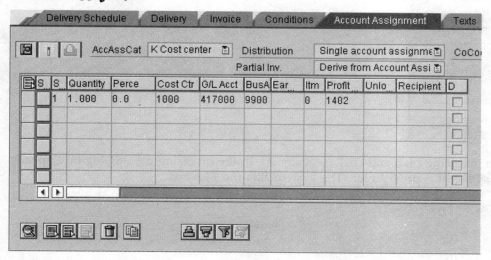

The item must have an account assignment.

Invoice

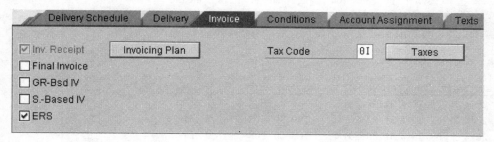

Goods receipt based invoice verification

☐ GR-Bsd IV must not be selected.

ERS

☑ ERS must be selected.

Invoicing plan

Click [Invoicing Plan]. The system gives the following dialog box:

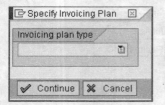

Specify the invoicing plan and click [✔ Continue]. In the invoicing plan dialog box, specify Start date, End date and press Enter. The system fills the Deadlines.

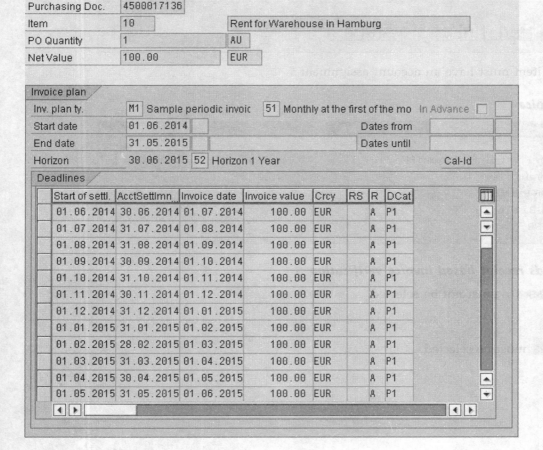

Save the purchase order.

15.1.3 Transaction

MRIS—Invoicing Plan Settlement

15.1.4 Initial Screen

Document Selection

Company Code	1000	to	
Plant	1000	to	
Vendor	1002	to	
Purchasing Document	4500017136	to	
Item		to	

Processing Options

Doc. selection	3
Test Run	☑

Display Options

Layout	

15.1.5 Test Run

Select Test Run ☑. Execute. The system gives the list.

Pstable	Vendor	Purch.Doc.	Item	Mat. Doc.	MatYr	InfoText	FI Doc.	DC	B/Lading	Proc. Doc.
X	1002	4500017136	10							

15.1.6 Settlement Run

Go back to initial screen and deselect Test Run ☐. Execute.

Pstable	Vendor	Purch.Doc.	Item	Mat. Doc.	MatYr	Information Text	FI Doc.	DC	Proc. Doc.
X	1002	4500017136	10	5105608758	2014	Document created	5100000117		

The system creates invoicing plan settlement.

15.1.7 Invoice

Click <u>5105608758</u>.

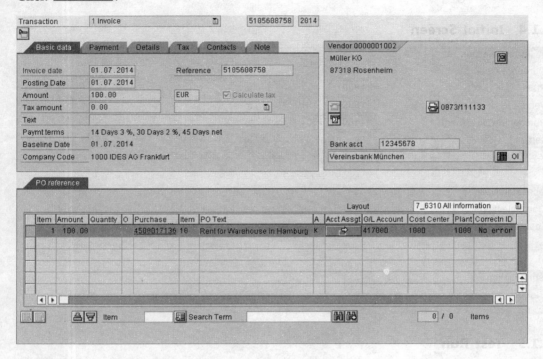

The system has automatically generated this invoice.

15.1.8 Accounting Entries

Click <u>5100000117</u>.

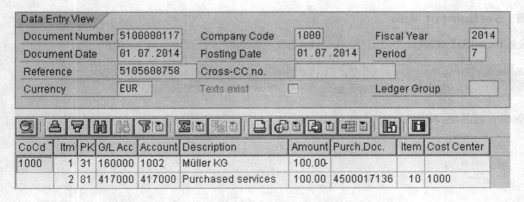

The vendor has been credited the amount due to him.

15.1.9 Message to Vendor

Run transaction MR90 to print the credit memo generated by the system.

Müller KG
87318 Rosenheim

```
Credit memo

                                    Page: 1 / 1

Document no. / Date              Currency
5105608758 / 01.07.2014         EUR
Your vendor number in our co.    Your tax ID number
1002
Our customer no. in your co.     Our tax ID number
                                 DE123456789
Processed by                     Your tax number
Mr. Agrawal
Telephone no.

Fax no.

E-mail address
```

As agreed, we have settled the following goods and services and
credited the amounts to your account in our company:

Item	Material	Description		
	EAN number	Vendor material/ext. service entry no.		
	Deliv. note /Ref./ of	GR doc./SEnt. / Item		
	PO (SA) / Item	Outline agrmt / Item		
	SEnt line	Service text		
	INT. SERVICE NO.	EXT. SERVICE NO.		
	QTY	UN		NET VALUE IN EUR
	Qty	**Un**	**TaxC**	**Net value in EUR**

Settlement items for plant: 1000, Werk Hamburg,
                                  22299 Hamburg, Alsterdorfer Strasse 13

00001
    4500017136   / 00010
                                        OI   100,00
              Settlement period 01.06.2014 bis 30.06.2014

Total net value			100,00
Input tax 0% (OI)		100,00	0,00

Total   **100,00**

Terms of payment: Related to 01.07.2014:
                      Within 14 days 3 % cash discount
                      Within 30 days 2 % cash discount
                      Within 45 days Due net

15.2 PARTIAL INVOICING PLAN

Functional Consultant	User	Business Process Owner	Senior Management	My Rating	Understanding Level
B	C	X	X		

15.2.1 Partial Invoicing Plan

An invoicing plan enables you to schedule invoice creation over a series of future due dates independently of individual procurement transactions and the actual receipt of goods or services. You do not wait for the vendor invoice for goods supplied or services performed every time. Instead you create invoices based on the dates scheduled in the purchase order and these trigger the payment to the vendor. You can inform the vendor when the invoice documents are created. In partial invoicing plan, the total amount is paid in different installments on specified dates.

15.2.2 Purchase Order

For using invoicing plan, you need to ensure the following for a purchase order item:

Services

	Line	D	Service No.	Short Text	Quantity	Un	Gross Price	Crcy
	10	☐		Installation of 10 T Crane in Hamburg	1	AU	10,000.00	EUR
	20	☐						EUR
	30	☐						EUR
	40	☐						EUR
	50	☐						EUR
	60	☐						EUR
	70	☐						EUR
	80	☐						EUR
	90	☐						EUR
	100	☐						EUR

Service Sel.   Line 10

Invoicing plans are generally used for services. If you select item category 'Service', specify the details of services here.

Delivery

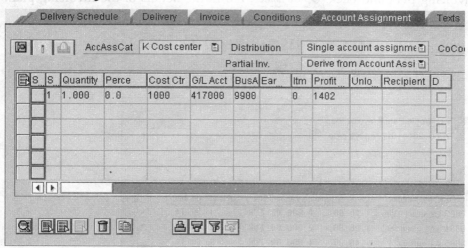

Goods receipt

☐ Goods Receipt must not be selected

Account Assignment

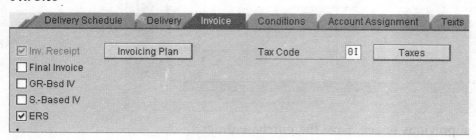

The item must have an account assignment.

Invoice

Goods receipt based invoice verification

☐ GR-Bsd IV must not be selected.

ERS

☑ ERS must be selected.

Invoicing plan

Click ⬚ Invoicing Plan . The system gives the following dialog box:

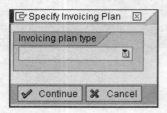

Specify the invoicing plan and click ✔ Continue . Fill in the details of the invoicing plan.

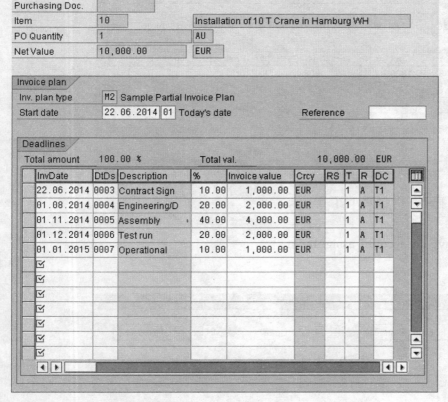

Go back to the previous screen. Save the purchase order.

15.2.3   Transaction

MRIS—Invoicing Plan Settlement

15.2.4   Initial Screen

Document Selection

Company Code	1000	to	
Plant	1000	to	
Vendor	1002	to	
Purchasing Document	4500017137	to	
Item		to	

Processing Options

Doc. selection	3
Test Run	☑

Display Options

Layout	

15.2.5   Test Run

^	Pstable	Vendor	Purch.Doc.	Item	Mat. Doc.	MatYr	InfoText	FI Doc.	DC	B/Lading	Proc. Doc.
⊡	X	1002	4500017137	10							

15.2.6   Settlement Run

Go back to initial screen and deselect `Test Run` ☐. Execute.

^	Pstable	Vendor	Purch.Doc.	Item	Mat. Doc.	MatYr	Information Text	FI Doc.	DC	B/	Pr
⊡	X	1002	4500017137	10	5105608757	2014	Document created	5100000116			

The system creates the invoicing plan settlement.

15.2.7 Invoice

Click 5105608757.

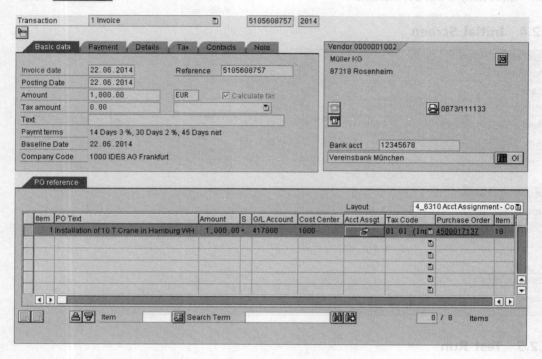

The system has automatically generated this invoice.

15.2.8 Accounting Entries

Click 5100000116.

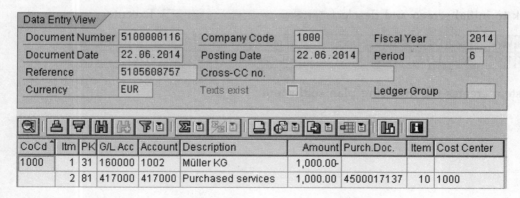

The vendor has been credited the amount due to him.

15.2.9 Message to Vendor

Run transaction MR90 to print the credit memo generated by the system.

Müller KG
87318 Rosenheim

Credit memo

Page: 1 / 1

Document no. / Date
5105608757 / 22.06.2014

Currency
EUR

Your vendor number in our co.
1002

Your tax ID number

Our customer no. in your co.

Our tax ID number
DE123456789

Processed by
Mr. Agrawal

Your tax number

Telephone no.

Fax no.

E-mail address

As agreed, we have settled the following goods and services and
credited the amounts to your account in our company:

Item	Material	Description		
	EAN number	Vendor material/ext. service entry no.		
	Deliv. note /Ref./ of	GR doc./SEnt. / Item		
	PO (SA) / Item	Outline agrmt / Item		
	SEnt line	Service text		
	INT. SERVICE NO.	EXT. SERVICE NO.		
	QTY	UN		NET VALUE IN EUR
	Qty	**Un**	**TaxC**	**Net value in EUR**

Settlement items for plant: 1000, Werk Hamburg,
22299 Hamburg, Alsterdorfer Strasse 13

00001
4500017137 / 00010

OI 1.000,00

Settlement period bis 22.06.2014

Total net value		1.000,00
Input tax 0% (OI)	1.000,00	0,00
Total		**1.000,00**

Terms of payment: Related to 22.06.2014:
Within 14 days 3 % cash discount
Within 30 days 2 % cash discount
Within 45 days Due net

16

Credit Memo

Credit memo

After receiving material from a vendor, you receive invoice from the vendor. Similarly, after returning goods to the vendor, you receive credit memo.

Goods return before invoice posting

If the goods are returned before the vendor sends invoice for goods, there will be no invoice either for goods sent, or for goods returned.

Goods return after invoice posting

If the goods are returned after the invoice for the goods receipt has been posted, the vendor will send a credit memo for goods returned. The material may be returned using goods return movement type 122, or goods receipt reversal movement type 102.

Positive quantity variance

You may also receive credit memo to correct an invoice with positive quantity variance (invoice quantity greater than the goods receipt quantity). When you post a credit memo, the total quantity in the purchase order history is reduced by the credit memo quantity.

Positive price variance

However, in the case of positive price variance (invoice price greater than the purchase order price), enter it as ⃞ 4 Subsequent credit 🔲 , and not as credit memo because you do not want to change the quantity of goods received. When you post a credit memo, the total quantity in the purchase order history is reduced by the credit memo quantity.

Checks in credit memo

➤ When you post a credit memo, the system performs the following checks:

➤ The maximum quantity you can credit is the quantity that has already been invoiced. If you enter a larger quantity, the system gives an error message.

➤ If you post a credit memo for the same quantity as was invoiced so far, the system expects that the total amount invoiced so far is also credited. Otherwise, a situation might arise where you have no stock for a material, but a stock value. If you do not enter the amount invoiced so far, the system automatically replaces your entry and proceeds to the item screen. A warning message informs you that your entry has been changed.

➤ If you post a credit memo for a smaller quantity than that invoiced to date, the amount of the credit memo cannot be larger than the amount invoiced so far. If you post a larger amount, the system displays an error message.

The system does not check that the price, computed by the `Amount` divided by the `Quantity`, corresponds to the purchase order price or the invoice price.

16.1 GOODS RECEIPT REVERSAL

Functional Consultant	User	Business Process Owner	Senior Management	My Rating	Understanding Level
A	A	A	A		

16.1.1 Scenario

You have reversed a goods receipt and returned the material to the vendor after invoice posting.

16.1.2 Reversal of Goods Receipt

Transaction

MIGO—Goods Movement

Selecting the Goods Receipt to be Reversed

Selection of goods receipt to be reversed using purchase order

| A01 Goods Receipt 🗎 | R01 Purchase Order🗎 | 4500017087 | | Plant | 1000 | ⊕🖩 | | Reversal of GR | 102 |

Specify the purchase order number, movement type 102 and press Enter. The system shows the goods receipts. Select the goods receipt you want to reverse.

Specifying goods receipt to be reversed directly

Alternatively, you specify the goods receipt number directly.

| A03 Cancellation 🖺 | R02 Material Docum 🖺 | 5000000015 | 2014 | ⊕ 🛗 | ▦ |

Reversal Goods Movement

Reference document of the reversal goods movement

| Material | Quantity | Where | Purchase Order Data | Partner | Account Assignment |

Purchase Order	4500017087	10	🖼		Item Category	Standard
Reference Document	5000000015	1
"Del.Completed" Ind.	1 Set automatic 🖺		☐ Del. Compl. Ind. PO Item

Incoterms   CPT

The **Purchase Order Data** tab shows the goods receipt being reversed in the **Reference Document** field. Select ☑ Item OK. Save the goods movement. The goods receipt is reversed.

Material Document of Goods Receipt Reversal

Display the material document using transaction MB02.

Change Material Document 5000000046 : Details 0001 / 0001

| ◀ ▶ 🖾 🕮 🖾 Messages | Material | WM Details... |

Purchase Order	4500017087	10		Movement Type	102	Reversal of GR
Ref. Document	5000000015	1
Plant	1000		Werk Hamburg
Vendor	1002		Müller KG
Incoterms	CPT
Material	100-100		Casing

Quantity in

| Unit of Entry | 2 | . | PC | Stor. Location | 0001 |

Further Information

Unloading Point

Company Code 1000 Fiscal Yr 2014

Text

Accounting Entries of Goods Receipt Reversal

Click Accounting Documents... and double-click Accounting document .

Document Number	5000000043	Company Code	1000	Fiscal Year		2014
Document Date	17.05.2014	Posting Date	17.05.2014	Period		5
Reference		Cross-CC no.				
Currency	EUR	Texts exist	☐	Ledger Group		

Data Entry View

CoCd	Itm	PK	S	G/L Account	Account	Description	Amount	Curr.	Tx	Cost Center
1000	1	99		790000	790000	Unfinished products	227.52-	EUR		
	2	86		191100	191100	Goods Rcvd/Invoice R	200.00	EUR		
	3	83		281500	281500	Income from price di	27.52	EUR		

16.1.3   Credit Memo

Transaction

MIRO—Enter Invoice

Purchase Order Structure

Display the purchase order structure by clicking Show PO structure .

Display - PO structure	Qty	Amount	Posting date	Doc. No.
🧑 Müller KG				
⤷ 4500017087				
⤷ 10 Gehäuse	100.000 PC	10,000.00 EUR	24.03.2014	
▷ Delivery note				
▷ Delivery note				
▷ Delivery note				
▷ Delivery note				
▷ Delivery note				
▷ Delivery note				
▷ Delivery note				
▷ Delivery note				
▷ Delivery note				
▷ Delivery note				
⤷ Delivery note				
📄 WE	2.000 PC	200.00 EUR	31.03.2014	5000000015
📄 WE	- 2.000 PC	- 200.00 EUR	17.05.2014	5000000046
📄 RE-L	2.000 PC	200.00 EUR	31.03.2014	5105608654

The system shows the goods receipt reversal entry.

Credit Memo Entry

Specify Transaction 2 Credit memo, enter the purchase order number and select the goods receipt that was reversed.

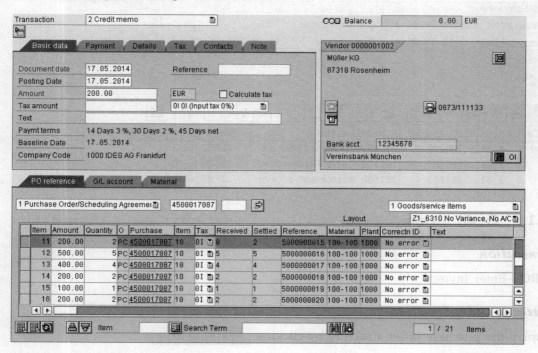

Note that the system shows the received quantity zero (because of goods receipt reversal) and the settled quantity 2. Post the credit memo.

Credit Memo Document

Display the posted credit memo using transaction MIR4. Display the purchase order structure by clicking | Show PO structure |.

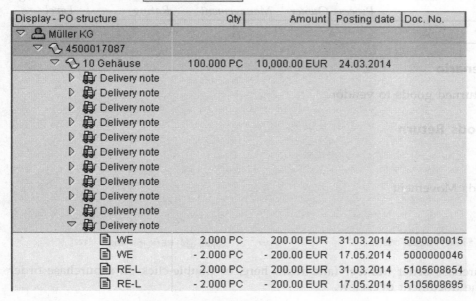

Display - PO structure	Qty	Amount	Posting date	Doc. No.
▽ 👤 Müller KG				
▽ 🔄 4500017087				
▽ 🔄 10 Gehäuse	100.000 PC	10,000.00 EUR	24.03.2014	
▷ 🚚 Delivery note				
▷ 🚚 Delivery note				
▷ 🚚 Delivery note				
▷ 🚚 Delivery note				
▷ 🚚 Delivery note				
▷ 🚚 Delivery note				
▷ 🚚 Delivery note				
▷ 🚚 Delivery note				
▷ 🚚 Delivery note				
▷ 🚚 Delivery note				
▷ 🚚 Delivery note				
▽ 🚚 Delivery note				
📄 WE	2.000 PC	200.00 EUR	31.03.2014	5000000015
📄 WE	- 2.000 PC	- 200.00 EUR	17.05.2014	5000000046
📄 RE-L	2.000 PC	200.00 EUR	31.03.2014	5105608654
📄 RE-L	- 2.000 PC	- 200.00 EUR	17.05.2014	5105608695

Note that the purchase order structure now shows the credit memo as well.

Accounting Entries of Credit Memo

Click | Follow-On Documents ... | and double-click | Accounting document |.

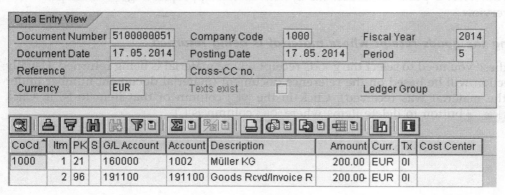

Data Entry View			
Document Number	5100000051	Company Code	1000	Fiscal Year	2014
Document Date	17.05.2014	Posting Date	17.05.2014	Period	5
Reference		Cross-CC no.			
Currency	EUR	Texts exist	☐	Ledger Group	

CoCd	Itm	PK	S	G/L Account	Account	Description	Amount	Curr.	Tx	Cost Center
1000	1	21		160000	1002	Müller KG	200.00	EUR	0I	
	2	96		191100	191100	Goods Rcvd/Invoice R	200.00-	EUR	0I	

This posting nullifies the debit on the | 191100 Goods Rcvd/Invoice R | account created by the goods receipt reversal and debits the vendor.

16.2 GOODS RETURN

Functional Consultant	User	Business Process Owner	Senior Management	My Rating	Understanding Level
A	A	A	A		

16.2.1 Scenario

You have returned goods to vendor.

16.2.2 Goods Return

Transaction

MIGO—Goods Movement

Selection

Enter the purchase order number (and item) here, or double-click on a purchase order number in the document overview.

Selecting the Goods Receipt of Return Item

Possible candidates

When you select a purchase order, the system inserts appropriate goods receipts in the item overview.

Selecting the goods receipt whose material is being returned

Out of these you need to select the goods receipt whose material is being returned. Usually the selection will be based on the reference document (material document number under which the material was received). Click in the $\boxed{\text{OK}}$ column of that item to ☑ it. Click $\boxed{\text{🗑 Delete}}$ button to delete items where $\boxed{\text{OK}}$ column is ☐.

Where

| Material | Quantity | Where | Purchase Order Data | Partner | Account Assignment |

Movement Type   `122` ☐ - RE return to vendor   Stock type   `Unrestricted use` 🖹

Plant	Werk Hamburg	`1000` 🔍
Storage Location	Materiallager	`0001`
Goods recipient		
Unloading Point		
Reason for Movement	`1`	Poor quality
Text		

Movement type

Movement type should be 122.

Stock type

Enter the stock type.

Storage location

Enter the storage location.

Reason for movement

You can select from the reasons for movement configured for this movement type. Configuration for a movement type also specifies whether reason for movement is mandatory, or optional, or whether the field is hidden.

Purchase Order Data

| Material | Quantity | Where | Purchase Order Data | Partner | Account Assignment |

Purchase Order	`4500017087` `10` 🖫	Item Category	Standard
Reference Document	`5000000012` `1`	
"Del.Completed" Ind.	`1 Set automatic` 🖹	☐ Del. Compl. Ind. PO Item

Incoterms   CPT

Purchase order

The system shows the purchase order number against which the goods were received, which is now being returned to the vendor.

Reference document number

Note that the reference document number refers to the material document number of the goods receipt.

Posting Goods Return

After the goods return is entered, post it by clicking | Post |. The system posts only those items for which ☑ Item OK indicator is set.

Material Document of Goods Return

Display the material document created by goods return using transaction MB02.

Change Material Document 5000000047 : Details 0001 / 0001

| ◀ | ▶ | 🔍 | 🖨 | 🖺 | Messages | Material | WM Details... |

Purchase Order	4500017087	10	Movement Type	122 RE return to vendor
Ref. Document	5000000012	1		
Plant	1000		Werk Hamburg	
Vendor	1002		Müller KG	
Incoterms	CPT			
Material	100-100		Casing	

Quantity in

Unit of Entry	3	PC	Stor. Location	0001

Further Information

Unloading Point				
Reason for Mvmt	1	Poor quality		
			Company Code	1000 Fiscal Yr 2014
Text				

Accounting Entries of Goods Return

Click [Accounting Documents...] and double-click [Accounting document].

Data Entry View

Document Number	5000000044	Company Code	1000	Fiscal Year	2014
Document Date	17.05.2014	Posting Date	17.05.2014	Period	5
Reference		Cross-CC no.			
Currency	EUR	Texts exist	☐	Ledger Group	

CoCd	Itm	PK	S	Account	Description	Amount	Curr.	Tx	Cost Center
1000	1	99		790000	Unfinished products	341.28-	EUR		
	2	86		191100	Goods Rcvd/Invoice R	300.00	EUR		
	3	83		281500	Income from price di	41.28	EUR		

16.2.3 Credit Memo

Transaction

MIRO—Enter Invoice

Purchase Order Structure

Display the purchase order structure by clicking [Show PO structure].

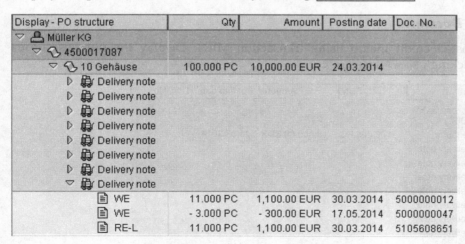

Display - PO structure	Qty	Amount	Posting date	Doc. No.
Müller KG				
4500017087				
10 Gehäuse	100.000 PC	10,000.00 EUR	24.03.2014	
Delivery note				
Delivery note				
Delivery note				
Delivery note				
Delivery note				
Delivery note				
Delivery note				
Delivery note				
WE	11.000 PC	1,100.00 EUR	30.03.2014	5000000012
WE	- 3.000 PC	- 300.00 EUR	17.05.2014	5000000047
RE-L	11.000 PC	1,100.00 EUR	30.03.2014	5105608651

The system shows the goods return entry.

Credit Memo Entry

Specify Transaction [2 Credit memo], enter the purchase order number and select the goods receipt that was returned.

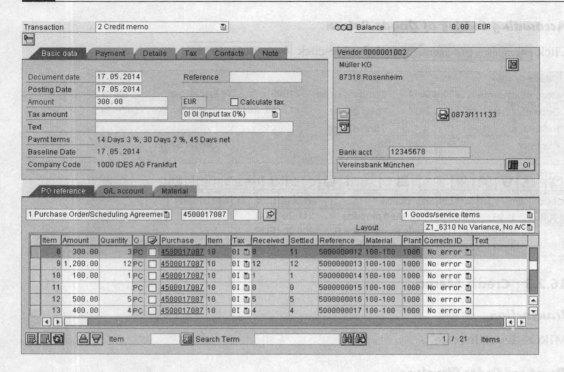

Note that the system shows the received quantity 8 (because of goods return) and the settled quantity 11. Post the credit memo.

Credit Memo Document

Display the posted credit memo using transaction MIR4. Display the purchase order structure by clicking | Show PO structure |.

Note that the purchase order structure now shows the credit memo as well.

Accounting Entries of Credit Memo

Click Follow-On Documents ... and double-click Accounting document.

Data Entry View

Document Number	5100000052	Company Code	1000	Fiscal Year	2014
Document Date	17.05.2014	Posting Date	17.05.2014	Period	5
Reference		Cross-CC no.			
Currency	EUR	Texts exist	☐	Ledger Group	

CoCd	Itm	PK	S	Account	Description	Amount	Curr.	Tx	Cost Center
1000	1	21		1002	Müller KG	300.00	EUR	0I	
	2	96		191100	Goods Rcvd/Invoice R	300.00-	EUR	0I	

This posting nullifies the debit on the 191100 Goods Rcvd/Invoice R account created by the goods return and debits the vendor.

16.3 QUANTITY VARIANCE

Functional Consultant	User	Business Process Owner	Senior Management	My Rating	Understanding Level
A	A	B	C		

16.3.1 Scenario

You may receive credit memo to correct an invoice with positive quantity variance (invoice quantity greater than the goods receipt quantity). When you post a credit memo, the total quantity in the purchase order history is reduced by the credit memo quantity.

16.3.2 Transaction

MIRO—Enter Invoice

16.3.3 Purchase Order Structure

Display the purchase order structure by clicking Show PO structure .

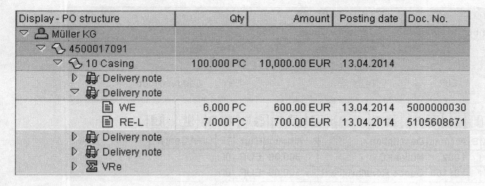

The purchase order structure shows the variance between the goods receipt quantity and invoice quantity.

16.3.4 Credit Memo Entry

Enter the credit memo.

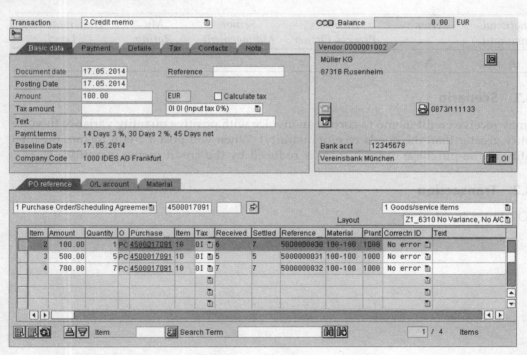

Enter the credit memo details. Select the goods receipt to be corrected. Enter the change in the Quantity and Amount fields. Post the credit memo.

16.3.5 Credit Memo Document

Display the posted credit memo using transaction MIR4. Display the purchase order structure by clicking | Show PO structure |.

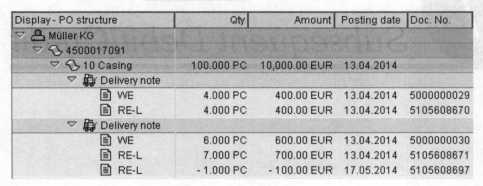

Display - PO structure	Qty	Amount	Posting date	Doc. No.
▽ 👤 Müller KG				
▽ 🔖 4500017091				
▽ 🔖 10 Casing	100.000 PC	10,000.00 EUR	13.04.2014	
▽ 🚚 Delivery note				
📄 WE	4.000 PC	400.00 EUR	13.04.2014	5000000029
📄 RE-L	4.000 PC	400.00 EUR	13.04.2014	5105608670
▽ 🚚 Delivery note				
📄 WE	6.000 PC	600.00 EUR	13.04.2014	5000000030
📄 RE-L	7.000 PC	700.00 EUR	13.04.2014	5105608671
📄 RE-L	- 1.000 PC	- 100.00 EUR	17.05.2014	5105608697

Note that the purchase order structure now shows the credit memo as well. Select the credit memo by double-clicking it.

16.3.6 Accounting Entries

Click | Follow-On Documents ... | and double-click | Accounting document |.

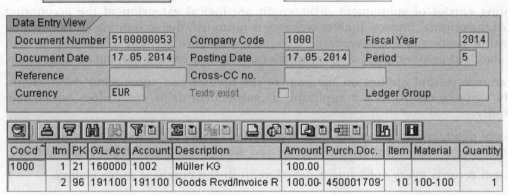

Data Entry View

Document Number	5100000053	Company Code	1000	Fiscal Year	2014	
Document Date	17.05.2014	Posting Date	17.05.2014	Period	5	
Reference		Cross-CC no.				
Currency	EUR	Texts exist	☐	Ledger Group		

CoCd	Itm	PK	G/L Acc	Account	Description	Amount	Purch.Doc.	Item	Material	Quantity
1000	1	21	160000	1002	Müller KG	100.00				
	2	96	191100	191100	Goods Rcvd/Invoice R	100.00-	4500017091	10	100-100	1

This corrects the mismatch in GR/IR account due to quantity variance.

CHAPTER

17

Subsequent Debit/Credit

Subsequent debit/credit

A subsequent debit/credit always refers to an additional invoice or credit memo that is received for a transaction that has already been invoiced. It is an error correction transaction.

Subsequent debit/credit does not change the quantity, it only changes value.

Accounting entries of subsequent debit/credit are logical extension of the accounting entries of the original invoice. If an overcharge is refunded, the accounting entries will be a reversal of posting of the overcharge, e.g. price difference account in the case of item having standard price or stock account in the case of item having moving average price.

Price variance control applies on the sum of the invoice and subsequent debit/credit. Quantity variance control is not applicable as subsequent debit/credit does not change the quantity.

Subsequent debit/credit entries are identified by the Subseq. Dr/Cr indicator at item level. An invoice can contain some normal entries and some subsequent debit/credit entries.

The system records every subsequent debit/credit in the purchase order history.

438

17.1 SUBSEQUENT CREDIT—MOVING AVERAGE PRICE

Functional Consultant	User	Business Process Owner	Senior Management	My Rating	Understanding Level
A	A	A	A		

17.1.1 Scenario

You had received and settled an invoice. You subsequently receive a credit for the same invoice. The material for which the credit is received is managed at moving average price.

17.1.2 Transaction

MIRO—Enter Invoice

17.1.3 Subsequent Credit Entry

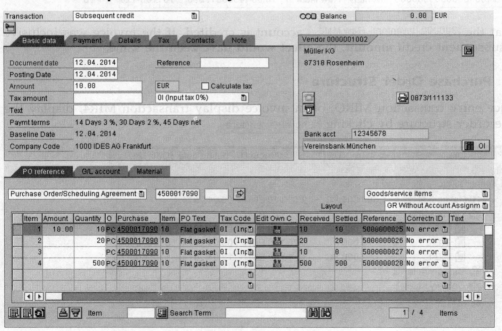

Subsequent debit/credit indicator

When you want to post subsequent debit/credit, the Subseq. Dr/Cr indicator of the items must be selected. This is possible even with Transaction 1 Invoice .

17.1.4 Accounting Entries

Display the invoice using transaction MIR4. Enter the Invoice Document No. and the Fiscal Year. Click 👓 Display Document. The system displays the invoice. Click Follow-On Documents ... . The system displays the list of accounting documents. Double-click the Accounting document to see the accounting entries.

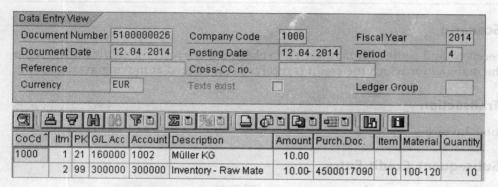

Note that the 300000 Inventory - Raw Mate account is credited. If the invoice was inclusive of this subsequent credit amount, the effect would have been the same.

17.1.5 Purchase Order Structure

In invoice entry transaction MIRO, or in invoice display transaction MIR4, display the purchase order structure by clicking Show PO structure.

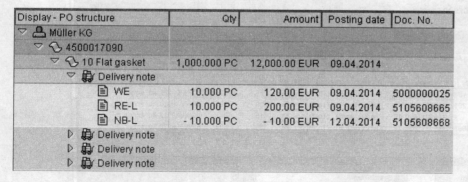

Interpretation

Legend	Interpretation
📄 NB-L	Subsequent debit/credit
Qty	Quantity for which subsequent debit/credit is received.
Amount	Amount of subsequent debit/credit
Sign of quantity and amount fields	Minus for subsequent credit, plus for subsequent debit.

17.2 SUBSEQUENT CREDIT—STANDARD PRICE

Functional Consultant	User	Business Process Owner	Senior Management	My Rating	Understanding Level
A	A	A	A		

17.2.1 Scenario

You had received and settled an invoice. You subsequently receive a credit for the same invoice. The material for which the credit is received is managed at standard price.

17.2.2 Transaction

MIRO—Enter Invoice

17.2.3 Subsequent Credit Entry

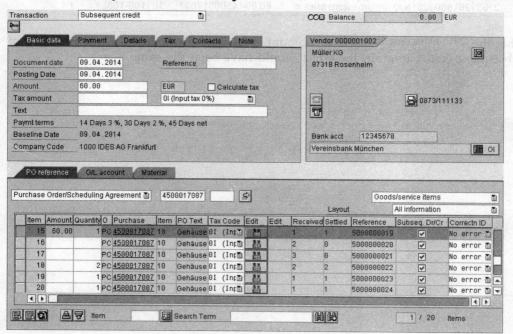

Subsequent debit/credit indicator

When you want to post subsequent debit/credit, the `Subseq. Dr/Cr` indicator of the items must be selected. This is possible even with `Transaction` `1 Invoice`.

17.2.4 Accounting Entries

Display the invoice using transaction MIR4. Enter the Invoice Document No. and the Fiscal Year . Click   Display Document . The system displays the invoice. Click Follow-On Documents ... . The system displays the list of accounting documents. Double-click the Accounting document to see the accounting entries.

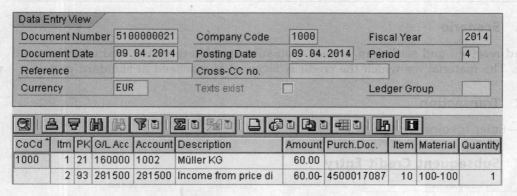

CoCd	Itm	PK	G/L Acc	Account	Description	Amount	Purch.Doc.	Item	Material	Quantity
1000	1	21	160000	1002	Müller KG	60.00				
	2	93	281500	281500	Income from price di	60.00-	4500017087	10	100-100	1

Note that the 281500 Income from price di account is credited. If the invoice was inclusive of this subsequent credit amount, the effect would have been the same.

17.2.5 Purchase Order Structure

In invoice entry transaction MIRO, or in invoice display transaction MIR4, display the
purchase order structure by clicking Show PO structure .

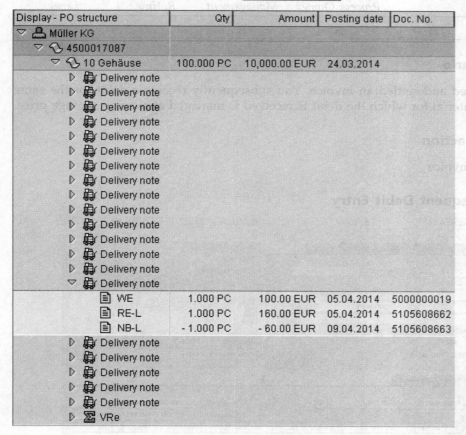

Interpretation

Legend	Interpretation
📄 NB-L	Subsequent debit/credit
Qty	Quantity for which subsequent debit/credit is received.
Amount	Amount of subsequent debit/credit
Sign of quantity and amount fields	Minus for subsequent credit, plus for subsequent debit.

17.3 SUBSEQUENT DEBIT—MOVING AVERAGE PRICE

Functional Consultant	User	Business Process Owner	Senior Management	My Rating	Understanding Level
A	A	A	A		

17.3.1 Scenario

You had received and settled an invoice. You subsequently receive a debit for the same invoice. The material for which the debit is received is managed at moving average price.

17.3.2 Transaction

MIRO—Enter Invoice

17.3.3 Subsequent Debit Entry

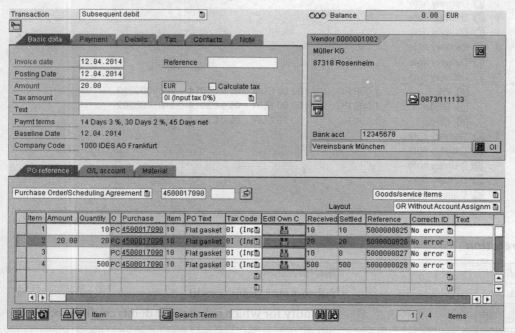

Subsequent debit/credit indicator

When you want to post subsequent debit/credit, the `Subseq. Dr/Cr` indicator of the items must be selected. This is possible even with `Transaction` `1 Invoice`.

17.3.4   Accounting Entries

Display the invoice using transaction MIR4. Enter the `Invoice Document No.` and the `Fiscal Year`. Click `Display Document`. The system displays the invoice. Click `Follow-On Documents ...`. The system displays the list of accounting documents. Double-click the `Accounting document` to see the accounting entries.

Data Entry View									
Document Number	5100000027	Company Code	1000		Fiscal Year	2014			
Document Date	12.04.2014	Posting Date	12.04.2014		Period	4			
Reference		Cross-CC no.							
Currency	EUR	Texts exist	☐		Ledger Group				

CoCd	Itm	PK	G/L Acc	Account	Description	Amount	Purch.Doc.	Item	Material	Quantity
1000	1	31	160000	1002	Müller KG	20.00-				
	2	89	300000	300000	Inventory - Raw Mate	20.00	4500017090	10	100-120	20

Note that the `300000  Inventory - Raw Mate` account is debited. If the invoice was inclusive of this subsequent debit amount, the effect would have been the same.

17.3.5   Purchase Order Structure

In invoice entry transaction MIRO, or in invoice display transaction MIR4, display the purchase order structure by clicking `Show PO structure`.

Display - PO structure	Qty	Amount	Posting date	Doc. No.
▽ 👤 Müller KG				
▽ 🔗 4500017090				
▽ 🔗 10 Flat gasket	1,000.000 PC	12,000.00 EUR	09.04.2014	
▷ 🚚 Delivery note				
▽ 🚚 Delivery note				
📄 WE	20.000 PC	240.00 EUR	11.04.2014	5000000026
📄 RE-L	20.000 PC	400.00 EUR	11.04.2014	5105608666
📄 NB-L	20.000 PC	20.00 EUR	12.04.2014	5105608669
▷ 🚚 Delivery note				
▷ 🚚 Delivery note				

Interpretation

Legend	Interpretation
📄 NB-L	Subsequent debit/credit
Qty	Quantity for which subsequent debit/credit is received.
Amount	Amount of subsequent debit/credit
Sign of quantity and amount fields	Minus for subsequent credit, plus for subsequent debit.

17.4 SUBSEQUENT DEBIT—STANDARD PRICE

Functional Consultant	User	Business Process Owner	Senior Management	My Rating	Understanding Level
A	A	A	A		

17.4.1 Scenario

You had received and settled an invoice. You subsequently receive a debit for the same invoice. The material for which the debit is received is managed at standard price.

17.4.2 Transaction

MIRO—Enter Invoice

17.4.3 Subsequent Debit Entry

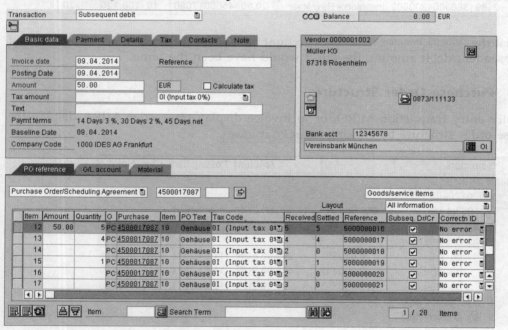

Subsequent debit/credit indicator

When you want to post subsequent debit/credit, the Subseq. Dr/Cr indicator of the items must be selected. This is possible even with Transaction 1 Invoice .

17.4.4 Accounting Entries

Display the invoice using transaction MIR4. Enter the Invoice Document No. and the Fiscal Year. Click &° Display Document. The system displays the invoice. Click Follow-On Documents ... The system displays the list of accounting documents. Double-click the Accounting document to see the accounting entries.

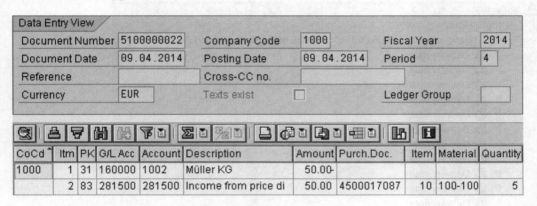

CoCd	Itm	PK	G/L Acc	Account	Description	Amount	Purch.Doc.	Item	Material	Quantity
1000	1	31	160000	1002	Müller KG	50.00-				
	2	83	281500	281500	Income from price di	50.00	4500017087	10	100-100	5

Note that the 281500 Income from price di account is debited. If the invoice was inclusive of this subsequent debit amount, the effect would have been the same.

17.4.5 Purchase Order Structure

In invoice entry transaction MIRO, or in invoice display transaction MIR4, display the purchase order structure by clicking Show PO structure .

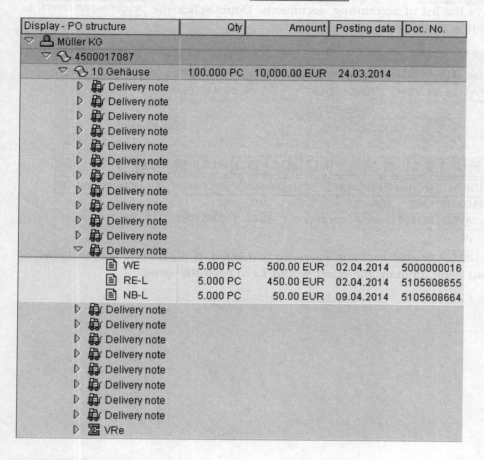

Display - PO structure	Qty	Amount	Posting date	Doc. No.
▽ 🔒 Müller KG				
▽ 🔗 4500017087				
▽ 🔗 10 Gehäuse	100.000 PC	10,000.00 EUR	24.03.2014	
▷ 📦 Delivery note				
▷ 📦 Delivery note				
▷ 📦 Delivery note				
▷ 📦 Delivery note				
▷ 📦 Delivery note				
▷ 📦 Delivery note				
▷ 📦 Delivery note				
▷ 📦 Delivery note				
▷ 📦 Delivery note				
▷ 📦 Delivery note				
▷ 📦 Delivery note				
▽ 📦 Delivery note				
📄 WE	5.000 PC	500.00 EUR	02.04.2014	5000000016
📄 RE-L	5.000 PC	450.00 EUR	02.04.2014	5105608655
📄 NB-L	5.000 PC	50.00 EUR	09.04.2014	5105608664
▷ 📦 Delivery note				
▷ 📦 Delivery note				
▷ 📦 Delivery note				
▷ 📦 Delivery note				
▷ 📦 Delivery note				
▷ 📦 Delivery note				
▷ 📦 Delivery note				
▷ 📦 Delivery note				
▷ Σ VRe				

Interpretation

Legend	Interpretation
📄 NB-L	Subsequent debit/credit
Qty	Quantity for which subsequent debit/credit is received.
Amount	Amount of subsequent debit/credit
Sign of quantity and amount fields	Minus for subsequent credit, plus for subsequent debit.

GR/IR Account Maintenance

18.1 GR/IR ACCOUNT MAINTENANCE

Functional Consultant	User	Business Process Owner	Senior Management	My Rating	Understanding Level
B	C	X	X		

18.1.1 Scenario

The quantity differences between goods receipt and invoice receipt for a purchase order result in a balance on the GR/IR clearing account.

➢ If the quantity invoiced is larger than the quantity received, the system expects further goods receipts for this purchase order to clear the balance.

➢ If the quantity received is larger than the quantity invoiced, the system expects further invoices for this purchase order to clear the balance.

If no more goods or invoices are to be received, you must clear the balance manually. This can be done in different ways:

➢ You can return the extra goods to the vendor.

➢ You can cancel the invoice and post a corrected invoice or a credit memo for the surplus posted quantity.

➢ You can clear the GR/IR clearing account manually.

➢ You can also clear differences in delivery costs.

The GR/IR clearing account is usually cleared at the end of a period or a fiscal year for those order items for which no further goods receipts or invoices are expected.

18.1.2 Transaction

MR11—Maintain GR/IR Clearing Account

18.1.3 Selection Screen

Document Header Data

Company Code	☑
Posting Date	31.05.2014
Reference	
Doc.Header Text	

Choose

Vendor		to		⇨
Freight vendor		to		⇨
Purch. Organization		to		⇨
Purchasing Group		to		⇨

Plant		to		⇨
Purchasing Document		to		⇨
Item		to		⇨
Purchase Order Date	01.01.2013	to	01.04.2014	
Purch. Doc. Category		⇨		
Order Type		to		⇨

Surplus Types

- ☑ Delivery surplus
- ☐ Invoice surplus

Clear

☑ GR/IR Clearing Account	☐ ERS Purchase Orders
☑ Delivery Cost Accounts	☐ ERS - Delivery Costs

Last movement before key date	01.06.2014
Qty Var. Less Than/Equal To	100.0 Percentage
Value Variance Less Than/= To	

Processing

Automatic clearance	○
Prepare List	◉ Layout

Default values for the selection screen in user parameters

You can maintain the following default values for the selection screen of transaction MR11 in user parameters:

Parameter	Meaning
MR11_AUSGL_BZNK	Delivery costs clearing
MR11_AUSGL_WERE	GR/IR clearing
MR11_BEDAT_HIGH	PO date upper limit
MR11_BEDAT_LOW	PO date lower limit
MR11_ BUDAT	Posting date
MR11_DPROZ	Quantity variance as a percentage
MR11_KDAY	Key date: last movement
MR11_WTABW	Value variance in local currency
MR11_XERSY	ERS purchase order
MR11_XREUE	Invoice surplus
MR11_XWEUE	Delivery surplus

18.1.4 List

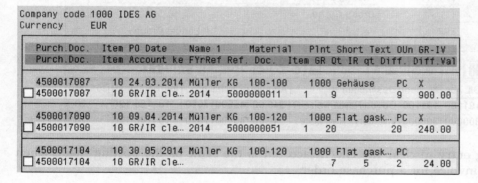

```
Company code 1000 IDES AG
Currency      EUR
```

Purch.Doc.	Item	PO Date	Name 1	Material	Plnt	Short Text	OUn	GR-IV
Purch.Doc.	Item	Account ke	FYrRef	Ref. Doc.	Item	GR Qt IR qt	Diff.	Diff.Val
4500017087	10	24.03.2014	Müller KG	100-100	1000	Gehäuse	PC	X
4500017087	10	GR/IR cle...	2014	5000000011	1	9	9	900.00
4500017090	10	09.04.2014	Müller KG	100-120	1000	Flat gask...	PC	X
4500017090	10	GR/IR cle...	2014	5000000051	1	20	20	240.00
4500017104	10	30.05.2014	Müller KG	100-120	1000	Flat gask...	PC	
4500017104	10	GR/IR cle...				7 5	2	24.00

18.1.5 Posting a GR/IR Account Entry

Select one or more entries in the list and click 🔲 Post .

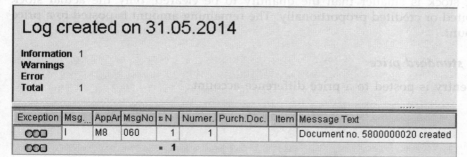

Log created on 31.05.2014

Information	1
Warnings	
Error	
Total	1

Exception	Msg.	AppAr	MsgNo	⌐ N	Numer.	Purch.Doc.	Item	Message Text
⊙⊙⊙	I	M8	060	1	1			Document no. 5800000020 created
⊙⊙⊙			■ 1					

18.1.6 Displaying an Account Maintenance Document

Run transaction MR11SHOW. Specify the `Acct maint. document` and `Fiscal year` and press Enter. The system shows the account maintenance document.

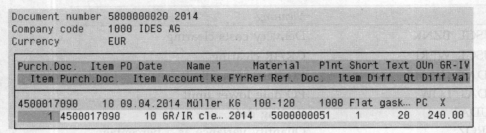

```
Document number 5800000020 2014
Company code     1000 IDES AG
Currency         EUR
```

| Purch.Doc. | Item PO Date | Name 1 | Material | Plnt Short Text OUn GR-IV |
| Item Purch.Doc. | Item Account ke FYrRef Ref. Doc. | Item Diff. Qt Diff.Val |

| 4500017090 | 10 09.04.2014 Müller KG | 100-120 | 1000 Flat gask... PC X |
| 1 4500017090 | 10 GR/IR cle... 2014 | 5000000051 | 1 | 20 | 240.00 |

18.1.7 Accounting Entries

Click `&° Follow-on Documents`. The system displays the list of accounting documents. Double-click the `Accounting document` to see the accounting entries.

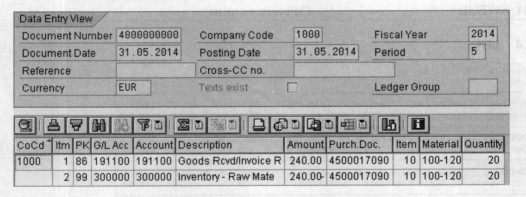

Data Entry View					
Document Number	4800000000	Company Code	1000	Fiscal Year	2014
Document Date	31.05.2014	Posting Date	31.05.2014	Period	5
Reference		Cross-CC no.			
Currency	EUR	Texts exist	☐	Ledger Group	

CoCd	Itm	PK	G/L Acc	Account	Description	Amount	Purch.Doc.	Item	Material	Quantity
1000	1	86	191100	191100	Goods Rcvd/Invoice R	240.00	4500017090	10	100-120	20
	2	99	300000	300000	Inventory - Raw Mate	240.00-	4500017090	10	100-120	20

The offsetting entry to clear the GR/IR account is the same as the posting made when you enter an invoice for a purchase order.

Material with moving average price (MAP)

The GR/IR account is cleared against the stock account, unless no stock coverage exists. If the material stock is smaller than the quantity to be cleared, only the actual stock quantity is debited or credited proportionally. The remaining amount is posted to a price difference account.

Material with standard price

The offsetting entry is posted to a price difference account.

Purchase orders assigned to an account

The offsetting entry is made to the cost or fixed asset account shown in the account assignments in the purchase order.

18.1.8 Purchase Order History

Run transaction ME22N to see the changes in the purchase order history.

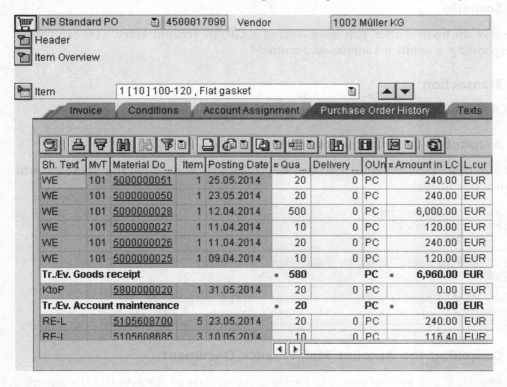

Note the following entry which is now included on account of GR/IR maintenance.

KtoP	5800000020	1 31.05.2014	20	0	PC		0.00	EUR
Tr./Ev. Account maintenance			**20**		**PC**	**=**	**0.00**	**EUR**

18.2   CANCELLING AN ACCOUNT MAINTENANCE DOCUMENT

Functional Consultant	User	Business Process Owner	Senior Management	My Rating	Understanding Level
B	C	X	X		

18.2.1   Scenario

If you receive an invoice after you have cleared a GR/IR account entry, you can cancel the corresponding account maintenance document.

18.2.2   Transaction

MR11SHOW—Display/Cancel Account Maintenance Document

18.2.3   Account Maintenance Document

Specify the Acct maint. document and Fiscal year and press Enter. The system shows the account maintenance document.

18.2.4   Cancelling the Account Maintenance Document

Click ⚙ Reverse... . The system prompts for the posting date of the reversal document.

Change Posting Date, if required. Click 💾.

18.2.5 Log

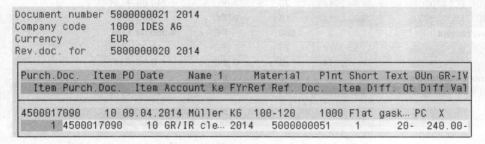

Log created on 01.06.2014

Information	1	
Warnings		
Error		
Total	1	

Exception	M	ApplicArea	Ms	Σ N	Numer.	Purch.Doc.	Item	Message Text
∞	I	M8	060	1	1			Document no. 5800000021 created
∞				▪ 1				

18.2.6 Cancellation Document

Run transaction MR11SHOW. Specify the Acct maint. document and Fiscal year and press Enter. The system shows the cancellation document.

```
Document number 5800000021 2014
Company code     1000 IDES AG
Currency         EUR
Rev.doc. for     5800000020 2014
```

| Purch.Doc. | Item PO Date | Name 1 | Material | Plnt Short Text OUn GR-IV |
| Item Purch.Doc. | Item Account ke FYrRef Ref. Doc. | Item Diff. Qt Diff.Val |

```
4500017090    10 09.04.2014 Müller KG  100-120     1000 Flat gask... PC  X
        1 4500017090    10 GR/IR cle... 2014    5000000051    1        20-   240.00-
```

18.2.7 Accounting Entries

Click 👆 Follow-on Documents . The system displays the list of accounting documents. Double-click the Accounting document to see the accounting entries.

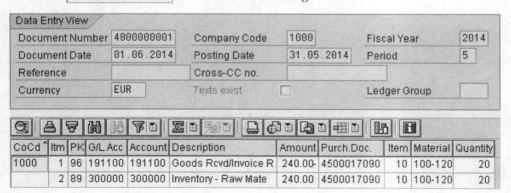

Data Entry View

Document Number	4800000001	Company Code	1000	Fiscal Year	2014
Document Date	01.06.2014	Posting Date	31.05.2014	Period	5
Reference		Cross-CC no.			
Currency	EUR	Texts exist	☐	Ledger Group	

CoCd	Itm	PK	G/L Acc	Account	Description	Amount	Purch.Doc.	Item	Material	Quantity
1000	1	96	191100	191100	Goods Rcvd/Invoice R	240.00-	4500017090	10	100-120	20
	2	89	300000	300000	Inventory - Raw Mate	240.00	4500017090	10	100-120	20

Note that the accounting entries are reversal of the accounting entries of the document that is cancelled.

18.2.8   Purchase Order History

Run transaction ME22N to see the changes in the purchase order history.

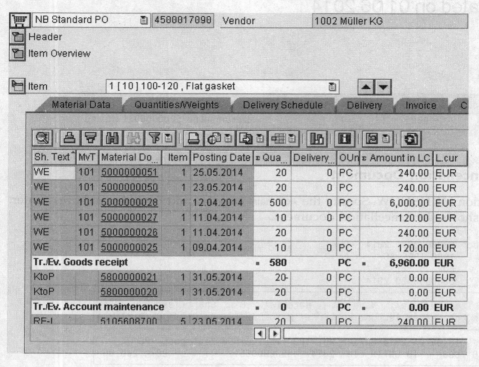

Note the new entry which is now included due to cancellation of the Account maintenance document.

| KtoP | 5800000021 | 1 | 31.05.2014 | 20- | 0 | PC | 0.00 | EUR |

18.3 NUMBER ASSIGNMENT FOR ACCOUNT MAINTENANCE DOCUMENTS

Functional Consultant	User	Business Process Owner	Senior Management	My Rating	Understanding Level
B	C	X	X		

18.3.1 Determination of Transaction from Transaction Code

Transactions are determined from transaction code in table T169. This table is SAP maintained; do not change it.

Transaction Code	TTyp	Transact.	Tr.	FunCls	Transaction Code
MR11	H	KP	RMRP		

18.3.2 Assignment of Number Ranges to Account Maintenance Transactions

In view VV_T003R_11, you assign number ranges to GR/IR account maintenance documents.

Transactn	No. range
KP	04
KS	04

18.3.3 Number Ranges for Account Maintenance Documents

In transaction OMRJ, you define number ranges for GR/IR account maintenance documents.

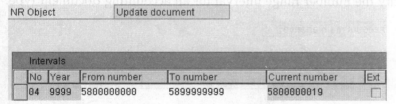

NR Object		Update document			
Intervals					
No	Year	From number	To number	Current number	Ext
04	9999	5800000000	5899999999	5800000019	☐

If number range is not specified for a year, the number is taken from the number range of the year 9999.

18.4 NUMBER ASSIGNMENTS FOR ACCOUNTING DOCUMENTS

Functional Consultant	User	Business Process Owner	Senior Management	My Rating	Understanding Level
B	C	X	X		

18.4.1 Accounting Document Type used in Account Maintenance

In view V_169F, you specify the default accounting document type that will get generated in invoice verification.

Transaction Code	MR11
Transaction Text	GR/IR account maintenance

Default Value			
Document Type		KP	Account maintenance

For the account maintenance document only internal number assignment is possible. Therefore, for the transaction code MR11, choose only the document type for which the number range is set to internal number assignment.

18.4.2 Number Range Assignment to Accounting Document Type

In view V_T003, you specify the number range interval for an accounting document type.

Document Type		KP	Account maintenance

Properties		
Number range	48	Number range information

18.4.3 Number Range Definition

In transaction MRM4, you define the number ranges for each interval and year.

NR Object	Accounting document
Subobject	1000

Intervals

	No	Year	From number	To number	Current number	Ext
	48	2014	4800000000	4899999999	4800000001	☐
	48	2015	4800000000	4899999999	0	☐

Account Determination

19.1 OVERVIEW

Functional Consultant	User	Business Process Owner	Senior Management	My Rating	Understanding Level
A	A	A	A		

19.1.1 Accounting Entries in Invoice Posting

When goods are received, accounting entries are passed debiting stock or consumption account and crediting GR/IR clearing account. When invoice is posted, the GR/IR clearing account is debited and the vendor is credited. When payment is done, the vendor is debited and the bank is credited.

Other accounting entries that take place during invoice posting pertain to taxes, planned or unplanned delivery costs, discounts, etc. Accounting entries similar to goods receipt are also passed, if there is variance between the invoice and the system suggested amounts.

19.1.2 Account Determination

When you post an invoice, the system updates various accounts in Financial Accounting. It determines automatically which amounts have to be posted to which accounts. Account assignment is based partly on your entries when you enter an invoice, partly on the information stored in the system and partly on the system settings.

19.1.3 Sources of Information

Your entries

➢ Which vendor account must be posted to?

➢ Which amounts must be posted?

➢ Is the invoice posted as a net or a gross amount?

Material master record

➢ Which valuation class does the material belong to?

➢ Which type of price control is required for the material?

➢ Is the stock available smaller than the quantity invoiced?

Posted documents

➢ What is the purchase order price?

➢ Has a goods receipt been posted for the purchase order?

System settings

➢ Is the invoice posted as a net or a gross amount (default value)?

➢ Which G/L accounts must be posted to?

19.1.4 Important Accounts in Invoice Verification

Vendor accounts

There is a separate account in the sub-ledger for each vendor that all amounts concerning this vendor are posted to. In invoice verification, a vendor's account is credited. This does not mean that the vendor receives payment. The vendor receives payment when your Finance department makes payment to the vendor, debiting the vendor account and crediting a bank account.

Stock accounts

In SAP, you do not set up a separate account for each material. Instead, different materials with similar features are grouped together in a common account (for example, raw materials). The materials are classified in valuation classes in the material master record, and different accounts are assigned to different valuation classes. Normally, posting to stock accounts takes place during goods receipt. However, posting to stock accounts may take place during invoice verification in the case of a price or quantity difference.

GR/IR clearing accounts

The GR/IR clearing account is an "intermediate" account between the stock account and the vendor account. At goods receipt, the net invoice amount expected is posted to the stock account. The offsetting entry is posted to the GR/IR clearing account. This posting is then cleared by an offsetting entry on the vendor account at invoice receipt.

Tax accounts

The system makes postings to special tax accounts when invoices include tax.

Price difference accounts

In the case of materials managed using standard price, as against moving average price, goods receipts are debited to stock accounts at standard rate. But the GR/IR account must be credited at the purchase order rate because that is the amount to be paid to the vendor. The difference is charged to a price difference account.

Cash discount clearing account

When you post an invoice net, the cash discount amount is taken into account in the invoice, it reduces the value of the items; the offsetting posting is made to the cash discount clearing account, which is then cleared when payment is made.

Freight clearing account

The stock account is debited with the planned delivery costs at goods receipt and the system makes the offsetting posting to a freight clearing account. This posting is then cleared by an offsetting entry to the vendor account at invoice receipt.

Small differences account

Sometimes the difference between the invoice and system calculation may be so small that it is not worth investigating. Therefore, many companies have a policy of accepting the amount in the vendor's invoice and posting the difference to a small difference account.

19.1.5   Different Views of Account Determination

You may look at three different views of account determination. All these show that the G/L account can depend on as many as five factors. Further, the G/L accounts for debit amounts and credit amounts can be different.

Simulation View

In transaction OMR0, click ⎡ Simulation ⎤. Select a plant, valuation class and transaction type.
Click ⎡ Account Assignments ⎤.

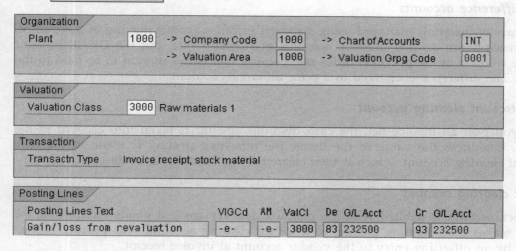

Data Storage View

Use transaction SE11 to see the data for G/L account determination stored in table T030.

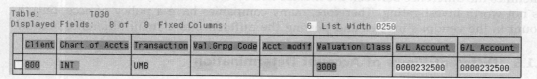

It shows that a debit G/L account and a credit G/L account are defined for a combination
of five factors.

Configuration View

In transaction OMR0, click ⎡ Account Assignment ⎤; then double-click UMB. Specify chart of
accounts.

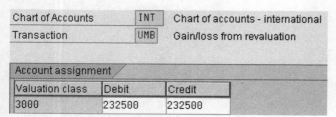

If you want the G/L accounts to depend on more or less number of factors, do so by
clicking ⎡ Rules ⎤.

19.1.6 Determination of Debit and Credit G/L Accounts

The image below shows that the G/L account to which posting takes place depends on five factors. Also, it is possible to post to one G/L account, if the amount is to be debited, and to another, if the amount is to be credited. It also shows how these factors are determined.

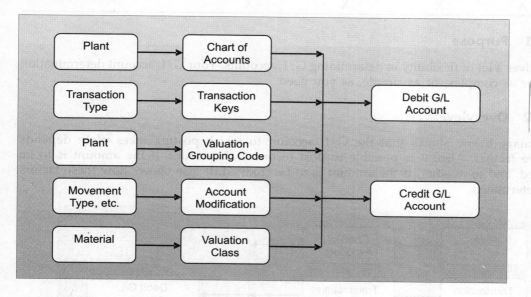

19.1.7 Determination of Debit and Credit Posting Keys

Debit and credit posting keys depend only on the transaction key discussed earlier. A debit posting key and a credit posting key is defined for each transaction key.

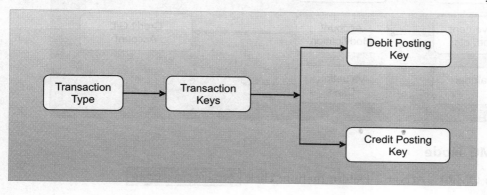

19.2 G/L ACCOUNTS

Functional Consultant	User	Business Process Owner	Senior Management	My Rating	Understanding Level
A	X	X	X		

19.2.1 Purpose

SAP gives a lot of flexibility in determining G/L accounts. Your G/L account determination may be as complex, or as simple, as you need.

19.2.2 Overview

The image below shows that the G/L account to which posting takes place depends on five factors. Also, it is possible to post to one G/L account, if the amount is to be debited, and to another, if the amount is to be credited. It also shows how these factors are determined.

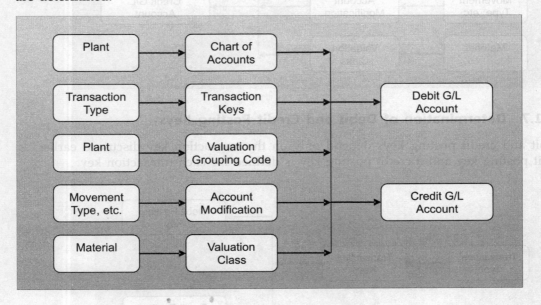

19.2.3 IMG Node

Transaction OMR0 - Account Determination; click Account Assignment .

19.2.4   Factors in Account Determination

Simplest Scenario

Chart of Accounts	INT	Chart of accounts - international
Transaction	WRX	GR/IR clearing account

Account assignment

Account
191100

The above screenshot shows the G/L account assigned to transaction key GR/IR clearing account. Since a G/L account is always defined within a chart of accounts, the chart of accounts is specified as well.

Most Complex Scenario

Chart of Accounts	INT	Chart of accounts - international
Transaction	GBB	Offsetting entry for inventory posting

Account assignment

Valuation modif.	General modification	Valuation class	Debit	Credit
0001	AUI	7920	895000	895000
0001	BSA	3000	399999	399999
0001	BSA	3001	399999	399999
0001	BSA	3030	399999	399999
0001	BSA	3040	399999	399999
0001	BSA	3050	399999	399999
0001	BSA	3100	399999	399999
0001	BSA	7900	799999	799999
0001	BSA	7920	799999	799999
0001	BSA	7925	799999	799999

In the most complex scenario, in addition to the transaction key, the G/L account also depends on the valuation area (valuation modification), general modification, and valuation class. It is also possible to post to one account, if the posting is a debit posting, and to another, if the posting is a credit posting.

Control of Factors

For each transaction key, you can decide the factors based on which the G/L account will be determined. To see or set the factors, click | Rules |. For some transaction keys, you can select all four factors.

Chart of Accounts	INT	Chart of accounts - international
Transaction	WRX	GR/IR clearing account

Accounts are determined based on

Debit/Credit	☐
General modification	☐
Valuation modif.	☐
Valuation class	☐

But, for some transaction keys, you can select fewer factors as illustrated below:

Chart of Accounts	INT	Chart of accounts - international
Transaction	BSX	Inventory posting

Accounts are determined based on

Debit/Credit	☐	Not changeable
Valuation modif.	☐	
Valuation class	☑	

19.2.5   Determination of Chart of Accounts

Overview

Account determination always takes place in a chart of accounts. Another company, which uses a different chart of accounts, is free to specify its own account determination process. But if two company codes use the same chart of account, they also share the account determination process. The chart of accounts is determined in the following sequence:

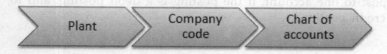

Assignment of Plant to Company Code

After you create a plant, you can assign it to a company code in view V_T001K_ASSIGN, or using transaction OX18.

CoCd	Plnt	Name of Plant	Company Name	Status
0001	0001	Werk 0001	SAP A.G.	
0005	0005	Hamburg	IDES AG NEW GL	
0006	0006	New York	IDES US INC New GL	
0007	0007	Werk Hamburg	IDES AG NEW GL 7	
0008	0008	New York	IDES US INC New GL 8	
1000	0099	Werk für Customizing-Kurse SCM	IDES AG	
1000	1000	Werk Hamburg	IDES AG	

Assignment of Chart of Accounts to Company Code

In view V_001_S, you can assign a chart of account to a company code.

CoCd	Company Name	City	Chrt/Accts	Cty ch/act
1000	IDES AG	Frankfurt	INT	GKR
1002	Singapore Company	Singapore		
2000	IDES UK	London	INT	CAGB
2100	IDES Portugal	Lisbon	INT	
2200	IDES France	Paris	CAFR	INT

Use of Chart of Accounts

All G/L accounts are defined within a chart of accounts. You, therefore, always specify chart of accounts in determination of G/L accounts.

19.2.6 Determination of Transaction Key

Purpose

When an invoice is posted, it may generate two or more accounting entries. In its simplest form, an invoice debits the GR/IR clearing account and credits the vendor. The system identifies each of these entries as a transaction key. For each item in an invoice, two or more transaction keys are involved. The transaction keys, and their determination, are predefined by SAP and cannot be changed. The purpose of this section is to show you the underlying linkages so that you know how transaction keys are determined.

Sequence of Determination of Transaction Keys

The transaction keys are determined in the following sequence:

Determination of Transaction Type

Transaction type is determined from transaction code in table T169.

Transaction Code	Transactn Type
MIR6	RD
MIR7	RD
MIRA	RD
MIRO	RD
MR8M	RS
MRDC	RS
MRIS	RS
MRNB	RS
MRRL	RS

Determination of Value String

Table T169W determines the value string.

Table: T169W
Displayed Fields: 3 of   3 Fixed Columns

Transactn Type	Line item ID	Value string
RD	8	RE16
RD	B	RE21
RD	C	RE02
RD	F	RE09
RD	G	RE10
RD	H	RE22
RD	I	RE10
RD	L	RE01
RD	M	RE07
RD	N	RE02
RD	S	RE08
RD	X	RE11
RD	Y	RE13

Transaction type

Transaction type is determined from transaction code in table T169. For logistics invoice verification, transaction types are `RD Logistics invoice` and `RS Logistics invoice, cancel`.

Line item id

Line item id is determined based on business scenario. Line item ids and their descriptions are given below. Value string is indicated for transaction type RD.

Line item ID	Description	Value string
8	Revaluation	RE16
A	Asset	
B	Warehouse stock order	RE21
C	Warehouse stock order assigned	RE02
K	Vendor	
F	Delivery costs	RE09
G	Assigned delivery costs	RE10
H	Delivery costs—warehouse stock order	RE22
I	Delivery costs—assigned warehouse stock order	RE10
L	Warehouse order	RE01
M	Material	RE07
N	Assigned order	RE02
P	Price difference	
S	General G/L account	RE08
T	Tax	
W	GR/IR item	
X	Purchase order—assigned asset	RE11
Y	Delivery costs—assigned asset	RE13
Z	Cash discount clearing	

Value string

The value string is determined based on the transaction type and the line item id. The master list of value strings for invoice verification is in table T169X.

```
Table:          T169X
Displayed Fields:   3 of   3  Fixed Columns:
```

Language	Value string	Description
E	ML01	Material ledger settlement
E	RE01	Invoice receipt, stock material
E	RE02	Inv. receipt, acct assgt/non-stock
E	RE03	Acct maint. Stock material
E	RE04	Acct maint. Acct assgt/non-stock
E	RE05	Material price change
E	RE06	Invoice receipt, vendor
E	RE07	Direct posting, material
E	RE08	Direct posting, G/L account/asset
E	RE09	Posting of freight costs
E	RE10	Pstg of fr. costs, acct assgt/non-stock
E	RE11	Inv. receipt, acct assgt to asset
E	RE12	Account maintenance, acct assgt to asset
E	RE13	Freight posting assigned to asset
E	RE14	Debit/credit material
E	RE17	Account maintenance, freight, warehouse
E	RE18	Account maintenance, freight acct assgt
E	RE19	Acc. maint. freight acct assgt to asset
E	RE20	Account maintenance: freight, warehouse
E	RE21	Invoice receipt: warehouse
E	RE22	Delivery costs: warehouse
E	RE24	Acct. Maint. Stock Mat. Subcontr.

Invoices for material received in warehouse get value string RE01.

Invoices for material assigned to cost centre, etc. get value string RE02.

Invoices for delivery cost get value string RE02.

Value strings in simulation

When you do simulation of account determination in transaction OMR0, you choose a value string (called transaction type there).

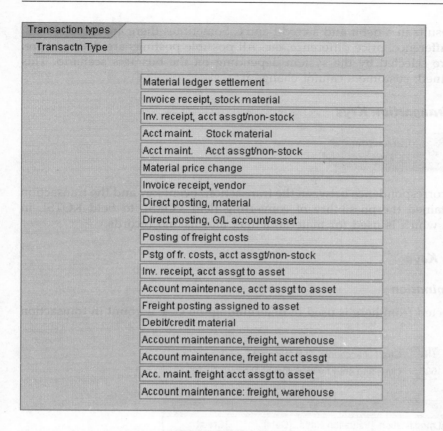

Determination of Transaction/Event Keys

A business scenario may result in multiple postings. Each posting is identified by a transaction/event key. For each value string, possible transaction/event keys are defined by SAP in table T169A.

```
Table:              T169A
Displayed Fields:   4 of   4   Fixed Columns:
```

Value string	x	Trans./ev. key	Line item ID
RE01	01	WRX	W
RE01	02	BSX	M
RE01	03	PRD	P
RE01	04	KDM	P
RE01	05	EIN	S
RE01	06	EKG	S
RE01	07	BSX	M
RE01	08	UMB	S

A posting usually results in a debit and a credit entry. Sometimes there are more entries, e.g. exchange rate difference, price difference, etc. All possible postings are defined here. Appropriate lines are selected by the system depending on the business scenario. This table is SAP maintained; customers cannot change it.

Determination of Transaction Keys

There is one-to-one correspondence between the transaction/event key and the transaction key. SAP has maintained the possibility of converting field VORSL to field KOTSL in table TCKMLBNKS, which is used for material ledger and has no records.

Use of Transaction Keys

G/L account determination

Transaction key selected from here is used in determining the G/L account in transaction OMR0 (table T030).

| Chart of Accounts | INT | Chart of accounts - international |
| Transaction | GBB | Offsetting entry for inventory posting |

Account assignment				
Valuation modif.	General modification	Valuation class	Debit	Credit
0001	AUI	7920	895000	895000
0001	BSA	3000	399999	399999

Posting key determination

Transaction key selected from here is used in determining the posting keys in transaction OMR0 (table T030B).

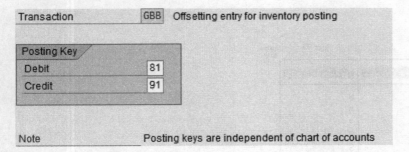

| Transaction | GBB | Offsetting entry for inventory posting |

Posting Key	
Debit	81
Credit	91

| Note | Posting keys are independent of chart of accounts |

19.2.7   Determination of Valuation Modification

Purpose

It is great, if all company codes and plants of an enterprise agree to the same account determination process. But if they do not and there may be good reasons for it, in SAP, you can define account determination process that is plant specific. This is done via valuation area and valuation grouping code.

Valuation Area

In SAP, you can specify whether valuation area is at plant level or company code level in transaction OX14.

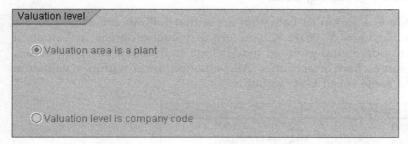

Valuation area serves two purposes:

➤ Through valuation area, you can define plant specific account determination.

➤ Valuation area also determines whether a material has the same moving average price at plant level or at company code level.

Sequence of Determination of Valuation Grouping Code

Valuation area is a plant

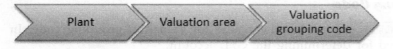

Valuation area is a company code

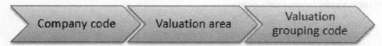

Determination of Valuation Area

Once you have defined whether valuation area is at plant level or company code level, SAP automatically creates valuation areas. The name of the valuation area is the same as the plant or the company code depending on whether valuation area is plant level or company code level.

Activation of Valuation Grouping Code

If you want to use the concept of valuation grouping code, you need to activate it using transaction OMWM.

Valuation grouping code
⦿ Valuation grouping code active
○ Valuation grouping code not active

Determination of Valuation Grouping Code

A valuation grouping code is a group of valuation areas that follows the same process of account determination. In view V_001K_K, you group valuation areas in valuation grouping codes. Valuation areas being grouped may belong to different company codes, but they must have the same chart of accounts. All valuation areas within a valuation grouping code post to the same set of G/L accounts.

Val. Area	CoCode	Company Name	Chrt/Accts	Val.Grpg Code
1000	1000	IDES AG	INT	0001
1100	1000	IDES AG	INT	0001
1200	1000	IDES AG	INT	0001
1300	1000	IDES AG	INT	0001
1400	1000	IDES AG	INT	0001
2000	2000	IDES UK	INT	0001
2010	2000	IDES UK	INT	0001
2100	2100	IDES Portugal	INT	0001
2200	2200	IDES France	CAFR	FR01

Use of Valuation Grouping Code

Valuation modification Valuation modif. is another name for valuation grouping code. In transaction OMR0, it is used for determining the G/L account.

Chart of Accounts	INT	Chart of accounts - international
Transaction	GBB	Offsetting entry for inventory posting

Account assignment				
Valuation modif.	General modification	Valuation class	Debit	Credit
0001	AUI	7920	895000	895000
0001	BSA	3000	399999	399999

Same material in different valuation grouping codes can post to different accounts.

19.2.8   Determination of General Modification

Purpose

For certain transaction keys, it is necessary to divide the posting transaction according to a further key: account modification. Account modification allows posting to different G/L accounts for different business scenarios. These keys are predefined by SAP and cannot be changed.

Account Modification

Account modification is applicable only for transaction/event keys GBB, PRD and KON. The value of account modification is automatically determined by the system. You have to only decide whether it is relevant for account determination in your company. Account modification is defined in view V_156X_KO.

MvT	S	Val.Update	Qty update	Mvt	Cns	Val.strng	Cn	TEKey	Acct modif	C
101		☑	☐	B	V	WE06	1	KBS		☑
101		☑	☑	B	A	WE06	1	KBS		☑
101		☑	☑	B	V	WE06	1	KBS		☑
101		☑	☑	F		WF01	2	GBB	AUF	☑
101		☑	☑	F		WF01	3	PRD	PRF	☐
101	E	☑	☑	B		WE01	3	PRD		☐

You can see that the account modification depends on several factors, e.g. movement type, special stock indicator, etc.

Account Modification for Consignment Liabilities

In transaction OMR0, you can assign one account to consignment material and another to pipeline material.

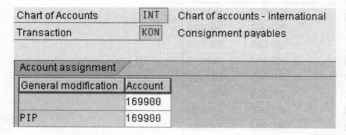

Chart of Accounts	INT	Chart of accounts - international
Transaction	KON	Consignment payables

Account assignment	
General modification	Account
	169900
PIP	169900

Account Modification	*Description*
Blank	Consignment liabilities
PIP	Pipeline liabilities

Account Modification for Cost (Price) Differences

In transaction OMR0, you can assign one account to goods receipts for purchase orders, another to goods receipts for production order, and a third to goods issues.

Chart of Accounts	INT	Chart of accounts - international
Transaction	PRD	Cost (price) differences

Account assignment

General modification	Debit	Credit
	281500	281500
PRA	281500	281500
PRF	281500	281500

Account Modification	Description
Blank	Goods receipts and invoice receipts for purchase orders
PRF	Goods receipts for production orders
PRA	Goods issues and other goods movements

Account Modification for Offsetting Entry for Inventory Posting

In transaction OMR0, you can assign different accounts to different scenarios of inventory posting.

Chart of Accounts	INT	Chart of accounts - international
Transaction	GBB	Offsetting entry for inventory posting

Account assignment

Valuation modif.	General modification	Valuation class	Debit	Credit
	AUF	7900	895000	895000
	AUF	7920	895000	895000
	AUI		895000	895000
	AUI	7920	895000	895000
	BSA	3000	399999	399999
	BSA	7900	399999	399999
	VBR	3000	400000	400000
	VBR	7920	892000	892000
0001	AUA	7900	895000	895000
0001	AUA	7910	895000	895000
0001	AUA	7920	895000	895000
0001	AUF	3040	895000	895000

Account Modification	Description
AUF	Goods receipts for production orders with account assignment
BSA	Initial entries of stock balances
INV	Expense/revenue from inventory differences
VAX	Goods issues for sales orders without account assignment object
VAY	Goods issues for sales orders with account assignment object
VBO	Consumption from stock of material provided to vendor
VBR	Internal goods issues (e.g. for a cost centre)
VKA	Consumption for sales order without SD
VNG	Scrapping/destruction
VQP	Sampling
ZOB	Goods receipts without purchase orders
ZOF	Goods receipts without production orders

19.2.9   Determination of Valuation Class

Classification of Inventory in Financial Accounting

Run transaction S_PL0_86000032 to see the account balances in structured form.

Commercial balance sheet

OL	Ledger
10	Currency type Company code currency
EUR	Amounts in Euro (EMU currency as of 01/01/1999)
2013.01 -2013.16	Reporting periods
2012.01 -2012.16	Comparison periods

F.S. item/account	Tot.rpt.pr
▽ ☐ A S S E T S	1,423.41
▽ ☐ Current assets	1,423.41
▽ ☐ Stocks	1,423.41
▽ ☐ Raw materials and supplies	198.14-
▷ ⤥ 0000300000 Inventory - Raw Material 1	198.14-
▽ ☐ Work in process	1,484.42
▷ ⤥ 0000790000 Unfinished products	2,622.02
▷ ⤥ 0000799999 Inventory (own goods)	1,137.60-
▽ ☐ Finished goods and merchandise	137.13
▷ ⤥ 0000310000 Trading Goods	142.24
▷ ⤥ 0000792000 Finished goods inventory	5.11-

A company usually has multiple G/L accounts that represent the stock of different types of materials. These accounts are usually grouped into categories as illustrated above.

Classification of Materials in Materials Management

Corresponding to the two-level structure of stock accounts in Financial Accounting, there is a two-level structure in Materials Management.

Financial accounting	Materials management
▽ ☐ Stocks	
▽ ☐ Raw materials and supplies	Account category reference 1
▷ 🖼 0000300000 Inventory - Raw Material 1	Valuation class 11
▽ ☐ Work in process	Account category reference 2
▷ 🖼 0000790000 Unfinished products	Valuation class 21
▷ 🖼 0000799999 Inventory (own goods)	Valuation class 22
▽ ☐ Finished goods and merchandise	Account category reference 3
▷ 🖼 0000310000 Trading Goods	Valuation class 31
▷ 🖼 0000792000 Finished goods inventory	Valuation class 32

Account Category Reference

Account category references are defined in view V_025K. An account category reference is a group of valuation classes. It is assigned to a material type in view V_134_K. When a material is created using this material type, it can only use valuation classes belonging to the corresponding account category reference. This ensures that you do not wrongly classify a raw material as finished goods .

Valuation Class

Valuation classes classify materials so that their inventory is managed in appropriate G/L accounts, e.g. 0000310000 Trading Goods , 0000792000 Finished goods inventory , etc. Valuation classes are defined in view V025.

Determination of Valuation Class

Valuation class is directly assigned to a material.

Valuation Classes for a Material

Run transaction MM02 and select Accounting 1 view.

| Quality management | ⊙ Accounting 1 | Accounting 2 | Costing 1 | Costing 2 |

Material	100-302	Hollow shaft	ℍ
Plant	1000	Werk Hamburg
Val. type	EIGEN

General data

Base Unit of Measure	PC	piece(s)	Valuation Category	B
Currency	EUR		Current period	10 2013
Division	01		Price determ.		☐ ML act.

Current valuation

Valuation Class	☑
VC: Sales order stk		Proj. stk val. class	
Price control	S	Price Unit	1
Moving price		Standard price	
Total Stock	0	Total Value	0.00
		☐ Valuated Un
Future price		Valid from	

| Previous period/year | | Std cost estimate |

Valuation class

Valuation classes classify materials so that their inventory is managed in appropriate G/L accounts such as Raw material, Finished goods, WIP, etc. Using this feature, you can post raw materials to one stock account and bought out parts to another. Valuation classes possible for a material are restricted by the account category reference of the material type of the material.

Valuation class: sales order stock

You can use this valuation class to maintain a set of G/L accounts for sales order stock. Valuation classes possible for a material are restricted by the account category reference of the material type of the material.

Valuation class: project stock

You can use this valuation class to maintain a set of G/L accounts for project stock. Valuation classes possible for a material are restricted by the account category reference of the material type of the material.

Use of Valuation Class

In transaction OMR0, you can use valuation class to determine the G/L account.

Chart of Accounts	INT	Chart of accounts - international
Transaction	BSX	Inventory posting

Account assignment

Valuation class	Account
3000	300000
3001	300010
3002	300010
3030	303000

Thus, goods movements of different materials will be posted to different G/L accounts depending on their valuation class.

Features of Valuation Classes

Valuation classes classify materials so that their inventory is managed in appropriate G/L accounts such as Raw material, Finished goods, WIP, etc.

Valuation classes are used for account determination, not for material valuation.

A valuation class classifies materials that post to the same set of G/L accounts.

If a material is subject to split valuation, valuation classes for different valuation types of the same material can be different and can, therefore, post to different set of G/L accounts.

Project stock and sales order stock of a material can have different valuation classes and can, therefore, post to different set of G/L accounts.

Valuation classes are assigned to a material in a valuation area. It is, therefore, possible that the same material has different valuation classes in different valuation areas.

19.2.10 Determination of Debit Account and Credit Account

If you are using standard price, and not moving average price, the price differences are posted to a price difference account. Usually you post both debit and credit entries to the same account. But some companies want to post debit entries to one G/L account and credit entries to another. SAP lets you to do that. This data is maintained using transaction OMR0.

Chart of Accounts	INT	Chart of accounts - international
Transaction	GBB	Offsetting entry for inventory posting

Account assignment

Valuation modif.	General modification	Valuation class	Debit	Credit
0001	AUI	7920	895000	895000
0001	BSA	3000	399999	399999
0001	BSA	3001	399999	399999
0001	BSA	3030	399999	399999
0001	BSA	3040	399999	399999
0001	BSA	3050	399999	399999
0001	BSA	3100	399999	399999
0001	BSA	7900	799999	799999
0001	BSA	7920	799999	799999
0001	BSA	7925	799999	799999

19.3 POSTING KEYS

Functional Consultant	User	Business Process Owner	Senior Management	My Rating	Understanding Level
A	X	X	X		

19.3.1 Purpose

Another important use of transaction key is to determine posting keys. Posting keys determine the manner in which a G/L account is updated. Posting keys, and their determination, is predefined by SAP.

19.3.2 IMG Node

Transaction OMR0—Account Determination

Click Posting Key .

19.3.3   Screen

Transaction	GBB	Offsetting entry for inventory posting

Posting Key	
Debit	81
Credit	91

Note	Posting keys are independent of chart of accounts

As the screenshot notes, posting keys are defined for a transaction key and are applicable to all charts of accounts.

19.3.4   Database Table

The linkage of posting keys to transaction is stored in table T030B. This table is maintained by SAP and cannot be changed.

```
Table:          T030B
Displayed Fields:   5 of   5 Fixed
```

Client	Transaction	Debit	Credit
800	BSX	89	99
800	EIN	40	50
800	EKG	40	50
800	KDM	40	50
800	PRD	83	93
800	UMB	83	93
800	WRX	86	96

19.3.5   Important Posting Keys

Transaction key	Transaction key name	Debit posting key	Credit posting key
BSX	Inventory posting	89	99
GBB	Offsetting entry for inventory posting	81	91
KBS	Account-assigned purchase order	81	91
KON	Consignment payables	81	91
PRD	Cost (price) differences	83	93
WRX	GR/IR clearing account	86	96

In reversal of goods movement, G/L accounts remain the same, but posting keys are different.

19.3.6 Posting Key Definition

You may see the definition of a posting key by running transaction OB41.

Posting Key	81	Costs

Debit/credit indicator
- ◉ Debit
- ○ Credit

Account type
- ○ Customer
- ○ Vendor
- ◉ G/L account
- ○ Assets
- ○ Material

Other attributes
- ☐ Sales-related
- ☐ Special G/L
- Reversal posting key 91
- ☐ Payment transaction

19.4 SIMULATION OF ACCOUNT DETERMINATION

Functional Consultant	User	Business Process Owner	Senior Management	My Rating	Understanding Level
A	X	X	X		

19.4.1 Purpose

Since account determination is a complex process, SAP provides a tool to simulate it. You can use this tool to see the G/L accounts to which posting will take place in a given scenario.

19.4.2 IMG Node

Transaction OMR0—Account Determination

19.4.3 Simulation

Click | Simulation |, select | Invoice receipt, stock material | and click | Account Assignments | to see the screenshot below.

19.4.4 Screen

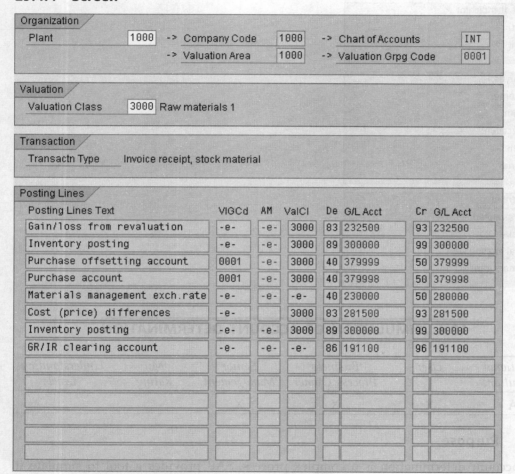

Organization					
Plant	1000	-> Company Code	1000	-> Chart of Accounts	INT
		-> Valuation Area	1000	-> Valuation Grpg Code	0001

Valuation		
Valuation Class	3000	Raw materials 1

Transaction	
Transactn Type	Invoice receipt, stock material

Posting Lines

Posting Lines Text	VlGCd	AM	ValCl	De	G/L Acct	Cr	G/L Acct
Gain/loss from revaluation	-e-	-e-	3000	83	232500	93	232500
Inventory posting	-e-	-e-	3000	89	300000	99	300000
Purchase offsetting account	0001	-e-	3000	40	379999	50	379999
Purchase account	0001	-e-	3000	40	379998	50	379998
Materials management exch.rate	-e-	-e-	-e-	40	230000	50	280000
Cost (price) differences	-e-		3000	83	281500	93	281500
Inventory posting	-e-	-e-	3000	89	300000	99	300000
GR/IR clearing account	-e-	-e-	-e-	86	191100	96	191100

19.5 SOURCES OF POSTING TO A G/L ACCOUNT

Functional Consultant	User	Business Process Owner	Senior Management	My Rating	Understanding Level
A	X	X	X		

19.5.1 Purpose

Since account determination automates the process of determining G/L accounts to which posting take place, business managers responsible for a G/L account may experience loss of control over the entries being passed in that G/L account. They may want to know which business processes are passing entries to their G/L accounts.

19.5.2 Where Used List of G/L Accounts

For each G/L account in a chart of accounts, you can see the sources of posting in the Materials Management module. In transaction OMR0, click `⇨ G/L Accounts` and specify the `Company Code` and the `Valuation Area`. The system shows the where used list of G/L accounts.

Company Code 1000   **Chart of Accounts** INT
Valuation Area 1000   **Valuatn Grouping Code** 0001

Ch.Acc. / Acc / ValClass / TEK / AG	Description	Acc...	Val.Gr.Cde	Status	Error
▽ 📄 INT					
▽ 📄 0000086100	Freight provision (MM)	Bal...			
📄 FR2	Freight provisions				
▽ 📄 0000086200	Customs provision (MM)	Bal...			
📄 FR4	Customs provisions				
▽ 📄 0000086300	Delivery costs provision (MM)	Bal...			
📄 RUE	Neutral provisions				
▽ 📄 0000169900	Accounts Payable - consigment ...	Bal...			
▽ 📄 KON	Consignment payables				
📄	Consignment Liabilities				
📄 PIP	Pipeline Liabilities				
▽ 📄 0000191100	Goods Rcvd/Invoice Rcvd (third p...	Bal...			
📄 WRX	GR/IR clearing account				
▽ 📄 0000191110	Take over Goods Rcvd/Invoice R...	Bal...	0001		
📄 WRY	GR/IR clearing acct (mat. ledger)...		0001		
▽ 📄 0000191120	Clearing-invoice reduction	Bal...			
📄 RKA	Inv.reductions from log.inv.verific...				
▽ 📄 0000192100	Freight Clearing Account (MM)	Bal...			
📄 FR1	Freight clearing				
▽ 📄 0000192300	Customs Duty Clearing Account ...	Bal...			
📄 FR3	Customs clearing				

19.5.3   Account Detective

Purpose

If you want to know other sources of posting to a G/L account, you can use the Account Detective.

Transaction

S_ALR_87101048—Account Detective

Selection Screen

In the selection screen apart from other selection criteria, you specify the areas whose account determination entries are to be shown.

Area	Tables
☑ Output FI Account Assignments	T030C, T030D, T030G, T030H, T030K, T030S, T030U, T074
☑ Output MM/HR Account Assignmnt	T030
☑ Output Cost Element Categories	
☑ Output AA Account Assignments	T095, T095B, T095P
☑ Output SD/EK Account Assignmnt	C001, C002, C003, C004, C005

List of Tables Posting to an Account

G/L acct Account	Name Assignment	Account	Assignment	Account	Assignment	B/S acct Account	AT AcGp Crc Assignment Accour
399999	Bestandsaufnahme					X	MAT EUR
T030	GBB					BSA	3000
T030	GBB					BSA	7900
T030	GBB		0001			BSA	3000
T030	GBB		0001			BSA	3001
T030	GBB		0001			BSA	3030
T030	GBB		0001			BSA	3040
T030	GBB		0001			BSA	3050
T030	GBB		0001			BSA	3100
T095	02		00010000			BSA	3100
T095	02		00020000			BSA	3100
T095	03		00020000			BSA	3100

Messages

20.1 OVERVIEW

Functional Consultant	User	Business Process Owner	Senior Management	My Rating	Understanding Level
A	A	A	A		

Messages

During the invoice verification process, the system generates certain communications for vendors and buyers. Some of these are electronic messages, while some are printed documents. Collectively, they are called messages. These messages to internal and external partners should not be confused with the information/warning/error messages that the system gives to the online user.

Printed documents

SAP provides predefined printed documents that can be customized to your requirements. The messages can be generated in different languages.

Electronic mails

SAP provides predefined electronic mails that can be customized to your requirements. The messages can be generated in different languages.

Flexible messages

SAP lets you create the output in different languages. It also lets you use different methods of communication, e.g. printed document and e-mail. These choices can be different for different companies in a business group. You can even specify a different language or communication medium for a specific vendor. SAP provides a flexible method called condition technique for this purpose. Most part of this configuration is supplied by SAP. You need to only understand it so that you can debug the problem if things do not work as expected.

Conditions records

This is the data you need to maintain to take full advantage of the flexibility offered by the conditions technique. This is explained in detail in Section 20.5.

20.2 MESSAGE SCHEMAS

Functional Consultant	User	Business Process Owner	Senior Management	My Rating	Understanding Level
A	X	X	X		

20.2.1 Purpose

Schemas are the starting point of message determination using condition technique. The system determines the schema automatically based on the business process you are carrying out.

20.2.2 IMG Node

SM34 ➤ VVC_T683_XX_MR

20.2.3 Schemas

Dialog Structure
▽ Schemas
 Control Data

Usage: B
Application: MR

Schemas

Proce	Descript.
MR0001	Invoice Verification
MR0002	Logistics Inv. Ver. (MR1M)
MR0003	Consignment (MRKO)
MR0004	ERS Procedure
MR0005	Revaluation (MRNB)
MR0006	Invoicing plan (MRIS)

20.2.4   Condition Types in Logistics Invoice Verification

Select [MR0002] Logistics Inv. Ver. (MR1M) and double-click ☐ Control Data .

Procedure	[MR0002] Logistics Inv. Ver. (MR1M)

Reference Step Overview

	Step	Counter	CTyp	Description	Requiremnt	Manual only
	10	0	MLPP	Mail Price Deviation	180	☐
	20	0	REKL	Complaint	181	☐

In logistics invoice verification, the system generates a complaint letter which you can see in section 6.3.5. It also generates a mail in the case of price deviation.

20.2.5   Condition Types in Consignment

Select [MR0003] Consignment (MRKO) and double-click ☐ Control Data .

Procedure	[MR0003] Consignment (MRKO)

Reference Step Overview

	Step	Counter	CTyp	Description	Requiremnt	Manual only
	10	0	KON6	Consignment		☐
	20	0	KONS	Consignment		☐

In consignment settlement, the system generates a message which you can see in section 14.1.9. Condition type KON6 is for EDI.

20.2.6   Condition Types in ERS Procedure

Select [MR0004] ERS Procedure and double-click ☐ Control Data .

Procedure	[MR0004] ERS Procedure

Reference Step Overview

	Step	Counter	CTyp	Description	Requiremnt	Manual only
	10	0	ERS6	ERS procedure, EDI		☐
	20	0	ERS	ERS Procedure		☐

In evaluated receipt settlement, the system generates a message which you can see in section 13.2.8. Condition type ERS6 is for EDI.

20.2.7 Condition Types in Revaluation

Select MR0005 Revaluation (MRNB) and double-click ☐ Control Data.

| Procedure | MR0005 Revaluation (MRNB) |

Reference Step Overview

	Step	Counter	CTyp	Description	Requiremnt	Manual only
	10	0	RAP6	New value method		☐
	20	0	RAP	New value method		☐

In revaluation, the system generates a message which you can see in section 4.19.10. Condition type RAP6 is for EDI.

20.2.8 Condition Types in Invoicing Plan

Select MR0006 Invoicing plan (MRIS) and double-click ☐ Control Data.

| Procedure | MR0006 Invoicing plan (MRIS) |

Reference Step Overview

	Step	Counter	CTyp	Description	Requiremnt	Manual only
	10	0	INS	Invoice plan		☐

In invoicing plan, the system generates a message which you can see in section 15.1.9.

20.2.9 Condition Types in Conventional Invoice Verification

Select MR0001 Invoice Verification and double-click ☐ Control Data.

| Procedure | MR0001 Invoice Verification |

Reference Step Overview

	Step	Counter	CTyp	Description	Requiremnt	Manual only
	10	0	EINK	Mail to Purchasing		☐

This is the old procedure for invoice verification. The new procedure is called logistics invoice verification.

20.3 MESSAGE/OUTPUT TYPES

Functional Consultant	User	Business Process Owner	Senior Management	My Rating	Understanding Level
A	X	X	X		

20.3.1 Purpose

Here you can see the message/output types relevant to invoice verification.

20.3.2 IMG Node

SM34 ➤ VN_T685B

20.3.3 Output Types

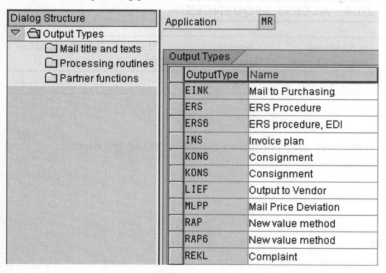

20.3.4 Access Sequence

Select [REKL Complaint] and click [🔍].

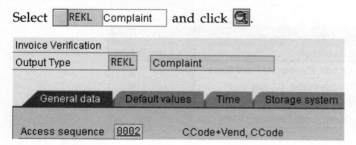

Note that an output type has an access sequence. Access sequences used by all output types are given below.

Usage	Application	Condition Type	Access sequence
B	MR	EINK	0001
B	MR	ERS	0002
B	MR	ERS6	0002
B	MR	INS	0004
B	MR	KON6	0002
B	MR	KONS	0002
B	MR	LIEF	
B	MR	MLPP	0003
B	MR	RAP	0003
B	MR	RAP6	0003
B	MR	REKL	0002

20.4 ACCESS SEQUENCES

Functional Consultant	User	Business Process Owner	Senior Management	My Rating	Understanding Level
A	X	X	X		

20.4.1 Purpose

Here you can see the access sequences and condition tables accessed by them.

20.4.2 IMG Node

SM34 ≻ VVC_T682_MR

20.4.3 Access Sequences

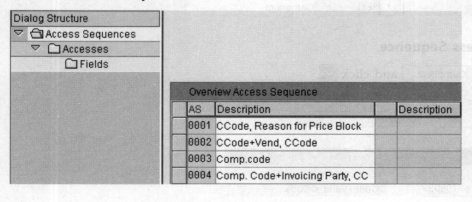

Dialog Structure
▽ 🗁 Access Sequences
  ▽ 🗀 Accesses
    🗀 Fields

	Overview Access Sequence		
AS	Description		Description
0001	CCode, Reason for Price Block		
0002	CCode+Vend, CCode		
0003	Comp.code		
0004	Comp. Code+Invoicing Party, CC		

20.4.4 Condition Tables

Select ☐ 0002 CCode+Vend, CCode and click ☐ Accesses.

Access sequence 0002 CCode+Vend, CCode

	No.	Tab	Description	Requiremnt	Exclusive
Overview Accesses					
	10	48	CoCode, Vendor		☑
	20	49	CoCde		☑

The above screenshot shows that for generating the complaint letter, the system first accesses condition table B048. If a record is found there, the system uses the information found in it to generate the complaint letter. If a record is found in table B048, it does not search for a record in table B049 (since the Exclusive indicator is ☑). However, if a record is not found in table B048, it searches for a record in table B049. Condition tables accessed by all access sequences are given below.

	Usage	Application	Access sequence	Table
☐	B	MR	0001	046
☐	B	MR	0002	048
☐	B	MR	0002	049
☐	B	MR	0003	049
☐	B	MR	0004	172
☐	B	MR	0004	049

20.5 CONDITION RECORDS

Functional Consultant	User	Business Process Owner	Senior Management	My Rating	Understanding Level
A	A	B		X	

20.5.1 Purpose

The system generates output based on the data found in condition tables. You need to maintain this data so as to generate output as per your requirement.

20.5.2 Transactions

MRM1—Create Message: Invoice Verification
MRM2—Change Message: Invoice Verification
MRM3—Display Message: Invoice Verification

20.5.3 Initial Screen

In the initial screen, you select the output type | Output Type | REKL | Complaint for which you want to maintain condition records.

20.5.4 Key Combination

Click | Key combination |.

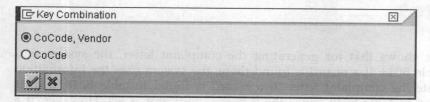

The system shows you the condition tables that can be maintained for the output type.

20.5.5 Condition Records in Table B048

Select ⦿ CoCode, Vendor and click ✓.

Company Code	1000	IDES AG

Condition Recs.							
Vendor	Name	Funct	Partner	Medium	Date/Time	Language
T-K515A01	Sapsota Company Limi	IP		1	3	
T-K515A02	Sapsota Company Limi	IP		1	3	
T-K515A03	Sapsota Company Limi	IP		1	3	

The system shows the condition records maintained in table B048.

20.5.6 Condition Records in Table B049

Select ⦿ CoCde and click ✓.

Condition Recs.							
CoCode	Name	Funct	Partner	Medium	Date/Time	Language
1000	IDES AG	IP		1	3	
R300	IDES Retail INC US	IP		1	3	

The system shows the condition records maintained in table B049.

20.5.7   Condition Technique

A condition table consists of two parts: the input part and the output part.

Input Part of the Condition Table

The input part is different for different condition tables.

Condition table	Input parameters
B048	Company Code , Vendor
B049	Company Code

The system accesses a condition table with the input information and seeks a record that matches the input information.

Output Part of the Condition Table

The output part is the same for all condition tables: Funct Partner Medium Date/Time Language .

Using the Output Part of the Condition Table

If a record is found in the condition table with matching input, the system collects the output parameters and uses them to generate the output. If no match is found in a condition table, the next condition table is searched. If no match is found in any condition table in the access sequence of the output type, no output is generated.

Significance of the Output Parameters

You need to understand how the output parameters are used, so that you can correctly maintain the condition records.

Partner function

In the condition record, you specify the partner function who will receive the message. If you use only one partner function, usually VN, you can specify that here. Actual partner number is determined by the system. Apart from external business partners, you can also specify an internal business partner, e.g. an organizational unit or a position.

Partner

Usually the system determines the partner function from the condition record, and the partner number for the partner function from the purchasing document. However, if a partner number is specified here, that partner number is used directly. This may be needed when the partner function is an internal business partner, e.g. an organizational unit or a position.

Medium

The transmission medium specifies how the message will be transmitted. SAP supports a variety of transmission media.

Transmission Medium	Short text
1	Print output
2	Fax
4	Telex
5	External send
6	EDI
7	Simple Mail
8	Special function
9	Events (SAP Business Workflow)
A	Distribution (ALE)
T	Tasks (SAP Business Workflow)

Transmission medium print

For transmission medium 1 click Communication to enter medium dependent communication data.

Variabler Key

CoCode	Vendor		Description
1000	1000		C.E.B. BERLIN

Print output

Output Device		☐ Print immediately
Number of messages		☐ Release after output
Spool request name		
Suffix 1		
Suffix 2		
SAP cover page	Do Not Print	
Recipient		
Department		
Cover Page Text		
Authorization		
Storage Mode		

Print settings

Layout module	
Form	
SmartForm	

Transmission medium simple mail

For transmission medium 7, click [Communication] to enter medium dependent communication data.

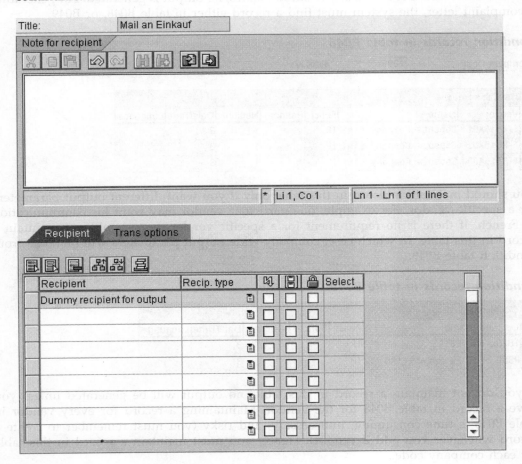

Date/time

Here you can specify when the messages will be transmitted.

1	Send with periodically scheduled job
2	Send with job, with additional time specification
3	Send with application own transaction
4	Send immediately (when saving the application)

Language

Here you can specify the language of the message.

How to Maintain Condition Records

In order to generate an output, the system must find a record in one of the condition tables. If no record is found in any condition tables, no output is generated. For generating a complaint letter, the system must find a record either in table B048, or B049.

Condition records in table B048

Company Code	1000	IDES AG

Condition Recs.

	Vendor	Name	Funct	Partner	Medium	Date/Time	Language
	T-K515A01	Sapsota Company Limi	IP		1	3	
	T-K515A02	Sapsota Company Limi	IP		1	3	
	T-K515A03	Sapsota Company Limi	IP		1	3	

You should maintain a record in this table only if you want different output parameters for a specific vendor. For example, one particular vendor may want his communication in French. If there is no requirement for a specific vendor, you should not maintain a record in this table. In which case, company-wide output parameters will be taken from condition table B049.

Condition records in table B049

Condition Recs.

	CoCode	Name	Funct	Partner	Medium	Date/Time	Language
	1000	IDES AG	IP		1	3	
	R300	IDES Retail INC US	IP		1	3	

If you do not maintain a record in this table, no output will be generated unless you have a record in table B048 for the vendor. Maintaining a record for every vendor in table B048 is time consuming, unnecessary, and risky (you must remember to create a record whenever you add a vendor). Hence, you must maintain a record in this table for each company code.

Flexibility and ease of maintenance

Through condition technique, SAP gives you both flexibility and ease of maintenance. By maintaining just one record in table B049, you can generate complaint letters. You can also decide whether you want to print the complaint letter, or send it through e-mail.

However, if some vendor has a specific requirement, he wants an e-mail while you normally print, that can be done by maintaining a record in table B048. If you do maintain a record in table B048, its output parameters should be different from the output parameters in table B049. If you do not want different output parameters, there is no need to maintain a record in table B048. The system will anyway get them from table B049.

The Condition Records that Need to be Maintained

You need to maintain condition records in tables B046, B048, B049, and B172, which are used by the following output types:

Output type	Description	Access sequence	Tables accessed
EINK	Mail to purchasing	0001	B046
ERS	ERS procedure	0002	B048, B049
ERS6	ERS procedure, EDI	0002	B048, B049
INS	Invoice plan	0004	B172, B049
KON6	Consignment	0002	B048, B049
KONS	Consignment	0002	B048, B049
LIEF	Output to vendor		
MLPP	Mail price deviation	0003	B049
RAP	New value method	0003	B049
RAP6	New value method	0003	B049
REKL	Complaint	0002	B048, B049

20.6 PRINTED MESSAGES

Functional Consultant	User	Business Process Owner	Senior Management	My Rating	Understanding Level
A	A	B	X		

20.6.1 Assignment of Forms to Output Types

The content of a message is specified in a form, and the form is processed by a program. In view VV_TNAPR_MR, you specify the program, the form routine and the form for every output type and medium.

Messages: Output Programs

Out.	Name	Med	Program	FORM routine	Form
EINK	Mail to Purchasing	7	RSNASTSO	SAPOFFICE_AUFRUF	
ERS	ERS Procedure	1	RM08NAST	ENTRY_ERS	MR_PRINT
ERS	ERS Procedure	2	RM08NAST	ENTRY_ERS	MR_PRINT
ERS6	ERS procedure, EDI	6	RSNASTED	EDI_PROCESSING	
INS	Invoice plan	1	RM08NAST	ENTRY_INS	MR_PRINT
INS	Invoice plan	2	RM08NAST	ENTRY_INS	MR_PRINT
KON6	Consignment	6	RSNASTED	EDI_PROCESSING	
KONS	Consignment	1	RM08NAST	ENTRY_KONS	MR_PRINT
KONS	Consignment	2	RM08NAST	ENTRY_KONS	MR_PRINT
MLPP	Mail Price Deviation	7	RSNASTSO	SAPOFFICE_AUFRUF	
RAP	New value method	1	RM08NAST	ENTRY_RAP	MR_PRINT
RAP	New value method	2	RM08NAST	ENTRY_RAP	MR_PRINT
RAP6	New value method	6	RSNASTED	EDI_PROCESSING	
REKL	Complaint	1	RM08NAST	ENTRY_REKL	MR_REKL

20.6.2 Content of Printed Messages

The content of printed messages is defined in forms using transaction SE71 by an ABAP consultant.

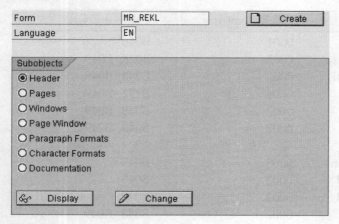

Windows

Select ⦿ Windows, click ⟨Display⟩.

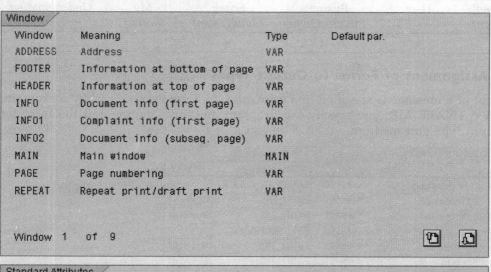

Window	Meaning	Type	Default par.
ADDRESS	Address	VAR	
FOOTER	Information at bottom of page	VAR	
HEADER	Information at top of page	VAR	
INFO	Document info (first page)	VAR	
INFO1	Complaint info (first page)	VAR	
INFO2	Document info (subseq. page)	VAR	
MAIN	Main window	MAIN	
PAGE	Page numbering	VAR	
REPEAT	Repeat print/draft print	VAR	

Window 1 of 9

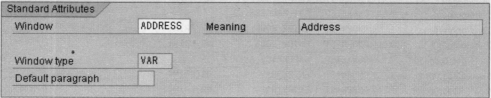

Standard Attributes		
Window	ADDRESS	Meaning	Address

Window type	VAR
Default paragraph	

Main Window

Click `MAIN        Main window`, then click 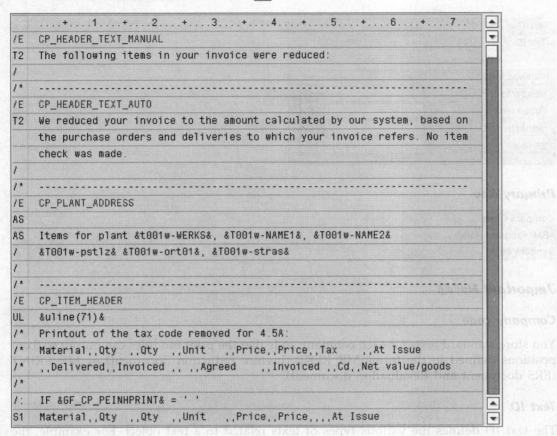.

```
      ....+....1....+....2....+....3....+....4....+....5....+....6....+....7..
/E    CP_HEADER_TEXT_MANUAL
T2    The following items in your invoice were reduced:
/
/*    --------------------------------------------------------------------
/E    CP_HEADER_TEXT_AUTO
T2    We reduced your invoice to the amount calculated by our system, based on
      the purchase orders and deliveries to which your invoice refers. No item
      check was made.
/
/*    --------------------------------------------------------------------
/E    CP_PLANT_ADDRESS
AS
AS    Items for plant &t001w-WERKS&, &T001W-NAME1&, &T001W-NAME2&
/     &T001w-pstlz& &T001w-ort01&, &T001w-stras&
/
/*    --------------------------------------------------------------------
/E    CP_ITEM_HEADER
UL    &uline(71)&
/*    Printout of the tax code removed for 4.5A:
/*    Material,,Qty  ,,Qty  ,,Unit   ,,Price,,Price,,Tax    ,,At Issue
/*    ,,Delivered,,Invoiced ,, ,,Agreed    ,,Invoiced ,,Cd,,Net value/goods
/*
/:    IF &GF_CP_PEINHPRINT& = ' '
S1    Material,,Qty  ,,Qty  ,,Unit    ,,Price,,Price,,,,At Issue
```

Here you can see the main content of a printed message. This format can be changed to meet your requirement. You can also use customer exit MRMN0001 to change the message output in invoice verification.

20.6.3   Sender Texts

Purpose

Forms are common for all companies. But the sender details vary from company code to company code. Here, for every company code, you define which standard texts are used for letter headers, footers, signature, and the sender address in the window of the envelope.

IMG Node

SM30 ➢ V_001G_R

Screen

Company Code	1000	IDES AG Frankfurt

Text ID

Text ID	

Standard texts

Header text		
Footer text		
Signature text		
Sender		

Primary Key

Company Code
ABAP Program Name
Sender Variant

Important Fields

Company code

You store standard texts for each company code that the print modules can output to fixed positions defined in the forms MR_REKL (Invoice reduction document) or MR_PRINT (ERS document and Revaluation document).

Text ID

The text ID defines the various types of texts related to a text object. For example, the object "TEXT" (standard texts) can have the following text IDs:

> ST for user-specific standard texts (individual texts). Standard texts must be created using transaction SO10 before assigning the texts in this view.
> SYST for cross-application system texts
> Various IDs for specific application departments. You must have the appropriate access authorization in order to access these texts.

Header text

Header text, e.g. company logo, is output at top right of the form.

Footer text

Footer text, e.g. company address, is output at the bottom of each page of the form.

Signature text

The signature text contains the name of the company and/or the name of an accounting clerk, for example. The details are generally printed at the end of the letter after the closing form.

Sender

The sender text contains a summary of the company address. The details are generally printed in the first line in the letter window, if no preprinted paper is used.

20.7   ELECTRONIC MAIL

Functional Consultant	User	Business Process Owner	Senior Management	My Rating	Understanding Level
A	A	B	X		

20.7.1   Assignment of Forms to Output Types

In view VV_TNAPR_MR, you specify the program and the form routine that will process the message.

Messages: Output Programs

	Out.	Name	Med	Program	FORM routine	Form
	MLPP	Mail Price Deviation	7	RSNASTSO	SAPOFFICE_AUFRUF	

20.7.2   Content of Electronic Mails

Note that there is no Form defined for Mails. The content of Mail is defined in view cluster VN_T685B.

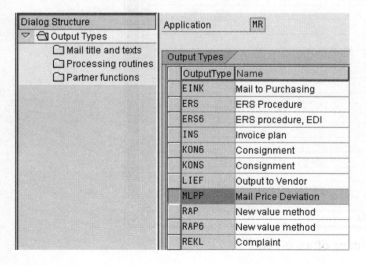

Dialog Structure	Application	MR	
▽ 🗁 Output Types			
🗀 Mail title and texts	**Output Types**		
🗀 Processing routines	OutputType	Name	
🗀 Partner functions	EINK	Mail to Purchasing	
	ERS	ERS Procedure	
	ERS6	ERS procedure, EDI	
	INS	Invoice plan	
	KON6	Consignment	
	KONS	Consignment	
	LIEF	Output to Vendor	
	MLPP	Mail Price Deviation	
	RAP	New value method	
	RAP6	New value method	
	REKL	Complaint	

Mail Title and Texts

Select ▐ MLPP ▐ Mail Price Deviation ▌ and double-click 🗀 Mail title and texts .

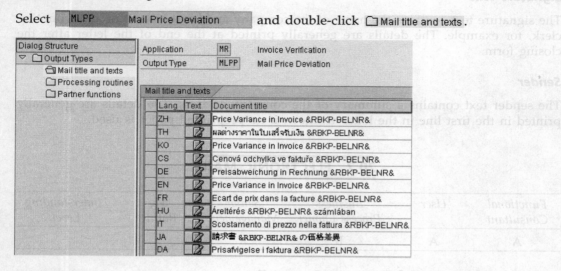

Mail Text

Click .

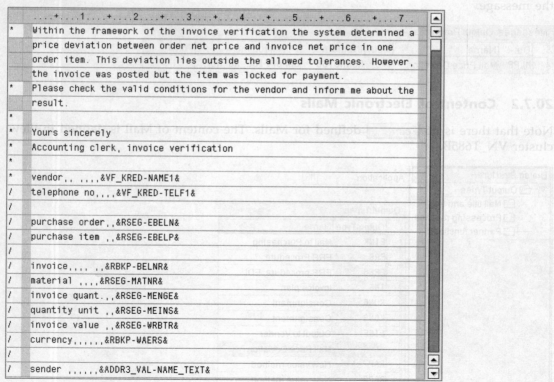

This is where you define the content of an e-mail.

20.7.3 Activation of Mail to Purchasing When Price Variances Occur

Output type MLPP generates a mail to purchasing when price variances occur. You can switch on, or switch off, this feature in view V_169P_A.

CoCd	Company Name	Auto. MAIL
1000	IDES AG	☑
2000	IDES UK	☐
2200	IDES France	☐

If you select the checkbox above, mail is generated; if you leave it blank, mail is not generated.

20.8   PRINTER DETERMINATION

Functional Consultant	User	Business Process Owner	Senior Management	My Rating	Understanding Level
A	A	B	X		

In invoice verification, the printer is determined in the following sequence:

20.8.1 Specifying the Printer while Processing the Output

In transaction MR90, select the messages and click Edit ➤ Printer default.

Printer default for output	⊠
Output Device	LP01
Number of messages	
Spool request name	
Suffix 1	
Suffix 2	
SAP cover page	Do Not Print
Recipient	
Department	
Cover Page Text	
Authorization	
☐ Print immediately	
☐ Release after output	

✓ ✗

You can specify a printer here.

20.8.2 Specifying the Printer while Processing the Invoice

When you are processing an invoice in transaction MIRO, click Message ➤ Header / Item. The system gives the list of messages.

Doc. No. 5105608650

	Stat	Output	Description	Medium		Fun	Partner	La	C	Pro	Time	Date/Time	Sa
	◌◯◌	REKL	Complaint	1 Print output	🗐	IP	1002	EN	☐		00:00	3	☐

Select the messages and click [🔩 Communication method].

Invoice presented by	1002	Müller KG
Output type	REKL	Complaint

Printing information

Logical destination	LP01	[⎙]
	Beispieldrucker. Mit SPAD anpassen.	

Number of messages		☐ Print immediately
Spool request name		☐ Release after output
Suffix 1		
Suffix 2		
SAP cover page	Do Not Print	
Recipient		
Department		
Cover Page Text		
Authorization		
Storage Mode		

Format

Form	

You can specify a printer here.

20.8.3 Specifying the Printer in the Condition Record

Select a condition record in transaction MRM2.

CoCode	Name	Funct	Partner	Medium	Date/Time	Language
1000	IDES AG	IP		1	3	

Click [Communication].

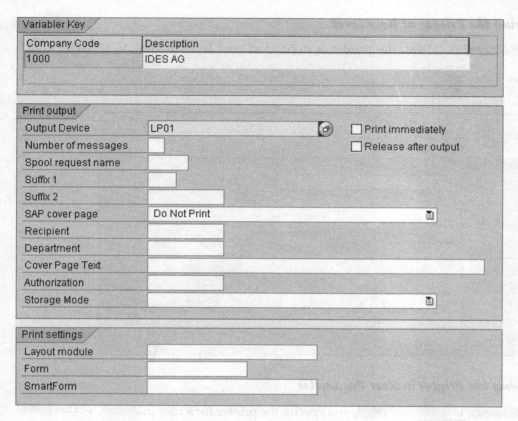

You can specify a printer here.

20.8.4 Specifying the Print Parameter in Output Type

Maintain output types in view VN_T685B. Select an output type and click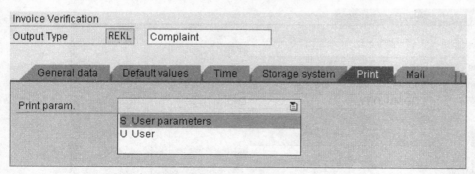

Choose the print parameter S or U.

Specifying the Printer at User Level

If the `Print param.` is U User , the printer is defined at user level in view V_TNADU.

Application	MR
Condition Type	REKL

User	SAPUSER

Printing Information

OutputDevice	LP01

Name		☐ Print immed.
Suffix 1		☐ Rel.after print
Suffix 2		
SAP cover page		
Recipient		
Department		
Cover Page Text		
Authorization		

Specifying the Printer in User Parameter

If the `Print param.` is S User parameters , you specify the printer for a user in `System` ➢ `User Profile` ➢ `Own Data` ➢ `Defaults` ➢ `OutputDevice` .

User	SAPUSER
Last Changed On	SAPUSER	29.03.2020	12:01:51	Status	Saved

Address | **Defaults** | **Parameters**

Start menu	
Logon Language	EN
Decimal Notation	X 1,234,567.89
Date format	1 DD.MM.YYYY

Spool Control

OutputDevice	
☐ Output Immediately	
☐ Delete After Output	

20.9   MESSAGE PROCESSES

Functional Consultant	User	Business Process Owner	Senior Management	My Rating	Understanding Level
A	A	B	X		

20.9.1   Message Creation

Messages are created automatically, when appropriate conditions arise, e.g. posting of invoices that result in a complaint letter.

20.9.2   Message Display

You can see the actual message using transaction MR90. For Consignment and Pipeline settlement, use transaction MR91.

20.9.3   Message Transmission

Invoice verification messages may be transmitted using one of the following processes:

Immediate transmission

Messages are transmitted immediately, if the date/time settings so require.

Batch transmission

Messages that are not transmitted immediately can be transmitted at predefined time intervals using a batch job. Usually, this is the preferred method, as this job can be run during lean hours. If the output is to be printed, the printing job can be done centrally, freeing the users from this task. To use this method, run transaction SA38, enter program RSNAST00, and create the appropriate variant. Then schedule the job using transaction SM36. The status of the messages is stored in table NAST.

Manual transmission

You can also run transaction MR90 (program MM70AMRA) to print/transmit the messages. Enter the selection criteria in the selection screen, choosing Processing mode 1 First processing.

Message Data			
Output Type		to	
Transmission Medium		to	
Created on		to	
Sort order	01	Vendor/Partner function/Document number	
Processing mode	1	First processing	

Invoice Doc. Data			
Invoice Document No.		to	
Fiscal Year	☑		
Company Code		to	
Invoicing Party		to	
User		to	

The system displays the list of selected messages.

Inv. Doc. No.	Item	CoCd	Vendor	Role	Name 1	Out.	Created on	Med	Status	User
5105608649		1000	1002	RS	Müller KG	REKL	30.03.2014	1	0	SAPUSER
5105608652		1000	1002	RS	Müller KG	REKL	31.03.2014	1	0	SAPUSER
5105608660		1000	1002	RS	Müller KG	REKL	08.04.2014	1	0	SAPUSER
5105608661		1000	1002	RS	Müller KG	REKL	08.04.2014	1	0	SAPUSER
5105608670		1000	1002	RS	Müller KG	REKL	13.04.2014	1	0	SAPUSER

You can see the message by selecting the message and clicking 🔲. You can process the messages by selecting the messages and clicking 🔲.

20.9.4   Message Retransmission

Processing mode 1 filters messages which have been outputted. If you want to reoutput a message, select processing mode 2.

20.10   CONDITION TABLES

Functional Consultant	User	Business Process Owner	Senior Management	My Rating	Understanding Level
A	X	X	X		

20.10.1   Maintaining Condition Tables

Usually SAP's predefined condition tables should meet your requirements. However, if you want, you can create condition tables using transaction M811. You can display a condition table using transaction M813. You may change your own condition table using transaction M812, but it is not advisable to change SAP's predefined condition tables.

20.11   REQUIREMENTS

Functional Consultant	User	Business Process Owner	Senior Management	My Rating	Understanding Level
A	X	X	X		

20.11.1   Maintaining Requirements

If a step has a requirement, that step is executed only if the requirement is fulfilled.

Routine	Description
83	Internet com.
180	Mail to buyer
181	Complaint

Requirement routines can be maintained using transaction M802.

Routine number	Description	Active	Application
83	Internet com.	☑	MR
180	Mail to buyer	☑	MR
181	Complaint	☑	MR

Archiving

20.10 CONDITION TABLES

21.1 ARCHIVE ADMINISTRATION

Functional Consultant	User	Business Process Owner	Senior Management	My Rating	Understanding Level
A	B	X	X		

21.1.1 Purpose

You archive invoice documents to free database space and to improve performance. In this section, the general framework for archiving is discussed. Specific transactions for archiving invoice documents are discussed in subsequent sections.

21.1.2 Transaction

SARA—Create Archive

21.1.3 Control Screen

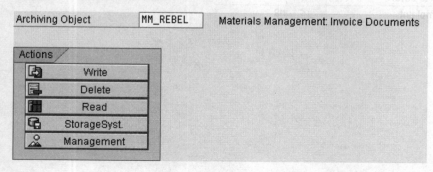

Archiving object

In transaction SARA, you can specify the archiving object. The archiving object for invoice documents is MM_REBEL.

Write

In this action, the archive file is created.

Delete

In this action, the archived data is deleted from the database.

Read

In this action, you can read the archived data from archive files.

Storage system

In this action, the archive files are stored in content repository.

Management

In this action, you can see the status of various archiving sessions.

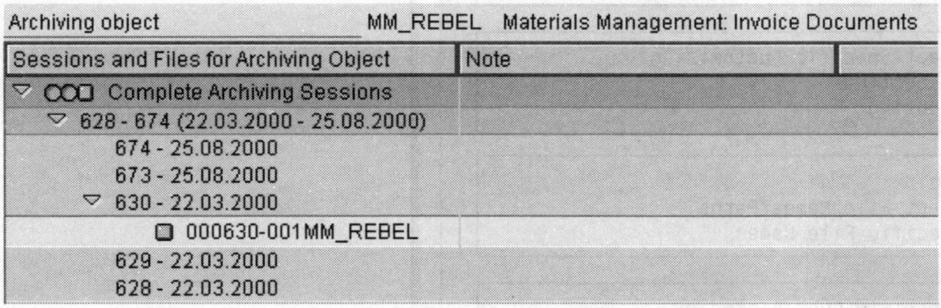

Archiving object	MM_REBEL Materials Management: Invoice Documents	
Sessions and Files for Archiving Object	Note	
▽ ◯◯▢ Complete Archiving Sessions		
▽ 628 - 674 (22.03.2000 - 25.08.2000)		
674 - 25.08.2000		
673 - 25.08.2000		
▽ 630 - 22.03.2000		
▢ 000630-001MM_REBEL		
629 - 22.03.2000		
628 - 22.03.2000		

You can also see the above screen using transaction MRA4 for invoice documents.

21.2 ARCHIVING CUSTOMIZING

Functional Consultant	User	Business Process Owner	Senior Management	My Rating	Understanding Level
A	B	X	X		

21.2.1 Purpose

You can customize the data archiving process for invoices.

21.2.2 Transaction

In archive administration transaction SARA or MRA4, click Customizing .

21.2.3 Screen

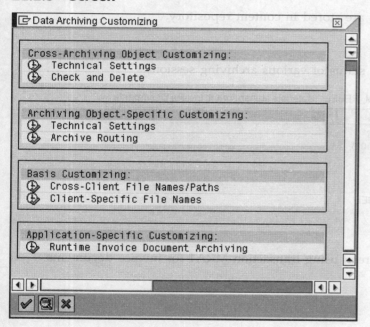

21.2.4 Cross-archiving Object Customizing

This customizing is for all archiving objects. You should not change these settings without concurrence from other users.

21.2.5   Archiving Object-specific Customizing: Technical Setting

Purpose

After the data is archived, it is deleted from the database using the delete program, and the file is stored in the storage system. Both these activities can happen automatically after archiving.

IMG Node

SM30 ➤ V_ARC_USR

In archive administration transaction SARA or MRA4, click ⎡ Customizing ⎤, and in `Archiving Object-Specific Customizing`, click ⊕ `Technical Settings`.

Screen

Object Name	MM_REBEL	Materials Management: Invoice Documents
Logical File Name	ARCHIVE_DATA_FILE	

Archive File Size

Maximum Size in MB	1
Maximum Number of Data Objects	1,000

Settings for Delete Program

Test Mode Variant	TESTLAUF	Variant
Production Mode Variant	PRODUKTIVLAUF	Variant

Delete Jobs
- ○ Not Scheduled
- ◉ Start Automatically
- ○ After Event   Event _____
                   Parameter _____

Place File in Storage System

Content Repository	MA

☑ Start Automatically

Sequence
- ◉ Delete Before Storing
- ○ Store Before Deleting   ☐ Delete Program Reads from Storage System

Primary Key

Archiving Object

Important Fields

Object name

For archiving invoice documents, the object is MM_REBEL.

Logical file name

At runtime, the logical file name is converted by the FILE_GET_NAME function module to a platform-specific path and file name. You can find out more about this setting in Basis customizing under Cross-client Maintenance of File Names and Paths.

Maximum size in MB

This parameter controls the maximum size of an archive file. Before an object is written to an archive file, the system checks whether the maximum permitted size is exceeded. If so, the current archiving file is closed and another is opened to accommodate the object.

Maximum number of data objects

This parameter controls the maximum number of data objects per archive file. Before a data object is written to an archive file, the system checks whether the maximum number allowed would be exceeded. If this is the case, the current archive file is closed and a new one opened for the data object.

Test mode variant

If you run the delete program (transaction MRA2) in ☑ Test Mode, the system uses the variant specified here.

Production mode variant

If you run the delete program (transaction MRA2) in ☐ Test Mode, the system uses the variant specified here.

Delete jobs

Here you do settings for running the delete program.

Archiving program modes

When the archiving program (transaction MRA1) is run, you specify a variant. In the variant you specify whether the program will be run in the ⊙ Test Mode , or in the ⊙ Production Mode .

Archiving program in test mode

When the archiving program (transaction MRA1) is run in test mode, objects are selected for archiving only for test purposes. No archive file is generated and, therefore, there is no deletion of the selected objects.

Archiving program in production mode

When the archiving program (transaction MRA1) is run in production mode, an archive file is generated and the selected objects get archived. The delete program may be run manually, or automatically as explained below:

Delete jobs	Explanation
⊙ Not Scheduled	You can run the delete program (transaction MRA2) later, select the archive file, and schedule the deletion job.
⊙ Start Automatically	The deletion job starts immediately after archiving without any intervention from the user.
⊙ After Event	The deletion job starts without any intervention from the user after the specified event.

Content repository

Here you specify the storage repository of physical archive files.

Start automatically

This checkbox indicates that archive files, after successful processing, are automatically transferred to a connected storage system.

Delete before storing

This radio button indicates that the data is deleted from the database before the archive file is stored in the content repository.

Store before deleting

This radio button indicates that the data is deleted from the database after the archive file is stored in the content repository.

Delete program reads from storage system

If the archive file is stored before deleting, here you can specify that the deletion program should read the file from the storage system for deleting the data from the database.

21.2.6   Archiving Object-Specific Customizing: Archive Routing

You can use this function to create rules and conditions, based on which archive files are automatically routed to specific areas in the file or storage system.

21.2.7   Basis Customizing: Cross Client File Names/Paths

These cross-client settings are done by your Basis administrator to determine physical file names and paths from their logical counterparts. If there is a problem with these settings, storage of archive files may be affected.

21.2.8   Basis Customizing: Client-specific File Names

These client-specific settings are done by your Basis administrator to determine physical file names from their logical counterparts. If there is a problem with these settings, storage of archive files may be affected.

21.2.9   Life of Invoice Documents before Archiving

Purpose

Here you define the minimum life of invoice documents for each company code. After the minimum life of a document has been reached, the document can be archived.

IMG Node

SM30 ➤ V_169R

In archive administration transaction SARA, MRA1, or MIAR, click `Customizing`, and in `Application-Specific Customizing`, click ⬙ `Runtime Invoice Document Archiving`.

Screen

CoCd	Life
1000	100
2000	100
2100	100
2200	100

Primary Key

Company Code

21.3 ARCHIVING INVOICE DOCUMENTS

Functional Consultant	User	Business Process Owner	Senior Management	My Rating	Understanding Level
A	B	X	X		

21.3.1 Purpose

You archive invoice documents to free database space and to improve performance. While archiving data, the system ensures that the data can be read, analyzed, and reloaded, if required. When you use this transaction, deletion and storage may happen automatically, if specified in `Archiving Object-Specific Customizing`.

21.3.2 Transaction

MRA1—Create Archive (Invoice Documents)

21.3.3 Selection Screen

```
Materials Management: Invoice Documents
Client            800
Variant                           [⇄] [⇅]    Maintain
User Name         SAPUSER

[▣]     Start Date       ●○○   Not Maintained
[⎙]     Spool Params.    ●○○   Not Maintained
```

Variant

Click [⇅   Maintain] to specify the selection parameters in a variant.

```
[⇲ ABAP: Variants                    ⊠]


  Create variant                      [⇄]


[🗋 Create] [✖]
```

Enter the variant name and click [🗋 Create].

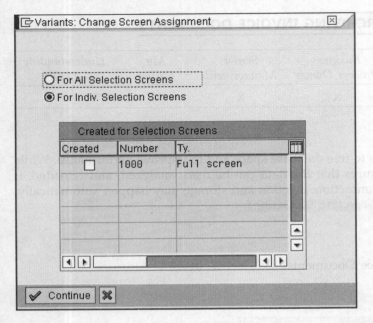

Select the checkbox and click ✔ Continue .

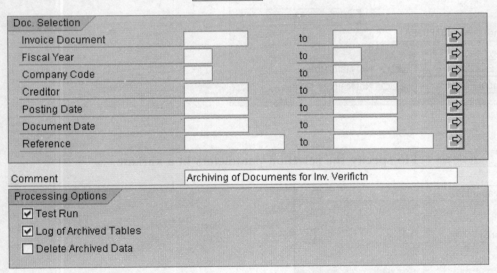

Specify the invoice documents to be archived.

Start Date

Click [🖩 Start Date] to define when you want processing to commence. You can specify [Immediate], [Date/Time], [After job], etc.

Spool Parameters

Click [🖨 Spool Params.] to specify background print parameters.

```
┌─ Background Print Parameters ─────────────────────── ⊠ ─┐
│                                                          │
│   Output Device      [                    ]              │
│   Number of copies   [1  ]                               │
│                                                          │
│   ┌─ Number of pages ──────────────────────────────┐    │
│   │  ⦿ Print all                                    │    │
│   │  ○ Print from page      [0       ]   To [0     ]│    │
│   │                                                 │    │
│   │                                                 │    │
│   └─────────────────────────────────────────────────┘   │
│                                                          │
│                                                          │
│                                                          │
│                                                          │
│  ┌──────────────┐                                        │
│  │ ✓  Properties │ ✖  ⓘ                                  │
│  └──────────────┘                                        │
└──────────────────────────────────────────────────────────┘
```

Specify the output device and other parameters.

21.3.4   Archiving

After maintaining the variant and specifying time and spool parameters, click ⊕. The background job for archiving is created.

21.3.5   Job

Click [🖳] to see the archiving jobs.

Job	Ln	Job CreatedBy	Status	Start date
☐ ARV_MM_REBEL_SUB20140529170533		SAPUSER	Released	
*Summary				

You can see the [🖳 Spool] and [📄 Job log].

21.3.6 Archive Directory

Click | Archive Directory | to see the archive directory and the space in it.

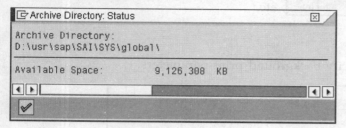

21.3.7 Customizing

Click | Customizing | to see the customizing for archiving. For details, see Section 21.2.

21.3.8 Management

Click | Management | to see the status of various archiving sessions.

Archiving object	MM_REBEL Materials Management: Invoice Documents	
Sessions and Files for Archiving Object	Note	
▽ ◯◯◻ Complete Archiving Sessions		
▽ 628 - 674 (22.03.2000 - 25.08.2000)		
674 - 25.08.2000		
673 - 25.08.2000		
▽ 630 - 22.03.2000		
◻ 000630-001MM_REBEL		
629 - 22.03.2000		
628 - 22.03.2000		

You can also see the above screen using transaction MRA4 for invoice documents.

21.3.9 Database Tables

Click Database Tables .

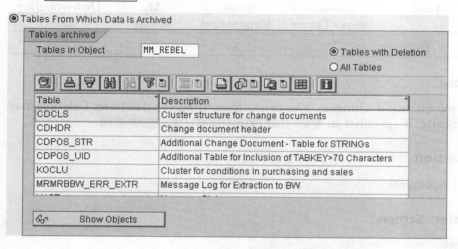

You can select a table and click Show Objects to show the objects through which that table is archived.

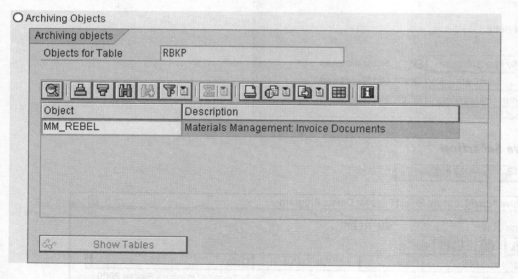

21.3.10 Information System

Click Information System to see information about archived data.

21.4   DELETING ARCHIVED INVOICE DOCUMENTS

Functional Consultant	User	Business Process Owner	Senior Management	My Rating	Understanding Level
A	B	X	X		

21.4.1   Purpose

After archiving the invoice documents, you delete them from the database. Deletion may happen automatically, if specified in `Archiving Object-Specific Customizing`.

21.4.2   Transaction

MRA2—Delete Documents

21.4.3   Selection Screen

Materials Management: Invoice Documents	
Client	800
User Name	SAPUSER

☐ Test Mode

🔳 Archive Selection	◉◯◯	Not Maintained
📅 Start Date	◉◯◯	Not Maintained
🖨 Spool Parameters	◉◯◯	Not Maintained

Archive Selection

Click  .

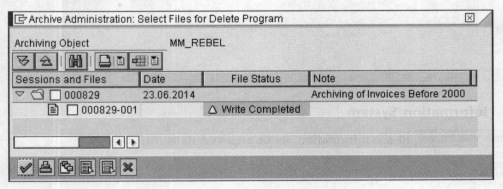

Select a file and click ✅ .

Start Date

Click 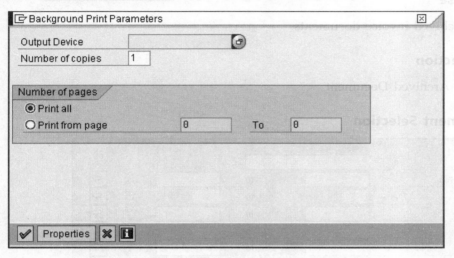 to define when you want processing to commence. You can specify Immediate , Date/Time , After job , etc.

Spool Parameters

Click Spool Parameters to specify background print parameters.

Background Print Parameters	⊠
Output Device	
Number of copies	1

Number of pages
- ⦿ Print all
- ○ Print from page   θ   To   θ

✔ Properties ✖ ℹ

Specify the output device and other parameters.

21.4.4   Deleting Documents

After specifying the archive selection, time and spool parameters, click ⊕.The background job for deletion is created.

21.4.5   Job

Click 🔳 to see the deletion jobs.

Job	Ln	Job CreatedBy	Status	Start date
ARV_MM_REBEL_DEL20140623111631	🖨	SAPUSER	Finished	23.06.2014
ARV_MM_REBEL_DEL20140623144523		SAPUSER	Active	23.06.2014
ARV_MM_REBEL_SUB20140623111506		SAPUSER	Finished	23.06.2014
ARV_MM_REBEL_SUB20140623143809		SAPUSER	Finished	23.06.2014
ARV_MM_REBEL_WRI20140623111514	🖨	SAPUSER	Finished	23.06.2014
ARV_MM_REBEL_WRI20140623143811	🖨	SAPUSER	Finished	23.06.2014
ARV_MM_REBEL_SUB20140529170533		SAPUSER	Finished	30.05.2014
ARV_MM_REBEL_WRI20140530080708	🖨	SAPUSER	Finished	30.05.2014
*Summary				

21.5 READING ARCHIVED INVOICE DOCUMENTS

Functional Consultant	User	Business Process Owner	Senior Management	My Rating	Understanding Level
A	B	X	X		

21.5.1 Purpose

You can read archived invoice documents.

21.5.2 Transaction

MRA3—Display Archived Document

21.5.3 Document Selection

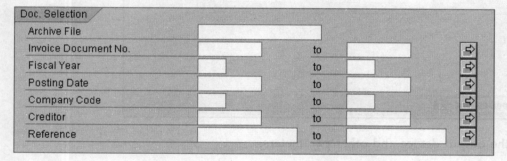

21.5.4 Archive Files

You can specify an invoice document or click 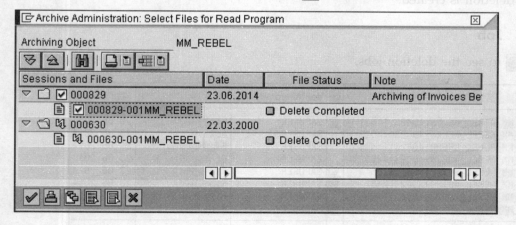 to select from the archive files.

21.5.5   Invoice Documents in a File

Select a file, and click ✓ to display invoice documents in the file.

Doc. Number	Year	CoCo	Doc. Date	Postg Date	Vendor	Gross Amount	Crcy
5105602001	1999	1000	03.02.1999	03.02.1999	1005	501,107.40	DEM
5105602002	1999	1000	03.02.1999	03.02.1999	1005	62,283.86	DEM
5105602003	1999	1000	03.02.1999	03.02.1999	1005	63,620.15	DEM
5105602004	1999	1000	03.02.1999	03.02.1999	1005	48,581.38	DEM

21.5.6   Invoice Document

Select an invoice document, and click 🔍 Invoice doc. .

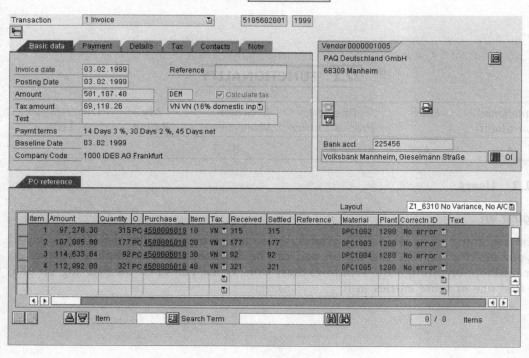

Utilities

22.1 FUNCTIONALITY

Functional Consultant	User	Business Process Owner	Senior Management	My Rating	Understanding Level
A	A	A	B		

22.1.1 Users

Logging on

If you are going to work in SAP, your system administrator creates a SAP log on pad on your desktop/laptop. The log on pad can be accessed either through a shortcut on your desktop, or through the Windows Start icon. When you open the SAP log on pad, you find one or more entries in it.

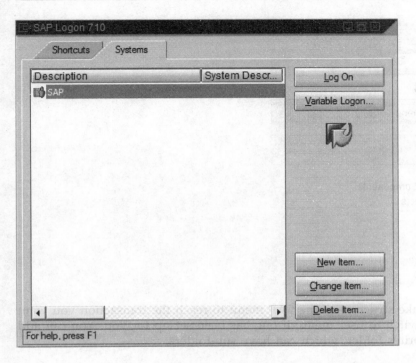

Each entry represents a server. Your system administrator tells you the purpose for which each server is to be used. You select the server you want to work on, and click the Log On icon. The system gives you the log on screen.

You enter the details given to you by your system administrator. You can change your password or press 'Enter' to log on. The system gives you the SAP menu.

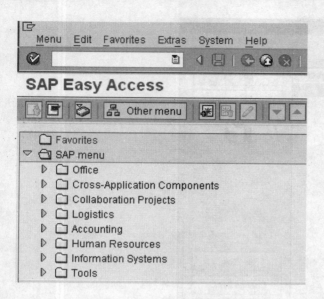

You can open the tree like structure of the SAP menu to reach the transaction you want to carry out. You can switch to user menu, if one has been set up for you. You can add transactions to the Favorites folder, which can have sub-folders.

Executing a transaction in the command field

An important part of all SAP screens is the command field, located in the top left corner of the screen. Here, you can enter a transaction directly, instead of going through a menu. If you are already in some transaction which you want to leave, prefix the transaction with /n, e.g. /nME21N. If you want to run the new transaction in a new session, prefix the transaction with /o, e.g. /oME21N.

Aborting the current transaction

You can abort the current transaction by entering /n in the command field.

Opening multiple sessions

You can open another session of SAP (same server and client) by clicking ▨ icon, or by entering /o in the command field.

Closing a session

You can close a session by entering /i in the command line or by closing the window. If the session you are closing is the only session on a client, you are logged off. The system asks you to confirm that you want to log off.

Logging off

You can log off by entering /nend or /nex in the command line. In the former case, the system asks you to confirm that you want to log off. All the sessions on the client are closed.

Displaying transactions

You work in SAP either through menu, or through transactions. Experienced users often prefer the latter method. Therefore, they need to know the transaction codes of various transactions. You can display the transaction codes in the menu by ticking the checkbox ☑ Display technical names in Extras ➤ Settings. The menu display changes as shown below.

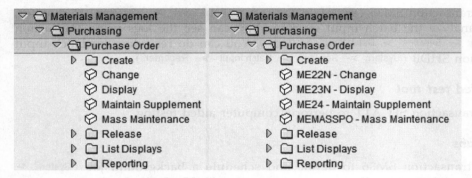

Business workplace

SAP provides a wide range of office functionality, e.g. mail, workflow, etc., in business workplace. You can access it using transaction SBWP, or by clicking the icon as shown.

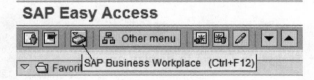

You can create and send a document by clicking 🗑 New message in business workplace. You can also do the same by running transaction SO00, or through menu System ➤ Short Message.

Maintaining own data

You can maintain your own data using transaction SU3 (System ➤ User Profile ➤ Own Data).

Running ABAP programs

You can run ABAP programs using transaction SA38 (System ➤ Services ➤ Reporting). It is recommended to avoid doing this by creating a transaction for every program.

Quick viewer

You can run quick viewer using transaction SQVI (System ➤ Services ➤ QuickViewer).

Output control

You can run transaction SP01 (System ➤ Services ➤ Output Control) to list the spool requests and output requests for a user id in a specific period. You can display their contents, print them and delete them. You can run transaction SP02 (System ➤ Own Spool Requests) to list your own spool requests.

Batch input

You can run transaction SM35 (System ➤ Services ➤ Batch Input ➤ Sessions) to monitor, process, and analyze the batch input sessions. You can see the logs using transaction SM35P (System ➤ Services ➤ Batch Input ➤ Logs). You can do recording for batch input using transaction SHDB (System ➤ Services ➤ Batch Input ➤ Recorder).

Computer aided test tool

You can use transaction SECATT to perform computer aided testing.

Background jobs

You can use transaction SM36 to define and schedule a background job (System ➤ Services ➤ Jobs ➤ Define Job). You can use transaction SM37 (System ➤ Services ➤ Jobs ➤ Job Overview) to monitor and manage jobs. You can release a job, stop an active job, delete a job, display spool list, display job log and display step list. You can also check status, change status from released to scheduled, copy job, change job, repeat scheduling, and move the job to a different server. You can also run transaction SMX to see your own jobs (System ➤ Own Jobs).

Queue

You can use transaction SM38 (System ➤ Services ➤ Queue) to display queue.

Reporting authorization problems

You can use transaction SU53 (System ➤ Utilities(H) ➤ Display Authorization Check) to see details of authorization problems and to report to the Basis team for resolution. Immediately after you encounter an authorization problem, enter /nSU53. The system shows a comparison between authorization available and authorization required.

Archived documents

You can use transaction OAAD to store and assign a new document in the content server. The transaction also provides a facility to search the archived documents.

Downloading file

You can use transaction CG3Y to download a file from the application server to your desktop.

Uploading file

You can use transaction CG3Z to upload a file from your desktop to the application server.

SAP query

You can start SAP queries using transaction SQ00.

22.1.2 Functional Consultants

Customizing

Transaction SPRO is used for accessing the customizing environment. You can customize the SAP system using the SAP Reference IMG, or you can define projects for customization, e.g. adapting the SAP Reference IMG to the needs of your company and/or subdivide the customization task into different subprojects.

View maintenance

Transactions SM30 (System ➤ Services ➤ Table Maintenance ➤ Extended Table Maintenance) and SM31 are used for maintaining data in one or more tables through a maintenance view. This transaction also provides a facility to navigate to the underlying IMG node for a particular maintenance view. Transaction SM34 (System ➤ Services ➤ Table Maintenance ➤ View Cluster Maintenance) is used for maintaining view clusters.

Customizing comparison

You can compare customizing of two systems or two clients in the same system by using transaction SCMP. You can also create comparison runs involving multiple objects using transaction SCU0 or OY19.

Transport management

You can use transactions SE09 and SE10 for creating and releasing a customizing or workbench transport request.

Data migration, computer aided testing, BDC

You can use transaction LSMW to migrate legacy data to SAP. You can use transaction SCAT or SECATT for creating a test case by recording a transaction and creating and loading test data. You can record or modify a BDC and run it using transaction SHDB.

Viewing data in tables

You can view data in a table using transaction SE11, SE16, SE16N, or SE17.

Logging on to OSS

You can use transaction OSS1 (System ➤ Services ➤ SAP Service) to log on to OSS. It is generally used to import and apply SAP notes.

Searching string in programs

You can use program RPR_ABAP_SOURCE_SCAN to search strings in programs.

Searching in SAP menu

You can use transaction SEARCH_SAP_MENU to search in SAP menu.

Searching in user menu

You can use transaction SEARCH_USER_MENU to search in user menu.

SAP query

You can use transaction SQ01 to maintain SAP queries, transaction SQ02 to maintain infoset, and SQ03 to maintain user groups. You can start SAP queries using transaction SQ00.

Workflow builder

You can use transaction SWDD for creating and editing workflows.

System status

You can see versions of SAP, operating system, and database by clicking System ➤ Status... . You can also see the transaction, program, and screen number.

Translation

You can use transaction SE63 to translate texts for various ABAP and non-ABAP objects.

22.1.3 ABAP

ABAP programs

You can create, modify, delete, and display source code of ABAP programs using transaction SE38. You can also execute ABAP programs using transaction SA38 or SE38. You can compare ABAP programs using transaction SE39.

Function modules

You can create, modify, delete, display, and test function modules using transaction SE37. You can also maintain a function group.

Dialog modules

You can create, modify, delete, display, and test dialog modules using transaction SE35. You can create menus using transaction SE41. Screens can be painted using transaction SE51 and its underlying flow logic defined.

Classes

You can create, modify, delete, display, and test classes using transaction SE24.

Logical databases

You can create, modify, delete, display, and test logical databases using transaction SE36. SAP provides several logical databases for materials, e.g. CKM and CMC. If you use logical databases in your ABAP programs, authorization checks are automatically taken care of; otherwise you must explicitly build authorization checks in your programs.

Enhancements

You can create enhancements through transaction CMOD. Enhancements are created in projects, which are logical groups of enhancements. You can test the enhancements using transaction SMOD.

BAdIs

You can use transaction SE19 to implement a Business Add-In. SAP provides predefined BAdIs for use by the customers. If you want to define your own BAdI, you can use transaction SE18.

Area menus

You can create area menus using transaction SE43. Area menus can be used in creating role menus in transaction PFCG.

Tables and views

You can create, modify, delete, and display tables and table fields using transaction SE11. You can view data in a table using transaction SE11, SE16, SE16N, or SE17. You can display/change technical settings of a table in transaction SE13.

Documentation

You can create documentation using transaction SE61.

SAP scripts

You can create SAP scripts using transaction SE71. Other transactions related to SAP script are SE72, SE73, SE74, SE75, SE75TTDTGC, SE75TTDTGD, SE76, SE77, and SO10.

Messages

You can maintain messages using transaction SE91. You can then call them in your own programs. You can also use SAP defined messages in your own programs.

Transactions

You can maintain transactions using transaction SE93. It is recommended that you have a transaction for every program so that the users are not required to run programs using transaction SA38 or SE38. This provides better control on authorizations. It is also recommended that you keep the transaction same as the program name.

Repository information

SAP has created lot of software objects. You can use transaction SE15/SE85/SE84 to find them.

BAPIs

You can see the BAPIs provided by SAP using transaction BAPI.

Object navigator

You use transaction SE80 to organize your programming in an integrated development environment. Development objects are arranged together in object lists. Each object list contains all of the objects in a certain category such as package, program, and global class. From the object list, you can select an object by double-clicking it. When you open an object, the workbench calls up the development tool with which the object was created.

ABAP dump analysis

You can use transaction ST22 to see details of any runtime error or short dump. This helps in analyzing the root cause of the dump and finding its solution.

22.1.4   Basis

System administration

You can use transaction S002 to get the menu for system administration.

Users

You can maintain users using transaction SU01 or SU01_NAV. You can get a variety of information about users, roles, and authorizations using transaction SUIM. You can view users' log on dates and password changes using transaction RSUSR200. You can use transaction SM04 to check the status of the users; for example, how many users are logged on and how many sessions a user is working on.

Roles

You can maintain roles using transaction PFCG. The system automatically inserts authorization objects based on transactions selected by you (These can be maintained using transaction SU22 or SU24). You update them with appropriate values. You can see change documents for roles using transaction RSSCD100_PFCG. The same program is called by transaction RSSCD100_PFCG_USER. Transaction S_BCE_68001403 gives the list of critical authorizations.

Transport management

You can manage transports using transactions SE01, SE03, SE09, and SE10. You can enable/disable transport using transaction SCC4.

SAP connect

You can use transaction SCOT for monitoring the status of the inbound and outbound traffic through SAPconnect.

ALE

Customizing of ALE can be done using transaction SALE. You can monitor ALE messages using transaction BD87.

Displaying and deleting locks

Transaction SM12 is used for checking and releasing lock entries.

Locking/unlocking transactions

You can use transaction SM01 to lock/unlock transactions.

Allowed menus for users

You can disable user menu or SAP menu at user level in view USERS_SSM.

22.2   TABLES AND VIEWS

Functional Consultant	User	Business Process Owner	Senior Management	My Rating	Understanding Level
A	A	A	B		

22.2.1 Data Dictionary

Domains

View DD01V contains the list of domains. View DD07V contains values for domains.

Data elements

View DD04V contains data elements and their descriptions.

Tables

View DD02V contains the list of tables.

Table fields

Table DD03L contains table fields and DD03T their descriptions. Table DD03M contains table fields with data elements, text, and domains. View DDVAL contains fixed values for table fields.

Foreign key fields

View DD08V contains foreign key relationship definitions.

Pool/cluster structures

View DD06V contains pool/cluster structures.

Technical settings of tables

Table DD09L contains technical settings of tables.

Matchcode objects

View DD20V contains matchcode objects. Table DD24S contains fields of a matchcode id.

Views

Table TVDIR contains directory of views. Table DD25T contains views, matchcode objects, and lock objects. Table DD27S contains fields in a view, matchcode object, or lock object.

22.2.2 Software Repository

Packages

All objects are developed under Packages (earlier called Development Classes), which are logical grouping of objects. Table TDEVC contains list of Packages. Package MB is for Inventory Management.

Repository objects

Table TADIR contains the directory of repository objects, along with their development class. Tables and structures are identified by object type TABL.

Objects

Objects are stored in OBJ series of tables.

ABAP programs

Table TRDIR contains list of ABAP programs. Table D010TAB contains the tables used by ABAP programs.

Transactions

View TSTCV contains list of transactions and programs associated with them.

22.2.3 Users, Roles and Authorization

User data

User data is stored in USR series of tables. Table USR01 stores the master list of users. Table USR04 contains the profiles attached to a user. A user's parameter IDs and their values are stored in table USR05.

Role maintenance

You can create, delete, or modify roles using transaction PFCG. Role related data is stored in tables starting with AGR.

Authorization objects

Authorization objects and their field names are in table TOBJ.

Authorization objects for roles

Table AGR_1250 contains authorization objects for a role which you see in transaction PFCG.

Master list of roles

Table AGR_DEFINE contains master list of roles.

Transactions for a role

Table AGR_TCODES contains transactions for roles.

Users having a role

Table AGR_USERS contains users for roles. Also see table AGR_USERT.

22.2.4 IMG Menu

Table CUS_IMGACH contains master list of IMG activities including documentation object and transaction.

22.2.5 SAP scripts

SAP scripts

SAP scripts are stored in STX series of tables.

22.2.6 Others

Documentation

Documentation header is stored in table DOKHL and text in table DOKTL.

Reserved names

Reserved Names for Customizing Tables/Objects are stored in table TRESC.

22.2.7 Delivery Classes of Tables

SAP stores data in tables. The tables are classified in delivery classes that determine which tables are controlled by SAP, and which tables are controlled by customers.

Code	Delivery class	Explanation
A	Application table (master and trans-action data)	A Support Pack of SAP is not expected to update these tables in any client.
L	Table for storing temporary data, delivered empty	A Support Pack of SAP is not expected to update these tables in any client.
G	Customizing table, protected against SAP Upd., only INS all.	A Support Pack of SAP is not expected to update these tables in any client.
C	Customizing table, maintenance only by cust., not SAP import	A Support Pack of SAP updates these tables in client 000 only. In other clients, these tables have to be adjusted from client 000 to get these entries.
E	Control table, SAP and customer have separate key areas	A Support Pack of SAP updates these tables in all clients.
S	System table, maint. only by SAP, change = modification	A Support Pack of SAP updates these tables in all clients.
W	System table, contents transportable via separate TR objects	A Support Pack of SAP updates these tables in all clients.

22.2.8 Search Help

When SAP designs tables, for each column it tries to provide search help. If search help is provided, you can select a value from it. By assigning search help to table columns, the help becomes standardized. There are different types of search help. In transaction

SE11, if you display a table and go to tab `Entry help/check` tab, you can see which columns have got entry help, and of which type in the column `Origin of the input help`. Different types of search help are listed below.

Fix.Val.	Short text
X	Explicit search help attachment to field
P	Input help implemented with check table
D	Explicit search help attachment to data element
F	Input help with fixed values
T	Input help based on data type
	No input help exists

Code	Search help	Explanation
X	Explicit search help attachment to field	Data integrity is checked against search help assigned to the field. There is no check table.
P	Input help implemented with check table	Data integrity is checked using a check table.
D	Explicit search help attachment to data element	Search help is attached to the data element assigned to the field.
F	Input help with fixed values	The field can take values only from a fixed list, which is defined in the Domain.
T	Input help based on data type	For example, Date (Calendar), Time.
Blank	No input help	There is no input help.

22.3 AUTHORIZATION

Functional Consultant	User	Business Process Owner	Senior Management	My Rating	Understanding Level
A	A	A	A		

22.3.1 Authorization Concepts

Authorization Objects

Creating a test role

The best way to understand how SAP controls authorizations is to create a test role for purchasing using transaction PFCG. After creating the role, you go to the `Menu` tab, and add a transaction, e.g. ME21N. You then go to the `Authorizations` tab, and click `Change Authorization Data`. You will see the following screen.

```
Z:PURCHASING                          ⟁ Test Role for Purchasing
   ┌─ ⊞ ☐☐☐ Standard   Cross-application Authorization Objects      AAAB
   └─ ☐ ⟁ Standard    Materials Management: Purchasing             MM_E

        ┌─ ⊞ ⟁ ▦ ☊ Standard   Document Type in Purchase Order        M_BEST_BSA
        ├─ ⊞ ☐☐☐ ▦ ☊ Standard   Purchasing Group in Purchase Order     M_BEST_EKG
        ├─ ⊞ ☐☐☐ ▦ ☊ Standard   Purchasing Organization in Purchase O  M_BEST_EKO
        └─ ⊞ ☐☐☐ ▦ ☊ Standard   Plant in Purchase Order                M_BEST_WRK
```

Object classes

The role has two object classes: AAAB and MM_E.

Authorization objects

The role has four authorization objects. Expand the authorization object M_BEST_BSA.

```
Z:PURCHASING                          ⟁ Test Role for Purchasing
   ┌─ ⊞ ☐☐☐ Standard   Cross-application Authorization Objects      AAAB
   └─ ☐ ⟁ Standard    Materials Management: Purchasing             MM_E

        ┌─ ☐ ⟁ ▦ ☊ Standard   Document Type in Purchase Order        M_BEST_BSA

             └─ ☐ ⟁ ▦ Standard   Document Type in Purchase Order    T-SI55039400

                  ┌─ ✱ ✎ Activity                      01, 02, 03, 08, 09
                  └─ ✱ ✎ Purchasing Document Type
```

Authorization fields

The screenshot above shows authorization fields in one authorization object. An authorization object groups up to ten authorization fields that are checked in an AND relationship. In this object, you specify the authorization given to a role (or profile), which will become the authorization for one or more users through assignment of the role to users. In this object, you specify the activity that can be performed and the purchasing document type for which it can be performed.

If a user tries to create a purchase order of document type NB, the system will check whether the user has the authorization for `Activity 01(Create)` and `Purchasing Document Type` `NB`. If any of the tests fail, the user will not be able to carry out the action. In other words, the final result is determined by applying AND operation to the result of all tests within an authorization object.

Multiple copies of the same authorization object

But, what would you do if you want to give create authorization for purchasing document type NB and display authorization for purchasing document type UB? You can do that by creating two authorization objects in the same role, one for each purchasing document type. If the user satisfies any one authorization object fully, he will be able to perform the transaction.

Adding an authorization object manually

You can add an authorization object manually. If you do not know the technical name of the authorization object, click [🗐 Selection criteria]. It opens the following screen:

```
Choose the authorizations you want to insert
├─ 🗀 Materials Management: Purchasing                    MM_E
│
│   ├─ 🗐 ⊖ Approved Manufacturer Parts List             M_AMPL_ALL
│   ├─ 🗐 ⊖ Approved Manufacturer Parts List - Plant     M_AMPL_WRK
│   ├─ 🗐 ⊖ Document Type in RFQ                          M_ANFR_BSA
│   ├─ 🗐 ⊖ Purchasing Group in RFQ                       M_ANFR_EKG
│   ├─ 🗐 ⊖ Purchasing Organization in RFQ                M_ANFR_EKO
│   ├─ 🗐 ⊖ Plant/Storage Location in RFQ                 M_ANFR_LGO
│   └─ 🗐 ⊖ Plant in RFQ                                   M_ANFR_WRK
```

This screenshot shows the authorization objects, grouped under object classes. You find the authorization object and add. The system shows the authorization objects that were manually added, and those, that were added by the system.

Default authorization objects and values

When you generated authorization profile, the system automatically added certain authorization objects, and in some cases, it also put values for the fields. SAP has created these defaults, but you can change the default settings, if you want. You are advised not to do so, unless you have adequate mastery over the subject.

Authorization object for transactions

In authorization control, authorization object S_TCODE under object class AAAB is very important. This authorization object controls the transactions that a user can run.

```
🗀 OOО 🗐 🧍 Standard Transaction Code Check at Transaction Start   S_TCODE
│
└─ 🗀 OOО 🗐 Standarc Transaction Code Check at Transaction Start   T-SI55039500
   │
   └─ ✂ Transaction Code                        ME21N
```

Roles and Profiles

You can create a role using transaction PFCG. You can also create a menu for a role. This is displayed in user menu of all users who are assigned that role.

If you go to the authorizations tab and click [Change Authorization Data], SAP proposes a set of authorization objects, along with their default values. You fill up the missing values, and check whether the proposed values are okay. If necessary, you may change them. Finally, when you save them, all authorization objects should be green, as only those authorization objects are active.

You can also see all users who have been granted the role in the [User] tab. If the [🔲 User comparison] button on the [User] tab is not green, click it. Otherwise, the authorizations may not work correctly.

Authorization for User

You can use transaction SU01 to assign roles to users. You can assign him one or more roles, which govern user authorization in SAP. You can also specify a reference user, whose authorizations will be available to the current user. You can also assign a user one or more profiles, which also grant him authorization in SAP.

Troubleshooting Authorization Problems

When a user faces authorization failure, you need to know what authorization he required, and what authorization he had. This is displayed by executing transaction SU53 immediately after an authorization failure.

22.3.2   Authorization Design Challenge

In SAP, the users can only do what they are authorized to do. If they have less authorization than they need, they will not be able to perform the tasks they are required to perform. If they have more authorization than they need, they may do something they are not expected to do. Ensuring that the business is not overexposed becomes particularly important in the current environment with its emphasis on regulatory compliance. At the operating level, this business challenge manifests itself in the following ways.

Stability of roles

Despite constantly changing business needs, you need to provide a stable regime of authorizations. This is very important because there is nothing more irritating to a user than discovering that he cannot do today, what he could do till yesterday, particularly when he has not asked for any change.

This problem is faced by the members of your Basis team, who actually create authorizations in the system. When you add a transaction in an existing role, SAP adds a lot of authorization objects. These persons must look at each authorization object, decide whether it is needed or not and, if needed, what should be its values. Only those who have performed this task themselves would know what a terrible task it is. And, if by some chance, they delete an authorization object that is required, or change its values inappropriately, they can be rest assured that all hell will break loose.

Number and complexity of roles

In a production environment, it is common to find a very large number of roles, each containing a large number of authorization objects. Remember that a role is a set of authorization objects, with values assigned to each authorization field. If two users are assigned a role, and one user needs a different value in one authorization object, you have to create another role. Typical culprits are organizational objects. Two persons perform identical tasks but for different plants, and one role becomes two roles. When the number of roles becomes too many, you lose control and give up.

Authorizers' understanding problem

The authorizers are business managers. They do not understand authorization objects. Usually, they are presented a paper document, which they sign with varied understanding level. This is then translated into roles by the members of the Basis team. Is this translation right? Can the members of the Basis team show authorization for each value they have assigned? These are uncomfortable questions, and no one asks them.

Role-based or person-based authorizations

Technically, every authorization you create is a role-based authorization. Here, the question is not from a technical viewpoint, but from the business perspective. In your organization, do you create role for Cashiers, or do you create role for the person who is a cashier? Somehow, it is fashionable and politically correct to say that 'authorizations should be role-based'. There are no votaries for person-based authorizations. What are the advantages and disadvantages of role-based authorizations and person-based authorizations? Is one inherently superior to the other? Is it possible that some authorizations are role-based, and some person-based? If yes, how do you decide which authorizations should be role-based, and which person-based?

Generic access

There are some transactions which provide generic access. You can use transaction SA38 or SE38 to run any program. If a user has access to these transactions, he effectively has access to all transactions. Similarly, using SE16 or SE11, you can view data in tables. Access to these transactions exposes the data in your system.

Authorization control in Z programs

SAP builds authorization control in the programs it provides. The responsibility of doing the same in your own programs lies with you. If authorizations are not controlled properly in Z programs, your carefully created authorization control can come to naught.

22.3.3 Authorization Design Strategy

Fortunately, each of the problems listed above has a solution.

Authorization control in Z programs

Your ABAP development team needs to create a policy which ensures that no data can be accessed by a program without checking for authorizations. Walkthrough and testing of a program should ensure and document that the policy has indeed been followed.

Generic access

Use of transactions SA38, SE38, SE16, SE11, and their equivalents should be banned. For each Z program, there should be a transaction code (preferably same as the program name), and authorization to run any program should be given via its transaction code. By doing this, you can ensure that a user cannot run any programs other than those assigned to him through transaction codes.

Role-based or person-based authorizations

It is futile to argue for or against role-based authorization. No organization can have authorizations which are fully role-based, or fully person-based. Whether an authorization should be role-based or person-based has a very simple intuitive answer. Thinking of an authorization, does the organization think role-based, or does it think person-based? Users accessing Employee Self Service would have role-based authorization because you do not think of a specific employee for whom you are creating the authorization.

If the work content of positions in your organization is very precisely and firmly defined and a change in the person holding that position has little or no impact on its functioning, perhaps all your authorizations can be role-based. But many organizations are somewhat flexible in this. They allow the holder of a position to redefine his role to an extent. The emphasis is on results, and if one wants to do things differently, or even different things, he is allowed to do so. The Sales Manager of one zone may not work exactly in the same way as the Sales Manager of another zone. If this is the case, you should have person-based authorizations for them. You cannot, and do not want to, force them to work in the same manner. You cannot deny some authorization to one because the other does not want it. Nor should you give authorization to the other, even when he does not want it.

The critical attribute that should determine whether authorization should be role-based or person-based, is the number of persons who would use an authorization. If the number of persons is large, it is a clear candidate for role-based authorization. If the number of persons is small, it is better to have person-based authorization. Person-based authorization is easier to design and implement. It also results in better user satisfaction.

Separating transaction authorization object from other authorization objects

Even if you add a single transaction in an existing role, SAP adds a number of authorization objects. The process of cleaning up these authorization objects creates the stability problem. This problem can be solved by creating two roles: one which contains only transactions, and another which contains other authorization objects. You would add a transaction in the role that contains only transactions. The system will add a number of other authorization objects. You would review these authorization objects with the role that contains other authorization objects, to make changes in the latter as required. You then delete other authorization objects from the role that contain only transactions. By doing so, the role that contains other authorization objects remains clean. Addition and changes in authorizations are well considered; and so are deletions, if any.

Separating utility authorization objects from other authorization objects

In a production environment, you will find that each role contains a large number of authorization objects under object class AAAB. These authorization objects are needed for a variety of utility transactions and actions. Typically, these authorization objects would have the same value in all roles. Since these authorization objects get repeated so many times, they make the task of maintaining roles appear very heavy and unmanageable. If all these authorization objects are grouped into two utility roles, one for utility transactions and the other for the remaining utility authorization objects, all other roles will become much lighter.

Separating organizational objects

Many a times, users have identical roles but different jurisdictions. One user may do purchasing activities for one plant, while another user may do the same activities for another plant. This affects only one authorization object, but the entire role gets replicated. It is, therefore, prudent to separate authorization objects involving organizational elements into a separate role.

Separation and simplification of roles

Considering the separation of authorization objects in different roles discussed above, each user will have at least five roles.

Role	Purpose
Utility transactions	This role will contain all utility transactions, e.g. SU53. This role will be assigned to all users. It will have no authorization objects other than transactions. Any user needing extra authorization will be given as person-based authorization.
Utility authorization objects	This role will contain all authorization objects other than transactions belonging to object class AAAB. This role will be assigned to all users and provide them authorization needed to run utility transactions. Any user needing extra authorization will be given as person-based authorization.
Business transactions	This role will contain all business transactions needed by a user to perform his business tasks. It will have no authorization objects other than transactions. If this authorization is role-based, extra authorization will be given as person-based authorization.
Business authorization objects	This role will contain all authorization objects other than transactions needed by a user to perform his business tasks. If this authorization is role-based, extra authorization will be given as person-based authorization.
Business organizational objects	All organizational authorization objects will be compulsorily person-based authorizations.

It may sound contradictory that a strategy which requires five roles to be assigned to each user will actually reduce the number and complexity of roles. Note that the first two roles are common company-wide. Therefore, they are much better controlled. Also, they make all other roles much lighter.

The business role being bifurcated doubles the number of roles, but the roles are much lighter than your current composite role. The issue is not just the number of roles, but the complexity of roles, and your ability to comprehend it.

The key to reducing the number of roles lies in the roles containing organizational authorization objects. This ensures that a role is never duplicated because the organizational authorization objects are different. These roles will also be extremely light.

Solving the understanding problem

The strategy discussed above creates roles that are much lighter. The first two roles are utility roles and your CIO can understand and approve them. No other business authorizer needs to bother about them. The other three roles will be much lighter, but the authorizer still needs to understand them. Understanding authorizations is not very difficult, but the authorizers need to familiarize themselves with the basic concepts. It will then be easy for them to authorize with understanding.

22.3.4   Release Criteria for Parked Documents

See Section 11.6.3.

22.3.5   FI Tolerance Groups for Users

Purpose

Here you can specify various limits that are enforced by the system. The limits can be different for different group of users. Permitted payment differences is important only for employees in Financial Accounting.

IMG Node

SM30 ➤ V_T043T

Screen

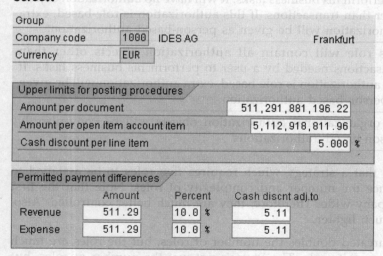

Group			
Company code	1000	IDES AG	Frankfurt
Currency	EUR		

Upper limits for posting procedures

Amount per document	511,291,881,196.22
Amount per open item account item	5,112,918,811.96
Cash discount per line item	5.000 %

Permitted payment differences

	Amount	Percent	Cash discnt adj.to
Revenue	511.29	10.0 %	5.11
Expense	511.29	10.0 %	5.11

Primary Key

Tolerance Group for Financial Accounting Employees
Company Code

Important Fields

Group

You can group your users in FI tolerance groups for users in view V_T043.

User name	Tolerance group
BC_RFC	1000
JUTZE	1000
WEISSJ	

With reference to the key, tolerances for the entry of documents and the granting of cash discounts can be determined for all employees of the group for payment settlement.

Company code

The limits can be different for different company codes.

Currency

This is the currency for all the amounts on the screen.

Amount per document

Here you specify the maximum permitted posting amount per document. The posting amount is the total of all debit items or, similarly, the total of all credit items.

Amount per open item account item

Here you specify the maximum posting amount permitted per invoice item. This restriction does not apply to automatically created line items.

Cash discount per line item

Here you specify the maximum cash discount percentage rate. The percentage rate is checked during the entry, change, and clearing of open items.

22.3.6   Configuration of System Messages

You can set the properties of messages as per your requirement in view V_T100C. These properties can be user dependent. If properties of messages are not defined here, they are taken from view T100S.

| Area | M8 | Invoice Verification/Valuation |

Message Control by User

	Msg	Message text	User Name	Online	Batchl	Standard
	155	Standard cost estimate exists in period & &		E	E	E
	155	Standard cost estimate exists in period & &	SCHAFFT	I	E	E
	298	Value exceeds limit & & in PO		I	I	I

You can set a message to error in table T100S and warning or information here for some users. By doing so, only specified users will be able to execute a scenario that results in this message.

22.4   PERSONALIZATION

Functional Consultant	User	Business Process Owner	Senior Management	My Rating	Understanding Level
A	A	A	A		

22.4.1   User Details

You can choose   System ➤ User Profile ➤ Own Data   to maintain your personal details.

User	SAPUSER				
Last Changed On	SAPUSER	29.03.2020	12:01:51	Status	Saved

Address   Defaults   Parameters

Person

Title	Mr.
Last name	Agrawal
First name	Prem
Academic Title	
Format	Prem Agrawal
Function	
Department	
Room Number		Floor		Building	

Communication

Language	EN English		Other communication...
Telephone		Extension	
Mobile Phone			
Fax		Extension	
E-Mail			
Comm. Meth	RML Remote Mail		

Assign other company address...   Assign new company address...

Company

22.4.2   User Defaults

You can choose System ➤ User Profile ➤ Own Data to maintain your personal default values.

User	SAPUSER				
Last Changed On	SAPUSER	29.03.2020	12:01:51	Status	Saved

Address | Defaults | Parameters

Start menu	
Logon Language	EN
Decimal Notation	X 1,234,567.89
Date format	1 DD.MM.YYYY

Spool Control

OutputDevice

☐ Output Immediately

☐ Delete After Output

Personal Time Zone

of the User

Sys. Time Zone   CET

CATT

☐ Check Indicator

For each output type there is a Print param.. If the Print param. is S User parameters, the printer is taken from here. However, if the Print param. is U User, the printer defined at user level in view V_TNADU is taken.

22.4.3   User Parameters

You can choose System -> User Profile -> Own Data to maintain user parameters to personalize the system.

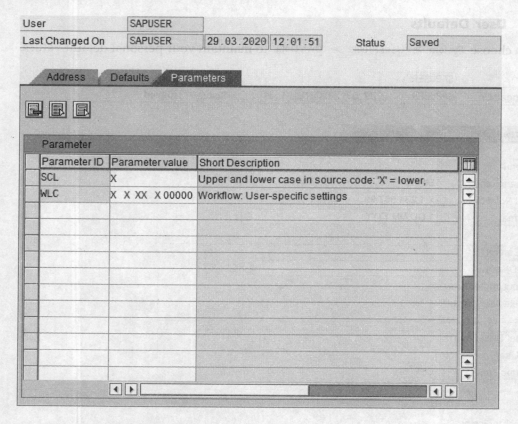

Automatic amount correction parameter RBB

When quantity changes occur, you can perform automatic correction of an item amount using the user parameter RBB. You can use automatic amount correction in transaction MIRO, MIR7, etc. The user parameter contains 13 characters. The thirteenth character is relevant for setting automatic amount correction.

If you maintain user parameter RBB and enter an X for the thirteenth character, automatic amount correction takes place for an invoice item. This means that if you change the quantity of an invoice item and then choose Enter, the system automatically calculates the new item amount. If you have already entered the quantity and item amount manually, and you change the quantity afterwards, the system does not calculate the amount again.

If you enter a blank for the thirteenth character of the user parameter, you have to enter the values for quantities and amounts manually.

Default values for the selection screen of transaction MR11

You can maintain default values for the selection screen of transaction MR11 in user parameters. For more details, see Section 18.1.3.

22.4.4   Customize Local Layout

You can click 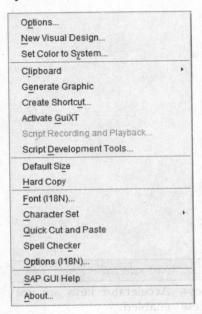 to customize the system to your liking. You choose from the following options:

Options...
New Visual Design...
Set Color to System...
Clipboard   ▶
Generate Graphic
Create Shortcut...
Activate GuiXT
Script Recording and Playback...
Script Development Tools...
Default Size
Hard Copy
Font (I18N)...
Character Set   ▶
Quick Cut and Paste
Spell Checker
Options (I18N)...
SAP GUI Help
About...

Some important settings are explained here. You may explore the rest.

Options

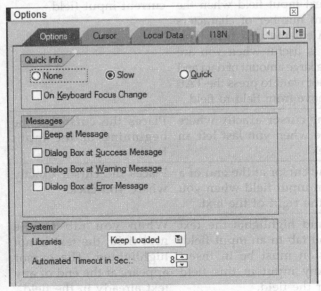

Options
| Options | Cursor | Local Data | I18N |

Quick Info
○ None   ◉ Slow   ○ Quick
☐ On Keyboard Focus Change

Messages
☐ Beep at Message
☐ Dialog Box at Success Message
☐ Dialog Box at Warning Message
☐ Dialog Box at Error Message

System
Libraries   Keep Loaded
Automated Timeout in Sec.:   8

Messages

SAP gives you messages in the message bar. If you want the system to display the message in a dialog box, you can tick the appropriate checkbox. You can also get a beep at a message.

Cursor

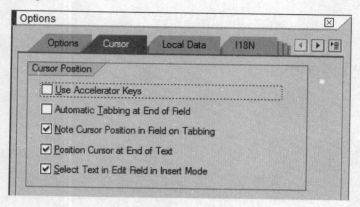

Cursor position	Selected	Not selected
Use Accelerator Keys	You can use numerous keys or key combinations to access frequently performed commands or operations quickly.	Accelerator keys are not enabled.
Automatic Tabbing at End of Field	The cursor automatically moves to the next input field when the maximum number of characters has been entered in a field. This function is useful when you are entering a large amount of data and you do not want to press the TAB key to move from field to field.	The cursor remains in the current input field.
Note Cursor Position in Field on Tabbing	Places the cursor exactly where you were when you last left an input field.	Places the cursor at the beginning of the input field.
Position Cursor at End of Text	Places the cursor at the end of a text in an input field when you click to the right of the text.	Places the cursor exactly where you click.
Select Text in Edit Field in Insert Mode	Selects and highlights the text when you tab to an input field. The session must be in insert mode. Any input in this field will clear the field.	When you tab to the next field, the text is not highlighted. The cursor appears at the end of any text already in the field.

Local Data

History

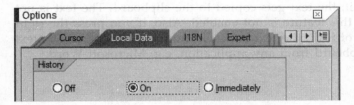

When you start entering data in a field, history shows you previously entered data matching your input as shown below.

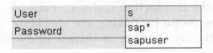

History	Description
Off	No input history is available.
On	Input history is available. Your input will be stored in the database locally. A list will be shown to the input field with focus when you make input or press the Backspace key.
Immediately	The history list will be shown immediately to the field with the focus before input is made.

Expert

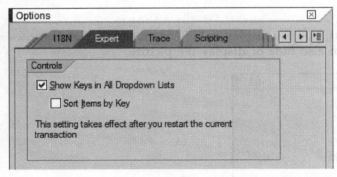

Displaying keys in drop down lists

In many fields, SAP provides a drop down list from which you can choose a value. These lists of values usually have a key and a description. Users who like to see the key in addition to the description can tick ☑ Show Keys in All Dropdown Lists . They can even sort the dropdown list by the key by ticking ☑ Sort Items by Key .

Quick Copy and Paste

SAP provides a method of quick copy and quick paste. You enable this by ticking ✔ <u>Q</u>uick Cut and Paste in 🔲. After that, if you press the left button of the mouse, move the mouse on some text, and release it, the text gets copied to the clipboard. The text is not selected, as would be the case, if this feature is not enabled. Also, if you press the right button of the mouse in any field of SAP, the text is pasted from the clipboard. The text may have been copied on the clipboard from any application, e.g. Microsoft Word.

22.4.5   User Settings

Displaying transactions

You work in SAP either through menu, or through transactions. Experienced users often prefer the latter method. Therefore, they need to know the transaction codes of various transactions. You can display the transaction codes in the menu by ticking the checkbox ☑ Display technical names in <u>Extras</u> ➤ S<u>e</u>ttings. The menu display changes as shown below.

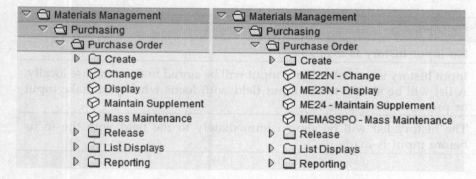

Menu settings

Through menu path <u>Extras</u> ➤ S<u>e</u>ttings, you can display or hide menu and display favorites at the top or at the bottom. You can also hide or display the picture.

┌─ Settings	☒
This is used to specify settings	
☐ Display favorites at end of list	
☐ Do not display menu, only display favorites	
☐ Do not display picture	
☑ Display technical names	
✔ 🔳 🔳 🔳 ✖	

Set start transaction

You can also set a start transaction, which is executed automatically when you log on to the system through menu path Extras ➤ Set start transaction .

⤷ Set start transaction	⊠
Transaction code	

✓ ✗

22.4.6   Defaults in the Material Master

You can set your own default values in the material master as explained in sections 2.1.2 to 2.1.4.

22.5   IMPLEMENTATION GUIDE

Functional Consultant	User	Business Process Owner	Senior Management	My Rating	Understanding Level
A	C	X	X		

When a consultant implements SAP MM Invoice Verification for a client, how does the consultant determine the client requirement and do configuration, and how does the client know that the right configuration is done for him? The answers to these twin questions lie in the methodology you follow:

The consultant can use the structure of this book to guide the implementation. He can ask specific questions to the users, record their answers and use the answers to do the configuration. Having done the configuration, he can explain it to the users and get it approved. If the users do not have enough SAP knowledge to confirm the configuration, the consultant should record the user input and get it signed off. An auditor should then confirm that the configuration reflects the user input. The source of all configuration should be user input.

Whereas many factual inputs can come from a knowledgeable power user, policy inputs should come from senior management. In large companies, senior management is often surprised at the diversity of practices followed in different parts of the company. The implementation of SAP provides an opportunity to senior management to either commonize the practice, or approve diversity. Even when there is no diversity, decisions on policy should be approved by management.

Both user inputs and corresponding configuration should be recorded in a configuration manual. The configuration manual should explain what has been configured and, if necessary, why. If you use the following table as the Table of Content of your configuration manual, your configuration manual will be easy to understand. Apart from what you configure, you should also indicate what is not implemented (NR) and what is SAP standard (SS). You should also add all Z developments done by you in respective sections. Feel free to add sections in the table of contents, but do not delete any line which has configuration in it. The support team needs to know if something is not implemented. If some configuration is not implemented, you can keep the section number blank, instead of creating empty sections in the configuration manual. The Reference column contains the section number in the book.

In the 'Approved by' column you should record the name of the person who has approved that particular configuration. If users are not knowledgeable enough to sign off the configuration, the users should sign off their input, and the auditor should sign off the configuration.

Section	Description	Configuration	NR/SS/ Done	Reference	Approved by
1	**Enterprise Structure**				
1.1	Company Code	V_T001		1.2	
1.2	Plant	V_T001W		1.3	
1.3	Factory Calendar	Transaction SCAL		1.3.5	
1.4	Assignment of Plant to Company Code	V_T001K_ASSIGN		1.3.6	
1.5	Storage Location	VC_T001L		1.4	
2	**Material**				
2.1	External Material Group	V_TWEW		2.1.5	
2.2	Laboratory/Office	V_024L		2.1.5	
2.3	Basic Materials	TWSPR		2.1.6	
2.4	Units of Measure Groups	V_006M		2.1.8	
2.5	Temperature Conditions	V_143		2.1.10	
2.6	Storage Conditions	V_142		2.1.10	
2.7	Container Requirements	V_144		2.1.10	
2.8	Screen Sequence Determination	V_CM2		2.4.1	
2.9	Screen Sequence Definition	V_CM1		2.4.1	
2.10	Creating Your Own Subscreens	Transaction OMT3C		2.4.2	
2.11	Additional Screens	V_T133S_ZUORD		2.4.3	
2.12	Sequence of Main and Additional Screens	V_T133S_REIHF		2.4.4	
2.13	Field References for Industry Sectors	V137		2.4.5	

Section	Description	Configuration	NR/SS/ Done	Reference	Approved by
2.14	Field References for Plants	V_130W		2.4.5	
2.15	Assignment of Fields to Field Selection Group	V_130F		2.4.5	
2.16	Field Properties	V_T130A_FLREF		2.4.5	
2.17	Field Attributes	V_130F		2.4.6	
2.18	Lock-relevant Fields	Transaction OMSFIX		2.4.7	
2.19	Maintenance Status of a Field	V_130F		2.5.5	
2.20	Maintenance Status Determination in Data Transfer	V_T133S		2.5.6	
2.21	Maintenance Status for Plants	V_130W		2.5.7	
2.22	Number Ranges for Material	Transaction MMNR		2.6	
2.23	Output Format of Material Numbers	V_TMCNV		2.6.10	
2.24	Material Type	MTART		2.7	
2.25	Material Creation Transactions for Specific Material Types	V_134K		2.7.13	
2.26	Material Group	V023		2.8.1	
2.27	Entry Aids for Items without a Material Master	V023_E		2.8.2	
2.28	Material Status	Transaction OMS4		2.9	
2.29	Purchasing Value Keys	V_405		2.10	
2.30	Shipping Instructions	VC_T027A		2.11	
3	**Procure-to-pay Cycle**				
4	**Invoices having System Amount matching Vendor Amount**				
4.1	Posting Unplanned Delivery Costs to a Specified G/L Account	V_169P_B		4.8.2	
4.2	Activation of Purchase Order Text Notification	V_169P_MB		4.18.3	
4.3	Text IDs Relevant for Purchase Order Text Notification	V_T169B_ASSIGN		4.18.4	
4.4	Enabling Prepayment at Company Code Level	V_WRF_ PREPAYMENT		4.20.5	
4.5	Field Status Group for Prepayment	V_WRF_PREPAY_ FCH		4.20.5	

Section	Description	Configuration	NR/SS/ Done	Reference	Approved by
4.6	BAdI for Prepayment	WRF_PREPAY_ INVOICE		4.20.5	
5	**Invoices having System Price more than Vendor Price**				
5.1	Small Difference Tolerance at Company Code Level	V_169G, Tolerance key BD		5.1.2	
5.2	Negative Difference Tolerance at Vendor Group Level	V_169L		5.1.3	
6	**Invoices having System Price less than Vendor Price**				
6.1	Positive Difference Tolerance at Vendor Group Level	V_169L		6.1.3	
6.2	Upper Limit of Invoice Reduction	V_169L		6.8.2	
6.3	Tax Treatment in Invoice Reduction	V_169P_IRTAX		6.10.2	
7	**Invoices having System Quantity more than Vendor Quantity**				
8	**Invoices having System Quantity less than Vendor Quantity**				
9	**Invoices without Purchase Order Reference**				
9.1	Activation of Direct Posting to G/L Account	TCULIV		9.1.2	
9.2	Activation of Direct Posting to Material Account	TCULIV		9.2.2	
10	**Invoice Payment Block**				
10.1	Payment Block Keys	V_008		10.2.2	
10.2	Activating Stochastic Block	V_169P_SA		10.4.2	
10.3	Setting Probability of Stochastic Block	V_169P_S		10.4.3	
10.4	Activating Item Amount Check at Company Code Level	V_169P_PA		10.5.2	
10.5	Activating Item Amount Check at Item Category Level	V_169D		10.5.2	
10.6	Amount Check for Items with Order Reference	V_169G, Tolerance key AP		10.5.2	

Section	Description	Configuration	NR/SS/ Done	Reference	Approved by
10.7	Amount Check for Items without Order Reference	V_169G, Tolerance key AN		10.6.3	
10.8	Tolerance for Price Variance	V_169G, tolerance key PP		10.7.2	
10.9	Tolerance for Price Variance—Estimated Price	V_169G, tolerance key PS		10.8.2	
10.10	Tolerance for Delivery Cost Variance	V_169G, tolerance key KW		10.9.2	
10.11	Amount Check of Blanket Purchase Order	V_169G, tolerance key LA		10.10.3	
10.12	Tolerance for Quantity Variance	V_169G, tolerance key DQ		10.11.2	
10.13	Tolerance for Quantity Variance when Goods Receipt Quantity is Zero	V_169G, tolerance key DW		10.12.2	
10.14	Tolerance for Order Price Unit Variance	V_169G, tolerance key BW		10.13.5	
10.15	Tolerance for Order Price Quantity Variance (IR before GR)	V_169G, tolerance key BR		10.14.4	
10.16	Tolerance for Schedule Variance	V_169G, tolerance key ST		10.15.2	
10.17	Tolerance for Blanket Purchase Order Validity Period	V_169G, tolerance key LD		10.16.3	
11	**Invoice Processes**				
11.1	Workflow for Completion of Incomplete Parked Invoices	Transaction MIRU_ W O R K F L O W _ VERV		11.5.6	
11.2	Workflow for Releasing Completed Invoices	Transaction MIRU_ W O R K F L O W _ FREIG		11.6.3	
11.3	Release Criteria for Completed Invoices	T169WF01		11.6.3	
11.4	Master List of Release Groups	V_VBWF08		11.6.3	
11.5	Status of Invoices Verified Correct in Background	V_169P_K		11.7.7	
11.6	Assignment Test Group	V_WRF_ASSIGN_ GRP		11.7.8	

Section	Description	Configuration	NR/SS/ Done	Reference	Approved by
11.7	Business Add-In: Assignment Test	BAdI WRF_MRM_ ASSIGN_TEST		11.7.8	
11.8	Reversal Reasons	T041C		11.8.3	
11.9	Workflow for Invoices whose Payment is Blocked for Price	Transaction MIRO_ WORKFLOW		11.9.4	
12	**Invoice Customizing**				
12.1	Item List Variants	Transaction OLMRLIST		12.1.2	
12.2	Aggregation List Variants	Transaction OLMRVERDLIST		12.2.2	
12.3	Aggregation Criteria	T169Y		12.2.3	
12.4	Assignment of Number Ranges to Transactions	VV_T003R_01		12.3.2	
12.5	Number Ranges for Invoice Documents	Transaction OMRJ		12.3.3	
12.6	Accounting Document Types used in Invoice Verification	V_169F		12.4.1	
12.7	Number Range Assignment to Accounting Document Type	V_T003		12.4.2	
12.8	Number Range Definition	Transaction MRM4		12.4.3	
12.9	Tax Procedure for a Country	V_005_E (transaction OBBG)		12.5.1	
12.10	Tax Codes for a Country	T007A		12.5.2	
12.11	Tax Rates	Transaction FTXP		12.5.5	
12.12	Account Keys	V_T007B		12.5.7	
12.13	Default Values for Tax Codes	V_169V_ST		12.5.8	
12.14	Configurable System Messages	T100S		12.6.2	
12.15	Attributes of System Messages	V_T100C		12.6.3	
12.16	Customer Exit for EDI Data Conversion	Customer exit EXIT_ SAPLMRMH_011		12.7.1	
12.17	Determining the Company Code	V_T076B		12.7.2	
12.18	Determining the Tax Code	T076M		12.7.4	
12.19	Determining Program Parameters for EDI Data Conversion	V_076S_M		12.7.5	

Section	Description	Configuration	NR/SS/ Done	Reference	Approved by
12.20	Treatment of Exchange Rate Differences	V_169P_PK		12.8	
12.21	Document Type for Bar Code Entry	T003S		12.9	
12.22	Start Logo	V_169P_LOGO		12.10	
12.23	Message Control	V_T100C		12.11.3	
12.24	Customizing the Duplicate Invoices Check	V_169P_DC		12.11.4	
12.25	Variance Types	V169VARIANCE-TYP		12.12.1	
12.26	Filling Variance Type Field	BAdI MRM_VARIANCE_TYPE		12.12.2	
12.27	ERS (Conventional Invoice Verification)	Customer Exit MM08R001		12.13	
12.28	Tolerance Checks	Customer Exit MM08R002		12.13	
12.29	Transfer of Document Header and Item Data, Account Assignment Proposal for Invoices for Blanket POs	Customer Exit LMR1M001		12.13	
12.30	Account Grouping for GR/IR Account Determination	Customer Exit LMR1M002		12.13	
12.31	Number Assignment in Logistics Invoice Verification	Customer Exit LMR1M003		12.13	
12.32	Item Text in Follow-on Documents	Customer Exit LMR1M004		12.13	
12.33	Change Criteria for Releasing Parked Documents for Posting	Customer Exit LMR1M005		12.13	
12.34	Change XML Data for BAPI Call CreateFromData	Customer Exit LMR1M006		12.13	
12.35	Consignment/Pipeline Settlement	Customer Exit RMVKON00		12.13	
12.36	ERS (Logistics Invoice Verification)	Customer Exit MRMH0001		12.13	
12.37	EDI Invoice Receipt (Logistics Invoice Verification)	Customer Exit MRMH0002		12.13	

Section	Description	Configuration	NR/SS/ Done	Reference	Approved by
12.38	Revaluation (Logistics Invoice Verification)	Customer Exit MRMH0003		12.13	
12.39	Message Output for Invoice Verification	Customer Exit MRMN0001		12.13	
12.40	BAdI before Updating, during Updating, and Saving an Invoice Document	BAdI INVOICE_ UPDATE		12.14	
12.41	BAdI to Prepopulate various Header Fields	BAdI MRM_ HEADER_ DEFAULT		12.14	
12.42	BAdI to Set Terms of Payment	BAdI MRM_ PAYMENT_ TERMS		12.14	
12.43	BAdI to Distribute Unplanned Delivery Costs	BAdI MRM_UDC_ DISTRIBUTE		12.14	
12.44	BAdI to Prepopulate various Transaction Fields	BAdI MRM_ TRANSACT_ DEFAULT		12.14	
12.45	BAdI to Change the Withholding Tax Data and the Data during a Vendor Split	BAdI MRM_WT_ SPLIT_UPDATE		12.14	
12.46	BAdI to Set Vendor-specific Tolerance Groups	BAdI MRM_ TOLERANCE_ GROUP		12.14	
12.47	BAdI for Additional Checks before Invoices are Released	BAdI MRM_ RELEASE_CHECK		12.14	
12.48	BAdI to Change Document Header Data in Invoicing Plans	BAdI MRM_MRIS_ HDAT_MODIFY		12.14	
12.49	BAdI to Change Document Header Data in Consignment Settlement	BAdI MRM_ MRKO_HDAT_ MODIFY		12.14	
12.50	BAdI to Change Customer's Own Fields	BAdI MRM_ITEM_ CUSTFIELDS		12.14	
13	**Evaluated Receipt Settlement**				
13.1	BAdI to Change Document Header Data in ERS	BAdI MRM_ERS_ HDAT_MODIFY		13.1.5	
13.2	BAdI to Change Document Lines in ERS	BAdI MRM_ERS_ IDAT_MODIFY		13.1.5	

Section	Description	Configuration	NR/SS/ Done	Reference	Approved by
13.3	Activate Automatic Settlement of Planned Delivery Cost	V_T169DC_ERS		13.3.2	
14	**Consignment and Pipeline Settlement**				
15	**Invoicing Plan Settlement**				
16	**Credit Memo**				
17	**Subsequent Debit/Credit**				
18	**GR/IR Account Maintenance**				
18.1	Assignment of Number Ranges to Account Maintenance Transactions	VV_T003R_11		18.3.2	
18.2	Number Ranges for Account Maintenance Documents	Transaction OMRJ		18.3.3	
18.3	Accounting Document Type used in Account Maintenance	V_169F		18.4.1	
18.4	Number Range Assignment to Accounting Document Type	V_T003		18.4.2	
18.5	Number Range Definition	Transaction MRM4		18.4.3	
19	**Account Determination**				
19.1	Account Determination	Transaction OMR0		19	
20	**Messages**				
20.1	Message Schemas	VVC_T683_XX_ MR		20.2	
20.2	Message/Output Types	VN_T685B		20.3	
20.3	Access Sequences	VVC_T682_MR		20.4	
20.4	Condition Records	Transactions MRM1, MRM2 and MRM3		20.5	
20.5	Assignment of Forms to Output Types	VV_TNAPR_MR		20.6.1	
20.6	Content of Printed Messages	SE71		20.6.2	
20.7	Sender Texts	V_001G_R		20.6.3	
20.8	Assignment of Forms to Output Types	VV_TNAPR_MR		20.7.1	
20.9	Content of Electronic Mails	VN_T685B		20.7.2	

Section	Description	Configuration	NR/SS/ Done	Reference	Approved by
20.10	Activation of Mail to Purchasing When Price Variances Occur	V_169P_A		20.7.3	
20.11	Specifying the Printer in the Condition Record	Transaction MRM2		20.8.3	
20.12	Specifying the Print Parameter in Output Type	VN_T685B		20.8.4	
20.13	Specifying the Printer at User Level	V_TNADU		20.8.4	
20.14	Maintaining Condition Tables	Transactions M811, M812 and M813		20.10.1	
20.15	Maintaining Requirements	Transaction M802		20.11.1	
21	**Archiving**				
21.1	Archiving Object-specific Customizing: Technical Setting	V_ARC_USR		21.2.5	
21.2	Life of Invoice Documents before Archiving	V_169R		21.2.9	
22	**Utilities**				
22.1	FI Tolerance Groups for Users	V_T043T		22.3.5	
22.2	Users in FI Tolerance Groups	V_T043		22.3.5	

22.6 TRANSACTIONS

Functional Consultant	User	Business Process Owner	Senior Management	My Rating	Understanding Level
A	X	X	X		

22.6.1 Invoice Verification

Category	Transaction	Description	Page number
User	FB03	Display Accounting Document	364
User	FTXP	Maintain Tax Code	375
Consultant	M802	Maintain Requirements	511
Consultant	M811	Create Message Condition Table (IV)	511
Consultant	M812	Change Message Condition Table (IV)	511
Consultant	M813	Display Message Condition Table (IV)	511

Category	Transaction	Description	Page number
User	MIR4	Display Invoice Document	338
User	MIR5	Display List of Invoice Documents	363
User	MIR6	Invoice Overview	349
User	MIR7	Park Invoice	340
User	MIRA	Enter Invoice for Invoice Verification in Background	346
User	MIRO	Enter Invoice	99
Consultant	MIRO_WORKFLOW	Customizing for Logistics IV: Workflow	358
Consultant	MIRU_WORKFLOW_FREIG	Customizing for Logistics IV: Workflow	345
Consultant	MIRU_WORKFLOW_VERV	Customizing for Logistics IV: Workflow	344
Consultant	MMNR	Define Material Master Number Ranges	64
User	MR11	Maintain GR/IR Clearing Account	450
User	MR11SHOW	Display/Cancel Account Maintenance Document	454
User	MR8M	Cancel Invoice Document	353
User	MR90	Messages for Invoice Documents	509
User	MR91	Messages for Consignment and Pipeline Settlement	409
User	MRA1	Archive Invoice Documents	519
User	MRA2	Delete Archived Invoice Documents	524
User	MRA3	Display Archived Invoice Documents	526
User	MRA4	Manage Invoice Document Archive	522
User	MRBR	Release Blocked Invoices	359
User	MRDC	Automatic Delivery Cost Settlement	401
User	MRIS	Invoicing Plan Settlement	415
User	MRKO	Consignment and Pipeline Settlement	406
User	MRM1	Create Output Condition Records IV	493
User	MRM2	Change Output Condition Records IV	493
User	MRM3	Display Output Condition Records IV	493
Consultant	MRM4	Number Ranges, Accounting Documents IV	373
User	MRNB	Revaluation	169

Category	Transaction	Description	Page number
User	MRRL	Evaluated Receipt Settlement	398
Consultant	OLMRLIST	Maintain List Variant	368
Consultant	OLMRVERDLIST	Maintain Aggregation Variant	369
Consultant	OMR0	Configure Automatic Postings	464
Consultant	OMRJ	Maintain Number Range Intervals for Invoice Documents	371
User	S_ALR_87101048	Account Detective	486
Consultant	SCAL	Factory Calendar	5

22.6.2 Utility

Category	Transaction	Description	Page number
ABAP	BAPI	Bapi Explorer	536
Basis	BD87	Status Monitor for ALE Messages	537
User	CG3Y	Download File	533
User	CG3Z	Upload File	533
ABAP	CMOD	Enhancements	535
Consultant	LSMW	Legacy System Migration Workbench	533
User	OAAD	Archivelink Administration Documents	532
Consultant	OSS1	Log on to SAPNet	534
Consultant	OY19	Customizing Cross-system Viewer	533
Basis	PFCG	Role Maintenance	541
Basis	RSSCD100_PFCG	Change Documents for Role Admin.	537
Basis	RSSCD100_PFCG_USER	For Role Assignment	537
Basis	RSUSR200	List of Users per Login Date	536
Basis	S_BCE_68001403	With Critical Authorizations	537
Basis	S002	Menu Administration	536
User	SA38	ABAP Reporting	531
Basis	SALE	Display ALE Customizing	537
User	SBWP	SAP Business Workplace	531
Consultant	SCAT	Computer Aided Test Tool	533
Basis	SCC4	Client Administration	537
Consultant	SCMP	View/table Comparison	533

Category	Transaction	Description	Page number
Basis	SCOT	SAPconnect—Administration	537
Consultant	SCU0	Customizing Cross-system Viewer	533
Basis	SE01	Transport Organizer (extended)	537
Basis	SE03	Transport Organizer Tools	537
Consultant, Basis	SE09	Transport Organizer	533
Consultant, Basis	SE10	Transport Organizer	533
Consultant, ABAP	SE11	ABAP Dictionary Maintenance	533
ABAP	SE13	Maintain Technical Settings (tables)	535
ABAP	SE15	ABAP/4 Repository Information System	536
Consultant, ABAP	SE16	Data Browser	533
Consultant, ABAP	SE16N	General Table Display	533
Consultant, ABAP	SE17	General Table Display	533
ABAP	SE18	Business Add-ins: Definitions	535
ABAP	SE19	Business Add-ins: Implementations	535
ABAP	SE24	Class Builder	535
ABAP	SE35	ABAP/4 Dialog Modules	535
ABAP	SE36	Logical Database Builder	535
ABAP	SE37	ABAP Function Modules	534
ABAP	SE38	ABAP Editor	534
ABAP	SE39	Splitscreen Editor: (new)	534
ABAP	SE41	Menu Painter	535
ABAP	SE43	Maintain Area Menu	535
ABAP	SE51	Screen Painter	535
ABAP	SE61	SAP Documentation	535
Consultant	SE63	Translation: Initial Screen	534
ABAP	SE71	SAPscript Form	535
ABAP	SE72	SAPscript Styles	535
ABAP	SE73	SAPscript Font Maintenance	535

Category	Transaction	Description	Page number
ABAP	SE74	SAPscript Format Conversion	535
ABAP	SE75	SAPscript Settings	535
ABAP	SE75TTDTGC	SAPscript: Change Standard Symbols	535
ABAP	SE75TTDTGD	SAPscript: Display Standard Symbols	535
ABAP	SE76	SAPscript: Form Translation	535
ABAP	SE77	SAPscript Styles Translation	535
ABAP	SE80	Object Navigator	536
ABAP	SE84	Repository Information System	536
ABAP	SE85	ABAP/4 Repository Information System	536
ABAP	SE91	Message Maintenance	536
ABAP	SE93	Maintain Transaction	536
Consultant	SEARCH_SAP_MENU	Find in SAP Menu	534
Consultant	SEARCH_USER_MENU	Find in User Menu	534
User, Consultant	SECATT	Extended Computer Aided Test Tool	532
User, Consultant	SHDB	Batch Input Transaction Recorder	532
Basis	SM01	Lock Transactions	537
Basis	SM04	User List	536
Basis	SM12	Display and Delete Locks	537
Consultant	SM30	Call View Maintenance	533
Consultant	SM31	Call View Maintenance like SM30	533
Consultant	SM34	View Cluster Maintenance Call	533
User	SM35	Batch Input Monitoring	532
User	SM35P	Batch Input: Log Monitoring	532
User	SM36	Schedule Background Job	532
User	SM37	Job Overview	532
User	SM38	Queue Maintenance Transaction	532
ABAP	SMOD	SAP Enhancement Management	535
User	SMX	Display Own Jobs	532
User	SO00	SAPoffice: Short Message	531

Category	Transaction	Description	Page number
ABAP	SO10	SAPscript: Standard Texts	535
User	SP01	Output Controller	532
User	SP02	Display Spool Requests	532
Consultant	SPRO	Customizing - Edit Project	533
User, Consultant	SQ00	SAP Query: Start Queries	534
Consultant	SQ01	SAP Query: Maintain Queries	534
Consultant	SQ02	SAP Query: Maintain Infoset	534
Consultant	SQ03	SAP Query: Maintain User Groups	534
User	SQVI	Quickviewer	532
ABAP	ST22	ABAP Dump Analysis	536
Basis	SU01	User Maintenance	536
Basis	SU01_NAV	User Maintenance	536
Basis	SU22	Auth. Object Usage in Transactions	537
Basis	SU24	Auth. Object Check Under Transactions	537
User	SU3	Maintain Users Own Data	531
User	SU53	Display Authorization Check	532
Basis	SUIM	User Information System	536
Consultant	SWDD	Workflow Builder	534

Index

World Government
For a World Free from War, Terrorism and Poverty

Facts

- The world spends trillions of dollars every year on military and war equipment, while its people go hungry.
- Today the world is incapable of resolving any dispute through military actions.
- Terrorism thrives because of covert support of country governments.
- Enormous expenditure on militaries all over the world is not only a waste, but also extremely dangerous as it increases the destructive power of country governments.

We want

- A world free from war, terrorism and poverty.

How can it be done?

- Establish a world parliament, a world government and a world court.
- Disband militaries of all countries simultaneously.
- Use the savings to alleviate poverty.

Will all countries agree?

- Yes! When people of the countries want it.
- We have to awaken the people of the whole world.

How will it work?

- The world parliament will be formed through direct election of members of parliament all over the world. These members of parliament will form the world government.
- The world government will have limited but sufficient power to provide security to all countries, manage global environment and combat terrorism all over the world.
- The world government will secure the borders of all countries to ensure that there is no unauthorized entry or exit.
- The country governments will continue to manage their affairs.
- Disputes between countries will be resolved with the help of the world parliament and the world court.
- No country will disband its military first. All countries will disband their

militaries simultaneously in a phased manner, under the supervision of the world government, which will verify that the militaries are actually disbanded.

- Countries will retain their police to maintain law and order.
- Countries may have special forces to deal with terrorism and to provide relief in the event of natural disasters.

Is it possible?

- Many people say that this is an impossible task because other people will not agree.
- This task is possible if we talk only about ourselves, and not about others. This task is big but not impossible.
- We have only one world, we can't give up on it.
- We can succeed only if we try.

What should I do?

- Level 1: Register with WIII and become a world citizen. Even children can join.
- Level 2: Spread the message to your family, friends and neighbours. Convince five persons to join.

- Level 3: Convince five persons that each one of them would enroll five more persons.
- Level 4: Become an active volunteer.

Act now

- Act now. Don't give up because of enormity of the task.

You have nothing to lose

- There is no membership fee.
- You are not required to work unless you want to. But if you want, there is a lot of work to do.
- You are not required to follow any person or any belief.

Contact

World Integration and Improvement Initiative (WIII)
E-mail: agrawal.prem@gmail.com

World Language

Need for a World Language

Perhaps the most important gift of nature to mankind is the ability to communicate using a language. However, this gift is not unmitigated, because we have got too much of it. We do not have a single language, but a large number of them, which sometimes is as bad as not having any language.

Lack of a common world language can greatly handicap a person, as more and more people travelling around the world discover to their dismay. With the world becoming smaller and smaller, as a result of advances in transportation and communication, the need for a common world language is felt more and more acutely. One option to overcome this handicap is for a person to learn multiple languages, which is not only wasteful, but can be done only to a limited extent. Another way to overcome this handicap is through translation and interpretation, for which we pay a heavy price in terms of cost, time, and timeliness, and achieve at best partial communication. Scientific and technical literature available in one language cannot be used by people who do not know that language.

There is probably no one, who does not agree with the need for a world language. Only, people do not want to discuss it, fearing that accepting any language, other than their own, as world language will put them at a disadvantage. Also, people are strongly attached to their mother tongue, often considering it as revered as their mother, and feel a sense of guilt in accepting another language.

While there are some, who do not want to discuss this issue fearing that they may have to accept another language, there are others who do the same hoping that their language may become world language by default. This may well happen, but is it desirable even for them?

Importance of a good world language

A language is a tool for communication, and we must evaluate it as we would evaluate any other tool. How effective is it in meeting its objective; and how much resources does it consume in doing so? People who hope that their language may become world language, should think again. Do we just want a common language, or do we want a really good world language—a language which provides effective, unambiguous communication with minimum effort.

This article shows that existing languages score quite badly in a rational evaluation. Let us remember that many of us use almost our entire non-sleeping time in reading, writing, and thinking—activities which depend on the efficiency of language. If we can design a language, which is more efficient than our existing language, we will gain that much extra time, which can be used for productive or recreational purposes. It has also been well accepted that languages influence our thinking, making the role of language even more important.

We must, therefore, consider ourselves lucky that we do not have a single language in the world. This gives us a choice. It is possible for us to have a well designed world language. If we had only one language, we would not have this choice, as we have no choice today in numbering system, computer keyboard, etc. We must not squander this choice away, by letting an existing language become the world language. It will be like losing a fortune, just because we refused to decide. It is also important that we decide to develop a world language as early as possible. The more time we lose, the more will be the backlog of translation, which must necessarily be done.

Should an existing natural language be world language?

Some of the existing natural languages, particularly English, aspire to become world language. Their claim is based primarily on their widespread use in dominant segments of society all over the world, e.g. science, law, business, industry, government, etc. However, if we objectively examine their effectiveness and efficiency, they do not perform too well. Let us take a look at 'English'.

Let us start from the alphabet. English does not have a phonetic alphabet. The same letter is associated with different sounds in different words. This puts tremendous load on people learning the language. They have to learn both the pronunciation as well as the spelling. Many languages of the world have this problem, while many are free from it.

The length of the words in a language determines the effort in communication to a large extent. If the words are long, the communication time and effort is more. Natural languages being product of evolution, have not paid much attention to length of words. Consequently, the words tend to be long. The best proof of this defect in a language is the existence of short forms for long words. 'Info' for information, and 'ad' for advertisement, amply demonstrate that words can be shorter.

All languages use prefixes and suffixes to add additional meaning to the meaning of a word. By doing so, they avoid the need to define and learn a word. This practice is very good, but often there are exceptions, which are not desirable. Also, usually this concept is not utilized fully. We do not need separate words for boy and girl. We need only one word with a prefix or a suffix for gender.

The meanings of words is another area of concern. Many times the words have contextual meanings. This increases the learning effort, as all the meanings of the words have to be learnt. Also, the words often suffer from overprecision, and underprecision. There are many words which mean exactly, or nearly, the same. On the other hand there are some words, whose meaning is not precise enough.

Grammars of natural languages are usually quite complex. Agreement of number and gender between noun and verb is a case in point. Really speaking, there is no need to alter the verb for number and gender; they should be attributes of noun alone. If that was done, the language will become simpler. By unnecessarily modifying the verb for number and gender, we make the language complex, and introduce the possibility of making mistakes. Needless complexity of grammar is best understood by learners of a foreign language, who constantly compare the grammar of the new language with that of their mother tongues.

Ambiguity or lack of clarity in the meaning of a sentence also exists.

It might be argued that the defects of English may be removed to prepare it for the role of world language. However, the changes may be so many, that we may not recognise it as English at all. Also, however much we improve it, it can never be as good as a language designed from scratch. We are going to build the world language only once, and it must be the best. Evaluation of other natural languages is likely to bring us to the same conclusion.

Also, we must remember that adopting an existing language as world language will be more repugnant to the rest of the world, than adopting a newly designed language.

Should Esperanto be world language?

If natural languages do not qualify to be the world language, what about Esperanto? After all it was created precisely for this purpose. There is no doubt that Esperanto is better suited to be the world language, than any other natural language. However, the question remains: is it possible to design a language better than Esperanto? The answer would be in affirmative, primarily because even Esperanto is based on some natural languages, and has not exercised freedom of choice in design to the fullest. However, Esperanto has definitely proved

a major point—that it is possible to design a language.

How to develop a world language?

Designing a language is not a very difficult job, but designing a good language is. Designing a language involves making a large number of decisions. How much effort is put in arriving at these decisions will determine the quality of language. Also, the process should involve wide ranging consultations with experts in various fields. After an initial decision is made based on expert opinion, it should be widely publicized, and feedback and comments of all the people should be considered, before finalizing the decision. Even then, if there is a good reason to alter a decision previously made, it should be done. In no case should we compromise on the quality of the world language. Some ideas are discussed here to illustrate the kind of improvements possible. Obviously, they are at best the tip of the iceberg.

Objectives of the world language

Some of the objectives of the world language would be as under. These need to be debated and enlarged. They also need to be interpreted for each sub-activity.

1. Achieve effective and unambiguous communication
   1.1 Between humans
   1.2 Between humans and machines
2. Minimize effort in communication
   2.1 Minimize effort in speaking and hearing
   2.2 Minimize effort in writing and reading
3. Minimize effort in learning the language
   3.1 Minimize the length and number of words
   3.2 Maximize the use of rules to form words and sentences. Have no exceptions.

Designing alphabet and script

One of the most fundamental components of a language is its alphabet. The alphabet is in two forms—written and spoken. While designing the alphabet, the spoken alphabet should be designed first. The sounds produced by human beings are not discrete. From a continuous spectrum, we have to select a set of sounds. If we select too few sounds, the alphabet will be small and words will be longer. On the other hand, too many sounds may cause problems in distinguishing between them. Fortunately, this science, called phonetics, is well developed, and can be used for selecting a set of sounds. The sounds should be selected in such a way that we get the maximum distinction between sounds, and the effort required in production of sound is minimum. In addition, pleasantness of sound in hearing may also be considered. The ability of machines to produce these sounds, and distinguish between them on hearing may also be considered.

In order to minimize learning effort, each sound should be assigned a character. Frequently occurring sound combinations may also be assigned an additional character, as in shorthand. The language should be phonetic. We already have natural languages which are phonetic, and they demonstrate the advantages offered by a phonetic language.

The script for the world language should be designed keeping in mind the ability of human hand for writing, and human eye for reading. In writing, the script should provide continuity. There should be no dotting the 'i', or cutting the 't'. This will minimize the movement of hand, and save effort. Each character should be independent, and combined sequentially. In some scripts, a part of the character is outside the main writing area, e.g. a part of 'g' is below the main line of writing. This should be avoided to conserve space. Characters should be as uniform in size as possible. Each character should be written in only one way. There should be no concept of upper and lower case, wherein the same character is written in two ways.

The effort in writing can be greatly reduced, if natural movements of body are used in the design of characters. Research should be conducted to determine which movements are easy for human hands, and which are not. For example, it is common experience that people find it easier to write 'u' than to write 'n'. So much so, that often 'n' looks like 'u'. This is not accidental, because its opposite never happens. This is an interesting example, because the two characters are mirror images of one another. It can perhaps be said that human hand can turn in quickly, but cannot turn out as quickly. Perhaps it has a natural tendency to move towards the chest as observed in case of an electric shock. Similarly, research should be conducted to determine if the human eye has any preferences in pattern recognition. We should also consider, whether the writing will be from left to right, right to left, top to bottom, or bottom to top. The suitability of the script for machine production and recognition should also be considered.

Designing words

Words, even in natural languages, consist of parts which have independent meaning. For example, both 'un' and 'well' in unwell have independent meanings, which determine the meaning of unwell. These parts are called morphemes by linguists; we may call them roots. All languages use the concepts of roots, prefixes, suffixes, etc. But they do not use it to the fullest. For example, the word 'bad' is not needed; 'ungood' could be used in its place.

We should design word roots in such a way that their meanings are, as far as possible, independent of each other. For the same meaning there should not be more than one word root. If word roots are well defined, the learning effort will greatly reduce. Let me illustrate.

We need word roots to indicate the number and the gender. We may decide that there will be three genders—masculine, feminine, and unknown or unspecified. Similarly, we may decide that there will be three numbers—singular, plural, and unknown or unspecified. We may combine both these attributes, and assign a vowel to each of the nine combinations. We then use these vowels to suffix nouns and pronouns. Let us see the power of this simple design. We now need only one word for father, mother, and parent. Similarly, only one word will be needed for brother, sister, and sibling. Not only that the number of words will be reduced, some new words will become available, e.g. a word for either son or daughter. Speakers of Hindi, will find new words like parent and sibling, which they never had before. Also, we do not often know the sex of a bird, and use masculine, feminine, or neuter gender, depending on convention. In the new scheme, we can use the unspecified gender most of the time, and can specify it if we know the gender. Also, legal documents often use words like person(s). This is because there is no concept of unknown, or unspecified, number. We can, thus, see the power of a simple well-defined word root.

The above example is not an isolated one. By defining just three morphemes, for parent, child, and spouse, hundreds of existing and non-existing words for family relations can be eliminated. A large number of words describing young members of a species can be eliminated by using a single prefix with the word for species. Also, we can have a prefix each for first half, second half, first quarter, second quarter etc. of age, and so on. Thus, the communicator can choose the precision with which he wants to convey the age.

Word roots will be formed by assigning a sequence of characters to each concept. This should be done, using principles of classification and codification. In many branches of science, e.g. zoology and botany, such classification already exists. These should be used, so that there is no need to have a separate scientific name. Also, the frequency of their use should be considered. Highly used roots should be identified by few characters, so that the words are short.

Rules should be defined to combine roots into words. Where classification and codification gives a large word, but the frequency of use requires a small word, a synonym may be defined. Thus, synonyms will exist only for the purpose of making the language more efficient.

Designing grammar

Grammar defines how to combine words into sentences. These rules should be as simple as possible, and there should be no exceptions. The sequence of words in a sentence should not affect its meaning. Also, preferably the sequence of words should not change, as it happens in English, where changing a sentence from affirmative to inquisitive requires a change in the sequence of words.

In many existing languages, attributes which should affect only words, are defined at the level of sentence. Number and gender are attributes of noun, and they have nothing to do with verb. Similarly, tense is an attribute of verb, and should not affect the noun. We think that a sentence is affirmative, or inquisitive (asks a question). Let us consider a simple sentence, "Are you going?". This may be interpreted as, "Are you going? (or not going)", or as "Are you? (or someone else) going". Here we can see that the question is an attribute of word, and not of sentence. Research will be needed to determine whether enquiry is always at word level, or sometimes at word level, and sometimes at sentence level.

What do we do next?

There is no doubt that it is possible to develop a language, which is far superior to existing languages. The development of such a language will be an iterative process. It will go through several cycles of improvement, before it becomes reasonably good. If we can assign even 1% of resources being spent in linguistic research, we can easily build such a language. Then it can be improved, and compared with existing languages. Only after its superiority is clearly demonstrated, do we have to think of adopting it. This project is definitely worthy of research, and I call upon the world community to take it up.

Good Governance

Many countries of the world face a number of problems. Are there any solutions? I believe that there are. Here are some ideas that could be helpful in solving some of our problems. There could be a structured public debate on these, and those which meet public approval could be implemented.

Minimize government functions

- Often governments try to do too many things.
- It is not government's job to provide goods and services. It should facilitate their production and distribution and ensure competitiveness, efficiency and non-exploitation of customers.
- Government should not be looked upon to provide direct employment. It should ensure a vibrant economy in which people are gainfully engaged.

Minimize government expenditure

- Whatever functions the government must perform, must be performed in the most efficient way, thereby reducing the cost of governance to a minimum.

- Methods of governance should be regularly reviewed, debated in public, and benchmarked with other countries and states to ensure that they are most effective and efficient.

Taxation

- There should be a single authority in each country which can levy taxes. No one else should be allowed to collect tax from any one. However, governments should be allowed to sell specific goods and services, which the citizens should be free to buy, or not to buy.
- The taxes collected by the taxation authority should be distributed among country, state and local governments as per a pre-defined agreed formula.
- The distribution of revenue from taxes should consider both the needs of governments and their contribution to revenue.
- The needs should be determined by estimating the cost of functions the governments are expected to provide.
- It will be citizens' right to get the services for which money is provided by the tax authority.

- The tax structure should be simplified. There should be only two forms of taxes. Excise for all goods and services produced in the country, and Custom for all goods and services brought in a country from outside.
- Sales tax, octroi, income tax, etc. should be abolished.
- Collection of excise and custom should be made effective by allocating more resources which would become available because of abolition of other taxes. In addition, the penalty for tax evasion should be very heavy, and corruption should be severely dealt with.
- It may be argued that income tax is applicable to only affluent sections of population. But, the same effect can be achieved by levying more excise on items which are consumed by these sections.

Norm-based governance

- People have started thinking that what the government does for them is charity. As a result, while some people get too much, others don't get even the basic minimum.
- This tendency is clearly visible. Constituencies of VIPs, e.g. prime minister, railway minister, etc. get generous allocation, which suddenly dries up if the concerned minister no longer holds office.
- This tendency is often justified by saying that at least somewhere something is getting done. This argument shows how little we have come to expect from our governments.
- In order to ensure that justice is done to all, we must define the functions of government, the levels in each function, and the entitlement criteria.
- For example we may say that all villages with population between 100 and 1000

will be linked with brick road, while those with a population of more than 1000, will be linked with tar road.
- Such norms will ensure fairness to all.
- Along with norms, the mechanism to redress grievances arising from not following the norms should be specified. In case of deliberate victimization, those responsible should be punished.

Government as service provider

- Where the government provides service, e.g. water, health care, education, roads, etc. it should be paid by the government treasury to the concerned government department for quantity and quality of service provided. This mechanism should replace the current mechanism of budgetary allocation.
- Government departments should be run as business. Their units should earn revenue, pay bills, and make profit or loss. The employees of each individual unit should be rewarded based on the financial performance of the unit.
- Citizens should be treated as customers and given bills for the service provided, showing the amount payable by them and the subsidies.
- Where possible, the quantity and quality of service should be certified by the individual customers. Where it is not possible, it should be certified by customer bodies.
- If private parties offer to provide service at a cheaper rate, the job should be given to them.

Accountability

- Government functionaries seem to have all power but no accountability.
- For example, the encroachment department of a municipal corporation has powers to demolish an illegal building.

But such powers are often exercised selectively to demolish some and leave others. The municipal corporation is not accountable to people as to why rules are being applied selectively.

- Lack of accountability breeds corruption.
- Whenever someone is given power, he should also be made accountable, preferably to the public.
- For example, if an illegal construction is found in the jurisdiction of an anti-encroachment department, its officers should be punished.

Citizens role in governance

- Governance can be much better and easier if citizens are involved in it.
- Schemes to involve citizens in governance should clearly specify how the citizens are going to contribute.
- Citizens can contribute by providing information, monitoring situations and taking action.
- The schemes involving citizens' role should be planned keeping their convenience in mind and should utilize their contribution in a most effective way.
- For example, 'Each one teach one' is not a viable and effective method; but asking a citizen to teach for two hours in a week is both convenient to the citizen and also effective in spreading education.
- Citizens should be able to see the effect of their contribution.
- One way of involving citizens would be to have a well publicised telephone number, which citizens can use to report situations such as street lights being kept on in daytime, engine of a parked bus running, leakage in a water pipe, etc. The person manning such a telephone should contact the concerned officer, who in turn should remedy the

situation. Only when citizens see their involvement resulting in action, they would participate more and more.

- Another way to involve citizens would be to assign them a small neighbourhood, which they will look after to ensure its cleanliness and orderliness. If someone digs up a road in their area, they will ensure that it is mended. They will also ensure that conservancy staff keeps their area clean. There can be many ways in which citizens can help.

Innovation

- Innovation can greatly help in good governance. Chronic problems faced by government can be solved by innovative methods.
- For example, a municipal corporation should never award a contract merely for building roads. It should always be a contract to build and maintain roads. Then the contractor will do a good job in building the road, as he will have to spend less on its maintenance. This will benefit everyone.

Political system

- In many countries, political system is corrupt because politics is not an economically viable profession.
- Every profession, except politics, offers a regular income.
- It is futile to argue that MLAs and MPs are paid a salary. These are the highest levels to which people reach in politics. The corruptionalisation is completed much before such levels are reached.
- We cannot expect to have politicians for free. If we do, we pay through our nose.
- Unless politics can attract young men and women and provide them a descent secure career, it is futile to expect politicians to be honest.

- Many countries have administrative or civil services. They should also create a political service in which young men and women should be recruited in an open competition. This service should conduct competitive examinations on the lines of the administrative or civil services.
- Those qualifying in the competitive examination should be trained and given pay and perks at par with the administrative or civil services.
- Those selected for political service, should be barred from taking up any other job, or doing any business.
- They should not be given any regular work. They should do political or social work of their choice.
- Their work should be monitored by Judiciary to ensure that they do adequate amount of work. If the quantum of their work is found inadequate, they must be withdrawn from political service and assigned administrative work. If they are found to be corrupt, their services should be terminated.
- They will contest election like any other person, and if they get elected, they will be entitled to only one salary, either of the service or of the elected office.
- Only if we can attract young students, and allow them to make an honest career in politics, can we hope to end corruption some day.

Education

- The objective of the education system is not clearly defined.
- People claim that education system has failed without even defining what education is expected to achieve.
- The objective of primary and secondary education should be to impart skills in languages and mathematics, and to create general awareness and scientific temperament.

- The objective of higher level education should be to impart skills and knowledge which a person will need in his career.
- The availability of different courses should be based on the manpower needs of a country. Consequently, in a country like India a large number of students should be educated in agriculture, horticulture, fishery, cattle rearing, etc.
- Education should not be fashionable; it should be need based and add value. It should also be easy to obtain, preferably without sacrificing the earning capacity of students.

Judiciary

- The effectiveness of judiciary determines how civilized a society is.
- The objective of judiciary is not merely to hear cases and pronounce judgement, but also to create confidence in people that if they are wronged, judiciary will help remedy the problem. It should also create the impression that no one can do wrong and get away with it.
- From the above point of view, judiciary in many countries has failed miserably.
- Failure of judiciary is the primary reason of corruption in society.
- Judiciary must work out and implement a strategy to achieve the above objectives. Judicial management should be a part of judiciary.
- Judiciary must get its workload studied to see what part of it can be eliminated by improving the rules governing those situations. For example, Judiciary handles a large number of cases related to motor vehicle accident compensation. If rules are framed to determine this compensation based on relevant factors like age, earning capacity, number of dependants, etc. insurance companies will be able to settle most of the cases, and the number of such cases going to court will drastically reduce.

- Judiciary should work on cases in a time bound manner. It should fix time norms for different types of cases and endeavour to finish a case in the allotted time.
- Judiciary can work in a time bound manner only if it has a reasonable number of cases in hearing. Therefore, new cases should go in a queue from which they should be taken for hearing. The cases may not be taken for hearing on a first-come first-served basis, but based on some guidelines which take into account the importance and urgency of a case.
- Judiciary must augment its capacity to meet the workload. The major resource that the judiciary requires is manpower. It is ironic that even in countries with excess manpower, this function is poorly performed due to lack of resources.
- Judiciary may take help of retired citizens to augment its capacity.
- Judiciary should review its policies to ensure that they are concomitant with speedy and effective justice.

E-Governance

- Information Technology (IT) is having a major impact on governance. Many country and state governments are changing their business processes to take advantage of the benefits that IT offers. However, if we have to get the most efficient e-governance at minimum cost, we need to do two things: commonize business processes and develop soft IT infrastructure.

Commonize business processes

- At present, the same business process gets computerized by different agencies in different ways. This creates islands of information which cannot talk to each other.

- A case in point is the computerization of RTO (Regional Transport Office) operations in India. Initially, different RTOs created their systems independently, and now it is proposed to scrap all those systems and replace them with a common central system. Needless to say the expenditure in independent systems could have been avoided.

Develop soft IT infrastructure

- We are aware of the importance of IT infrastructure in the development of IT. However, we usually think only of hardware infrastructure. It is high time we start thinking of soft IT infrastructure as well, and understand its importance in the development of IT. Let me explain.
- Any computerization project requires creation of master data, e.g. citizens, business entities, real estate properties, etc. At present each system creates its own master data. In India, a citizen has one id for income tax department, another for his driving licence, and yet another for his bank. He also has an id in each of the hospitals he visits, and so on. Obviously, these systems cannot talk to each other. If each person in the world were to be given a unique person id, that id would get used by all these systems, instead of trying to create their own. This not only would save development effort but also would enable diverse systems to talk to each other.
- It is not only the persons we need to identify uniquely but also every legal entity such as businesses, each piece of land and real estate, etc. The list is endless and so are the benefits of creating such unique identities.
- Wherever possible, we should look for natural attributes in giving id to an entity. For example, we can give a number to land and real estate based on its longitude, latitude and altitude. Similarly, we can

codify the primary relation between two persons as Father (F), Mother (M), Brother (B), Sister (C), Husband (H), Wife (W), Son (S) and Daughter (D). All other relations can be derived by combining these primary relations.

- It is important that standards for master data creation and codification are discussed and agreed in international bodies such as International Standards Organization. If this is not done, the world will have to incur additional cost later either in changing the systems, or in building interfaces.

- The benefits of unique identification are enormous. If each person is given a unique numeric id, we can store a telephone number and an e-mail id against him. For calling a person, you would make the call on his person id with a prefix, say 1. The prefix will indicate to the telephone system that the following number is a person id which has to be converted into telephone number. If the person's telephone number changes, only the link needs to be changed. The callers will still call the same number. Similarly, a person can be contacted on the same e-mail id, even if he changes his service provider.

- E-governance should not be creating islands of computer systems. We must

have a clear vision, strategy and master plan. We must understand what to do and what not to do, if we are not to waste our precious time and resources.

Pledge your time (samay daan)

- We citizens only criticize. We do nothing concrete.
- Things are not going to change if we expect others to change them. They will change if we act to change them.
- Those who want to change the world for better should pledge 1% of their time for society. This works out to less than 15 minutes a day and less than two hours a week.
- They can spend this time to pursue the cause of their choice. They can join an NGO, or form local groups to discuss and debate what can be done.
- Even if they just meet once a week to discuss what can be done, ideas will emerge and things will begin to happen.
- Their own efforts will shape their actions and organizations.
- The key thing is commitment and doing; not idle criticism.
- Register your time pledge (samay daan) with World Integration and Improvement Initiative (agrawal.prem@gmail.com)

City without Traffic Lights

Are you fed up with traffic lights? Traffic lights at every junction. Stop, start. Stop, start. Stop, start. Do you sometimes wish that the roads of your city were like expressway. Where your car would compete with the wind and you would reach your destination in minutes.

Fortunately, this is possible. In order to use this plan, the main roads of the city need to be like a grid, as shown in Figure 1.

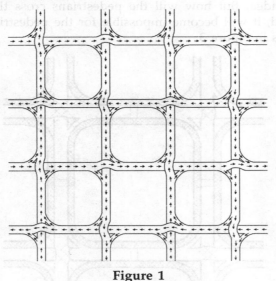

Figure 1

All roads will be one-way. When one road meets another at an intersection, there are two possibilities; you may either continue on your road, or you may turn on the other road in the direction of the traffic on that road. This is shown in Figure 2.

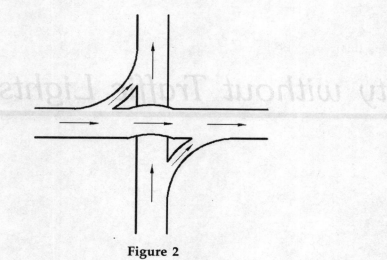

Figure 2

If you turn on the other road, there is no problem. But if you continue on your road, you will run into the traffic going straight on the other road. This is solved by a flyover or grade separator. Traffic on one road will go above the flyover, and the traffic on the other road will go under the flyover. This will ensure smooth flow of traffic without traffic light. This will be done on all intersections. Figure 1 shows this arrangement.

Sounds like a good idea. But how will the pedestrians cross the road? If the traffic moves at a fast speed, it will become impossible for the pedestrians to cross the road. The solution to this is in Figure 3.

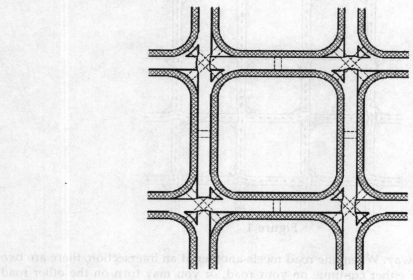

Figure 3

There will be a ring road for pedestrians and cyclists in each sector (the area bounded by main roads on all four sides). This pedestrian ring road will be connected to the pedestrian ring roads of adjoining sectors through subways. Thus, no pedestrian or cyclist will ever come on the main roads, allowing the vehicles to move freely on the main roads. Pedestrian roads will not be one-way. Pedestrians and cyclists will move on the pedestrian roads in both directions.

But how will a person take public transport, e.g. bus or taxi? This is explained in Figure 4.

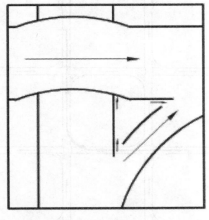

Figure 4

At each intersection, there are two triangular areas. Buses and taxis will go inside these triangular areas. There they will drop and pickup the passengers and come out of the triangle on the road they wish to take. These triangular areas will be connected to the pedestrian roads through subways.

Figure 5 shows the vehicle ring roads inside the sectors. This ring road will be connected to all the four main roads as well as to the internal roads of the sector. These roads will be two-way.

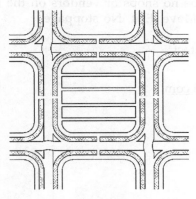

Figure 5

Figure 6 shows how the vehicles will move from one sector to another sector. Draw a horizontal and a vertical line from the source sector to the destination sector. You can do this in two ways. You can take either of these two ways to travel to your destination. You come out of the source sector taking the exit according to your travel path, move to the destination sector and enter it.

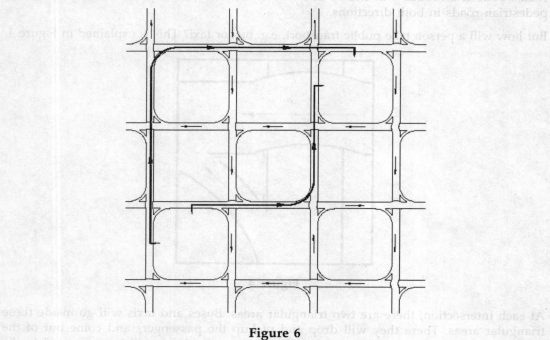

Figure 6

The main roads will be fenced on both sides so that no one can enter or exit them except through designated entry and exit roads. No pedestrian or cyclist will enter these roads. The vehicles will enter these roads, move to their destination and exit. Vehicles will neither stop on the main roads, nor be parked on it. Public transport will not stop on the main roads. There will be no shops or vendors on the main roads. Main roads will be like expressways. Enter, Move, Exit. No stoppage.

For further information, contact

P K Agrawal
E-mail: agrawal.prem@gmail.com

City without Traffic Lights and with Metro Rails

Public Transport

What should be the mode of public transport in a city? Experience shows that Metro rail is a better mode of public transport than buses. If a new city is planned with a grid structure it would be great to have Metro rails running parallel to the roads. To keep the costs low, Metro rails should be laid on ground, parallel to roads. However, that would prevent the traffic from taking right turn. We may, therefore, use the following design.

Grid

The city roads will have a grid structure.

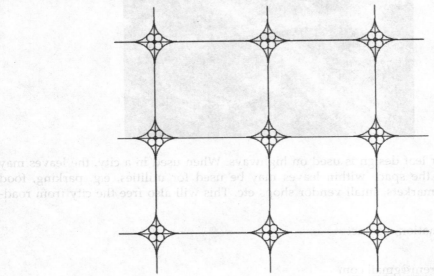

Road

In this design each road is a two-way road with a two-way Metro rail track in its center.

Road ⟶

Metro ⟶

⟵ Metro

⟵ Road

Junction

At each junction there will be a clover leaf interchange and Metro stations. Thus, it will be feasible to walk to a Metro station from anywhere in the city. The clover leaf interchange is a classic design which fully separates the traffic on a crossing of two two-way roads.

Usually the clover leaf design is used on highways. When used in a city, the leaves may be smaller. Also, the space within leaves may be used for utilities, e.g. parking, food courts, vegetable markets, small vendor shops etc. This will also free the city from road-side vendors.

For further information, contact

P K Agrawal
E-mail: agrawal.prem@gmail.com

INDEX
(573–578)